THE JOHN HARVARD LIBRARY

Bernard Bailyn

Editor-in-Chief

THE ELEMENTS OF MORAL SCIENCE

By

FRANCIS WAYLAND

Edited by Joseph L. Blau

THE BELKNAP PRESS OF
HARVARD UNIVERSITY PRESS
Cambridge, Massachusetts
1963

EDITOR'S PREFACE

In presenting this new edition of Francis Wayland's *The Elements of Moral Science* to a twentieth-century audience, I can do no better than to repeat words its author wrote in his preface to its first edition, in 1835: "If I have not been so happy as to elucidate truth, I have endeavored to express myself in such a manner that the reader shall have as little trouble as possible in detecting my errors." My hope is that this will not be merely an additional volume on already over-burdened library shelves but rather a continuous help to students of the American tradition attempting to understand the educational patterns of our nineteenth-century colleges and the intellectual heritage bequeathed to our own day by the leaders of education of a century and more ago.

A great part of the work of preparing this edition was done during my tenure as a Visiting Scholar in Residence at the Blaisdell Institute, Claremont, California. I have had the privilege of using the Honnold Library of the Associated Colleges of Claremont and the Henry E. Huntington Library of San Marino, California, in addition to my "home" library at Columbia University. To the directors and staffs of these various libraries I should like to express my thanks for un-reserved consideration and assistance. Three young ladies of Suffern, New York, Carol Jean Walsh, Eileen Murphy and Mary G. Preble, helped immeasurably in the long task of detailed comparison of the three chief editions of Wayland's book. Mary Lou Anewalt and Judith Blau have also given me assistance.

Finally, no work of mine would be complete without acknowledging the share of Eleanor W. Blau in its preparation. The many burdens she assumes for me and removes from me make her, in the truest sense, a help meet for a scholar and writer.

J. L. B.

CONTENTS

INTRODUCTION

"I AM built railroad fashion," said Francis Wayland in a moment of self-analysis. "I can go forwards, and, if necessary, back; but I can't go sideways."[1] Wayland knew himself; this is an apt characterization of a man who could not bear to mark time. Born in 1796 while George Washington was still President of the United States, Wayland lived through the chief formative years of his country; he died, a respected leader, in September 1865, a short while after the assassination of President Lincoln. As a young minister of twenty-seven, he won wide acclaim for his sermon on "The Moral Dignity of the Missionary Enterprise," the manifesto of a new era in Christian missions.[2] Yet, less than three years later, Wayland resigned his pastorate to enter upon a distinguished career in education, first and very briefly, as Professor of Mathematics and Natural Philosophy at his *alma mater,* Union College, and then, for many years, as President of Brown University.

Wayland was a central figure in the first great movement for reform of higher education in the United States. The colleges founded in the colonial era had taken over from their British analogues a curriculum dedicated largely to instruction in classical languages and inculcation of religious orthodoxy. Essentially the course of study was a Protestant version of the humanistic education developed during the Renaissance.[3] Admirable as a training for the forensic professions of the church, the law, and politics this education certainly was;

[1] Quoted by J. Lewis Diman, "The Late President Wayland," *Atlantic Monthly,* 21 (1868), 72.
[2] Henry Barnard, "Francis Wayland," *American Journal of Education,* 13 (1863), 773. For a fuller discussion, see James O. Murray, *Francis Wayland* (Boston and New York: Houghton, Mifflin and Company, 1891), pp. 44–50.
[3] See Paul Oskar Kristeller, *Renaissance Thought: The Classic, Scholastic, and Humanistic Strains* (Harper Torchbooks, The Academy Library, New York: Harper and Brothers, 1961), *passim* but especially chaps. 1 and 5, for indications of the educational theory and practice of the Humanists.

in England it had also become the distinguishing background of the cultured gentleman, the very foundation of a caste society. In the United States, however, within a quarter of a century after independence, the pressures for advanced education on a practical or utilitarian basis began to be felt. Union College, under the presidency of Eliphalet Nott (1773–1866; president of Union 1804–1866), was the first college to respond in any degree to those pressures from the public.

True, Nott's innovations were minor. Study of modern languages was permitted as a partial substitute for the study of Latin and Greek; there was some slight increase in the concern for training in science and its practical engineering and technological applications; and it was at least theoretically possible for a student to be admitted to Union with no intention of proceeding to a degree, perhaps for the study of one subject only.[4] Trivial as these modifications may seem when viewed from a perspective in which education for immediate usefulness has become a commonplace, in their own day they seemed major cracks in the barrier between theoretical studies and the applied arts and sciences.

Not even on the frontier, twenty-five years later, had the practical spirit moved as far as had Nott at Union College. In 1829, Robert Hamilton Bishop (1777–1855) who had left Transylvania University, in Kentucky, to assume the presidency of Miami University, Oxford, Ohio, "advertised a 'Farmer's College' but he did not mean courses in agriculture." What he meant was a rapid and intensive study of the traditional classical course, so that farmers' sons, who could not afford four years of college, might achieve culture in three. " 'Literary and scientific knowledge is no longer to be the exclusive property of a few professional men,' he declared. 'It is to become the common property of the mass of the human family . . . It is of vast importance . . . that a reasonable proportion of the farming interest

---

[4] R. Freeman Butts, *The College Charts Its Course: Historical Conceptions and Current Proposals* (New York and London: McGraw-Hill Book Company, Inc., 1939), p. 133. An interesting brief account of Nott's innovations and the consequent priority of Union in significant educational reform is Harold A. Larrabee, "Electives Before Eliot," *Harvard Alumni Bulletin*, April 26, 1940, pp. 893–897. Larrabee includes also some material on Wayland's reforms.

should be qualified to move on at the head of all improvements in their immediate neighborhood.' Education for leadership by providing the solid substance of traditional learning was his ideal." [5] Bishop's way of distributing education was to make classical training more readily available, not to change its content.

At about the same time as Bishop announced his plan for developing cultured farmer-leaders, President Jeremiah Day (1773–1867, president of Yale 1817–1843) and Professor James L. Kingsley (1778–1852) wrote the celebrated "Yale Report" of 1828, an emphatic reply to critics of the classical curriculum, stressing the educational importance of retaining thorough training in Latin and Greek. The Report was the bulwark of conservative educational thinkers until late in the nineteenth century. Its authors argue that exponents of the classical course cannot be accused of "a blind opposition to salutary reform," since they have made piecemeal modifications and improvements in the college as these proved necessary, even to the introduction of new subjects of study. Despite the reluctant readiness of the educational establishment to acknowledge the need of "salutary reform," however, criticism of the collegiate curriculum is heard on all sides. "From different quarters, we have heard the suggestion that our colleges must be *new-modelled;* that they are not adapted to the spirit and wants of the age; that they will soon be deserted, unless they are better accommodated to the business character of the nation." The *gravamen* of the Report is a defense of Yale's administrative and educational policy against this demand for a thorough overhaul.[6]

Despite this defense of conservatism, there was a strong counter-spirit of educational experimentation abroad in the land. George Ticknor (1791–1871), after his return from postgraduate study in

---

[5] Louis B. Wright, *Culture on the Moving Frontier* (Bloomington: Indiana University Press, 1955), pp. 105–106, quoting James H. Rodabaugh, *Robert Hamilton Bishop* (Ohio Historical Collections, IV, Columbus, 1935), p. 65.

[6] Richard Hofstadter and Wilson Smith, *American Higher Education, a Documentary History* (Chicago: The University of Chicago Press, 1961), I, 275–291, contains the central argument of the Yale Report of 1828 in excerpt. For further discussion, see Butts, *The College Charts Its Course,* especially pp. 118–125, and George P. Schmidt, *The Liberal Arts College, a Chapter in American Cultural History* (New Brunswick, N.J.: Rutgers University Press, 1957), pp. 54–57.

Germany, became an ardent advocate of German methods of teaching and of study; Harvard College, under the leadership of President John T. Kirkland (1770–1840, president of Harvard 1810–1828) and under Ticknor's influence, took an early step towards the elective system in 1824. Thomas Jefferson's program for the University of Virginia (1825) was radical for its time. Attempts to modify the traditional course of study were made at Amherst College and at the University of Vermont. Perhaps the most striking experimental program was that introduced by Wilbur Fisk (1792–1839), the first president of Wesleyan University. In 1831, when Wesleyan was founded, Fisk set up its programs departmentally and permitted each student to advance at his own best rate. This implied the abandonment of stated work, done in lockstep, for each of the four years of the college course, and led inevitably to the elimination of a fixed time requirement for completion of a degree. After Fisk's death, his program was dropped and "subsequently Wesleyan became an outstanding example of adherence to a classical prescribed curriculum." [7]

There is little question that Wayland was an adherent of the "modern" party from the beginning of his academic career as a tutor under (and personal favorite of) Eliphalet Nott at Union College. Indeed, Nott's concern to help Wayland's campaign for the presidency of Brown University may have been motivated by the older man's desire to extend the influence of his educational ideas to his own alma mater, for Nott had received his M.A. from Rhode Island College (as Brown was then called) in 1795. It is certainly clear that Wayland held to a theory of democracy that led inevitably to a conception of universal education. Even in Wayland's two discourses, delivered in 1825 and published under the title "The Duties of an American Citizen," the young preacher had asserted that, "The paramount duty of an American citizen is, to put in requisition every possible means for elevating universally the intellectual and moral

[7] See Butts, *The College Charts Its Course, passim;* Schmidt, *The Liberal Arts College,* chap. 3; and William G. Roelker, "Francis Wayland: a Neglected Pioneer of Higher Education," *Proceedings of the American Antiquarian Society, April 21, 1943–October 20, 1943* (Worcester, Mass.: published by the Society), 53 (1944), 47–50.

character of our people." [8] Yet he seems to have proposed no major changes at Brown until he had been its president for nearly fifteen years. The suggestion that he presented ideas for modernizing privately and found neither the faculty nor the corporation of the university prepared to accept them is the most probable explanation, based on Wayland's own reminiscences.[9]

In 1840, Wayland visited Europe and gave particular attention to an examination of Oxford and Cambridge Universities. This experience apparently crystallized his determination to make public his views on the changes that he considered desirable in higher education. This he did, briefly, in his 1841 Report to the Fellows of Brown University, and more extensively and significantly in his book *Thoughts on the Present Collegiate System in the United States,* a year later. Although Wayland asserted the necessity for improvement in many aspects of college management and college life and even proposed that American colleges should be transformed into "real" universities, a curious spirit of reluctance breathes through the pages of this little book. The Preface begins with a statement most uncharacteristic of its author: "The following pages are submitted to the public with great diffidence because they propose changes; and the author has lived too long to be a passionate admirer of innovation." Perhaps, since the author lived long enough once more to become an admirer of innovation, we may ascribe his temporary revulsion to the effects of the Dorr Rebellion (1842), to which he was heartily opposed. Indeed, this possibility is heightened by his statement that, if native talent does not find an outlet through advanced education, it is likely to break out in agitation.

The defects in the system of collegiate education in the United States to which Wayland called attention at this time were chiefly those of rigidity. He was concerned because, despite the relative recency of most of the American institutions of higher education, their boards of trustees and their faculties seem inclined merely to

[8] Francis Wayland, *Occasional Discourses, including several never before published* (Boston: James Loring, 1833), p. 70.
[9] Roelker, "Francis Wayland," pp. 50–51; see Murray, *Francis Wayland,* pp. 164–166, for the quotation from Wayland's autobiographical reminiscences on which Roelker's suggestion is based.

follow the old patterns rather than to develop new patterns to meet new conditions. He argued that rethinking should take place before traditionary roots had sunk too deep. He criticized especially the torpor of "the Visitorial Power," that is, of the body of corporate supervisors under whatever name. Members of these boards should serve the college community as goads and spurs to advance, yet precisely here he detected the greatest inertia. Partly, he thought, this was a consequence of tenure; "A body chosen for life is peculiarly liable to attacks of somnolency." Partly, too, he regarded the irresponsibility of boards of trustees as an inevitable moral consequence of their size. "That corporations have no conscience I would by no means assert, but I believe it will generally hold true that their conscience is inversely as their number. In large bodies responsibility is too much divided."

He argued, in addition, for greater professionalization of the faculties. Far too many of those engaged in collegiate instruction were only temporary members of the academic community, serving it for a few years while preparing for their own professional careers in law, medicine, or religion. Neither the salaries of professors nor the opportunities for training available encouraged young men to regard college teaching as their life's work. To remedy these two basic deficiencies Wayland proposed the establishment of decent pay scales for college teachers and the foundation of "a class of higher seminaries, seminaries capable of teaching teachers, in other words institutions for professional education." If more adequate preparation and better pay led young men to regard college teaching as a career, they would devote more time and thought to the curriculum in general and to the quality of their own teaching.

The next major element to be considered in an educational program is the student body. Here Wayland's view was uncompromising: the primary responsibility of the college to its student is character-building. "The most important end to be secured in the education of the young is moral character. Without this, brilliancy of intellect will only plunge its possessor more deeply in temporal disgrace and eternal misery." [10] These were not mere words flung out

[10] Francis Wayland, *Thoughts on the Present Collegiate System in the United States* (Boston: Gould, Kendall & Lincoln, 1842), pp. 7, 8–9, 51, 5, 115.

to catch the eye of the pious public. They represent, rather, the dis-
tillation of Wayland's own practice as a teacher. One of his biog-
raphers is unusually frank in describing him. "He was never spoken
of as a learned man in philosophy, or ethics, or political economy . . .
But his classroom was made the place where constant lessons were
given on the conduct of life." [11] James Burrill Angell (1829–1916),
who studied under Wayland at Brown and later taught there before
going on to distinction as a university president (University of
Vermont, 1866–1871; University of Michigan, 1871–1909), defined
Wayland's "greatness and his influence" as "more conspicuously
moral than intellectual." [12]

Beyond the centrality of moral discipline, Wayland was committed to a belief in intellectual discipline. He espoused the faculty
psychology that was a commonplace of his times, even as did the
authors of the Yale Report of 1828. His distinction was to have
utilized this psychological theory to sustain a reformist rather than
a traditionary outlook.[13] The objects of education may be grouped
under the two heads of "discipline of the faculties" and "acquisition
of knowledge," and "while both these were included in his idea of
education, he directed his chief efforts as a teacher towards the
former." [14] Where Wayland differed from the traditionalists was
in seeing that there is no special value to the study of Greek and
Latin for the discipline of the faculties. The achievement of disci-
plined minds is dependent upon the way in which study and teaching are done, not upon what is studied or taught. Nor, he was convinced, is there any special educational merit in the fixed, four-year
course, the same for all students in the first three years and permitting
a minimum of elective variation in the fourth. Wayland urged the
abolition of the fixed course. He would have allowed each student
to carry as many subjects as he wanted, choosing those subjects only
that he wished to study and pursuing them as long and as deeply
as possible. To provide the opportunity for this much elective freedom, he advocated that each college should add to its regular cur-

[11] Murray, *Francis Wayland,* pp. 190–191.
[12] Angell's article, "Francis Wayland," was published in *Hours at Home,* II (1865),
189.
[13] See Butts, *The College Charts Its Course,* p. 213.
[14] Barnard, "Francis Wayland," p. 776.

riculum full courses in those subjects for which there was a community demand.[15]

No doubt some part of the motivation of Wayland's desire to expand the college offerings and thus to attract more students was prudential. As president of Brown, he was a successful fund raiser. Certainly he had had little difficulty in getting money to put up new buildings, and one of the chief achievements of his first few years at Brown was the development of a major library. Yet he saw the number of students declining and annual expenses exceeding annual income. A possible solution was to appeal to the public for more funds to carry on the traditional type of college training; this most of the colleges were doing, without signal response. The alternative to which Wayland adhered was to redesign the college course to make it more responsive to community needs and thus to draw more students, more fees and, possibly, more liberal endowments. This prudential motivation seems to have been uppermost in his mind at the time of his 1850 *Report to the Corporation of Brown University*. That this is so is clear from his departure from his earlier insistence on proper remuneration for college teachers and his recommendation, instead, of a free trade system under which faculty members would be paid a base salary and a proportion of the fees of the students attracted to their classes. "Like every other man, the instructor will be brought directly in contact with the public, and his remuneration will be made to depend distinctly upon his industry and skill in his profession." [16]

Yet it would be less than fair to insist upon this prudential motive to the exclusion of an equal emphasis on Wayland's firm and principled commitment to a wider diffusion of educational opportunities and advantages. "God," he declared, "has scattered the seeds of pre-eminent ability as profusely among the poor as among the rich." Later in the same address he presented a well-nigh Jeffersonian

---

[15] See the summary in Butts, *The College Charts Its Course*, p. 147.

[16] Francis Wayland, *Report to the Corporation of Brown University, on Changes in the System of Collegiate Education, read March 28, 1850* (Providence, R.I., 1850). Excerpts from this *Report* are printed in Hofstadter and Smith, *American Higher Education*, II, 478–487; the quoted sentence, p. 486. See also Barnard, "Francis Wayland," p. 777, and Butts, *The College Charts Its Course*, pp. 146–147.

picture of the intimate connection between educational opportunity and republican stability. He thought it obvious that "a very high degree of universal intelligence is absolutely demanded by the very theory of our republican institutions." As long as "the *many,* and not the *few,*" rule, enact the laws and execute them, a republican government must rest on an educated electorate. If provision for adequate education is not made, republican government will work no better than hereditary monarchy or aristocracy. "The education of princes in other countries must be the education of the people in this. Unless this be substantially the case, the permanency of our institutions has not yet been secured." [17]

In 1849, seeing no hope of more than temporary and minor ameliorations of the condition of Brown University and little indication that his earlier suggestions for basic changes were taken seriously, Francis Wayland precipitated action by presenting a letter of resignation to the Brown corporation. The resignation was not accepted. Instead, a committee was appointed, with Wayland himself as its chairman, to report the changes that would have to be made to keep Wayland in the presidency.[18] The general theoretical base of the 1850 *Report* presented by this committee differs in no significant detail from Wayland's earlier statements. If the available supply of collegiate education exceeds the current demand, the reason is that something is wrong with the system, which is not directed broadly enough at the needs of all classes in the community. "We must carefully survey the wants of the various classes of the community in our own vicinity, and adapt our courses of instruction, not for the benefit of one class, but for the benefit of all classes."

Wayland presented eight principles for reorganization, permitting far more scope to student option than the classical college curriculum allowed. Indeed, he suggested a philosophy and a program that closely resemble those advocated by the extension divisions of many institutions of higher education in the twentieth century. In illustration of his design he sketched a "curriculum" consisting of fifteen

[17] Francis Wayland, *A Discourse, delivered at the opening of the Providence Athenaeum,* July 11, 1838. Published at the request of the Directors of the Athenaeum. (Providence: Knowles, Vose & Company, 1838), pp. 6, 32–33.

[18] See Barnard, "Francis Wayland," p. 778.

different "courses of instruction," but he was careful to add that it would not necessarily be the case that every college would offer the same courses of instruction or pursue them to the same extent. The criterion was the fulfillment of local needs; the ultimate goal, to create "opportunity for diversified forms of excellence." The method proposed, he thought, would tend to make all colleges more nearly self-supporting. More fee-paying students would attend because the college would be offering better preparation for entry into the learned professions. Moreover there was a possibility that some students, after completing the courses essential to their careers, might remain in attendance for an additional period, in order to pursue "a more generous course of professional education."

Behind the text of Wayland's *Report,* underlying even its most practical, businesslike aspects, there glows a Jeffersonian republicanism, dimmed only slightly by a consciousness of class superiority. The potential students and fee payers, by and large, will "come from classes who now receive no benefit whatever from the college system, as it at present exists." By modifying the college program Wayland hoped to relieve some of the financial difficulties with which his administration was beset. In addition, the *Report* points out, "We should be carrying the blessings of scientific and literary education to portions of society from which they have thus far been practically excluded." To do so is a matter of justice, for each man has a right to the fullest opportunities for developing his potential. Wayland's sentiments seem better than his logic when he argues, after this, that "If every man who is willing to pay for them, has an *equal* right to the benefits of education, every man has a *special* right to that kind of education which will be of the greatest value to him in the prosecution of useful industry."

Besides being just, Wayland claims, an educational program of the sort proposed is expedient and necessary. Civilization, he asserts, advances in the development of the useful arts, and it is, therefore, in the national interest to spread as widely as possible the knowledge that promotes and leads to the perfecting of the useful arts. Again, "Anyone who will observe the progress which, within the last thirty years, has been made by the productive classes of society . . . must be convinced that a system of education, practically restricted to a class vastly smaller, and rapidly decreasing in influence, cannot possibly continue." If the existing colleges maintain an aristocratic class bias, the mass of society will foster new kinds of colleges, teaching everything the old-line colleges do, except ancient languages which would be replaced by agricultural science or other practical courses preparing students for other "productive departments." "In New York and Massachusetts," the *Report* notes, "incipient measures have been taken for establishing agricultural colleges." [19] Wayland's "free trade" ideas, expressed most fully in his *Elements of Political Economy* (1837),[20] crop up in the context of his educational writings. His plan for incentive payments for teachers has already been noted. He applies the same principle to the course of study: "If, by placing Latin and Greek upon their own merits, they are unable to retain their present place in the education of civilized and Christianized man, then let them give place to something better." [21]

When Union College celebrated a half century under Nott's presidency, in 1854, Wayland was asked to deliver the feature address. Seemingly Nott himself—"him," said Wayland, "to whom I owe more than to any other living man"—proposed that Wayland fill this central role. The subject to which the speaker was urged to address himself was certainly congenial both to him and to Nott— "the principles which should govern the system of collegiate education in our age and country." Virtually all of Wayland's comments on higher education on this occasion were reaffirmations of points he had made in earlier discussions of the same theme. Here, however, he presented these ideas in a broader context of general principles, so that this address reveals much of its author's philosophy

---

[19] Hofstadter and Smith, *American Higher Education*, II, 478–484.

[20] Murray, *Francis Wayland*, p. 208: "In a community, the interests of which were bound up in manufactures, he was the outspoken advocate of Free Trade." And J. Lewis Diman, "The Late President Wayland," *Atlantic Monthly*, 21 (1868), 69, speaking of Wayland's decision to leave the active ministry for the presidency of Brown, says, "We can never regret a step which, at a time when the sophisms of the Protective system were held in New England as hardly less sacred than the injunctions of the decalogue, gave us, in one of our chief seats of learning, a bold advocate of correct principles of trade."

[21] Hofstadter and Smith, *American Higher Education*, II, 486.

of education, his theological insight and his conception of the nature of democracy.

Wayland's most comprehensive definition of education clearly evidences the moral bent of his mind with its emphasis, as in the ethical philosophy of Kant, on universality and on duty. Education is, he says, "that culture either of body or mind, which shall enable us the better to discharge the duties of our present probation and prepare for the results which shall emerge from that probation hereafter . . . It comprehends, therefore, every interest of humanity." There is an intimate and reciprocal relationship between knowledge and mental action. The outcome of any act of mind is a piece of knowledge; every piece of knowledge, therefore, presupposes a prior act of mind. Although this reciprocal relation holds always and everywhere, the distinction between knowledge, the outcome, and mental activity, the occasion, has led to two distinct ways of viewing the educational process. "Hence some have considered education to consist merely in the communication of knowledge; others almost entirely in the discipline of mind." The criteria of success that have been suggested depend upon which of these two is selected as the goal.

Furthermore, because there is this distinction of educational objectives, a similar division of subjects has been made. Some subjects are defended as contributory to mental discipline, while others are advocated for the sake of the knowledge they impart. Partisanship extends even further: "Some of them, *of which the results are acknowledged to be in general valueless,* are prosecuted on account of the mental discipline which they are supposed to impart. That they tend to nothing practical, has sometimes been deemed their appropriate excellence. Hence, some learned men have exulted rather facetiously in the 'glorious inutility' of the studies which they recommend. On the other hand; there are many studies which communicate knowledge, admitted by all men to be indispensable, *which are supposed to convey no mental discipline*" (italics supplied). The direction that Wayland's educational thought must take to resolve this highly artificial dilemma is obvious; he must reach toward a higher ground, asserting at the least that there is some mental discipline in all studies that eventuate in knowledge and possibly that some useful knowledge arises from even the most disciplinary of studies. Far more unexpected, however, is the way he takes to reach this conclusion, the way of theodicy, or the justification of God's moral governance of the universe. Wayland actually introduces a theological and metaphysical doctrine of pre-established harmony as the means of going beyond educational partisanship:

> It may, I think, be safely taken for granted that the system of which we form a part is the work of a Being of infinite wisdom and infinite benevolence. He made the world without us and the world within us, and he manifestly made each of them for the other. He has made knowledge, intellectual culture and progress, all equally necessary to our individual and social well-being . . . Is it then to be supposed that he has made for our brief probation two kinds of knowledge; one necessary for the attainment of our means of happiness, but incapable of nourishing and strengthening the soul; and the other tending to self-culture, but leading to no single practica[l] advantage?
>
> Is it not rather to be believed that he has made each of these ends to harmonize with the other, so that all intellectual culture shall issue in knowledge which shall confer benefits on the whole; and all knowledge properly acquired shall in an equal degree tend to intellectual development? Did God manifest himself in the flesh, in the form of a carpenter's son, to create an intellectual aristocracy, and consign the remaining millions of our race to daily toil, excluded from every opportunity for spiritual improvement?

Surely, Wayland has used heavy artillery here to crack a nut. Yet it is only an extreme instance of a persistent trait in his thinking. There is an arrogance in the way in which Wayland uses God as the cosmic guarantor of whatever Wayland believes. Further, since much of Wayland's belief arises out of the complex of ideas of the Enlightenment, God has a considerable work to do. He is, for example, in an almost Emersonian fashion, Wayland's device for escaping the heavy hand of "authority and precedent" handed down from the past. God "gives to every age the means for perceiving its own wants and discovering the best means of supplying them." He "intended us for progress, and we counteract his design when we deify antiquity, and bow down and worship an opinion, not because it is either wise or true, but merely because it is ancient." New inventions, particularly those utilizing steam power, are part of God's design to free the mind and liberate the emotions; "God is thus lifting off from us that oppressive severity of toil which paralyzes intellect and benumbs the power of emotion." [22]

All that the Enlightenment ascribed to the advance of human reason Wayland credited to the operations of God. Although his language occasionally suggested a belief in human agency and a conviction of man's capacity to affect his destiny, his more careful statements stressed the exclusive place of God as First Cause. He "most confidently believes that all power, efficiency, real causation in the universe, is the work of God, and God alone; and that what is considered causation in man is merely stated antecedency . . ." [23] He maintained this position, however, as we have seen, by a violation of the principle of parsimony; he brought God into his explanations after he had accounted for events on natural grounds or as supplementary justification for positions that he held antecedently. In all cases, he was guilty of the "speculative hybris" of professing "to be on intimate terms with God, to share his plans and secrets." [24]

Wayland's attitude toward science was profoundly influenced by his way of interpreting the relation of God to mundane events. At one time, after his graduation from Union College, he designed to enter the medical profession. He served a three-year apprenticeship (1813–1816) under Dr. Eli Burritt of Troy, New York, and was licensed to practice medicine. His conversion and decision to enter the ministry occurred at about the same time as the completion of his medical preparation. The professorship at Union College to which he was called in 1826, but in which he served only a part of one year (leaving it for the presidency of Brown), was in mathematics and natural philosophy. Certainly Wayland was not one of the outstanding scientists of his time; yet neither was he a scientific

[22] Francis Wayland, *The Education Demanded by the People of the U. States. A Discourse delivered at Union College, Schenectady, July 25, 1854, on The occasion of the fiftieth anniversary of the presidency of Eliphalet Nott* . . . (Boston: Phillips, Sampson, and Company, 1855), pp. 3, 4, 5–6, 8, 10, 16.

[23] Wayland, *Occasional Discourses*, p. 375.

[24] Hiram Haydn, *The Counter-Renaissance* (New York: Charles Scribner's Sons, 1950), p. 77, thus describes a typical attitude critical of Scholasticism pervading the "counter-Renaissance." Haydn quotes the phrase "speculative hybris" from Basil Willey, *The Seventeenth Century Background* (London, 1934), p. 261.

illiterate. His attitude toward science was, however, shaped by his religious beliefs rather than by his scientific views. In brief, he believed that "since all that exists is the work of God, and exists just as he wills, the more intimate our acquaintance with the author, the more readily shall we understand those works, which are nothing else than manifestations of his character." [25]

The implications of this view were set forth in some detail by Wayland in 1831, in his *Discourse on the Philosophy of Analogy*.[26] In its logical dimension, this address is an assertion of the importance of analogical reasoning, a type of reasoning that had been lightly regarded by most philosophers, though used by almost all, and highly commended by many theologians. Wayland's particular concern was to indicate the uses of analogy in the development of science. In line with the tradition of British empiricism, to which he adhered in the form of Scottish "common sense" realism, Wayland's starting point was a mind shorn of innate ideas but equipped with a set of faculties or powers awaiting occasions for their use. In addition, man has been "endowed with a universal appetite for knowledge, which, by a law of his nature, grows by what it feeds on." The universe in which man is placed is one "in all respects corresponding to this mental appetite, and adapted, at the same moment, both to gratify and to stimulate inquiry." The foreordained harmony in which Wayland believed provided an escape from the dilemmas of epistemology. Man's faculties and his appetite for knowledge are "the elements of which his intellectual character is composed"; the universe is man's environment, "the circumstances under which those elements are placed." From the combination of these elements and their circumstances, "knowledge must inevitably result." [27]

---

[25] Francis Wayland, *The Dependence of Science upon Religion. A Discourse Delivered at the Dedication of Manning Hall, the Chapel and Library of Brown University, February 4, 1835* (Providence: Marshall, Brown & Co., 1835), p. 8.

[26] This address was originally delivered before the Phi Beta Kappa Society of Rhode Island, September 7, 1831, and separately published (Boston: Hilliard, Gray, Little, and Wilkins, 1831). It was reprinted in Wayland, *Occasional Discourses*, pp. 319–343. A modern reprinting is available in Joseph L. Blau, ed., *American Philosophic Addresses, 1700–1900* (New York: Columbia University Press, 1946), pp. 344–363.

[27] Wayland, *Occasional Discourses*, pp. 320–321.

Wayland did not conceive of science as the special realm or domain inhabited by a special breed of men or as a concern for the quantitative as opposed to the qualitative. Science meant to him "the knowledge of the laws of nature and of the modes in which they may be applied to increase the happiness of man." [28] To speak, therefore, of "the progress of knowledge" is the same as to speak of "the advance of science." He described three steps in the progress of knowledge. The first, appropriate to his empirical orientation, is our sensory observation that "certain things exist, and that certain changes are taking place in them." Next, there is a recognition of orderliness in the succession of the changes, leading to "the first conception of a law of nature." This conception is refined and extended by "subsequent observation and more accurate experiments," determining what is essential and what accidental in its first rough formulation, until "a nearer and nearer approximation is made to pure and unchangeable truth." It is worthy of note, in this context, that Wayland considers the operation of a law of nature as necessary, so that we "are enabled to predict, under given circumstances, what, throughout the material universe, will be the certain result." Although probability theory and the problems inherent in induction had, by this time, become an important subject of discussion in the philosophy of science, Wayland was apparently unaware of these questions and faced the relation of observed data to natural laws with an unjustifiable naïveté. The third and final step to which he calls attention is the subsumption of the laws governing particular phenomenal changes under more and more general laws, on the basis of the discovery of "points of coincidence" in their operation. Thus, gravity, magnetism, and electricity are found to have points of coincidence, from which "we derive a general law of attraction." This, in its turn, may yet be discovered to be "subject to some more general law, which governs both attraction and repulsion, and every species of motion . . . And so on to infinity." [29] There is no end to the process of generalizing the laws of nature.

It is not merely the case that there is such a process of extending

---

[28] Wayland, *The Dependence of Science upon Religion,* p. 8.
[29] Wayland, *Occasional Discourses,* pp. 321–323.

and generalizing knowledge. A law of nature is not merely what men find in the external world, but also a statement of what God placed there. When the range of application of a law of nature is discovered, what man has done is to "extend its dominion to other changes placed by the Author of nature under its control." [30] Similarly, when human knowledge, or science, is found to be continually developing, it is "evident that a tendency to universal extension has been impressed upon it by its Creator." [31]

Given this intimate relationship between God's purposes and man's attainments (fallaciously established though it be),[32] Wayland correctly notes that deduction and induction "never discover a law of nature; they only show whether a law has or has not been discovered." [33] Neither can be the guarantor of continued progress in discovery. Something else is needed; Wayland identifies this as the act of skill of posing the right questions in the investigation of nature. He calls this skill "the philosophy of analogy" or the "science of analogy." "There is needed a science, which, standing on the confines of what is known, shall point out the direction in which truth probably lies, in the region that is unknown. This, when it has assumed a definite form, will be the science of analogy." This "science" has not yet been developed, and its development would require a man of mighty intellect, accomplished in all the sciences and familiar with their history, with sufficient analytic skill to be able to extract the laws of discovery from a close examination of the circumstances of those discoveries that have been made, and thus to gain a scientific understanding of "the yet unexplained process of original investigation. When God shall have sent that Genius upon earth who was born to accomplish this mighty labor, then, one of the greatest obstacles will have been removed to our acquiring an unlimited control over all the agents of nature." Once again we can see in this

[30] Wayland, *Occasional Discourses*, p. 321.

[31] Wayland, *Occasional Discourses*, p. 323.

[32] The fallacy is that known as *post hoc* reasoning; the fact that man has attained to knowledge is taken as evidence for the assertion that this was, from the beginning, God's intention.

[33] Wayland, *Occasional Discourses*, p. 327. Wayland's note to this passage, on p. 375, quotes Francis Bacon as saying "It is the office of the mathematics to determine truth in natural philosophy, not to create or produce it."

statement Wayland's translation into the terms of a nineteenth-century conservative theism of an ambition characteristic of the *illuminati* of the eighteenth century.

Although the science of analogy was but a dimly envisioned future possibility, Wayland was convinced that he could formulate the two "self-evident" principles upon which the laws of such a science of discovery would necessarily be based. The first of these is that "A part of any system which is the work of an intelligent agent, is similar, so far as the principles which it involves are concerned, to the whole of that system." Granted the assumption, unstated, that the universe is, in fact, the creation of an intelligent being, this is a principle of consistency. The second principle is that "The work of an intelligent and moral being must bear, in all its lineaments, the traces of the character of its Author." [34] Once again, the same unstated assumption is present; granting its validity, this second principle makes an assertion that is by no means self-evident, that any product will be an exemplification of the qualities of its producer, provided only that that producer be intelligent and moral.

Natural religion, wherever and whenever it has occurred, has made a principle of this sort its basis for reasoning from the characteristics of observed phenomena, considered as effects, to the existence and character of God. Wayland's use of the principle is an inversion of this traditional application. For what he asserts is that we know the character of God and are able to reason from this knowledge of the cause to a knowledge of God's effects. That investigator who is "most deeply penetrated with a conviction of the attributes of the First Cause of all things" (principle two) and at the same time "most thoroughly imbued with the spirit of the system" (principle one) will be best qualified to use "analogy the most skilfully." [35] If this is so, Wayland declares, it is probable that progress in the sciences will be made chiefly by scientists of the Christian faith. "I think that in-

[34] Wayland, *Occasional Discourses,* pp. 328–329.

[35] Wayland, *Occasional Discourses,* pp. 329–330. Wayland, in a note expanding on this point, asserts that "There is a certain character or *style* (if I may use the expression) in the operation of Divine Wisdom, something which everywhere announces, amidst an infinite variety of detail, an *inimitable unity and harmony of design;* and in the perception of which, *philosophical sagacity and genius* seems chiefly to consist." P. 376; italics in the original.

fidel philosophers generally will be found to have distinguished
themselves by the accurate use of the sciences, and Christian philosophers by the additional glory of foretelling when and how the
sciences may be used. I am not aware that infidelity hath presented
to the world any discoveries to be compared with those of Boyle and
Pascal, and Bacon and Newton, or of Locke, and Milton, and
Butler." [36]

Wayland foresaw no possibility of a conflict of science and religion.
His spiritual descendants, who saw the conflict develop in the after-
math of Darwinian biology, have fallen back into a modern version
of the medieval doctrine of the double truth. The truths of religion
and those of science, however they may diverge, can never contradict
each other because they are truths in different universes of discourse.
Wayland's more optimistic faith was that there was but one universe and that, within that universe, what the scientist found to be
true must be in complete accord with God's revealed truth; he
allowed, however, for progress in human understanding of the divine revelation in the reflected light of scientific advance. So, for
example, there was a reciprocal development of the science of astronomy and of a clearer understanding of God's plan:

> While men, measuring the universe by the standard of their own narrow
> conceptions, and surveying all things through the distempered medium of
> their own puerile vanity, placed the earth in the center of the system, and sup-
> posed sun, moon, and stars to revolve daily around it, the science of astronomy
> stood still, and age after age groped about in almost rayless darkness. It was
> only when humility had taught us how small a space we occupied in the bound-
> lessness of creation, and raised us to a conception of the plan of the Eternal,
> that light broke in, like the morning star upon our midnight, and a beau-
> teous universe rose out of void and formless chaos.

This is an instance of the "glory" that will result "when the full
blaze of every science shall be concentrated upon the page of everlasting Truth, and thence reflected, with undiminished effulgence,
upon the upward path of baptized philosophy." [37]

Wayland achieved, for his time, an excellent synthesis of religiously
inspired teleology with the empirical and inductive procedures val-

---

[36] Wayland, *Occasional Discourses*, p. 331.
[37] Wayland, *Occasional Discourses*, pp. 341–343.

ued by his philosophic school and, to a great extent, by the science of the age. "The confession of utter ignorance" with which scientific work begins, he equated with the religious spirit of humility. He declared that "our only business in Science is to understand and obey the laws to which the Creator has subjected the physical universe, as in Religion our only business is to understand and obey the laws to which He has subjected the moral universe." In both areas, progress is in proportion to the initial humility of the student; religion is primary because it taught humility ages before this virtue was applied to the study of physics. Again, religion is primary, because it "fosters the love of truth." Most importantly, however, religion is primary because of its concern with morality, and "Moral science lies at the foundation of all science." Wayland's enthusiasm for moral science leads him to the verge of imputing imperfection to God: "The distinguishing elements of the character of Deity are moral elements, that in general everything else is made *for the sake of developing moral character in himself* or his accountable creatures" (italics supplied). Of all religions, Christianity is most favorable to the advancement of science because of its moral emphasis on benevolence toward all men, expressing itself in a concern for the greatest possible happiness of all men, first, of course, in the form of moral concern, but also in the form of physical and intellectual concern.

Science can progress only in an advanced state of society and its progress is proportional to social advance. Society is held in balance by the tension and opposition of "impulsive" and "moral" forces in human nature. "In order to the constitution of society, both of these opposing principles must be in constant operation. They are to the social, what the centrifugal and centripetal forces are to the planetary system." Religion without revelation, natural religion, reinforcing the dictates of conscience, is inadequate to provide a sufficient counterbalance to the forces of impulse. A merely nominal Christianity, "allowed to degenerate into a mere system of forms and ceremonies, while its moral obligations were neglected and forgotten," is equally unsatisfactory for this purpose. But with the Reformation there came a revival of a true Christianity, to provide sufficient moral force to balance the impulsive forces in human nature. As a result, the Reformation was followed by a period of stability and of measured social progress, leading to an expansion of leisure and an extension of education. To these advances we owe the development of science. "It is not too much then to assert that to revealed religion we owe that state of civilization in which alone such science can exist, as renders the laws of nature instruments available to the production of the happiness of man." [38]

To "baptized science" and "revealed religion" Wayland added a third firm commitment: to "republican institutions." In his youth, in his parents' home, he had listened to many politico-religious discussions carried on by his father with other members of the Baptist denomination. The common, and not completely unwarranted, belief among the Baptists was that the Federalist party spoke for the "Standing Order" in New England, under which the members of the Baptist church had suffered in the past, whereas the Republicans, Jefferson's party, favored unrestricted freedom of religion, the "separation of church and state." [39] Needless to say, the Baptists of the early nineteenth century were overwhelmingly supporters of the party which spoke for their freedom, and Francis Wayland was no exception. As early as 1825, in two sermons preached before his Boston church and published under the title *The Duties of an American Citizen,* Wayland's political commitment to Jeffersonian democracy is completely explicit. He called his auditors' attention to two theories of government espoused in the European world: governments of will and governments of law.

Governments of will assume the division of society into a ruling class, invested with power "by divine appointment," and a class of the ruled, large in number but weak in the instruments of control, "bound to yield passive and implicit obedience" to its rulers. To illustrate the consequences of the principles on which governments of will are based, Wayland quotes from one of the declarations of the Holy Alliance: "All useful and necessary changes ought only

---

[38] Wayland, *The Dependence of Science upon Religion,* pp. 10, 14, 26, 29, 31.

[39] See Murray, *Francis Wayland,* pp. 5–6. It should be remembered that Jefferson used the phrase "separation of church and state," which has become the focus of much twentieth-century controversy, in his reply to a congratulatory letter addressed to him by a Baptist group from Danbury, Connecticut.

to emanate from the free will and intelligent conviction of those whom God has made responsible for power." In contrast with these principles and consequences, governments of law assume "that there is but one class of society, and that this class is the people; that all men are created equal, and therefore that civil institutions are voluntary associations, of which the sole object should be to promote the happiness of the whole." The people have a right to choose the form of government under which they wish to live and to make whatever later modifications they may desire. The authority of rulers is delegated to them by the people, to be exercised constitutionally, "according to a written code, which code is nothing more than an authentic expression of the people's will." The ruler's function, under a government of law, is to be "nothing more than the intelligent organ of enlightened public opinion." Needless to say, the government of the United States is "an illustrious example of the government of law" and an inspiration to the people of every land.[40]

By 1838, the screaming of the eagle had become a little less vociferous. Faced in his day-to-day life in Rhode Island by the existence of a considerable popular opposition to its constitutional government, Wayland saw the struggle as one arising from economic differentiation and warned against what he saw as a developing tyranny of the majority. Earlier, as we have seen, he considered a government of law the expression of a classless society; now he saw, as James Madison had in the tenth of the *Federalist Papers,* that economic differences could lead to political factionalism, and this, in turn, to the destruction of republicanism and constitutionalism.

It can have escaped the observation of no one that one of the greatest political dangers to which this country is exposed arises from a feeling of estrangement between the rich and the poor. I do not suppose, however, that the capitalist and laborer will ever be here arrayed in arms against each other. In a country where neither entail nor primogeniture can exist, the conditions of men change so rapidly that a contest between these two classes, by physical force, is scarcely to be apprehended. We have, however, reason to fear that this feeling of estrangement may lead the different classes of society to look with indifference upon the rights of each other. The majority, for the time being, will then trample upon the rights of the minority; constitutions, and law, and equity, will be forgotten, and the only rule recognized will be the will of the strongest. Each party, as in the mutation of politics it comes into

[40] Wayland, *Occasional Discourses,* pp. 49–50, 59–62.

power, will improve upon the example of its predecessor; and thus, each in turn will suffer and will inflict the most aggravated wrong. The result of this may be easily predicted. All men hate injustice when they themselves are the sufferers; and, as all in turn suffer, they will all in turn lightly esteem that form of government under which injustice may so easily be perpetrated. A growing disaffection toward republican institutions will thus be engendered, and all will consent to submit to the tyranny of one, in order to be delivered from the tyranny of many. This I hold to be the danger to which, at this moment, we are in this country exposed; and I almost fear that, from this very cause, some symptoms of a want of confidence in the permanence of our free institutions have already become apparent.[41]

Was this jeremiad addressed merely to local conditions in Rhode Island? Perhaps not; perhaps it is a reflection of a general situation to which Alexis de Tocqueville had called attention in *Democracy in America* (1835), or perhaps it is the plaint of an ardent Jeffersonian democrat after a decade of viewing the Jacksonian democracy in power.

Whatever may have induced Wayland to this prophetic diatribe, the passage just quoted serves admirably to explain the stand he took when, in 1842, Rhode Island was torn by the civil strife of the Dorr Rebellion. This is not the place to discuss the rights and wrongs of the situation that evoked so extreme a reaction; let it suffice to say that Rhode Island's constitution preserved obsolete limitations on the right of suffrage and that a popular party, headed by Thomas Wilson Dorr (1805-1854), believing that all legally authorized measures to remove the defect had been exhausted, took matters into its own hands. The actions of this group led to reprisals, and, in 1842, to what for a time threatened to be civil war. There were incidents of violence, and it was these that led Wayland, as a public leader, to deliver his celebrated discourse on *The Affairs of Rhode Island,* on May 22, 1842, and later sermons on "The Duty of Obedience to the Civil Magistrate." The position Wayland took was a difficult one to maintain. All the objectives sought by the popular party were congenial to his political ideals; it was the method of rebellion to which he here took exception. Yet he could not, consistently, appear as an opponent of all rebellion and revolution, since the 1825 sermons, of which we have spoken, and his 1826 eulogy on

[41] Wayland, *A Discourse . . . 1838*, pp. 28-29.

"The Death of the Ex-Presidents," John Adams and Thomas Jefferson,[42] praised the American Revolution and suggested that other nations follow the example of the American colonies. To understand Wayland's position, we must recur to his distinction between governments of will and those of law. Rebellion against a government of will for the sake of establishing a government of law is justifiable; rebellion against a government of law is unjustifiable because the proper, nonrevolutionary means of change are written into the constitution.

By making this distinction Wayland was able to rationalize the stand he took against the Dorr group. "This," he said, ". . . is no party question. It is a question affecting the very existence of society. During the past week we have been called upon to decide, not whether this party or that shall be in the ascendant, but whether law or anarchy shall bear sway; not at the ballot boxes, to express our peaceful wishes, but at the cannon's mouth, to determine whether we shall be governed by constitutional law or trampled under foot by a lawless soldiery." Wayland introduced an interesting addition to the classical theory of the social contract by arguing that "in any social compact, not only the rights but also the feelings of our fellow men should be strictly regarded." Yet his own emphasis belies this concern for human feelings, among the members of the popular party, at least. Indeed, we might say he showed great tenderness toward both the rights and the feelings of the minority and far less for the rights and feelings of the majority. Considering the extent to which the social contract theory had been used, in both Europe and America, as a philosophic foundation for the right of revolution, Wayland's interpretation of it comes as a shock. "We are not at liberty to enter a society and enjoy its advantages, and then conspire to overturn it; to swear allegiance, and when we please, to violate it. We have no more liberty to overturn the social compact when we will, than the marriage compact." [43] This view of the social contract would not have commended itself to Thomas Jefferson nor yet to

[42] Wayland, *Occasional Discourses*, pp. 80–97.
[43] Francis Wayland, *The Affairs of Rhode Island. A Discourse Delivered in the Meeting-House of the First Baptist Church, Providence, May 22, 1842* (Providence: B. Cranston & Co. and H. H. Brown, 1842), pp. 5–6, 13, 29.

John Locke. It is far closer to the version expounded by Thomas Hobbes and, we should add, to the theology of liberty in Calvin's *Institutes of the Christian Religion.*

The theological aspect of Wayland's zealous moderation comes to the fore in his three sermons on "The Duty of Obedience to the Civil Magistrate." He spoke of the apparent contradiction in the obligations of the Christian: his duty to obey the civil magistrate and his duty to obey God. When does one "Render unto Caesar the things that are Caesar's"? The civil magistracy, Wayland answered, is to be obeyed within the limits of its constituted authority only, and then only while its authority is exercised "innocently." [44] Civil government is constituted to protect the rights with which individuals were endowed by their Creator; it was ordained by God because men, in their innate injustice, attempt to appropriate the labor and the property of their fellow men to their own purposes and to limit the freedom of thought and conscience of other men. The purpose of civil government, established by social contract, is mutual restraint. Hence all must be placed under civil authority so that the force of the united whole may guarantee the individual rights of each. In protecting the rights of individuals, it is legitimate for society to use force. Both governments and individuals are, however, subject to the moral law and the Gospels, but in the last resort the individual conscience must be the judge of the rectitude of government enactments. When one is conscientiously convinced that the government is no longer performing its constituted functions but is using force to deprive individuals of their rights, then it has lost its authority and he is justified in resisting it for the sole purpose of instituting another government in its place.

Mere error on the part of a government is not enough to sanction revolt even though the error may lead to injustice. No government may properly be resisted "so long as it accomplishes, or honestly intends to accomplish, the purpose for which it was established." Indeed, the individual, in undertaking rebellion, is obligated to restrict

---

[44] Francis Wayland, *University Sermons* (Boston: Gould, Kendall, & Lincoln, 1849), pp. 256–258. My discussion in this section is indebted to an unpublished essay by Mr. George S. Rosenberg, on "The Social Philosophies of Francis Wayland and Job Durfee, and Their Relation to the Dorr Rebellion," in my possession.

his actions to the exercise of powers reserved to him in the original compact and is also bound by the principles of the Gospels, from which "all true freedom on earth springs essentially." At this stage in Wayland's thought, he virtually excluded the possibility of any justifiable revolt against duly constituted civil authorities, especially in the United States of America. Even when "Caesar" acts wrongfully, passive resistance is the limit of the citizen's recourse; the religious and moral obligation of the citizen does not extend to righting the wrongs done by the government. The individual's problem is how to "shun participation in the guilt of Caesar." [45]

Wayland reached a similar conclusion in a "little essay" published in 1838 under the title *Limitations of Human Responsibility*. Here his concern was with the methods by which reforms, desirable in themselves, were to be sought. He urged the need for a proper conception of individual moral responsibility that would not, on the one hand, merge the individual conscience into any sort of social conscience or, on the other hand, demand of the individual conscience responsibility that lies beyond its scope. Men should not be held responsible for the doing of good when this would require either more ability than they have or a kind of ability that they do not have. Furthermore, Wayland argued, even the possession of powers and abilities adequate to the accomplishment of any reform does not necessarily imply responsibility for its performance.[46] We may conjecture that the position taken by Wayland was a protest, born out of the Enlightenment, against the emphasis on the sense of guilt that was a major feature of the stock-in-trade of both religious and secular evangelists in the 1830's and 40's.

Needless to say, Wayland's position did not go unchallenged. Abolitionists were deeply disappointed by his emphasis on the limitations of individual responsibility for the social guilt of slavery. Protagonists of constitutional change in Rhode Island were vehement in denouncing his opposition to the Dorr Rebellion. In a typical attack, John Augustus Bolles (1809–1878), a Boston lawyer, com-

[45] Wayland, *University Sermons*, pp. 259–260, 264, 283ff., 256.
[46] See the discussion of *Limitations of Human Responsibility* in Murray, *Francis Wayland*, pp. 209–211.

mented on Wayland's extension of the doctrine of social contract to include sensitivity to the feelings as well as the rights of others by noting that he had "arrived at the conviction that suffrage is not so much a matter of *right* as of feeling; not an indubitable and most precious boon, but a fancy, 'a doubtful matter,' a thing not worth the quarreling for or about, upon the one side or the other." As for the religious doctrine of submission to the "powers that be," Bolles charged that they "would seem to have been taken entire from the manuscript sermon of some royal chaplain . . . not from the head and heart of an American preacher." In sum, "We miss that clearness of judgment, and that lofty tone of bold republicanism, which were so conspicuous in the splendid sermons 'on the Duties of an American Citizen,' and in the 'Eulogy' of July, 1826, on Adams and Jefferson." [47]

Such an appeal from Wayland's sober conservatism at the time of the Dorr revolt to his earlier intoxicated republicanism was vindicated by the stand Wayland took later, in 1848–1849, when he opposed the annexation of Texas and the Mexican War that followed. He had no scruples now about challenging the acts of duly constituted civil authority. The United States, he thought, had more territory than it could use with profit; to annex Texas would serve only to extend the range and power of slavery and to involve the nation in unnecessary and immoral war. The Mexican War, he declared, was "*ab origine,* wicked, infamous, unconstitutional in design, and stupid and shockingly depraved in its management." [48] These are scarcely the words of one who believed the citizen's only recourse to be passive resistance. Indeed, the sermons he preached at this time on "Obedience to the Civil Magistrate" [49] were deliberately intended to stir the moral sense of the nation. To his sister Wayland wrote, "I never felt more anxious about anything I have published; not, I trust, on my own account (for necessity was laid upon me, and

---

[47] [John Augustus Bolles], *"The Affairs of Rhode Island,"* being a Review of President Wayland's Discourse. A Vindication of the Sovereignty of the People and a Refutation of the Doctrines and Doctors of Despotism. By a Member of the Boston Bar. (Providence: B. T. Albro; Boston: B. B. Mussey, 1842), pp. 15, 16, 5.

[48] Quoted in Murray, *Francis Wayland,* p. 273.

[49] Wayland, *University Sermons,* pp. 252–293.

I could not but bear my testimony), but on account of my country." [50] Again, Wayland both acted and spoke in opposition to the Fugitive Slave Law of 1850, even to the point of sheltering, clothing, and feeding a fugitive slave and sending him on his way with a gift of money. Any charge of inconsistency or vacillation that might be laid against Wayland because of this is, however, disarmed by his calm insistence and assurance that whether he is urging silence and obedience to constituted authority, as in 1842, or counselling prophetic utterance and disobedience to law, as in 1850, he is doing as God would have him do.[51]

Wayland's last important statement of his theory of democracy, in 1854, occurs as a digression in his address at the celebration of Eliphalet Nott's half century in the presidency of Union College. On this occasion, without making specific reference to any of the agitations that had swept the nation or to those that were still matters of grave concern, Wayland reaffirmed his faith in a Jeffersonian limited government and in a society into which men entered voluntarily as a means to self-fulfillment. He proposed, in essence, a "social contract" view of a civil polity of mutual protection of every man's "right to himself." Beyond this protection, democratic society "leaves the individual to work out his own destiny for himself." A man's success or failure is his own; each man is permitted to "pursue his own happiness, in his own way." Each is "the architect of his own fortune."

The wheel had turned full circle. Wayland reverted to the vigorous individualistic republicanism of his early years as his career at Brown neared its end. Forcefully he declared the educational corollary of his political faith:

When our systems of education shall look with as kindly an eye on the mechanic as the lawyer, on the manufacturer and merchant as the minister; when every artizan, performing his process with a knowledge of the laws by which it is governed, shall be transformed from an unthinking laborer into a practical philosopher; and when the benign principles of Christianity shall

---

[50] Quoted in Murray, *Francis Wayland,* pp. 273–274.

[51] "I have always declared that I would never aid in arresting a fugitive, or do a thing to return him to slavery . . . This I have a right to do, on the principle that I must obey God rather than man." Quoted in Murray, *Francis Wayland,* p. 274.

imbue the whole mass of our people with the spirit of universal love, then, and not till then, shall we illustrate to the nations the blessings of Republican and Christian Institutions.[52]

No wonder that, in 1870, Noah Porter (1811–1892) of Yale, in re-affirming the traditionalism of the Yale Report of 1828 against later and freer educational ideals, still found it necessary to attempt to refute the principles underlying Wayland's "complete revolution . . . in the constitution of Brown University." [53]

When Henry Barnard lauded Wayland in *The American Journal of Education,* he spoke of Wayland's resignation of his Boston pastorate, in 1826, as a leaving of the ministry with the intention of resuming it within a short time.[54] Yet there seems to be little doubt that Wayland, with the aid of his sponsors, President Eliphalet Nott of Union College and Professor Moses Stuart (1780–1852) of the Andover Theological Seminary, had been jockeying for the presidency of Brown University for some time. He spent but one year, 1816–1817, as a student at Andover, under the tutelage and influence of Stuart, before returning to Union as a tutor. During part of his four years as a tutor, he filled the pulpit of a small church in the village of Burnt Hills. He left his post at Union to accept the pastorate of the First Baptist Church in Boston on the advice of Stuart, who wrote that the move would bring Wayland nearer to Brown University, "the center of Baptist activities." Even more revealingly, Stuart added, "The cause there absolutely and impe-riously demands a man like you." [55] So open a statement as this leaves little room for doubt that Wayland accepted the Boston pulpit as a stepping-stone to the presidency of Brown.

The incumbent president, Dr. Asa Messer (1769–1836) had, of course, to be forced out, with as much grace as possible. Messer was, so Wayland himself said, "a scholar of profound and varied learn-ing, as well as an instructor of singular ability." [56] This estimate, in

---

[52] Wayland, *The Education Demanded,* pp. 22–23, 29.

[53] Noah Porter, *The American Colleges and the American Public* (New Haven, Conn.: Charles C. Chatfield & Co., 1870), esp. pp. 14–16.

[54] Barnard, "Francis Wayland," p. 773.

[55] Roelker, "Francis Wayland," p. 31.

[56] Wayland, *Discourse on the Life and Character of Nicholas Brown,* p. 22, quoted in Barnard, "Francis Wayland," p. 773.

the course of a eulogy of Nicholas Brown, could have been intended merely as an indication of the distinctions that had come to Brown University through the funds supplied by its munificent patron. Or, possibly, it could have been a victor's gallant gesture to his vanquished foe. Conceivably, it could have been an overgenerous statement of the reality. However this may be, Messer had seemingly allowed himself two lapses from grace; he had consorted with the newly founded Unitarian Church, coming perilously close to an espousal of its position, and he had permitted student discipline at Brown to lapse. Messer's theological lapse was the ostensible official reason for his resignation being demanded. The charter of Brown was liberal, for its time. The majority voice in its government was reserved to the Baptists, but the faculty was "free and open for all denominations of Protestants"—the "President alone excepted." Once his Baptist affiliation was suspect, Messer could no longer serve as president.[57]

Yet so much emphasis is placed in the sources on Messer's failure to maintain student discipline, that the theological reason seems like a trumped-up charge. "The last two or three years of Dr. Messer's term of service were marked by a large share of idleness, dissipation and recklessness on the part of many students." [58] "A barrel of ale was always kept on tap in the cellar, to which all under-graduates had free access." [59] It is possible that the pressures and tensions of Dr. Messer's life during the years preceding his forced resignation, his own searching attempts to discover where he really stood in the theological spectrum, and the attacks upon him for his concessions to Unitarianism, led to lessened effectiveness as a disciplinarian. But it is also within the bounds of possibility that both his theological and his disciplinary difficulties were greatly exaggerated as part of a campaign of intrigue to dispose of him in the interest of Francis Wayland.[60]

[57] See quotations from Brown University Charter in Murray, *Francis Wayland*, pp. 59–60.
[58] Barnard, "Francis Wayland," p. 774.
[59] Quoted, from unindicated source, by Murray, *Francis Wayland*, p. 63.
[60] Although Wayland was appointed Professor at Union College on his resignation of his Boston pastorate, his move to Brown was, apparently, so certain that his wife

Once his election to the presidency of Brown had been achieved, Wayland introduced strict disciplinary measures, which produced extraordinarily rapid results and speedily gained Wayland a reputation for administrative firmness. The friendly interpretation given by Barnard suggests that the students were glad to be forced back to habits of order and study. "There are men now in high position who ascribe their success in life to the influence of Dr. Wayland in recalling them from the worse than waste of time, and inciting them to assert their manhood by a new course of conduct." [61] A less friendly interpretation might reflect, cynically, that the discipline under Dr. Messer could not have been as bad as it was painted if Wayland was so easily able to stem the tide.

Whatever Wayland did, in fact, achieve was not won by popularity contest methods. His influence over the students was not based on their affection for him. Among his intimates on the faculty and elsewhere, he was known as a man of warm heart and genial, even jovial, manner. This side of himself he never turned toward his students. "His influence over the young men arose partly from his majestic presence, but mainly from that imperial spirit, corresponding with the external presence, the existence and power of which every one perceived who came in contact with him." [62] Wayland, in his Reminiscences, noted that he never faced an important instance of student discipline without grave mental distress; so effectively did he control himself, however, that he gained the reputation of a martinet. "I went through it so coolly that I believe I acquired

---

never left Boston for Schenectady! "From the postscripts to Wayland's devoted, but routine, letters to his wife in Boston it is evident that he promptly engaged in an active, but very secret, campaign to obtain the appointment as president." Roelker, "Francis Wayland," p. 32. "About the time of my leaving Boston," Wayland himself recalled, "Dr. Messer, the President of Brown University, was on the point of resigning. I had been urged to become a candidate for the office. My friends in the vicinity of Boston, especially Dr. Sharp and Dr. Bolles, pressed it. In the course of the autumn, Dr. Messer resigned . . . There was some doubt as to the election, as one or two candidates beside myself had been presented. I had but little anxiety about the result, although the uncertainty was annoying." Quoted in Murray, *Francis Wayland*, pp. 60–61.

[61] Barnard, "Francis Wayland," p. 774.
[62] Barnard, "Francis Wayland," p. 775.

the reputation of being a stern, unfeeling disciplinarian, who was determined to carry out college regulations regardless of the pain he caused." [63]

In the relatively tiny and inadequately financed American colleges of the nineteenth century, there was little division of labor. The president, especially, had to be a man-of-all-work. Wayland, for example, took care of much of the everyday routine correspondence of Brown University, as well as being its chief fund raiser, meeting with its Board of Governors, personally selecting and directing its faculty, often preaching in its chapel, and acting as disciplinarian. He was a leading figure in the local community of Providence, participating in public ceremonies and serving on committees of citizens. He played a significant role on the national educational scene and took an important part in stimulating the development of elementary education in New England. He was one of the creators of the free public library system that was one of the glories of Massachusetts; the town of East Sudbury even changed its name to Wayland in his honor and in gratitude for a substantial cash contribution he made toward its public library.[64] Withal, like other college presidents of his day, Wayland taught, regularly and with devotion, the senior course in moral philosophy, described by Roelker as the "one garden spot" in "the arid waste of the curriculum." [65]

"The loosely organized moral philosophy course, with its core of ethics and its smattering of logic and literary criticism, of political, economic, and psychological data, offered limitless opportunities to the ingenious teacher. He could turn it in many directions and make it serve as a vehicle for anything he wanted the seniors to know before turning them out into the world." [66] For the college president thus to make a lasting impression on the students was a long-stand-

---

[63] Murray, *Francis Wayland*, p. 69. An extended presentation of Wayland's views on discipline, largely in his own words, is given by Murray, pp. 67–73.

[64] See Jared M. Heard, *Origin of the Free Public Library System of Massachusetts* (Clinton, Mass., 1860), and Roelker, "Francis Wayland," p. 53. For a general account of Wayland as a public figure and an educational leader, see Murray, *Francis Wayland*, especially chaps. vi and ix.

[65] Roelker, "Francis Wayland," p. 41.

[66] George P. Schmidt, "Intellectual Crosscurrents in American Colleges," *American Historical Review*, 42 (1936), 49.

ing tradition before Wayland came to Brown. His mentor, Eliphalet Nott, had been particularly skillful in using the opportunity to impress his views indelibly on Union College seniors. Nott's course was recorded simply as "Kames." [67] One of Nott's former students described the experience and its effects:

> Lord Kames himself would have rubbed his eyes in astonishment, if he could have seen and heard the use that was made of his book. He would have found it so amplified and expanded that, instead of a compend of aesthetics, it had become a comprehensive study of human nature, ranging over the whole field of physical, moral, and intellectual philosophy, and applied to practical use in business, politics, and religion . . . Many a clergyman, many an author, many a lawyer and statesman has found that Dr. Nott and "Kames" have given him the solution of some of the most perplexing problems of his life.[68]

Wayland's senior course probably rambled somewhat less than Nott's, but it was apparently equally effective. When he first came to Brown and undertook the teaching of this course, the textbook in use was the *Principles of Moral and Political Philosophy* of William Paley (1743–1805), English theologian and lecturer in Cambridge University. Paley's work is regarded as the best statement of the utilitarian ethics of the eighteenth century. Wayland's antipathy to basing moral judgments on the consequences of men's acts was already deeply ingrained. He inclined far more to sympathy with the views of Bishop Joseph Butler (1692–1752), whose moral emphasis was placed upon conscience as a faculty directing man's actions in accordance with moral law. At first, Wayland had his classes continue to use Paley's book as their text and presented his own objections, dissents and disagreements in the classroom discussions. Within a short time, however, he began to present his own ideas in the form of lectures and "In a few years, these lectures had become so far extended, that, to my surprise, they contained, by themselves, the elements of a different system from that of the textbook which I was teaching." [69]

---

[67] It was based on readings in *The Elements of Criticism* of the Scottish philosopher Henry Home, Lord Kames (1696–1782).

[68] Frederick W. Seward, *Reminiscences of a War-Time Statesman and Diplomat* (New York, 1916), p. 65.

[69] *The Elements of Moral Science,* Preface, below.

The rest of the story is a familiar one. Recovering from his surprise, Wayland set about the task of, first, amplifying his lectures and using them to replace Paley's book and, next, transforming the lectures into a book of his own, *The Elements of Moral Science,* first published by Cooke and Company in New York, in May 1835. This work was, for its time, phenomenally successful. Printing followed printing in America until, by the end of the nineteenth century, about 100,000 copies had been sold. An abridged version was prepared for use in secondary schools. An English edition was published and many translations into such languages as Modern Greek, Armenian and Hawaiian. In these various translations, Wayland's *Elements of Moral Science* was carried all over the world by missionaries.

Undoubtedly part of the reason for the widespread acceptance of Wayland's textbook was its extreme directness and simplicity of presentation. The book is better described as a didactic manual or handbook of precepts than as a philosophic discussion of ethical problems. Wayland deliberately and consciously avoided any extended discussions, illustrations or historical references. He set out "to state the moral law, and the reason of it, in as few and as comprehensive terms as possible . . . A work which should attempt to exhibit what was true appeared to me more desirable than one which should point out what was exploded, discuss what was doubtful, or disprove what was false." [70] Early as he was in the American textbook field, Wayland had already grasped, in essence, the principle of blandness by which it is still dominated.

As a result, this first American textbook in moral philosophy has far more value as a document illustrative of nineteenth-century ethics and of the history of moral education than as a contribution to the development of philosophy in America. Its first part, headed "Theoretical Ethics," has its philosophic roots in the Scottish version of an empiricism that, nevertheless, accepts certain principles as given prior to all experience. Among these *a priori* principles are the rules governing moral action, the laws of the moral life. We have already noted that Wayland accepted the faculty psychology current in his age; we must now add that he regarded conscience (or "moral sense")

[70] *The Elements of Moral Science,* Preface.

as one of these constituent powers of the human mind. The function of conscience is to give man a quasi-perceptual means of discriminating right actions from wrong. Since Wayland rejected utilitarianism, which permits this discrimination to be made by an evaluation of the consequences of an action, and replaced it with the view that the moral quality of an action resides in its intention, conscience may be described as a way of judging the intentions of an action. Conscience is the judiciary branch of the moral life, not its legislature. The laws of morality are made by God, not by man's moral sense. Men may learn some part of their duty by the "light of nature" or natural religion. This is, however, deficient in extent and inadequate in motivating them to the good life. Full knowledge of duty and adequate impulsion toward its performance can come only through the "additional light" of revealed religion, of the Holy Scripture.

The longer second part of Wayland's *Elements of Moral Science,* headed "Practical Ethics," is of more interest. It is founded on three commonplaces of popular American thought in the nineteenth century: the eternal validity of the moral law revealed in the Scriptures and man's consequent obligation to revere and worship the Divine Revealer; [71] the right of private judgment, a corollary of his theoretical views on the conscience and a central feature of the Protestant tradition; and the limitation of the powers of government, the political heritage of Jeffersonian republicanism as expressed in the Declaration of Independence. By applying these principles to moral practice, Wayland was able to vindicate and validate all the virtues he thought desirable to cultivate: justice, veracity, chastity, and benevolence.

For all of Wayland's careful colorlessness of presentation, one section of his text proved to be controversial in the extreme. Under the head of "Personal Liberty" he treated the question of slavery. The position to which he came is that slavery is morally unjust, because it is an invasion of the personal liberty of the slave and religiously

---

[71] Hence, a rigorous observance of the "Sabbath" is demanded and magistrates are declared to be obligated to enforce such observance. Wayland here acknowledges his debt to the British Quaker and abolitionist, Joseph John Gurney (1788–1847), whose *Brief Remarks on the History, Authority, and Use of the Sabbath* received American publication, with notes by Moses Stuart, in 1833.

unsanctioned, save to the extent and in the manner explicitly allowed by "the Law of Moses." After a long discussion he reaches the conclusion that the duty of masters to slaves is to manumit them; the duty of slaves to masters is to obey them and be faithful to them. Wayland's solution to the most crying social injustice of his time was to leave action entirely up to the Christian conscience of the individual master. He certainly intended no aid or comfort to the nascent abolitionist movement. We must understand his 1838 essay on "The Limitations of Human Responsibility" as, in part, a justification of the unorganized approach to the elimination of slavery proposed in *The Elements of Moral Science*. The Northern Abolitionist, he is saying, in effect, does not bear the burden of guilt for the Southern slaveowner; therefore it is not his responsibility but the Southerner's to put an end to slavery.[72]

Though Wayland's views on the justification of slavery seem moderate, by eighteenth- or twentieth-century standards, they were published during the very years of the nineteenth century when proslavery thought in the South was most energetically consolidating and defending its position.[73] Moreover, Wayland had struck at a most vulnerable point in the armor of the Southern way of life: its religiosity. Practically as soon as the book was published, one Southern theologian prepared a reply. Stephen Taylor (1796–1853), who was professor of ecclesiastical history and church government in the Union Theological Seminary, Richmond, Virginia, prepared a book entitled, *Relation of Master and Servant, as Exhibited in the New Testament: together with a Review of Dr. Wayland's Elements of*

---

[72] Wayland's "The Limitations of Human Responsibility" was most unfavorably received by the British press and, especially, the dissenting churches because of its antiabolitionist implications. His diary during his 1840 visit reflects this: "All the talk about abolition, etc.! It is amusing to perceive how this question seems to absorb every other among the dissenters, and to what extent they carry out their notions. A man who does not adopt their opinions is, it would seem, excommunicated from church and society." Quoted in Murray, *Francis Wayland*, p. 83. The same author (p. 211) remarks on the American reception of "The Limitations of Human Responsibility" that "His treatment of the slavery question . . . was a surprise and a disappointment to the best antislavery sentiment of the North."

[73] For an extended account of this process and especially of the impact of the Hegelianized argument of Thomas R. Dew, see William Sumner Jenkins, *Pro-Slavery Thought in the Old South* (Chapel Hill: The University of North Carolina Press, 1935).

Moral Science on the Subject of Slavery (Richmond, Va., 1836). Of course, Wayland's textbook of "moral science" could not be used in Southern colleges; Jasper Adams (1793–1841), a Brown graduate and former president of Charleston College, Charleston, South Carolina, hastened to publish a rival text presenting a fitter interpretation of the moral benefits of slavery and of the duties of masters and slaves.[74] It was not enough, however, to protect the South on its home grounds; the attack against Wayland had to be carried into "enemy" territory in the North. In pursuance of this aim the Reverend Richard Fuller (1804–1876), of Beaufort, South Carolina, wrote, in the form of a letter to the editor of *The Christian Reflector,* a sharp criticism of Wayland:

His position is this: the moral precepts of the gospel condemn slavery; it is therefore criminal. Yet he admits that neither the Saviour nor his apostles commanded masters to emancipate their slaves; nay, they "go further," he adds, "and prescribe the duties suited to both parties in their present condition;" among which duties, be it remembered, there is not an intimation of manumission, but the whole code contemplates the continuance of the relation. Here, then, we have the Author of the gospel, and the inspired propagators of the gospel, and the Holy Spirit inditing the gospel, all conniving at a practice which was a violation of the entire moral principle of the gospel! And the reason assigned by Dr. Wayland for this abstinency by God from censuring a widespread infraction of his law, is really nothing more nor less than expediency—the apprehension of consequences. The Lord Jesus and the apostles teaching expediency![75]

As late as 1857, Wayland was still a *bête noir* of Southern apologists; one of them, James A. Sloan, even managed to twist Wayland's arguments, in *The Elements of Moral Science,* on the sanctity of property into an attack on Wayland's views on slavery. Sloan's general position is that Wayland, who is representative of "another class of writers and declaimers," has first *"assumed* that the relation is morally and politically wrong—sinful in itself," and then sought out proofs

---

[74] Jasper Adams, *Elements of Moral Philosophy* (Cambridge, Mass.: Folsom, Wells, and Thurston, 1837).

[75] Fuller's original letter was reprinted as an introduction to the exchange of letters that it initiated. See *Domestic Slavery Considered as a Scriptural Institution:* in a correspondence between the Rev. Richard Fuller . . . and the Rev. Francis Wayland . . . Revised and corrected by the authors. Fifth edition (New York: Lewis Colby & Co.; Boston: Gould, Kendall and Lincoln, 1847), pp. 4–5. The first edition of this book was published in 1845.

for this assumption. The initial assumption, Sloan says, causes such men as Wayland to "look at all things pertaining to the subject through a false medium." [76]

In the meantime, Wayland's views on slavery had become more militant. The first major revision of his *Elements of Moral Science,* in 1837, the year before "The Limitations of Human Responsibility," showed a few changes from the chapters as originally written, generally with a view to sharpening his argument. A revealing footnote to one of the passages carried over from the first edition to the 1837 revision indicates, however, that Wayland had taken the views of his Southern critics into account but, in this instance, had decided to make no change. By 1842, his realization that the South was not apologizing for slavery but propagandizing for its extension made it clear that the earlier moderate stand he had taken would be of no avail. He read William Ellery Channing's pamphlet on *The Duty of the Free States.* Charles Sumner reported to Channing that Wayland "wished me to say to you that he had read both parts with great pleasure, and that he agreed with you entirely. His views on slavery, and with regard to the South, have materially changed lately." [77]

In his exchange of letters with Fuller, however, Wayland tried to leave the door open to a reconciliation of his views with those of his Christian colleagues in the South. He made, for example, a careful distinction between the inherent wrongness of an act and the guilt of the actor; "The *wrong* was ever the same. *Guilt* commenced as soon as he was convinced of the wrong, and continued in the practice of it." He asserted and emphasized that human understanding of the unchanging divine moral law is continually improving and deepening, "with the progress of light and knowledge," so that "It is much more difficult for a man at the present time to hold his fellow men in bondage, and be guiltless, through ignorance, than it was twenty years since"; nevertheless, he still declared that there was, "on this subject, wide ground for the exercise of Christian charity." He carried the argument for progress even to the belief in a

[76] James A. Sloan, *The Great Question Answered; or, Is Slavery a Sin in Itself (Per Se?) answered according to the teaching of the Scriptures* (Memphis: Hutton, Gallaway & Co., 1857), p. 8.

[77] Charles Sumner to William Ellery Channing, June 23, 1842, quoted in Murray, *Francis Wayland,* p. 213.

progressive revelation, that God revealed to the Hebrews "just as much of his moral law as he chose, and the law on this subject belonged to the part which he did not choose to make known" at that time.

For all this obvious attempt to pacify and mollify, it is clear in the letters to Fuller that Wayland's opposition to slavery had become firmer. In the interest of this more forceful stand, he was ready to compromise—or, at least, to rationalize—his cherished antagonism to utilitarianism, the morality of expediency. For, he argued, in response to Fuller's charge that he had accused "the Lord Jesus and the apostles" of teaching expediency, there are, indeed, many cases "in which the acting from expediency involves moral guilt, and frequently guilt of no ordinary turpitude." There are, however, many cases in which expedient action may not involve guilt, all of which fall under this rule: "We may innocently employ any means for the accomplishing of our purposes, which are innocent in themselves, and which we employ with a virtuous intention." One such "innocent" form of expediency is "the inculcating of a fundamental truth, rather than of the duty which springs immediately out of it." Wayland argues that the "gospel of Christ" is a representative of expediency of this sort. "It is a treasure house of elementary and all-controlling moral truth. This truth it presents to the understanding, and presses upon the conscience, leaving it to every individual to carry it into practice according to the peculiarities of his individual situation, provided only he do it *honestly, earnestly,* with pure love to God and ardent charity to man." [78] Thus the exigencies of the controversy over slavery led Wayland to a partial reconciliation of Paley and Butler.

The ultimate fruits of Wayland's increasing conviction of the evil of slavery can be found in his opposition to the annexation of Texas, his support of Abraham Lincoln's nomination for the presidency, and his recognition of the necessity of Northern military action to put down secession in 1861. He wrote his son, on January 18, 1861,

God is about to bring slavery forever to an end. He has taken it into his own hands, and allowed the South to have its own way. They proclaim slavery as a most religious thing, for which they are willing to die. God is taking

[78] Fuller and Wayland, *Domestic Slavery,* pp. 38–39, 40–41, 49–50, 69, 72–73.

this way to free us from complicity, and to let them try it by themselves. Greater madness never existed.[79]

The final revision of *The Elements of Moral Science,* undertaken during the last year of the Civil War and the last of Wayland's life, presents a largely rewritten chapter on slavery with a far more decisive stress on its immorality.[80]

Wayland had, however, another conviction of long standing, against the use of force, against war. He had been an advocate of international arbitration. At the time of the Mexican War, he had preached that a citizen was under no obligation to support his government in a war of aggression. He often declared that all war, except in self-defense, was forbidden by the Gospels. One of his chief complaints against the Dorr rebels had been their resort to violence. From the first edition of *The Elements of Moral Science,* he had included a brief but sharp condemnation of war. The American Peace Society elected him as its president for several terms. Yet he all but welcomed the Civil War when it burst upon the nation:

Can it be doubted on which side God will declare himself? Can we doubt that, if we look to him in faith, he will bring forth judgment into victory? If you want to see how God looks on oppression, read the ninety-fifth Psalm. I hope all our friends will continue firm, and sacrifice no principle for present advantage. The best place to meet a difficulty is just where God puts it. If we dodge it, it will come in a worse place.[81]

He regretted "the death of men who have made themselves enemies, but to whom I have no feeling of enmity." [82] Yet he gave the war his unswerving support in every way in which a man of his age in poor physical condition could, even to "march with a regiment of troops to their embarkation, and send them forth with the benediction of his prayer." [83] And when, in 1865, he came to review the

[79] Murray, *Francis Wayland,* p. 147.

[80] In 1862, he wrote to the editors of the *Atlantic Monthly* declining an invitation to write for that magazine, on the ground of ill health. He took the occasion to commend the editors for their strong antislavery position, ALS, May 2, 1862, F. Wayland to the Editors of the *Atlantic Monthly,* Huntington Library, San Marino, California.

[81] Francis Wayland to the Hon. Lafayette Foster, quoted in Murray, *Francis Wayland,* pp. 146–147.

[82] Quoted from a letter to his sister, in Murray, *Francis Wayland,* p. 149.

[83] Murray, *Francis Wayland,* p. 150.

penultimate section of his *Elements of Moral Science,* he moderated somewhat the antiwar attitude of his earlier editions.

These two related changes in Wayland's "practical ethics" spell out the extent to which his moral views, however doctrinaire they may seem to the casual modern reader, were actually forged on the anvil of large public affairs. Absolutist though he was, the living issues of his day forced him to modify his absolutism. Perhaps his early moral views were oversimplified; he had not yet faced the crisis that comes from the conflict of two ideals. In the thirty years that separate the first edition of *The Elements of Moral Science* from the last revision to bear the impress of the author's hand, he learned by his experience and that of his country the vital lesson that no moral system is worth the statement that has not been hammered out in the teeth of recalcitrant fact.

Joseph L. Blau

Columbia University

A NOTE ON THE TEXT

THERE were three main editions of Wayland's *Elements of Moral Science*. The original text was published in 1835. Wayland himself was dissatisfied with it; he quickly revised it and published what became the standard edition in 1837. It was this version that entered into the curriculum of innumerable colleges and which sold at least 75,000 copies. A final version was published in 1865 when the author was in the last few months of his life and was isolated to a considerable extent from the currents of the time. The book in this form did not repeat its earlier popularity.

The text reprinted in the present edition is that of 1837, with minor changes: archaic punctuation and spelling have been modernized and typographical errors have been corrected. Some of the variations from edition to edition are important, however, and an effort has been made to provide the reader with the texts of revisions that represent significant shifts in Wayland's thinking. Major differences between the 1837 edition and those of 1835 and 1865, bearing particularly on the questions of slavery and of war, have been noted in numbered footnotes and the variant passages reprinted in their entirety in the Appendix. There are in addition some 1050 minor changes—verbal alterations within sentences which Wayland made in an effort to increase the precision of his statements. These revisions, of value to the advanced student of nineteenth-century philosophy and linguistics, were compiled in the course of preparing this volume, and have been recorded on microfilm and deposited in the Brown, Columbia, and Harvard University Libraries.

J. L. B.

THE ELEMENTS OF MORAL SCIENCE

PREFACE

In presenting to the public a new treatise upon Moral Science, it may not be improper to state the circumstances which led to the undertaking and the design which it is intended to accomplish.

When it became my duty to instruct in Moral Philosophy in Brown University the textbook in use was the work of Dr. Paley. From many of his principles I found myself compelled to dissent, and at first I contented myself with stating to my classes my objections to the author and offering my views, in the form of familiar conversations, upon several of the topics which he discusses. These views, for my own convenience, I soon committed to paper and delivered in the form of lectures. In a few years these lectures had become so far extended that, to my surprise, they contained by themselves the elements of a different system from that of the textbook which I was teaching. To avoid the inconvenience of teaching two different systems, I undertook to reduce them to order and to make such additions as would render the work in some measure complete within itself. I thus relinquished the work of Dr. Paley and for some time have been in the habit of instructing solely by lecture. The success of the attempt exceeded my expectations, and encouraged me to hope that the publication of what I had delivered to my classes might in some small degree facilitate the study of moral science.

From these circumstances the work has derived its character. Being designed for the purposes of instruction, its aim is to be simple, clear, and purely didactic. I have rarely gone into extended discussion, but have contented myself with the attempt to state the moral law, and the reason of it, in as few and as comprehensive terms as possible. The illustration of the principles and the application of them to cases in ordinary life I have generally left to the instructor, or to the student himself. Hence, also, I have omitted everything which relates to the history of opinions, and have made but little allusion even to the opinions themselves of those from whom I dissent. To have acted otherwise would have extended the undertaking greatly beyond the limits which I had assigned to myself; and it seemed to me not to belong to the design which I had in view. A work which should attempt to exhibit what was true appeared to me more desirable than one which should point out what was exploded, discuss what was doubtful, or disprove what was false.

In the course of the work I have quoted but few authorities, as in preparing it I have referred to but few books. I make this remark in no manner for the sake of laying claim to originality, but to avoid the imputation of using the labors of others without acknowledgment. When I commenced the undertaking I attempted to read extensively, but soon found it so difficult to arrive at any definite results in this manner that the necessities of my situation obliged me to rely upon my own reflection. That I have thus come to the same conclusions with many others, I should be unwilling to doubt. When this coincidence of opinion has come to my knowledge I have mentioned it. When it is not mentioned it is because I have not known it.

The author to whom I am under the greatest obligations is Bishop Butler. The chapter on Conscience is, as I suppose, but little more than a development of his ideas on the same subject. How much more I owe to this incomparable writer I know not. As it was the study of his sermons on human nature that first turned my attention to this subject, there are doubtless many trains of thought which I have derived from him but which I have not been able to trace to their source, as they have long since become incorporated with my own reflections. The article on the Sabbath, as is stated in the text, is derived chiefly from the tract of Mr. J. J. Gurney on the same subject. Entertaining those views of the Sacred Scriptures, which I have expressed in the work itself, it is scarcely necessary to add here that I consider them the great source of moral truth; and that a system of ethics will be true just in proportion as it develops their meaning. To do this has been my object; and to have, in ever so humble a manner, accomplished it, I shall consider as the greatest possible success.

It is not without much diffidence that I have ventured to lay before the public a work on this important subject. That something of this sort was needed has long been universally confessed. My professional duty led me to undertake it; and I trust that the hope of usefulness has induced me to prepare it for publication. If I have not been so happy as to elucidate truth, I have endeavored to express myself in such a manner that the reader shall have as little trouble as possible in detecting my errors. And if it shall be found that I have thrown any light whatever upon the science of human duty, I shall have unspeakable cause for gratitude to that Spirit whose inspiration alone teacheth man understanding. And my cause for gratitude will scarcely be less should my failure incite someone better able than myself to do justice to the subject to a more successful undertaking.

BROWN UNIVERSITY, April 1835.

PREFACE
TO THE
SECOND EDITION

A SECOND edition of the Elements of Moral Science having been demanded within a much shorter period than was anticipated, I have given to the revisal of it all the attention which my avocations have permitted.

The first edition, owing to circumstances which could not be foreseen, was unfortunately in several places inaccurate in typographical execution. I have endeavored, I hope with better success, to render the present edition in this respect less liable to censure. In a few cases, single words and modes of expression have also been changed. I have, however, confined myself to verbal corrections, and have in no case that I remember intentionally altered the sense.

Having understood that the work has been introduced as a textbook into some of our highest seminaries of education, I hope that I may be forgiven if I suggest a few hints as to the manner in which I suppose it may be most successfully used for this purpose.

1. In the recitation room, let neither instructor nor pupil ever make use of the book.

2. Let the portion previously assigned for the exercise be so mastered by the pupil, both in plan and illustration, that he will be able to recite it in order and explain the connection of the different parts with each other without the necessity of assistance from his instructor. To give the language of the author is not, of course, desirable. It is sufficient if the idea be given. The questions of the instructor should have respect to principles that may be deduced from the text, practical application of the doctrines, objections which may be raised, &c.

3. Let the lesson which was recited on one day be invariably reviewed on the day succeeding.

4. As soon as any considerable progress has been made in the

work, let a review from the beginning be commenced. This should comprehend for one exercise as much as had been previously recited in two or three days; and should be confined to a brief analysis of the argument, with a mere mention of the illustrations.

5. As soon as the whole portion thus far recited has been reviewed, let a new review be commenced, and continued in the same manner; and thus on successively until the work is completed. By pursuing this method a class will, at any period of the course of study, be enabled with the slightest effort to recall whatever they have already acquired; and when the work is completed, they will be able to pursue the whole thread of the argument from the beginning to the end; and thus to retain a knowledge, not only of the individual principles, but also of their relations to each other.

But the advantage of this mode of study is not confined to that of a more perfect knowledge of this or of any other book. By presenting the whole field of thought at one view before the mind, it will cultivate the power of pursuing an extended range of argument; of examining and deciding upon a connected chain of reasoning; and will, in no small degree, accustom the student to carry forward in his own mind a train of original investigation.

I have been emboldened to make these suggestions not in the least because I suppose the present work worthy of any peculiar attention from an instructor, but simply because, having been long in the habit of pursuing this method and having witnessed its results in my own classes, I have thought it my duty to suggest it to those who are engaged in the same profession with myself. Other instructors may have succeeded better with other methods. I have succeeded best with this.

At the suggestion of some of his friends, the author has it in contemplation to prepare a small abridgement of the present work, in duodecimo, for the use of schools and academies. It will be published as soon as his engagements will permit.

BROWN UNIVERSITY, September 1835.

PREFACE
TO THE
FOURTH EDITION

THE publishers having thought proper to give to the Elements of Moral Science a more permanent form, I have revised the work with all the care that my engagements would allow. In doing this I have made many verbal alterations; I have modified some paragraphs; some I have transposed, and a few I have added.

I embrace with pleasure this opportunity of returning my grateful acknowledgments to those gentlemen who either privately or through the medium of the press have favored me with their critical remarks. I have endeavored to weigh their suggestions with all the impartiality in my power. Where I have been convinced of error, I have altered the text. Where I have only doubted, I have suffered it to remain; as it seemed profitless merely to exchange one doubtful opinion for another. Where, notwithstanding the arguments advanced, my views remained unchanged, I have also contented myself with allowing the text to stand without additional remark. The reasons for so doing may be very briefly stated: I supposed that those considerations in favor of what I had advanced which occurred to me would naturally occur to any other person; and I seem to myself to have observed that the public really take very little interest in the controversies of authors. A very considerable amount of manuscript which I had prepared for the purpose of publication in connection with this edition I have therefore suffered to lie quietly on my desk.

BROWN UNIVERSITY, January 1837.

CONTENTS
AND PLAN OF THE WORK

BOOK SECOND

PRACTICAL ETHICS

PART FIRST · LOVE TO GOD, OR PIETY

CHAPTER THIRD · JUSTICE AS IT RESPECTS CHARACTER   238

CHAPTER FOURTH · JUSTICE AS IT RESPECTS REPUTATION   244

OF VERACITY

CHAPTER FIRST · VERACITY OF THE PAST AND PRESENT   254

BOOK FIRST

THEORETICAL ETHICS

CHAPTER FIRST

OF THE ORIGIN OF OUR NOTION OF THE MORAL

QUALITY OF ACTIONS

Section I · Of Moral Law

ETHICS, or Moral Philosophy, is the Science of Moral Law.

The first question which presents itself is, What is moral law? Let us then inquire first what is *law;* and secondly what is *moral* law.

By the term *law,* I think, we generally mean a form of expression denoting either a mode of existence or an order of sequence.

Thus, the first of Sir Isaac Newton's laws, namely, that every body will continue in a state of rest or of uniform motion in a right line unless compelled by some force to change its state, denotes *a mode of existence.*

The third law of motion, that to every action of one body upon another there is an equal and contrary reaction, denotes *an order of sequence;* that is, it declares the general fact that if one event occur, the constitution of things under which we exist is such that another event will also occur.

The axioms in Mathematics are laws of the same kind. Thus, the axiom, "if equals be added to equals, the wholes will be equal," denotes an order of sequence in respect to quantity.

Of the same nature are the laws of Chemistry. Such, for instance, is the law that if soda be saturated with muriatic acid the result will be common salt.

Thus also in Intellectual Philosophy. If a picture of a visible object be formed upon the retina, and the impression be communicated by the nerves to the brain, the result will be an act of perception.

The meaning of law when referring to civil society is substantially

the same. It expresses an established order of sequence between a specified action and a particular mode of reward or of punishment. Such, in general, is the meaning of *law*.

Moral Philosophy takes it for granted that there is in human actions a moral quality; that is, that a human action may be either right or wrong. Everyone knows that we may contemplate the same action as wise or unwise; as courteous or impolite; as graceful or awkward; and also as right or wrong. It can have escaped the observation of no one that there are consequences distinct from each other which follow an action and which are connected, respectively, with each of its attributes. To take, for instance, a moral quality. Two men may both utter what is false; the one intending to speak the truth, the other intending to deceive. Now, some of the consequences of this act are common to both cases, namely, that the hearers may in both cases be deceived. But it is equally manifest that there are also consequences peculiar to the case in which the speaker *intended* to deceive; as, for example, the effects upon his own moral character and upon the estimation in which he is held by the community. And thus, in general, Moral Philosophy proceeds upon the supposition that there exists in the actions of men a moral quality, and that there are certain sequences connected by our Creator with the exhibition of that quality.

A moral law is, therefore, a form of expression denoting an order of sequence established between the moral quality of actions and their results.

Moral Philosophy, or Ethics, is the science which classifies and illustrates moral law.

Here it may be worthwhile to remark that an order of sequence established supposes of necessity an Establisher. Hence Moral Philosophy, as well as every other science, proceeds upon the supposition of the existence of a universal cause, the Creator of all things, who has made every thing as it is, and who has subjected all things to the relations which they sustain. And hence, as all relations, whether moral or physical, are the result of His enactment, an order of sequence once discovered in morals is just as invariable as an order of sequence in physics.

Such being the fact, it is evident that the moral laws of God can never be varied by the institutions of man, any more than the physical laws. The results which God has connected with actions will inevitably occur, all the created power in the universe to the contrary notwithstanding. Nor can these consequences be eluded or averted, any more than the sequences which follow by the laws of gravitation. What should we think of a man who expected to leap from a precipice, and by some act of sagacity elude the effect of the accelerating power of gravity? or of another, who by the exercise of his own will determined to render himself imponderable? Everyone who believes God to have established an order of sequences in morals must see that it is equally absurd to expect to violate with impunity any moral law of the Creator.

Yet men have always flattered themselves with the hope that they could violate *moral* law, and escape the consequences which God has established. The reason is obvious. In *physics* the consequent follows the antecedent, often immediately, and most commonly after a stated and well known interval. In *morals* the result is frequently long delayed; and the *time* of its occurrence is always uncertain. Hence, "because sentence against an evil work is not executed *speedily,* therefore the hearts of the sons of men are fully set in them to do evil." But time, whether long or short, has neither *power* nor *tendency* to change the order of an established sequence. The time required for vegetation in different orders of plants may vary; but yet wheat will always produce wheat, and an acorn will always produce an oak. That such is the case in morals, a heathen poet has taught us:

> Raro antecedentem scelestum
> Deseruit, pede pœna claudo.
> HOR. *Lib.* 3. *Car.* 2.

A higher authority has admonished us, "Be not deceived, God is not mocked; *whatsoever* a man *soweth, that shall he* also *reap."* It is also to be remembered that in morals as well as in physics the harvest is always more abundant than the seed from which it springs.

Section II · *What Is a Moral Action?*

Action, from *actum,* the supine of the Latin verb *ago,* I do, signifies something done; the putting forth of some power.

But under what circumstances must power be put forth in order to render it a *moral* action?

1. A machine is in common conversation said to be powerful. A vegetable is said to *put forth* its leaves, a tree to *bend* its branches, or a vine to *run* towards a prop; but we never speak of these instances of power as actions.

2. Action is never affirmed but of beings possessed of *a will;* that is, of those in whom the putting forth of power is immediately consequent upon their determination to put it forth. Could we conceive of animate beings whose exertions had no connection with their will, we should not speak of such exertions as actions.

3. Action, so far as we know, is affirmed only of beings possessed of *intelligence;* that is, who are capable of comprehending a particular end and of adopting the means necessary to accomplish it. An action is something done; that is, some change effected. But man effects change only by means of stated antecedents. An action, therefore, in such a being supposes some change in view and some means employed for the purpose of effecting it.

We do not, however, affirm this as essential. Suppose a being so constituted as to be able to effect changes without the use of means; action would then not involve the necessity of intelligence *in the sense in which it is here explained.* All that would be necessary would be the previous conception of the change which he intended to effect.

4. All this exists in man. He is voluntary and intelligent, capable of foreseeing the result of an exertion of power; and that exertion of power is subject to his will. This is sufficient to render man the subject of government. He can foresee the results of a particular action, and can will or not will to accomplish it. And other results can be connected with the action, of such a nature as to influence his will in one direction or in another. Thus a man may know that

stabbing another will produce death. He has it in his power to will or not to will it. But such other consequences may be connected by society with the act that, though on many accounts he would desire to do it, yet on other and graver accounts he would prefer not to do it. This is sufficient to render man a subject of government. But is this all that is necessary to constitute man a *moral* agent; that is, to render him a subject of *moral* government?

May not all this be affirmed of brutes? Are they not voluntary and even to some extent intelligent agents? Do they not, frequently at least, comprehend the relation of means to an end, and voluntarily put forth the power necessary for the accomplishment of that end? Do they not manifestly design to injure us, and also select the most appropriate means for effecting their purpose? And can we not connect such results with their actions as shall influence their will and prevent or excite the exercise of their power? We do this whenever we caress or intimidate them to prevent them from injuring us or to excite them to labor. They are, then, subjects of government as truly as man.

Is there, then, no difference between the intelligent and voluntary action of a brute and the moral action of a man? Suppose a brute and a man both to perform the same action; as, for instance, suppose the brute to kill its offspring and the man to murder his child. Are these actions of the same character? Do we entertain the same feelings towards the authors of them? Do we treat the authors in the same manner, and with the design of producing in them the same result?

I think no one can answer these questions in the affirmative. We *pity* the brute, but we *are filled with indignation* against the man. In the one case we say there has been *harm* done; in the other, *injury* committed. We feel that the *man deserves punishment:* we have no such feeling towards the brute. We say that the man has done *wrong;* but we never affirm this of the brute. We may attempt to produce in the brute such a recollection of the offense as may deter him from the act in future; but we can do no more. We attempt, in the other case, to make the man sensible of the act as wrong, and to produce in him a radical change of character; so that he not only would not commit the crime again, but would be inherently averse to the commission of it.

These considerations are, I think, sufficient to render it evident that we perceive an element in the actions of men which does not exist in the actions of brutes. What is this element?

If we should ask a child, he would tell us that the man *knows better*. This would be his mode of explaining it.

But what is meant by knowing better? Did not the brute and the man both know that the result of their action would be harm? Did not both intend that it should be harm? In what respect, then, did the one *know better* than the other?

I think that a plain man or a child would answer, the man *knew* that he *ought not to do it,* and that the brute did *not know* that he *ought not to do it;* or he might say, the man knew and the brute did not know that it was *wrong;* but whatever terms he might employ, they would involve the same idea. I do not know that a philosopher could give a more satisfactory answer.

If the question then be asked, what is a moral action? we may answer, it is the voluntary action of an intelligent agent who is capable of distinguishing between right and wrong, or of distinguishing what he ought from what he ought not to do.

It is, however, to be remarked that although action is defined to be the putting forth of power, it is not intended to be asserted that the moral quality exists only where *power is actually exerted.* It is manifest that our thoughts and resolutions may be deserving either of praise or of blame; that is, may be either right or wrong where they do not appear in action. When the will consents to the performance of an action, though the act be not done, the omniscient Deity justly considers us as either virtuous or vicious.

From what has been said it may be seen that there exists in the actions of men an element which does not exist in the actions of brutes. Hence, though both are subjects of government, the government of the one should be constructed upon principles different from that of the other. We can operate upon brutes only by fear of punishment and hope of reward. We can operate upon man not only in this manner, but also by an appeal to his consciousness of right and wrong, and by the use of such means as may improve his moral nature. Hence, all modes of punishment which treat men as we treat brutes are as unphilosophical as they are thoughtless, cruel, and vindictive. Such are those systems of criminal jurisprudence which have in view nothing more than the infliction of pain upon the offender. The leading object of all such systems should be to reclaim the vicious. Such was the result to which all the investigations of Howard led. Such is the improvement which Prison Discipline Societies are laboring to effect.

And it is worthy of remark that the Christian precept respecting the treatment of injuries proceeds precisely upon this principle. The New Testament teaches us to love our enemies, to do good to those that hate us, to overcome evil with good; that is, to set before a man who does *wrong* the strongest possible exemplification of the opposite moral quality, *right*. Now it is manifest that nothing would be so likely to show to an injurious person the turpitude of his own conduct, and to produce in him self-reproach and repentance, as precisely this sort of moral exhibition. Revenge and retaliation might or might not prevent a repetition of the injury to a particular individual. The requiting of evil with good, in addition to this effect, has an inherent *tendency* to produce sorrow for the act and dislike to its moral quality; and thus, by producing a change of character, to prevent the repetition of the offense under all circumstances hereafter.

Section III · In What Part of an Action Do We Discover Its Moral Quality?

In a deliberate action four distinct elements may be commonly observed. These are—

1. The outward act, as when I put money into the hand of another.

2. The conception of this act, of which the external performance is the mere bodying forth.

3. The resolution to carry that conception into effect.

4. The intention or design with which all this is done.

Now the moral quality does not belong to the external act, for the same external act may be performed by two men while its moral character is in the two cases entirely dissimilar.

Nor does it belong to the conception of the external act, nor to the resolution to carry that conception into effect: for the resolution to perform an action can have no other character than that of the action itself. It must, then, reside in the intention.

That such is the fact may be illustrated by an example. A and B both give to C a piece of money. They both conceived of this action before they performed it. They both resolved to do precisely what they did. In all this both actions coincide. A, however, gave it to C with the intention of procuring the murder of a friend; B, with the intention of relieving a family in distress. It is evident that in this case the *intention* gives to the action its character as right or wrong.

That the moral quality of the action resides in the intention may be evident from various other considerations.

1. By reference to the intention, we inculpate or exculpate others, or ourselves, without any respect to the happiness or misery actually produced. Let the result of an action be what it may, we hold a man guilty simply on the ground of intention, or, on the same ground, we hold him innocent. Thus also of ourselves. We are conscious of guilt or of innocence not from the result of an action, but from the intention by which we were actuated.

2. We always distinguish between being the instrument of good and intending it. We are grateful to one who is the cause of good, not in the proportion of the amount effected, but of the amount intended.

Intention may be wrong in various ways.

As, for instance, first, where we *intend to injure* another, as in cruelty, malice, revenge, deliberate slander.

Here, however, it may be remarked that we may intend to inflict pain without intending wrong; for we may be guilty of the violation of no right. Such is the case when pain is inflicted for the purposes of justice; for it is manifest that if a man deserve pain it is no violation of right to inflict it. Hence we see the difference between *harm, injury,* and *punishment.* We *harm* another when we actually inflict pain; we *injure* him when we inflict pain in violation of his rights;

we *punish* him when we inflict pain which he deserves and to which he has been properly adjudged—and in so doing there is, therefore, a violation of no right.

2. Intention is wrong where we act for the gratification of our own passions without any respect to the happiness of others. Such is the case of seduction, ambition, and, in nations, commonly of war. Every man is bound to restrain the indulgence of his passions within such limits that they will work no ill to his neighbor. If they actually inflict injury, it is no excuse to say that he had no ill will to the individual injured. The Creator never conferred on him the right to destroy another's happiness for his own gratification.

3. As the right and wrong of an action reside in the intention, it is evident that where an action is intended, though it be not actually performed, that intention is worthy of praise or blame as truly as the action itself, provided the action itself be wholly out of our power. Thus God rewarded David for intending to build the temple, though he did not permit him actually to build it. So he who intends to murder another, though he may fail to execute his purpose, is in the sight of God a murderer. The meditation upon wickedness with pleasure comes under the same condemnation.

4. As the right or wrong exists in the intention, wherever a particular intention is essential to virtuous action the performance of the external act without that intention is destitute of the element of virtue. Thus a child is bound to obey his parents, with the intention of thus manifesting his love and gratitude. If he do it from fear or from hope of gain, the act is destitute of the virtue of filial obedience and becomes merely the result of passion or self-interest. And thus our Saviour charges upon the Jews the want of the proper *intention* in all their dealings with God. "I know you," said he, "that ye have not the *love of God* in you."

And, again, it is manifest that our moral feelings, like our taste, may be excited by the conceptions of our own imagination scarcely less than by the reality. These, therefore, may develop moral character. He who meditates with pleasure upon fictions of pollution and crime, whether originating with himself or with others, renders it evident that nothing but opposing circumstances prevents him from being himself an actor in the crime which he loves. And still more, as the moral character of an action resides in the intention, and as whatever tends to corrupt the intention must be wrong, the meditating with pleasure upon vice, which has manifestly this tendency, must be wrong also.

And here let me add that the imagination of man is the fruitful parent both of virtue and vice. Thus saith the wise man, "Keep thy heart with all diligence, for out of it are the issues of life." No man becomes openly a villain until his imagination has become familiar with conceptions of villainy. The crimes which astonish us by their atrocity were first arranged, and acted, and reacted, in the recesses of the criminal's own mind. Let the imagination, then, be most carefully guarded if we wish to escape from temptation and make progress in virtue. Let no one flatter himself that he is innocent if he love to meditate upon anything which he would blush to avow before men, or fear to unveil before God.

Section IV · Whence Do We Derive Our Notion of the Moral Quality of Actions? [1]

To this question several answers have been given. Some of them we shall proceed to consider.

1. Is our notion of right and wrong a modification of any other idea?

The only *modifications* of which an idea is susceptible are, first, that *of greater or less vividness of impression,* or secondly, that *of simplicity or of composition.* Thus the quality of beauty may impress us *more or less forcibly* in the contemplation of different objects; or on the other hand, the idea of beauty may be *simple,* or else *combined* in our conceptions with the idea of utility.

Now if our notion of right and wrong be a *modification* of some other idea, in the first sense, then one degree of the original quality will be destitute of any moral element and another degree of it will possess a moral element; and by ascending higher in the scale it may at last lose all its original character and possess another having no remains of resemblance to itself. This would be to say that a quality,

[1] See Appendix (A) for the 1865 text included here between nn. 1 and 3.

by becoming more intense, ceased to be itself; as if a triangle, by becoming more perfect as a triangle, at last became a square. Thus if it be said that the idea of right and wrong is a modification of the idea of beauty, then the same object, if beautiful in one degree, would have no moral quality; if beautiful in another degree, would begin to be virtuous; and, if beautiful in the highest degree, would cease to be beautiful, and be purely virtuous or holy. What meaning could be attached to such an affirmation, I am not able to discover.

The other meaning of a *modification* of an idea is that it is compounded with some other idea. Now suppose our notion of right and wrong to be a modification in this latter sense. Then this notion either enters into the original elements of the compound idea, or it does not. If it does, then it is already present; and this supposition does not account for its existence. If it does not enter into the elements of the compound idea, then these elements must exist either merely combined, but each possessing its original character, in which combination the moral idea is not involved; or else they must lose their original character and be merely the stated antecedents to another idea, which is an idea like neither of them, either separately or combined. In this latter case it is manifest that the consequent of an antecedent is no *modification* of the antecedent, but an entirely different subject, coming into existence under these particular circumstances, and in obedience to the laws of its own organization. Do we ever term a salt a *modification* of an acid, or of an alkali, or of an acid and alkali united? Is the explosive power of gunpowder a modification of the spark and the gunpowder? We think, then, it may be safely concluded that the notion of right and wrong is not a *modification* of any other idea.

If anyone assert that this idea universally ensues upon the combination of two other ideas, it will become him to show what those *two ideas are,* neither of which involves the notion of right and wrong, but upon the combination of which this notion always arises, while the original elements which precede it entirely disappear.

2. Is our notion of the moral quality of actions derived from an exercise of the judgment?

Judgment is that act of the mind by which, a subject and a predicate being known, we affirm that the predicate belongs to the subject. Thus, he who knows what grass is, and what green is, may affirm that grass is green. But in this act of the mind, the notion of the two things of which the affirmation is made must exist before the act of judgment can be exerted. A man who had no notion either of grass or of green could never affirm the one of the other. And so of any other instance of this act. A man who had no notion of right or wrong could never affirm either quality of any subject; much less could he by this faculty acquire the original idea. And thus, in general, the judgment only affirms a relation to exist between two notions which previously existed in the mind; but it can give us no *original notions of quality,* either in morals or in anything else.

3. Is our notion of the moral quality of actions derived from association?

The term association is used to designate two habits of mind considerably alike. The first is that by which the sight or recollection of one object calls to recollection some other object to which it stands in some particular relation. Thus the sight of a hearse may recall to recollection the death of a friend; or the sound of his native language in a foreign country may awaken in the breast of an exile all the recollections of home. The second case is where a particular emotion, belonging to one train of circumstances, is awakened by another with which it has no necessary connection; and this first emotion comes at last to be awakened by the accidental instead of by the necessary antecedent. Thus the countenance of a person may be suited to awaken no emotion of pleasure in itself; but if I become acquainted with him and am pleased with his moral and intellectual character, a degree of pleasure is at last excited by his countenance, which in the end appears to me agreeable, or, it may be, beautiful.

Now in both these cases it is evident that *no new idea* is gained. In the one case a well known idea is revived; in the other, two known ideas are connected in a new relation; but this is all. Association is the faculty by which we transfer; but we can transfer nothing which did not previously exist. We could never use the idea of right and wrong by association unless we had already acquired it. In the acts of judgment and association, therefore, as the *existence* of the notion must be presupposed, neither of these acts will account for the origin of the notion itself

4. Is our notion of the moral quality of actions derived from the idea of the greatest amount of happiness?

Thus it is said that our notion of right and wrong is derived from our idea of productiveness of happiness, or in other words that an *action is right or wrong because it is productive or not productive of the greatest amount of happiness.*

When the affirmative of this question is asserted it is, I presume, taken for granted that the idea of right and wrong, and of productiveness of the greatest amount of happiness, are two distinct ideas. If they be not, then one cannot be derived from the other; for nothing can correctly be said to be a cause of itself. We shall, therefore, consider them as different ideas, and inquire in what sense it is true that the one is the cause of the other.

When we speak of two events in nature, of which one is *the cause* of the other, we use the word cause in one of the two following senses. First, we use it to denote *stated antecedency* merely; as when we say that sensation is the *cause* of perception, or that a man perceives an external object *because* an impression is made upon an organ of sense. Secondly, we use it to signify that the event or change of which we speak may be referred to some law or fact more general than itself. We say, in other words, that the fact in question is a *species* under some *genus,* with which it agrees as to generic qualities; and from which it is distinguished by its specific differences. Thus when asked why a stone falls to the earth we reply, *because* all matter is reciprocally attractive to all other matter. This is the generic fact under which the fact in question is to be comprehended; and its specific difference is that it is a particular form of matter attracted by a particular form of matter, and probably unlike the matter of the planets, the comets, or the sun.

First. When it is said that an action is right *because* it is productive of the greatest amount of happiness, suppose *because* to be used in the *first* of these senses. It will then mean that we are so constituted that the idea of the greatest amount of happiness is always the stated antecedent to the idea of right or moral obligation. Now this is a question purely of fact. It does not admit of a reason *a priori*. And if it be the fact, it must be the universal fact; that is to say, this consequent must always under similar conditions be preceded by this antecedent, and this antecedent be followed by this consequent.

1. To facts, then, let us appeal. Is it a fact that we are *conscious* of the existence of this connection? When we are conscious that an act is right, is this consciousness preceded by a conviction that this action will be productive of the greatest amount of happiness? When we say it is wrong to lie or to steal, do we find this consciousness preceded by the notion that lying or stealing will not produce the greatest amount of happiness? When we say that a murderer deserves death, do we find this notion preceded by the other that murder will *not produce* the greatest amount of happiness and that putting a murderer to death *will produce* it? When we say that a man ought to obey God, his Creator and Preserver, do we find this conviction preceded by the other—that the exercise of this affection will produce the greatest amount of happiness? Now I may have greatly mistaken the nature of moral affections; but I am much deceived if many persons will not be found who will declare that, often as they have formed these judgments, the idea of the greatest amount of happiness never actually entered into their conception.

2. Or, take the case of *children*. When you would impress upon a child the duty of obeying its parents or of loving God, do you begin by explaining to it the idea of the greatest amount of happiness? Are we obliged to make use of this antecedent in order to produce this consequent? If so, it surely would take a much longer time than is actually required to produce in a child any moral sensibility. Do we not find children well instructed into the consciousness of right and wrong who could not be made to comprehend the notion of the greatest amount of happiness?

3. How do we attempt to arouse the consciences of the *heathen*? When we tell them that they ought to obey God and believe on Jesus Christ, do we begin by explaining to them that this course of life will produce the greatest amount of happiness? Suppose we could

never arouse them to duty until we had produced[2] a conviction of
the amount of happiness which would result to the universe from
piety; would a single one of them ever listen to us long enough to
understand our doctrine?

4. Does the *Bible* anywhere assert, that the conviction of the
greatest amount of happiness is necessary to the existence of moral
obligation? If I mistake not, it presents a very different view of the
subject. It declares that the heathen are without excuse. But why?
Because disobedience to God interferes with the greatest amount of
happiness? No, but for a very different reason: *"Because that which
may be known of God is manifest in them, for God hath showed it
unto them;* so THAT *they are without excuse." Rom.* i. 19, 20. St. Paul
here seems to assume that the revelation of God's eternal power and
divinity and the manifestation of his will are sufficient of themselves,
without any other consideration, to make whatever he shall command obligatory upon his creatures.

It seems, then, to me by no means proved that an action is right
because it is productive of the greatest amount of happiness; if we
mean by it that in our conception the one idea is the stated antecedent to the other.

Secondly. But let us take the other meaning of *because*. Suppose
it said that the idea of moral obligation is an idea comprehended
under, and to be referred to, a more general idea, namely, that of
the productiveness of the greatest amount of happiness. Now if this
be the case, then, manifestly, either the notion of the greatest amount
of happiness and the notion of right must be equally extensive; that
is, must extend precisely to the same number of individual instances:
or else their extent must be different; that is, the generic notion of
the greatest amount of happiness must comprehend cases which
are excluded from its species, the idea of right. If the latter be the
case, then, there will be some cases in which an action would produce
the greatest amount of happiness which would not contain the moral
element; and besides, if this were the case it would become those
who made this assertion to show what is that other element which,

[2] The 1835 edition: "produced the greatest amount of happiness which would
result from piety"

combining with the idea of the greatest amount of happiness, designates the subordinate and different idea as the idea of moral obligation. This, however, would not be attempted, and it will be at once admitted that these two ideas are in their nature coextensive; that is, that whatever is productive of the greatest amount of happiness is right, and whatever is right is productive of the greatest amount of happiness.

Let us suppose it then to be assumed that the terms are precisely coextensive, viz., that they apply exactly to the same actions and in the same degrees. It would then be difficult to assign a meaning to the word *because* corresponding to either of the senses above stated. Nor, if two terms are precisely coextensive, do I see how it is possible to discover which of the two is to be referred to the other, or whether either is to be referred to either. If A and B are equally extensive I do not see how we can determine whether A is to be referred to B, or B to be referred to A.

The only other meaning which I can conceive as capable of being attached to the assertion is this; *that we are not under moral obligation to perform any action unless it be productive of the greatest amount of happiness;* thus making moral obligation rest upon this other idea, that of the greatest amount of happiness.

Now if this be asserted, it is surely, from what has been said above, not self-evident; for we manifestly do not instinctively and universally, as soon as this connection is asserted, yield our assent to it, nor is it absurd to deny it; and therefore the assertion is capable of proof and we may justly demand the proof before we believe it. Let us, then, examine the proof on which it rests.

It is, however, to be remarked that if the assertion be true that we are under obligation to perform an action only on the ground that it is productive of the greatest good, the assertion must be true in its widest sense. It must apply to actions affecting our relations not only to man, but also to God; for these are equally comprehended within the notion of moral obligation. And thus, the assertion is that we are not under obligation to perform any action whatever, under any circumstances, unless it be productive of the greatest amount of happiness.

1. It is said that these two always coincide; that is, that we always are under obligation to do whatever is productive of the greatest amount of happiness; and that whatever we are under obligation to do is productive of the greatest amount of happiness. Now granting the premises, I do not see that the conclusion would follow. It is possible to conceive that God may have created moral agents under obligations to certain courses of conduct, and have so arranged the system of the universe that the following of these courses shall be for the best, without making our obligation to rest at all upon their tendency to produce the greatest amount of happiness.

A parent may require a child to do that which will be for the good of the family; and yet there may be other reasons besides this which render it the *duty* of the child to obey his parent.

2. But secondly, how do we know that these premises are true— that whatever we are under obligation to do is productive of the greatest amount of happiness? It never can be known, unless we know the whole history of this universe from everlasting to everlasting. And besides, we know that God always acts right, that is, deals with all beings according to their deserts; but whether he always acts simply to promote the greatest happiness I do not know that he has told us. His government *could not be more perfectly right* than it is; but whether it could have involved less misery or have produced more happiness I do not know that we have the means of ascertaining. As, therefore, the one quantity so to speak is fixed, that is, is as great as it can be, while we do not certainly know that the other is as great as it can be we cannot affirm that right and the greatest amount of happiness always coincide: nor that we are under obligation to do nothing unless it would tend to produce the greatest amount of happiness.

3. Besides, suppose we are under no obligation to do any thing unless it were productive of the greatest amount of happiness, it would follow that we are under no obligation to obey God unless the production of the greatest amount of happiness were the controlling and universal principle of his government. That is, if his object in creating and governing the universe were any other, or if it were doubtful whether it might not be any other, our obligation

to obedience would either be annihilated or would be contingent; that is, it would be inversely as the degree of doubt which might exist. Now as I have before remarked, this may or may not be the ultimate end of God's government; it may be his own pleasure or his own glory or some other end which he has not seen fit to reveal to us; and, therefore, on the principle which we are discussing our obligation to obedience seems a matter yet open for discussion. Now if I mistake not, this is wholly at variance with the whole tenor of Scripture and reason. I do not know that the Scriptures ever give us a reason why we ought to obey God aside from his existence and attributes, or that they ever put this subject in a light susceptible of a question.

To this view of the subject the following remarks of Bishop Butler manifestly tend: "Perhaps divine goodness, with which, if I mistake not, we make very free in our speculations, may not be a bare single disposition to produce happiness; but a disposition to make the good, the faithful, the honest man happy. Perhaps an infinitely perfect mind may be pleased with seeing his creatures behave suitably with the nature which he has given them, to the relations in which he has placed them to each other, and to that in which they stand to himself; that relation to himself, which during their existence is ever necessary, and which is the most important one of all. I say, an infinitely perfect mind may be pleased with this *moral piety* of moral agents *in and for itself, as well as* upon account of its being essentially conducive to the happiness of his creation. Or the whole end for which God made and thus governs the world, may be utterly beyond the reach of our faculties: there may be somewhat in it, as impossible for us to have any conception of, as for a blind man to have a conception of colors." *Analogy,* part 1, ch. 2.

Again: "Some men seem to think the only character of the Author of nature, to be that of single, absolute benevolence. This, considered as a principle of action, and infinite in degree, is a disposition to produce the greatest possible happiness, without regard to persons' behavior, otherwise than as such regard would produce the highest degrees of it. And, supposing this to be the only character of God, veracity and justice in him would be nothing but benevolence, conducted by wisdom. Now, surely this *ought not to be asserted, unless it can be proved; for we should speak with cautious reverence upon such a subject.* There may possibly be, in the creation, beings, to whom the Author of nature manifests himself under this most amiable of all characters, this of infinite, absolute benevolence; for it is the most amiable, supposing it is not, as perhaps it is not, incompatible with justice; but he *manifests himself to us* under the character of a *Righteous* Governor. He *may*, consistently with this, be simply and absolutely benevolent, in the sense now explained; but he *is*, for he has given us a proof, in the constitution and government of the world, that he is, a *Governor over servants*, as he rewards and punishes us for our actions." *Analogy*, ch. 3.

"Nay, farther, were treachery, violence, and injustice, no otherwise vicious, than as foreseen likely to produce an overbalance of misery to society, then, if a man could procure to himself as great advantage by an act of injustice, as the whole foreseen inconvenience likely to be brought upon others by it would amount to, such a piece of injustice would not be faulty or vicious at all; because it would be no more than, in any other case, for a man to prefer his own satisfaction to another's in equal degrees. The fact then appears to be, that we are constituted so as to condemn falsehood, unprovoked violence, injustice, and to approve of benevolence to some in preference to others, abstracted from all consideration which conduct is likeliest to produce an overbalance of happiness or misery. And, therefore, were the Author of nature to propose nothing to himself as an end, but the production of happiness, were *his* moral character merely that of Benevolence, yet *ours* is not so. Upon that supposition, indeed, the only reason of his giving us the above mentioned approbation of benevolence to some persons rather than others, and disapprobation of falsehood, unprovoked violence, and injustice, must be that he foresaw this constitution of our nature would produce more happiness than forming us with a temper of mere general benevolence. But still, since this is our constitution falsehood, violence, injustice, must be vice in *us*, and benevolence to some, preferably to others, must be virtue, abstracted from all consideration of the overbalance of evil or good which they appear likely to produce.

"Now, if human creatures are endued with such a moral nature as we have been explaining, or with a moral faculty, the nature of which is action, moral government must consist in rendering them happy or unhappy, in rewarding or punishing them, as they follow, neglect, or depart from, the moral rule of action, interwoven in their nature, or suggested and enforced by this moral faculty, in rewarding or punishing them on account of their so doing." *Second Dissertation on Virtue.*

For these reasons I think it is not proved that an action is right because it is productive of the greatest amount of happiness. It may be so or it may not, but we ought not to believe it to be so without proof; and it may even be doubted whether we are in possession of the media of proof, that is, whether it is a question fairly within the reach of the human faculties; and so far as we can learn from the Scriptures I think their testimony is decidedly against the supposition. To me the Scriptures seem explicitly to declare that the *will of our God alone* is sufficient to create the obligation to obedience in all his creatures; and that this *will,* of itself, precludes every other inquiry. This seems to be the view of St. Paul in the passage which we have quoted as well as in several other places, in his Epistle to the Romans. To the same import is the prayer of our Saviour, "I thank thee, O Father, Lord of heaven and earth, because thou hast hid these things from the wise and prudent, and hast revealed them unto babes; even so, Father, *for so it seemed good in thy sight."*

It seems, therefore, to me that these explanations of the origin of our moral sentiments are unsatisfactory. I believe the idea of a moral quality in actions to be ultimate, to arise under such circumstances as have been appointed by our Creator, and that we can assign for it no other reason than that such is his will concerning us.

If this be true, our only business will be to state the circumstances under which our moral notions arise. In doing this, it would be presumption in me to expect that I shall be able to give an account of this subject more satisfactory to others than theirs has been to me. I merely offer it as that which seems to me most accurately to correspond with the phenomena.

The view which I take of this subject is briefly as follows: [3]

1. It is manifest to everyone that we all stand in various and dissimilar relations to all the sentient beings, created and uncreated, with which we are acquainted. Among our relations to created beings are those of man to man, or that of substantial equality, of parent and child, of benefactor and recipient, of husband and wife, of brother and brother, citizen and citizen, citizen and magistrate, and a thousand others.

2. Now it seems to me that as soon as a human being comprehends the relation in which two human beings stand to each other, there arises in his mind a consciousness of moral obligation connected by our Creator with the very conception of this relation. And the fact is the same whether he be one of the parties or not. The nature of this feeling is that the one *ought* to exercise certain dispositions towards the others to whom he is thus related; and to act towards them in a manner corresponding with those dispositions.

3. The nature of these dispositions varies, of course, with the relations. Thus those of a parent to a child are different from those of a child to a parent; those of a benefactor to a recipient from those of a recipient to a benefactor; and both of them differ from that of a brother to a brother, or of a master to a servant. But different as these may be from each other, they are all pervaded by the same generic feeling, that of *moral obligation;* that is, *we feel that we ought* to be thus or thus disposed and to act in this or that manner.

4. This I suppose to be our constitution in regard to created beings; and such do I suppose would be our feeling, irrespectively of any notion of the Deity. That is, upon the conception of these and such like relations, there would immediately arise this feeling of moral obligation to act towards those sustaining these relations in a particular manner.

5. But there is an Uncreated Being to whom we stand in relations infinitely more intimate and inconceivably more solemn than any of those of which we have spoken. It is that Infinite Being *who stands to us* in the relation of Creator, Preserver, Benefactor, Law-

[3] Concludes material shown in Appendix (A).

giver, and Judge; and *to whom we stand* in the relation of dependent, helpless, ignorant, and sinful *creatures*. *How much* this relation
involves we cannot possibly know; but so much as this we know,
that it involves obligations greater than our intellect can estimate.
We cannot contemplate it without feeling that, from the very fact
of its existence, we are under obligations to entertain the disposition
of filial love and obedience towards God, and to act precisely as he
shall condescend to direct. And this obligation arises simply from
the fact of the relation existing between the parties and irrespectively
of any other consideration; and if it be not felt when the relations
are perceived, it can never be produced by any view of the consequences which would arise to the universe from exercising it.

6. This relation and its consequent obligation *involve, comprehend,* and *transcend* every other. Hence it places obligation to man
upon a new foundation. For if we be ourselves thus under illimitable
obligations to God, and if, by virtue of the relation which he sustains
to the creation, he is the Protector, Ruler, and Proprietor of all, we
are under obligations to obey him in everything. And as every other
being is also his creature, we are bound to treat that creature as he
its Proprietor shall direct. Hence we are bound to perform the obligation under which we stand to his creatures not merely on account
of our relations to *them,* but also on account of the relations in which
we and *they* stand to *God*.

And hence, in general, our feeling of moral obligation is a peculiar
and instinctive impulse, arising at once by the principles of our
constitution as soon as the relations are perceived in which we stand
to the beings, created and uncreated, with whom we are connected.

The proof of this must rest, as I am aware, with every man's consciousness. A few illustrative remarks may, however, not be altogether useless.

I think, if we reflect upon the subject, that the manner in which
we attempt to awaken moral feelings confirms the view which I
have taken. In such a case, if I mistake not, *we always place before
the mind the relation in which the parties stand to each other*.

1. If we wish to awaken in ourselves gratitude to another, we do
not reflect that this affection will produce the *greatest good;* but we

remember the individual in the relation of benefactor; and we place this relation in the strongest possible light. If this will not produce gratitude our effort, of necessity, fails.

2. If we desire to inflame moral indignation against crime, we show the relations in which the parties stand to each other and expect hence to produce a conviction of the greatness of the obligation which such turpitude violates.

3. So if we wish to overcome evil with good, we place ourselves in the relation of benefactor to the injurious person; and in spite of himself he is frequently compelled to yield to the law of his nature; and gratitude for favors and sorrow for injury spontaneously arise in his bosom.

4. And in the plan of man's redemption it seems to me that the Deity has acted on this principle. Irrespectively of a remedial dispensation, he is known to us only as a Creator, all wise and all powerful, perfect in holiness, justice, and truth. To our fallen nature these attributes could minister nothing but terror. He therefore has revealed himself to us in the relation of a Saviour and Redeemer, a God forgiving transgression and iniquity; and thus by all the power of *this new relation* he imposes upon us *new obligations* to gratitude, repentance, and love.

5. And hence it is that God always asserts that as from the fact of this *new relation* our *obligations* to him are increased, so he who rejects the gospel is in a special manner a sinner, and is exposed to a more terrible condemnation. The climax of all that is awful in the doom of the unbelieving is expressed by the terms, "the wrath of the Lamb."

Again, I am not much accustomed to such refined speculations; but I think that obedience or love to God from any more ultimate motive than that this *affection is due to him because he is God, and our God,* is not piety. Thus if a child say, I will obey my father because it is for the happiness of the family; what the character of this action would be I am not prepared to say; but I think the action would not be *filial obedience. Filial obedience* is the obeying of *another* because *he is my father;* and it is FILIAL *obedience* only insofar as it proceeds from this motive. This will be evident if we substitute for the love of the happiness of the family the love of money or some other such motive. Everyone sees that it would not be *filial* obedience for a child to obey his parent because he would *be well paid for it.*

Now it seems to me that the same principle applies in the other case. To feel under obligation to love God because this affection would be productive of the greatest good, and not on account of what he is and of the relations in which he stands to us seems to me not to be *piety;* that is, not to be the feeling which a creature is bound to exercise towards his Creator. If the obligation to the love of God can really arise from anything more ultimate than the essential relation which he sustains to us, why may not this more ultimate motive be something else, as well as the love of the greatest good? I do not say that anything else would be as benevolent; but I speak metaphysically and say that if real piety, or love to God, may truly spring from anything more ultimate than God himself, I do not see why it may not spring from one thing as well as from another; and thus true piety might spring from various and dissimilar motives no one of which has any real reference to God himself.

My view of this subject, in few words, is as follows:

1. We stand in relations to the several beings with which we are connected such that some of them, as soon as they are conceived, suggest to us the idea of moral obligation.

2. Our relations to our *fellow men* suggest this conviction, in a limited and restricted sense, corresponding to the idea of general or essential equality.

3. The relation in which we stand to the Deity suggests the conviction of universal and unlimited love and obedience. This binds us to proper dispositions toward Him; and also to such dispositions toward his creatures as *he shalt appoint.*

4. Hence our duties to man are enforced by a twofold obligation; first, because of our relations to *man as man;* and secondly, because of our relation to man as being, with ourselves, a *creature of God.*

5. And hence an act which is performed in obedience to our obligations to man may be *virtuous;* but it is not *pious* unless it also be performed in obedience to our obligations to God.

6. And hence we see that two things are necessary in order to constitute any being a moral agent. They are, first, that he possess an intellectual power by which he can understand the relation in which he stands to the beings by whom he is surrounded; secondly, that he possess a moral power by which the feeling of obligation is suggested to him as soon as the relation in which he stands is understood. This is sufficient to render him a moral agent. He is *accountable* just in proportion to the opportunity which he has enjoyed for acquiring a knowledge of the relations in which he stands and of the manner in which his obligations are to be discharged.

Section I · Is There a Conscience?

BY conscience, or the moral sense, is meant that faculty by which we discern the moral quality of actions and by which we are capable of certain affections in respect to this quality.

By *faculty* is meant any particular part of our constitution by which we become affected by the various qualities and relations of beings around us. Thus by taste we are conscious of the existence of beauty and deformity; by perception we acquire a knowledge of the existence and qualities of the material world. And in general, if we discern any quality in the universe or produce or suffer any change, it seems almost a truism to say that we have a faculty, or power, for so doing. A man who sees must have eyes, or the faculty for seeing; and *if he have not eyes* this is considered a sufficient reason why *he should not see*. And thus it is universally admitted that there may be a thousand qualities in nature of which we have no knowledge, for the simple reason that we have not been created with the faculties for discerning them. There is a world without us and a world within us which exactly correspond to each other. Unless *both exist* we can never be conscious of the existence of either.

Now that we do actually observe a moral quality in the actions of men must, I think, be admitted. Every human being is conscious that from childhood he has observed it. We do not say that all men discern this quality with equal accuracy, any more than that they all see with equal distinctness; but we say that all men perceive it in some actions; and that there is a multitude of cases in which their perceptions of it will be found universally to agree. And moreover, this quality, and the feeling which accompanies the perception of it, are unlike those derived from every other faculty.

The question would then seem reduced to this, Do we perceive this quality of actions by a single faculty, or by a combination of faculties? I think it must be evident from what has been already stated that this notion is, in its nature, simple and ultimate, and *distinct from every other notion.* Now if this be the case, it seems self-evident that we must have a *distinct and separate faculty* to make us acquainted with the existence of this *distinct and separate quality.* This is the case in respect to all other distinct qualities: it is surely reasonable to suppose that it would be the case with this unless some reason can be shown to the contrary.

But after all, this question is to the moral philosopher of but comparatively little importance. All that is necessary to his investigations is that it be admitted that there is such a quality, and that men are so constituted as to perceive it and to be susceptible of certain affections in consequence of that perception. Whether these facts are accounted for on the supposition of the existence of a single faculty or of a combination of faculties will not affect the question of moral obligation.[4] All that is necessary to the prosecution of the science is that it be admitted that there is such a quality in actions, and that man is endowed with a constitution capable of bringing him into relation to it.

It may, however, be worthwhile to consider some of the objections which have been urged against the supposition of the existence of such a faculty.

I. It has been said, if such a faculty has been bestowed it must have been bestowed universally: but it is not bestowed universally; for what some nations consider right, other nations consider wrong, as infanticide, parricide, duelling, &c.

1. To this it may be answered, first, the objection seems to admit the universality of the existence of conscience, or the power of discerning in certain actions a moral quality. It admits that everywhere men make this distinction; but affirms that in different countries they refer the quality to different actions. Now *how this difference is to be accounted for* may be a question; but the *fact,* as stated in the objection, shows the universality of the power of observing such a quality in actions.

2. But secondly, we have said that we discover the moral quality

---

[4] The 1865 edition has a different final sentence: "If it be granted that we do actually recognize moral distinctions and feel the pressure of moral obligation, it matters little whether in this acting we make use of one power of the mind or several."

of actions in the *intention. Now it is not the fact* that this difference exists, as stated in the objection, if the *intention* of actions be considered. Where was it not considered right to *intend* the happiness of parents? Where was it not considered wrong to *intend* their misery? Where was it ever considered right to intend to requite kindness by injury? and where was it ever considered wrong to intend to requite kindness with still greater kindness? In regard to the *manner* in which these intentions *may be fulfilled* there may be a difference; but as to the moral quality of these *intentions themselves,* as well as of many others, there is a very universal agreement among men.

3. And still more, it will be seen on examination that in these very cases in which wrong actions are practised, they are justified on the ground of a good *intention* or of some view of the relations between the parties which, if true, would render them innocent. Thus if infanticide be justified it is on the ground that this world is a place of misery and that the infant is better off not to encounter its troubles; that is, that the parent wishes or intends well to the child: or else it is defended on the ground that the relation between parent and child is such as to confer on the one the right of life and death over the other; and therefore, that to take its life is as innocent as the slaying of a brute or the destruction of a vegetable. Thus also are parricide and revenge and various other wrong actions defended. Where can the race of men be found, be they ever so savage, who need to be told that ingratitude is wrong, that parents ought to love their children, or that men ought to be submissive and obedient to the Supreme Divinity?

4. And still more, I think one of the strongest exemplifications of the universality of moral distinctions is found in the character of many of the ancient heathen. They perceived these distinctions and felt and obeyed the impulses of conscience, even though at variance with all the examples of the deities whom they worshipped. Thus says Rousseau, "Cast your eyes over all the nations of the world, and all the histories of nations. Amid so many inhuman and absurd superstitions, amid that prodigious diversity of manners and characters, you will find every where the same principles and distinctions

of moral good and evil. The paganism of the ancient world produced, indeed, abominable gods, who, on earth, would have been shunned or punished as monsters; and who offered, as a picture of supreme happiness, only crimes to commit, or passions to satiate. But Vice, armed with this sacred authority, descended in vain from the eternal abode. *She found in the heart of man, a moral instinct* to repel her. The continence of Xenocrates was admired by those who celebrated the debaucheries of Jupiter. The chaste Lucretia adored the unchaste Venus. The most intrepid Roman sacrificed to fear. He invoked the god who dethroned his father, and died without a murmur by the hand of his own. The most contemptible divinities were served by the greatest men. The holy voice of nature, stronger than that of the gods, made itself heard, and respected, and obeyed on earth, and seemed to banish to the confines of heaven, guilt and the guilty." Quoted by Dr. Brown, *Lecture* 75.

II. Again, the objection has been made in another form. It is said that savages violate, without *remorse* or *compunction,* the plainest principles of right. Such is the case when they are guilty of revenge and licentiousness.

This objection has been partly considered before. It may, however, be added:

First. No men, nor any class of men, violate *every* moral precept without compunction, without the feeling of guilt and the consciousness of desert of punishment.

Secondly. Hence the objection will rather prove the existence of a *defective* or *imperfect conscience,* than that no such faculty exists. The same objection would prove us destitute of taste or of understanding; because these faculties exist, only in an imperfect state, among savages and uncultivated men.

III. It has been objected, again, that if we suppose this faculty to exist it is, after all, useless; for if a man please to violate it and to suffer the pain, then this is the end of the question, and, as Dr. Paley says, "the moral instinct [of] man has nothing more to offer."

To this it may be answered:

The objection proceeds upon a mistake respecting the function of conscience. Its use is to teach us to discern our moral obligations and to impel us towards the corresponding action. It is not pretended by the believers in a moral sense that man may not, after all, do as he chooses. All that they contend for is that he is constituted with such a faculty and that the possession of it is necessary to his moral accountability. It is in his power to obey it or to disobey it, just as he pleases. The fact that a man may obey or disobey conscience no more proves that it does not exist than the fact that he sometimes does and sometimes does not obey passion proves that he is destitute of passion.

Section II · Of the Manner in Which the Decision of Conscience Is Expressed.[5]

Whoever will attentively observe the operations of his own mind when deciding upon a moral question and when carrying that decision into effect will, I think, be conscious of several distinct forms of moral feeling. These I suppose to be the following:

I. Suppose we are deliberating respecting an action *before performing it.*

1. If we pause, and candidly consider the nature of an action which involves, in any respect, our relations with others, amidst the various qualities which characterize the action we shall not fail to perceive *its moral quality.* We may perceive it to be gratifying or self-denying, courteous or uncivil, in favor of or against our interest; but distinct from all these and differing from them all, we may always perceive that it seems to us to be either right or wrong. Let a man recollect any of the cases in his own history in which he has been called upon to act under important responsibility, and he will easily remember both the fact and the pain and distress produced by the conflict of these opposite impulsions. It is scarcely necessary to remark that we easily, or at least with much greater ease, perceive this quality in the actions of others. We discern the *mote* in our *brother's* eye much sooner than the *beam* in our *own* eye.

2. Besides this discriminating power, I think we may readily observe a distinct *impulse* to do that which we conceive to be right, and to leave undone that which we conceive to be wrong. This im-

⁵ See Appendix (B) for the 1865 text for this section.

pulse we express by the words ought and ought not. Thus we say it is *right* to tell the truth; and *I ought* to tell it. It is *wrong* to tell a lie; and *I ought not* to tell it. Ought and ought not seem to convey the *abstract* idea of right and wrong, together with the other notion of impulsion to do or not to do a particular action. Thus we use it always to designate a motive to action, as we do passion or self-love or any other motive power. If we are asked why we performed any action, we reply, we acted thus because it *gratified* our desires, or because it *was for our interest* upon the whole, or because we felt that *we ought to* act thus. Either of them is considered sufficient to account for the fact; that is, either of them explains the motive or impulse in obedience to which we acted. It is also manifest that we use the term, not merely to designate an impulse, but also an obligation to act in conformity with it. Thus we say, we *ought* to do a thing, meaning that we are not only impelled towards the action but that we are under an imperative obligation to act thus. This is still more distinctly seen when we speak of another. When we say of a friend that he ought to do anything, as we cannot judge of the impulses which move him, we refer principally to this conviction of obligation which, above every other, should govern him.

The power of this impulse of conscience is most distinctly seen when it comes into collision with the impulse of strong and vehement passion. It is then that the human soul is agitated to the full extent of its capacity for emotion. And this contest generally continues, specially if we have decided in opposition to conscience, until the action is commenced. The voice of conscience is then lost amid the whirlwind of passion; and it is not heard until after the deed is done. It is on this account that this state of mind is frequently selected by the poets as a subject for delineation. Shakespeare frequently alludes to all these offices of conscience, with the happiest effect.

The constant monitory power of conscience is thus illustrated by one of the murderers about to assassinate the Duke of Clarence: "I'll not meddle with it (conscience), it is a dangerous thing; it makes a man a coward; a man cannot steal, but it accuseth him; a man cannot swear, but it checks him. 'Tis a blushing, shamefaced spirit, that mutinies in a man's bosom: it fills one full of obstacles.

It made me once restore a purse of gold, that, by chance, I found. It beggars any man that keeps it." *Richard III,* Act i, Sc. 4. The whole scene is a striking exemplification of the workings of conscience even in the bosoms of the most abandoned of men. The wicked Clarence appeals to the *consciences* of his murderers; and they strengthen themselves against his appeals by referring to his own atrocities and thus awakening in their own bosoms the conviction that he *ought* to die.

The state of mind of a man meditating a wicked act and the temporary victory of conscience are seen in the following extract from Macbeth. He recalls the relations in which Duncan stood to him, and these produce so strong a conviction of the wickedness of the murder that he decides not to commit it.

> "If the assassination
> Could trammel up the consequence, and catch,
> With his surcease, success; that but this blow
> Might be the be-all and the end-all here,
> But here, upon this bank and shoal of time,—
> We'd jump the life to come.—But, in these cases,
> We still have judgment here; that we but teach
> Bloody instructions, which, being taught, return
> To plague the inventor. This even-handed justice
> Commends the ingredients of our poisoned chalice
> To our own lips. He's here in *double trust:*
> *First,* as I am his *kinsman* and his *subject,*
> *Strong both against the deed;* then, as his *host,*
> Who *should* against his murderer shut the door,
> Not bear the knife myself. Besides, this Duncan
> Hath *borne his faculties so meek,* hath been
> *So clear in his great office,* that *his virtues*
> Will plead like angels, trumpet-tongued, against
> The deep damnation of his taking off.
>
> *   *   *   *   *   *
>
> I have no spur
> To prick the sides of my intent, but only
> Vaulting ambition, which o'erleaps itself."
>
> *Macbeth,* Act i, Sc. 7

The anguish which attends upon an action not yet commenced but only resolved upon, while we still doubt of its lawfulness, is finely illustrated by the same author in the case of Brutus, who, though a man of great fortitude, was by the anguish of contending emotions deprived of sleep and so changed in behavior as to give his wife reason to suspect the cause of his disquietude:

> "Since Cassius first did whet me against Cæsar,
> I have not slept.
> Between the acting of a dreadful thing
> And the first motion, all the interim is
> Like a phantasma, or a hideous dream:
> The *genius,* and the *mortal instruments,*
> *Are then in council;* and the state of man,
> Like to a little kingdom, suffers then
> The nature of an insurrection."
>
> *J. Cæsar,* Act ii, Sc. 1

The same contest between conscience and the lower propensities is, as I suppose, graphically described by the Apostle Paul in the seventh chapter of his Epistle to the Romans.

II. Suppose now an action *to be done.* I think that everyone who examines his own heart will be conscious of another class of feelings consequent on those to which we have just alluded.

1. If he have obeyed the impulses of conscience and resisted successfully the impulses at variance with it, he will be conscious of a feeling of innocence, of self-approbation, of desert of reward. If the action have been done by another, he will feel towards him a sentiment of respect, of moral approbation, and a desire to see him rewarded and, on many occasions, to reward him himself.

2. If he have disobeyed the impulses of conscience, he will be conscious of guilt, of self-abasement, and self-disapprobation or remorse, and of desert of punishment. If it have been done by another he will be conscious of a sentiment of moral disapprobation and of a desire that the offender should be punished and, in many cases, of a desire to punish him himself. Of course, I do not say that all these feelings can be traced by reflection upon every action; but I think that in all cases in which our moral sensibilities are at all aroused we can trace some, and frequently all of them.

In accordance with these remarks several facts may be noticed.

The boldness of innocence and the timidity of guilt, so often observed by moralists and poets, may be thus easily accounted for. The virtuous man is conscious of deserving nothing but reward. Whom, then, should he fear? The guilty man is conscious of desert of punishment, and is aware that everyone who knows of his offense desires to punish him; and as he never is certain but that everyone knows it, whom can he trust? And still more, there is with the feeling of desert of punishment, a disposition to submit to punishment arising from our own self-disapprobation and remorse. This depresses the spirit and humbles the courage of the offender far more than even the external circumstances by which he is surrounded.

Thus, says Solomon, "the wicked flee when no man pursueth, but the righteous is bold as a lion."

> "What stronger breastplate than a heart untainted?
> Thrice is he *armed*, who hath his quarrel *just;*
> And he but *naked*, though *lock'd up in steel*,
> Whose *conscience* with *injustice* is *corrupted*."
> 2d Part Henry VI, Act iii, Sc. 2

> "*Suspicion* always haunts the *guilty* mind;
> The *thief* doth fear each bush an officer."
> 2d Part Henry VI, Act v, Sc. 6

> "I feel within me
> A peace, above all earthly dignities,—
> A *still* and *quiet* conscience."
> Henry VIII, Act iii, Sc. 2

The effect of guilt:

> "No wonder why
> I felt rebuked beneath his eye;
> I might have known, there was *but one*,
> Whose look could quell Lord Marmion."
> Marmion, Cant. vi, 17

> "Curse on yon base marauder's lance,
> And doubly curs'd my failing brand.
> A *sinful* heart makes *feeble* hand."
> Marmion, Cant. vi, St. 32

It is in consequence of the same facts that crime is with so great certainty detected.

A man, before the commission of crime, can foresee no reason why he might not commit it with the certainty of escaping detection.

He can perceive no reason why he should be even suspected; and can imagine a thousand methods in which suspicion, awakened, might with perfect ease be allayed. But as soon as he becomes guilty, his relations to his fellow men are entirely changed. He becomes suspicious of everyone, and thus sees every occurrence through a false medium. Hence he cannot act like an innocent man; and this very difference in his conduct is very often the sure means of his detection. When to this effect produced upon the mind by guilt is added the fact that every action must, by the condition of our being, be attended by antecedents and consequents beyond our control, all of which lead directly to the discovery of the truth, it is not wonderful that the guilty so rarely escape. Hence it has grown into a proverb, "murder will out;" and such we generally find to be the fact.

This effect of guilt upon human action has been frequently remarked.

Thus Macbeth, after the murder of Duncan:

"How is it with me when *every noise* appals me?"

Act ii, Sc. 2

"Guiltiness will speak, though tongues were out of use."

The same fact is frequently asserted in the sacred Scriptures. Thus, "The Lord is known by the judgment that he executeth; the wicked is *snared* in the *work of his own hands.*"

"Though hand join in hand, the wicked shall not go unpunished."

I hope that I need not apologize for introducing into such a discussion so many illustrations from poetry. They are allowed on all hands to be accurate delineations of the workings of the human mind and to have been made by most accurate observers. They were made, also, without the possibility of bias from any theory; and therefore are of great value when they serve to confirm any theoretical views with which they may chance to coincide. They show at least in what light poets, whose only object is to observe the human heart, have considered conscience, and what they have supposed to be its functions and its mode of operation.

Section III · The Authority of Conscience

We have thus far endeavored to show that there is in man a faculty denominated Conscience; and that it is not merely a discriminating, but also an impulsive faculty. The next question to be considered is, what is the authority of this impulse.

The object of the present section is to show that this is *the most authoritative impulse of which we find ourselves susceptible.*

The supremacy of Conscience may be illustrated in various ways.

I. It is involved in the very conception which men form of this faculty.

The various impulses of which we find ourselves susceptible can differ only in two respects, that of *strength* and that of *authority.*

When we believe them to differ in nothing but *strength,* we feel ourselves perfectly at liberty to obey the strongest. Thus if different kinds of food be set before us, all equally healthy, we feel entirely at liberty to partake of that which we prefer; that is, of that to which we are most strongly impelled. If a man is to decide between making a journey by land or by water, he considers it a sufficient motive for choice that the one mode of traveling is more pleasant to him than the other. But when our impulses differ in *authority,* we feel obliged to neglect the difference *in strength* of impulse, and to obey that, be it ever so weak, which is of the higher *authority.* Thus suppose our desire for any particular kind of food to be ever so strong, and we know that it would injure our health; self-love would admonish us to leave it alone. Now self-love being a more authoritative impulse than passion, we should feel an obligation to obey it, be its admonition ever so weak, and the impulse of appetite ever so vehement. If we yield to the impulse of appetite, be it ever so strong, in opposition to that of self-love, be it ever so weak, we feel a consciousness of self-degradation and of acting unworthily of our nature; and if we see another person acting in this manner, we cannot avoid feeling towards him a sentiment of contempt. " 'Tis not in folly not to scorn a fool." And in general whenever we act in obedience to a lower and in opposition to a higher sentiment, we feel this consciousness of degradation, which we do not feel when the impulses differ *only in degree*. And conversely, whenever we feel this consciousness of degradation for acting in obedience to one instead of to another, we may know that we have violated that which is of the higher authority.

If, now, we reflect upon our feelings consequent upon any moral action, I think we shall find that we always are conscious of a sentiment of self-degradation whenever we disobey the monition of conscience, be that monition *ever so weak,* to gratify the impulse of appetite or passion or self-love, be that impulse *ever so strong*. Do we consider it any palliation of the guilt of murder for the criminal to declare that his vindictive feelings impelled him much more strongly than his conscience? whereas, if we perceived in these impulses no other difference than that of *strength,* we should consider this not merely an excuse, but a justification. And that the impulse of conscience is of the highest authority is evident from the fact that we cannot conceive of any circumstances in which we should not feel guilty and degraded from acting in obedience to any impulse whatever in opposition to the impulse of conscience. And thus we cannot conceive of any more exalted character than that of him who, on all occasions, yields himself up implicitly to the impulses of conscience, all things else to the contrary notwithstanding. I think no higher evidence can be produced to show that we do really consider the impulse of conscience of higher authority than any other of which we are susceptible.

II. The same truth may, I think, be rendered evident by observing the feelings which arise within us when we compare the actions of men with those of beings of an inferior order.

Suppose a brute to act from appetite and injure itself by gluttony; or from passion and injure another brute from anger: we feel nothing like *moral* disapprobation. We pity it and strive to put it out of its power to act thus in future. We never feel that a brute is disgraced or degraded by such an action. But suppose a man to act thus, and we cannot avoid a feeling of disapprobation and of disgust; a conviction that the man has done violence to his nature. Thus to call a man a brute, a sensualist, a glutton, is to speak of him in the most insulting manner: it is to say, in the strongest terms, that he has acted unworthily of himself and of the nature with which his Creator has endowed him.

Again. Let a brute act from deliberate selfishness; that is, with deliberate caution seek its own happiness upon the whole, unmindful of the impulsions of present appetite, but yet wholly regardless of the happiness of any other of its species. In no case do we feel disgust at such a course of action; and in many cases we, on the contrary, rather regard it with favor. We thus speak of the cunning of animals in taking their prey, in escaping danger, and in securing for themselves all the amount of gratification that may be in their power. We are sensible in these cases that the animal has acted from the highest impulses of which the Creator has made it susceptible. But let a man act thus. Let him, careful merely of his own happiness upon the whole, be careful for nothing else and be perfectly willing to sacrifice the happiness of others to any amount whatsoever to promote his own to the least amount soever. Such has been frequently the character of sensual and unfeeling tyrants. We are conscious in such a case of a sentiment of disgust and deep disapprobation. We feel that the man has not acted in obedience to the highest impulses of which he was susceptible; and poets and satirists and historians unite in holding him up to the world as an object of universal detestation and abhorrence.

Again. Let another man, disregarding the impulses of passion and appetite and self-love, act under all circumstances in obedience to the monitions of conscience, unmoved and unallured by pleasure and unawed by power; and we instinctively feel that he has attained to the highest eminence to which our nature can aspire; and that he has acted from the highest impulse of which his nature is susceptible. We are conscious of a conviction of his superiority which nothing can outweigh; of a feeling of veneration allied to the reverence which is due to the Supreme Being. And with this homage to virtue all history is filled. The judge may condemn the innocent, but posterity will condemn the judge. The tyrant may murder the martyr, but after ages will venerate the martyr and execrate the tyrant. And if we will look over the names of those on whom all past time has united in conferring the tribute of praiseworthiness, we shall find them to be the names of those who, although they might differ in other respects, yet were similar in this, that they shone resplendent in the lustre of unsullied virtue.

Now as our Creator has constituted us such as we are, and as, by our very constitution, we do thus consider conscience to be the most authoritative impulse of our nature, it must be the most authoritative, unless we believe that He has deceived us or, which is the same thing, that He has so formed us as to give credit to a lie.

III. The supremacy of conscience may also be illustrated by showing the necessity of this supremacy to the accomplishment of the objects for which man was created.

When we consider any work of art as a system composed of parts and arranged for the accomplishment of a given object, there are three several views which we may have of it and all of them necessary to a complete and perfect knowledge of the thing.

1. We must have a knowledge of the several *parts* of which it is composed. Thus he who would understand a watch must know the various wheels and springs which enter into the formation of the instrument. But this alone, as, for instance, if they were spread separately before him upon a table, would give him a very imperfect conception of a watch.

2. He must, therefore, understand how these parts are put together. This will greatly increase his knowledge; but it will still be imperfect for he may yet be ignorant of the *relations* which the parts sustain to each other. A man might look at a steam engine until he was familiarly acquainted with its whole machinery and yet not know whether the paddles were designed to move the piston rod, or the piston rod to move the paddles.

3. It is necessary, therefore, that he should have a conception of the *relation* which the several parts sustain to each other; that is, of the effect which every part was designed to produce upon every other part. When he has arrived at this idea and has combined it with the other ideas just mentioned, then, and not till then, is his knowledge of the instrument complete.

It is manifest that this last notion, that of the relations which the parts sustain to each other, is frequently of more importance than either of the others. He who has a conception of the cause of motion in a steam engine and of the manner in which the ends are accomplished, has a more valuable notion of the instrument than he who has ever so accurate a knowledge of the several parts without a conception of the relation. Thus in the history of astronomy the existence of the several parts of the solar system was known for ages, without being productive of any valuable result. The progress of astronomy is to be dated from the moment when the relation which the several parts hold to each other was discovered by Copernicus.

Suppose, now, we desire to ascertain what is the relation which the several parts of any system are designed by its author to sustain to each other. I know of no other way than to find out that series of relations in *obedience to which* the system will accomplish the object for which it was constructed. Thus if we desire to ascertain the relation which the parts of a watch are designed to sustain to each other, we inquire what is that series of relations in obedience to which it will accomplish the purpose for which it was constructed, that is, to keep time. For instance, we should conduct the inquiry by trying each several part and ascertaining by experiment whether, on the supposition that *it was the cause of motion,* the result, namely, the keeping of time, could be effected. After we had tried them all, and had found that under no other relation of the parts to each other than that which assumes the mainspring to be the source of motion and the balance wheel to be the regulator of the motion, the result could be produced; we should conclude with certainty that this was the relation of the parts to each other intended to be established by the maker of the watch.

And again, if an instrument were designed for several purposes, and if it was found that not only a single purpose could not be accomplished, but that no one of them could be accomplished under any other system of relations than that which had been at first discovered, we should arrive at the highest proof of which the case was susceptible that such was the relation intended to be established between the parts by the inventor of the machine.

Now man is a system composed of parts in the manner above

stated. He has various powers and faculties and impulses; and he is manifestly designed to produce some result. As to the ultimate design for which man was created, there may be a difference of opinion. In one view, however, I presume there will be no difference. It will be allowed by all that he was designed for the production of his own happiness. Look at his senses, his intellect, his affections, and at the external objects with which these are brought into relation; and at the effects of the legitimate action of these powers upon their appropriate objects; and no one can for a moment doubt that this was *one* object for which man was created. Thus it is as clear that the eye was intended to be a source of pleasure as that it was intended to be the instrument of vision. It is as clear that the ear was intended to be a source of pleasure as to be the organ of hearing. And thus of the other faculties.

But when we consider man as an instrument for the production of happiness, it is manifest that we must take into the account man as a society, as well as man as an individual. The larger part of the happiness of the individual depends upon society; so that whatever would destroy society—or what is in fact the same thing, destroy the happiness of man as a society—would destroy the happiness of man as an individual. And such is the constitution under which we are placed that no benefit or injury can be, in its nature, individual. Whoever truly promotes his own happiness promotes the happiness of society; and whoever promotes the happiness of society promotes his own happiness. In this view of the subject it will then be proper to consider man as a society as an instrument for producing the happiness of man as a society; as well as man as an individual as an instrument for producing the happiness of man as an individual.

Let us now consider man as an instrument for the production of human happiness in the sense here explained.

If we examine the impulsive and restraining faculties of man, we shall find that they may generally be comprehended under three classes:

1. *Passion or appetite.* The object of this class of our faculties is to impel us towards certain acts which produce immediate pleasure.

Thus the appetite for food impels us to seek gratification by eating. The love of power impels us to seek the gratification resulting from superiority; and so of all the rest.

If we consider the nature of these faculties, we shall find that they impel us to immediate gratification without any respect to the consequences either to ourselves or to others; and that they know of no limit to indulgence until, by their own action, they paralyze the power of enjoyment. Thus the love of food would impel us to eat until eating ceased to be a source of pleasure. And where, from the nature of the case, no such limit exists, our passions are insatiable. Such is the case with the love of wealth and the love of power. In these instances, there being in the constitution of man no limit to the power of gratification, the appetite grows by what it feeds on.

2. *Interest or self-love.* This faculty impels us to seek our own happiness considered in reference to a longer or shorter period; but always beyond the present moment. Thus if appetite impelled me to eat, self-love would prompt me to eat such food, and in such quantity, as would produce for me the greatest amount of happiness upon the whole. If passion prompted me to revenge, self-love would prompt me to seek revenge in such a manner as would not involve me in greater distress than that which I now suffer; or to control the passion entirely unless I could so gratify it as to promote my own happiness for the future as well as for the present. In all cases, however, the promptings of self-love have respect solely to the production of our own happiness; they have nothing to do with the happiness of any other being.

3. *Conscience.* The office of conscience, considered in relation to these other impulsive faculties, is to restrain our appetites within such limits that the gratification of them will injure neither ourselves nor others; and so to govern our self-love that we shall act not solely in obedience to the law of our own happiness, but in obedience to that law which restricts the pursuit of happiness within such limits as shall not interfere with the happiness of others. It is not here asserted that conscience always admonishes us to this effect; or that when it admonishes us it is always successful. We may, if we please, disobey its monitions; or, from reasons hereafter to be mentioned,

its monitions may have ceased. What we would speak of here is the tendency and object of this faculty; and the result to which, if it were perfectly obeyed, it would manifestly lead. And that such is its tendency I think that no one who reflects upon the operations of his own mind can for a moment doubt.

Suppose, now, man to be a system for the promotion of happiness, individual and social; and that these various impelling powers are parts of it. These powers being frequently, in their nature, contradictory; that is, being such that one frequently impels *to* and another repels *from* the same action; the question is in what relation of these powers to each other can the happiness of man be most successfully promoted.

1. It cannot be asserted that when these impulsions are at variance, it is a matter of indifference to which of them we yield; that is, that a man is just as happy, and renders society just as happy, by obeying the one as the other. For as men always obey either the one or the other, this would be to assert that all men are equally happy; and that every man promoted his own happiness just as much by one course of conduct as by another; than which nothing can be more directly at variance with the whole experience of all men in all ages. It would be to assert that the glutton who is racked with pain is as happy as the temperate and healthy man; and that Nero and Caligula were as great benefactors to mankind as Howard or Wilberforce.

2. If, then, it be not *indifferent* to our happiness to *which* of them we yield the supremacy, the question returns, Under what relation of each to the other can the happiness of man be most successfully promoted?

1. Can the happiness of man be promoted by subjecting his other impulses to his appetites and passions?

By referring to the nature of appetite and passion as previously explained, it will be seen that the result to the individual of such a course would be sickness and death. It would be a life of unrestrained gratification of every desire until the power of enjoyment was exhausted, without the least regard to the future; and of refusal to endure any present pain no matter how great might be the subse-

quent advantage. Everyone must see that, under the present constitution, such a course of life must produce nothing but individual
misery.

The result upon society would be its utter destruction. It would
render every man a ferocious beast bent upon nothing but present
gratification, utterly reckless of the consequences which gratification
produced upon himself either directly or through the instrumentality
of others; and reckless of the havoc which he made of the happiness
of his neighbor. Now it is manifest that the result of subjecting man
to such a principle would be not only the destruction of society, but
also, in a few years, the entire destruction of the human race.

2. Can the happiness of man be best promoted by subjecting all
his impulses to self-love?

It may be observed that our knowledge of the future and of the
results of things around us is manifestly insufficient to secure our
own happiness even by the most sagacious self-love. When we give
up the present pleasure, or suffer the present pain, we must from
necessity be wholly ignorant whether we shall ever reap the advantage which we anticipate. The system of which every individual
forms a part was not constructed to secure the happiness of any
single individual; and he who devises his plans with sole reference
to himself must find them continually thwarted by that Omnipotent
and Invisible Agency which is overruling all things upon principles
directly at variance with those which he has adopted. Inasmuch, then,
as we can never certainly *secure* to ourselves those results which self-
love anticipates, it seems necessary that, in order to derive from our
actions the happiness which they are capable of producing, they
involve in themselves some element, irrespective of future result,
which shall give us pleasure, let the result be what it may.

The imperfection of self-love as a director of conduct is nobly
set forth in Cardinal Wolsey's advice to Cromwell:

> "Mark but my fall, and that which ruin'd me.
> Cromwell, I charge thee fling away ambition
> *Love thyself last.* Cherish the hearts that hate thee.
> Be just, and fear not,
> Let all the ends thou aim'st at, be thy country's,

Thy God's, and truth's; then, if thou fall'st, O Cromwell
Thou fall'st a blessed martyr."

Henry VIII, Act iii, Sc. 2

"May he do *justice,*
For *truth's* sake, and his *conscience;* that his bones
When he has run his course, and sleeps in blessings
May have a tomb of orphans' tears wept on them."

Ibid.

"For care and trouble set your thought,
Ev'n when your end's attained;
And all your plans may come to nought,
When every nerve is strained."

BURNS's *Epistle to a Young Friend*

"But, mousie! thou art not alone,
In proving *foresight* may be vain.
The best laid schemes of mice and men
Gang oft agley,
And *leave us nought but grief and pain
For promised joy."*

BURNS, *On turning up a Mouse's Nest*

Besides, a man acting from uncontrolled self-love knows of no other object than his *own* happiness. He would sacrifice the happiness of others to any amount, how great soever, to secure his own in any amount, how small soever. Now suppose every individual to act in obedience to this principle; it must produce universal war and terminate in the subjection of all to the dominion of the strongest; and in sacrificing the happiness of all to that of one: that is, produce the *least amount* of happiness of which the system is susceptible. And still more, since men who have acted upon this principle have been proverbially unhappy, the result of such a course of conduct is to render *ourselves miserable* by the *misery of everyone else;* that is, its tendency is to the *entire destruction of happiness.* It is manifest, then, that the highest happiness of man cannot be promoted by subjecting all his impulses to the government of self-love.

Lastly. Suppose, now, all the impulses of man to be subjected to *conscience.*

The tendency of this impulse so far as this subject is concerned

is to restrain the appetites and passions of man within those limits
that shall conduce to his happiness on the whole; and so to control
the impulse of self-love that the individual in the pursuit of his own
happiness shall never interfere with the rightful happiness of his
neighbor. Each one, under such a system, and governed by such an
impulse, would enjoy all the happiness which he could create by
the use of the powers which God had given him. Everyone doing
thus, the whole would enjoy all the happiness of which their constitution was susceptible. The happiness of man as an individual and
as a society would thus be, in the best conceivable manner, provided
for. And thus under the relation which we have suggested, that is,
conscience being supreme and governing both self-love and passion,
and self-love, where no higher principle intervened, governing passion, man individual and man universal, considered as an instrument
for the production of happiness, would best accomplish the purpose
for which he was created. This, then, is the relation between his
powers which was designed to be established by his Creator.

It can in the same manner be shown that if man, individual and
universal, be considered as an instrument for the production of
power, this end of his creation can be accomplished most successfully by obedience to the relation here suggested; that is, on the
principle that the authority of conscience is supreme.* This is conclusively shown in *Butler's Analogy,* Part i, Chapter 3. And thus let
any reasonable end be suggested for which it may be supposed that
man has been created; and it will be found that this end can be best
attained by the subjection of every other impulse to that of conscience; nay, that it can be attained in no other way. And hence the
argument seems conclusive that this is the relation intended by his
Creator to be established between his faculties.

If the preceding views be correct it will follow:

1. If God has given man an impulse for virtue it is as true that he

---

* Vis consili expers, mole ruit sua.
  Vim temperatam, di quoque provehunt
  In majus; idem odere vires
  Omne nefas animo moventes.
                              Ho r. *Lib.* 3, *Car.* 4

has designed him for virtue as for anything else; as, for instance, for seeing or for hearing.

2. If this impulse be the most authoritative in his nature, it is equally manifest that man is made for virtue *more than for anything else.*

3. And hence he who is vicious not only acts *contrary to his nature* but contrary *to the highest impulse of his nature:* that is, he acts as much in opposition to his nature as it is possible for us to conceive.

Section IV · The Law by Which Conscience Is Governed

Conscience follows the general law by which the improvement of all our other faculties is regulated. *It is strengthened by use, it is impaired by disuse.*

Here it is necessary to remark that by use we mean the *use of the faculty itself,* and not of *some other faculty.* This is so plain a case that it seems wonderful that there should have been any mistake concerning it. Everyone knows that the arms are not strengthened by using the legs, nor the eyes by using the ears, nor the taste by using the understanding. So the conscience can be strengthened, not by using the memory, or the taste, or the understanding; but by using the conscience, and by using it precisely according to the laws and under the conditions designed by our Creator. The conscience is not improved by the reading of moral essays nor by committing to memory moral precepts nor by imagining moral vicissitudes; but by hearkening to its monitions and obeying its impulses.

If we reflect upon the nature of the monition of conscience, we shall find that its office is of a threefold character.

1. It enables us to discover the moral quality of actions.

2. It impels us to do right, and to avoid doing wrong.

3. It is a source of pleasure when we have done right and of pain when we have done wrong.

Let us illustrate the manner in which it may be improved, and injured, in each of these respects.

I. Of the improvement of the discriminating power of conscience.

1. The discriminating power of conscience is improved by *reflecting upon the moral character* of our actions, both before and after we have performed them. If, before we resolve upon a course of conduct or before we suffer ourselves to be committed to it, we deliberately ask, *Is this right?* Am I now actuated by appetite, by self-love, or by conscience? we shall seldom mistake the path of duty. After an action has been performed, if we deliberately and impassionately examine it, we may without difficulty decide whether it was right or wrong. Now with every such effort as this, the discriminating power of conscience is strengthened. We discern moral differences more distinctly, and we distinguish between actions that before seemed blended and similar.

2. The discriminating power of conscience is improved by meditating upon characters of pre-eminent excellence, and specially upon the character of God our Creator and Christ our Redeemer, the Fountain of all moral excellence. As we cultivate taste, or our susceptibility to beauty, by meditating upon the most finished specimens of art or the most lovely scenery in nature, so conscience, or our moral susceptibility, is improved by meditating upon anything eminent for moral goodness. It is hence that example produces so powerful a moral effect; and hence that one single act of heroic virtue, as that of Howard, or of illustrious self-denial gives a new impulse to the moral character of an age. Men cannot reflect upon such actions without the production of a change in their moral susceptibility. Hence the effect of the Scripture representations of the character of God and of the moral glory of the heavenly state. The Apostle Paul refers to this principle when he says, "We all, with open face, beholding, as in a glass, the glory of the Lord, are *changed into the same image,* from glory to glory, even as by the Spirit of the Lord."

On the contrary, the discriminating power of conscience may be injured,

1. By neglecting to reflect upon the moral character of our actions both before and after we have performed them. As taste is rendered obtuse by neglect so that we fail to distinguish between elegance and vulgarity and between beauty and deformity, so if we yield to the

impulses of passion and turn a deaf ear to the monitions of conscience, the dividing line between right and wrong seems gradually
to become obliterated. We pass from the confines of the one into
those of the other with less and less sensation, and at last neglect
the distinction altogether.

Horace remarks this fact:

> Fas atque nefas, exiguo fine, libidinum
> Discernunt avidi.

This is one of the most common causes of the grievous moral imperfection which we everywhere behold. Men act without *moral reflection*. They will ask, respecting an action, every question before
that most important one, is it right; and, in the great majority of
cases, act without putting to themselves this question at all. "The ox
knoweth his owner, and the ass his master's crib; but Israel doth not
know, my people *do not consider*." If any man doubt whether this
be true, let him ask himself, How large is the portion of the actions
which I perform upon which I deliberately decide whether they be
right or wrong? And on how large a portion of my actions do I
form such a decision after they have been performed? For the want
of this reflection the most pernicious habits are daily formed or
strengthened; and when to the power of habit is added the seductive
influence of passion, it is not wonderful that the virtue of man should
be the victim.

2. The discriminating power of conscience is impaired by frequent meditation upon vicious character and action. By frequently
contemplating vice our passions become excited, and our moral
disgust diminishes. Thus also, by becoming familiar with wicked
men, we learn to associate whatever they may possess of intellectual
or social interest with their moral character; and hence our abhorrence
of vice is lessened. Thus men who are accustomed to view habitually
any vicious custom cease to have their moral feelings excited by
beholding it. All this is manifest from the facts made known in the
progress of every moral reformation. Of so delicate a texture has God
made our moral nature and so easily is it either improved or impaired. Pope says, truly,

Vice is a monster of so frightful mien,
As, to be dreaded, needs but to be seen;
But, seen too oft, familiar with her face,
We first endure, then pity, then embrace.

It is almost unnecessary to remark that this fact will enable us to estimate the value of much of our reading and of much of our society. Whatever fills the memory with scenes of vice or stimulates the imagination to conceptions of impurity, vulgarity, profanity, or thoughtlessness, must by the whole of this effect render us vicious. As a man of literary sensibility will avoid a badly written book for fear of injuring his taste, by how much more should we dread the communion with anything wrong, lest it should contaminate our imagination and thus injure our moral sense!

II. The *impulsive* power of conscience is improved by use and weakened by disuse.

To illustrate this law we need only refer to the elements of man's active nature. We are endowed with appetites, passions, and self-love in all their various forms; and any one of them, or all of them, may at times be found impelling us towards actions in opposition to the impulsion of conscience, and, of course, one or the other impulse must be resisted. Now as the law of our faculties is universal, that they are strengthened by use and weakened by disuse, it is manifest that when we obey the impulse of conscience, and resist the impulse of passion, the power of conscience is strengthened; and on the contrary, when we obey the impulse of passion, and resist that of conscience, the power of passion is strengthened. And yet more, as either of these is strengthened its antagonist impulse is weakened. Thus every time a man does right he gains a victory over his lower propensities, acquires self-control, and becomes more emphatically a free man. Every time a man does wrong, that is, yields to his lower propensities, he loses self-control, he gives to his passions power over him, he weakens the practical supremacy of conscience and becomes more perfectly a slave. The design of the Christian religion in this respect is to bring us under the dominion of conscience, enlightened by revelation, and to deliver us from the slavery of evil propensity. Thus our Lord declares, "If the Son shall make you free, ye shall be free indeed." And on the contrary, "Whosoever committeth sin, is the servant (the slave) of sin."

Again. It is to be remarked that there exists a reciprocal connection between the use of the discriminating and of the impulsive power of conscience. The more a man reflects upon moral distinctions, the greater will be the practical influence which he will find them to exert over him. And it is still more decidedly true that the more implicitly we obey the impulsions of conscience, the more acute will be its power of discrimination and the more prompt and definite its decisions. This connection between theoretical knowledge and practical application is frequently illustrated in the other faculties. He who delineates objects of loveliness finds the discriminating power of taste to improve. And thus also this effect, in morals, is frequently alluded to in the Scriptures.

Our Saviour declares, "If any man will *do* his will, he shall *know* of the doctrine."

Thus also, "Unto him that hath, shall be given, and he shall have abundance; but from him that hath not (that is, does not improve what he has), shall be taken away even that which he hath."

Thus also, the Apostle Paul: "I beseech you therefore, brethren, by the mercies of God, that ye present your bodies a living sacrifice, *holy and acceptable unto God,* which is your rational service; and be ye not conformed to this world, but be ye transformed unto the renewing of your mind, *that (so that, to the end that) ye may know* what is that good, and acceptable, and perfect will of the Lord."

III. The sensibility of conscience as a source *of pleasure or of pain* is strengthened by use and weakened by disuse.

The more frequently a man does right, the stronger is his impulse to do right and the greater is the pleasure that results from the doing of it. A liberal man derives a pleasure from the practice of charity of which the covetous man can form no conception. A beneficent man is made happy by acts of self-denial and philanthropy, while a selfish man performs an act of goodness by painful and strenuous effort and merely to escape the reproaches of conscience. By the habitual exercise of the benevolent affections, a man becomes more and more capacious of virtue, capable of higher and more disinterested and more self-denying acts of mercy, until he becomes an enthusiast in goodness, loving to do good better than anything else. And in the same manner, the more our affections to God are exercised, the more constant and profound is the happiness which they create and the more absolutely is every other wish absorbed by the single desire to do the will of God. Illustrations of these remarks may be found in the lives of the Apostle Paul, John Howard, and other philanthropists. Thus it is said of our Saviour, "He went about doing good." And he says of himself, *"My meat* is to *do the will of Him that sent me,* and to finish his work."

And it deserves to be remarked that in our present state opportunities for moral improvement and moral pleasure are incessantly occurring. Under the present conditions of our being, there are everywhere and at all times sick to be relieved, mourners to be comforted, ignorant to be taught, vicious to be reclaimed, and men by nature enemies to God to be won back to reconciliation to Him. The season for moral labor depends not, like that for physical labor, upon vicissitudes beyond our control: it depends solely upon our own will. This I suppose to be the general principle involved in our Saviour's remark to his Apostles: "Say ye not, There are *four months,* and *then* cometh the harvest? Lift up your eyes, and look upon the fields, for they *are white already to the harvest."* That is, the fields are always waiting for the laborer in the moral harvest.

And on the contrary, the man who habitually violates his conscience not only is more feebly impelled to do right, but he becomes less sensible to the pain of doing wrong. A child feels poignant remorse after the first act of pilfering. Let the habit of dishonesty be formed, and he will become so hackneyed in sin that he will perpetrate robbery with no other feeling than that of mere fear of detection. The first oath almost palsies the tongue of the stripling. It requires but a few months, however, to transform him into the bold and thoughtless blasphemer. The murderer, after the death of his first victim, is agitated with all the horrors of guilt. He may, however, pursue his trade of blood until he have no more feeling for man than the butcher for the animal which he slaughters. Burk, who was in the habit of murdering men for the purpose of selling their bodies to the surgeons for dissection, confessed this of himself. Nor is this true of individuals alone. Whole communities may become so accustomed to deeds of violence as not merely to lose all the milder sympathies of their nature, but also to take pleasure in exhibitions of the most revolting ferocity. Such was the case in Rome at the period of the gladiatorial contests; and such was the fact in Paris at the time of the French revolution.

This also serves to illustrate a frequently repeated aphorism, *Quem Deus vult perdere, prius dementat.* As a man becomes more wicked, he becomes bolder in crime. Unchecked by conscience he ventures upon more and more atrocious villainy and he does it with less and less precaution. As in the earliest stages of guilt he is betrayed by timidity, in the later stages of it he is exposed by his recklessness. He is thus discovered by the very effect which his conduct is producing upon his own mind. Thus oppressors and despots seem to rush upon their own ruin as though bereft of reason. Such limits has our Creator by the conditions of our being set to the range of human atrocity.

Thus we see that by every step in our progress in virtue the succeeding step becomes less difficult. In proportion as we deny our passions, they becomes less imperative. The oftener we conquer them, the less is the moral effort necessary to secure the victory and the less frequently and the less powerfully do they assail us. By every act of successful resistance we diminish the tremendous power of habit over us and thus become more perfectly under the government of our own will. Thus with every act of obedience to conscience our character is fixed upon a more immovable foundation.

And on the contrary, by every act of vicious indulgence we give our passions more uncontrolled power over us and diminish the power of reason and of conscience. Thus by every act of sin we not only incur new guilt, but we strengthen the bias towards sin during the whole of our subsequent being. Hence every vicious act renders our return to virtue more difficult and more hopeless. The tendency of such a course is to give to habit the power which ought to be exerted by our will. And hence it is not improbable that the conditions of our being may be such as to allow of our arriving at such a state that reformation may be actually impossible. That the Holy Scriptures allude to such a condition during the present life is evident. Such, also, is probably the *necessary* condition of the wicked in another world.

In stating the change thus produced upon our moral nature, it deserves to be remarked that this loss of sensibility is probably only temporary. There is reason to believe that no impressions made upon the human soul during its present probationary state are ever permanently erased. Causes operating merely upon man's physical nature frequently revive whole trains of thought, and even the knowledge of languages, which had been totally forgotten during the greater portion of a long life. This seems to show that the liability to lose impressions, once made upon us, depends upon some condition arising from our material nature only, and that this liability will cease as soon as our present mode of existence terminates. That is to say, if the power of *retaining* knowledge is always the same, but if our *consciousness of knowledge* is veiled by our material organs, when these have been laid aside our entire consciousness will return. Now indications of the same nature are to be found in abundance with respect to conscience. Wicked men, after having spent a life in prosperous guilt and without being in trouble like other men, are frequently, without any assignable cause, tormented with all the agonies of remorse; so that the mere consciousness of guilt has become absolutely intolerable and they have perished by derangement or by suicide. The horrors of a licentious sinner's death bed present a striking illustration of the same solemn fact. A scene of this sort has been no less vividly than accurately described by Dr. Young in the death of Altamont. All these things should be marked by us as solemn warnings. They show us of what the constitution under which we exist is capable; and it is in forms like these that the "coming events" of eternity "cast their shadows before."

> In such indexes,
>   There is seen
> The baby figures of the giant mass
> Of things to come at large.
>   SHAKES.

Section V · Rules for Moral Conduct, Derived from the Preceding Remarks

Several plain rules of conduct are suggested by the above remarks, which may more properly be introduced here than in any other place.

I. *Before you resolve upon an action or a course of action,*

1. Cultivate the habit of deciding upon its moral character. Let the first question always be, Is this action right? For this purpose God gave you this faculty. If you do not use it you are false to yourself and inexcusable before God. We despise a man who never uses his reason and scorn him as a fool. Is he not much more to be despised who neglects to use a faculty of so much higher authority than reason? And let the question, Is this right? be asked *first, before* imagination has set before us the seductions of pleasure, or any step has been taken which should pledge our consistency of character. If we ask this question *first* it can generally be decided with ease. If we wait until the mind is agitated and harassed by contending emotions, it will not be easy to decide correctly.

2. Remember that your conscience has become imperfect from your frequent abuse of it. Hence in many cases its discrimination will be indistinct. Instead of *deciding* it will frequently only *doubt. That doubt* should be, generally, as imperative as a decision. When you, therefore, doubt respecting the virtue of an action, do not perform it unless you as much doubt whether you are at liberty to refrain from it. Thus says President Edwards in one of his resolutions: "Resolved, never to do any thing, of which I so much question the lawfulness, as that I intend, at the same time, to consider and examine afterwards, whether it be lawful or not; except I as much question the lawfulness of the omission."

3. Cultivate on all occasions, in private or in public, in small or great, in action or in thought, the habit of obeying the monitions of conscience; all other things to the contrary notwithstanding.

> Its slightest touches, instant pause;
> Debar a' side pretences;

And, resolutely, keep its laws,
Uncaring consequences.

BURNS

The supremacy of conscience imposes upon you the obligation to act thus. You cannot remember in the course of your whole life an instance in which you regret having obeyed it; and you cannot remember a single instance in which you do not regret having disobeyed it. There can nothing happen to you so bad as to have done wrong; there can nothing be gained so valuable as to have done right. And remember that it is only by cultivating the practical supremacy of conscience over every other impulse that you can attain to that bold, simple, manly, elevated character which is essential to true greatness.

This has been frequently taught us, even by the heathen poets:

> Virtus, repulsæ nescia sordidæ,
> Intaminatis fulget honoribus:
>   Nec sumit aut ponit secures
>   Arbitrio popularis auræ:
>
> Virtus, recludens immeritis mori
> Cœlum, negata tentat iter via;
>   Cœtusque vulgares et udam
>   Spernit humum fugiente penna.

HOR. Lib. 3, Car. 2

A greater than a heathen has said, "If thine eye be single, thy whole body shall be full of light;" and has enforced the precept by the momentous question, "What shall it profit a man, though he should gain the whole world, and lose his own soul? or what shall a man give in exchange for his soul?"

II. *After an action has been performed,*

1. Cultivate the habit of reflecting upon your actions and upon the *intention* with which they have been performed and of thus deciding upon their moral character. This is called self-examination. It is one of the most important duties in the life of a moral, and specially of a probationary existence.

> 'Tis greatly wise, to talk with our past hours,
> And ask them what report they bore to Heaven,
> And how they might have borne more welcome news.

a. Perform this duty *deliberately.* It is not the business of hurry or of negligence. Devote time exclusively to it. Go alone. Retire within yourself and weigh your actions coolly and carefully, forgetting all other things, in the conviction that you are a moral and an accountable being.

b. Do it impartially. Remember that you are liable to be misled by the seductions of passion and the allurements of self-interest. Put yourself in the place of those around you and put others in your own place and remark how you would then consider your actions. Pay great attention to the opinions of your enemies: there is generally foundation, or at least the appearance of it, in what they say of you. But above all, take the true and perfect standard of moral character exhibited in the precepts of the gospel and exemplified in the life of Jesus Christ; and thus examine your conduct by the light that emanates from the holiness of heaven.

2. Suppose you have examined yourself and arrived at a decision respecting the moral character of your actions.

1. If you are conscious of having *done right,* be thankful to that God who has mercifully enabled you to do so. Observe the peace and serenity which fills your bosom and remark how greatly it overbalances the self-denials which it has cost. Be humbly thankful that you have made some progress in virtue.

2. If the character of your actions have been mixed, that is, if they have proceeded from motives partly good and partly bad, labor to obtain a clear view of each and of the circumstances which led you to confound them. Avoid the sources of this confusion; and when you perform the same actions again be specially on your guard against the influence of any motive of which you now disapprove.

3. If conscience convicts you of having acted wrongly,

1. Reflect upon the wrong, survey the obligations which you have violated until you are sensible of your guilt.

2. Be willing to suffer the pains of conscience. They are the rebukes of a friend and are designed to withhold you from the commission of wrong in future. Neither turn a neglectful ear to its monitions nor drown its voice amid the bustle of business or the gayety of pleasure.

3. Do not let the subject pass away from your thoughts until you have come to a settled resolution, a resolution *founded on moral disapprobation of the action,* never to do so any more.

4. If restitution be in your power, make it, without hesitation, and do it immediately. The least that a man ought to be satisfied with who has done wrong is to repair the wrong as soon as it is possible.

5. As every act of wrong is a sin against God seek in humble penitence his pardon, through the merits and intercession of his Son, Jesus Christ.

6. Remark the actions or the courses of thinking which were the occasions of leading you to do wrong. Be specially careful to avoid them in future. To this effect, says President Edwards, "Resolved, that when I do any conspicuously evil action, to trace it back, till I come to the original cause; and then both carefully endeavor to do so no more, and to fight and pray, with all my might, against the original of it."

7. Do all this, in humble dependence upon that merciful and everywhere present Being, who is always ready to grant us all assistance necessary to keep his commandments, and who will never leave us nor forsake us if we put our trust in him.

It seems, then, from what has been remarked, that we are all endowed with conscience, or a faculty for discerning a moral quality in human actions, impelling us towards right and dissuading us from wrong; and that the dictates of this faculty are felt and known to be of supreme authority.

The possession of this faculty renders us accountable creatures. Without it we should not be specially distinguished from the brutes. With it we are brought into moral relations with God and all the moral intelligences in the universe.

It is an ever present faculty. It always admonishes us if we will listen to its voice, and frequently does so even when we wish to silence its warnings. Hence we may always know our duty if we will but inquire for it. We can, therefore, never have any excuse for doing wrong, since no man need do wrong unless he chooses; and no man will do it ignorantly unless from criminal neglect of the faculty which God has given him.

How solemn is the thought that we are endowed with such a faculty and that we can never be disunited from it! It goes with us through all the scenes of life, in company and alone, admonishing, warning, reproving, and recording: and as a source of happiness or of misery it must abide with us forever. Well doth it become man, then, to reverence himself.

And thus we see that from his moral constitution, were there no other means of knowledge of duty, man is an accountable creature. Man is under obligation to obey the will of God in *what manner soever signified*. That it is signified in this manner I think there cannot be a question; and for this knowledge he is justly held responsible. Thus the Apostle Paul declares that "the Gentiles, who have not the law, are a law unto themselves, which show the *work of the law, written on their hearts,* their consciences being continually excusing or accusing one another." How much greater must be the responsibility of those to whom God has given the additional light of natural and revealed religion!

CHAPTER THIRD

THE NATURE OF VIRTUE

Section I · Of Virtue in General

IT has been already remarked that we find ourselves so constituted as to stand in various relations to all the beings around us, especially to our fellow men, and to God. There may be, and there probably are, other beings to whom, by our creation, we are related: but we as yet have no information on the subject; and we must wait until we enter upon another state before the fact and the manner of the fact be revealed.

In consequence of these relations, and either by the appointment of God or from the necessity of the case—if indeed these terms mean anything different from each other—there arise moral obligations to exercise certain affections towards other beings and to act towards them in a manner corresponding to those affections. Thus we are taught in the Scriptures that the relation in which we stand to Deity involves the obligation to universal and unlimited obedience and love; and that the relation in which we stand to each other involves the obligation to love, limited and restricted; and, of course, to a mode of conduct in all respects correspondent to these affections.

An action is right when it corresponds to these obligations, or, which is the same thing, is the carrying into effect of these affections. It is wrong when it is in violation of these obligations, or is the carrying into effect of any other affections.

By means of our intellect we become conscious of the relations in which we stand to the beings with whom we are connected. Thus by the exertion of our intellectual faculties, we become acquainted with the existence and attributes of God, his power, his wisdom, his goodness, and it is by these same faculties that we understand and verify those declarations of the Scriptures which give us additional knowledge of his attributes; and by which we arrive at a knowledge of the conditions of our being as creatures and also of the various relations in which we stand to each other.

Conscience, as has been remarked, is that faculty by which we become conscious of the obligations arising from these relations; by which we perceive the quality of right in those actions which correspond to these obligations and of wrong in those actions which violate them; and by which we are impelled towards the one and repelled from the other. It is manifestly the design of this faculty to suggest to us this feeling of obligation as soon as the relations on which it is founded are understood; and thus to excite in us the corresponding affections.

Now in a perfectly constituted moral and intellectual being, it is evident that there would be a perfect adjustment between these external qualities and the internal faculties. A *perfect eye* is an eye that, under the proper conditions, would discern every variety and shade of color in every object which it was adapted to perceive. The same remark would apply to our hearing or to any other sense. So a *perfectly constituted intellect* would, under the proper conditions, discern the relations in which the being stood to other beings; and a *perfectly constituted conscience* would, at the same time, become conscious of all the obligations which arose from such relations and would impel us to the corresponding courses of conduct. That is, there would exist a perfect adaptation between the external qualities which were addressed to these faculties and the faculties themselves to which these qualities were addressed.

Hence in a being thus perfectly constituted it is manifest that virtue, the doing of right, or obedience to conscience would mean the same thing.

When, however, we speak of the perfection of a moral organization, we speak of the perfection of adjustment between the faculty of conscience and the relations and obligations under which the particular being is created. Hence this very perfection admits of various gradations and modifications. For example:

1. The relations of the same being change, during the progress of its existence from infancy, through childhood and manhood, until old age. This change of relations involves a change of obligations; and the perfection of its moral organization would consist in the perfect *adjustment* of its moral faculty to its *moral relations* throughout the whole course of its history. Now the tendency of this change

is, manifestly, from less to greater; that is, from less imperative to more imperative and from less numerous to more numerous obligations. That is, the tendency of the present system is to render beings more and more capacious of virtue and of vice, as far as we are permitted to have any knowledge of them.

2. As it is manifestly impossible for us to conceive either how numerous or how important may be our relations to other creatures in another state, or how much more intimate may be the relations in which we shall stand to our Creator; and as there can be no limit conceived to our power of comprehending these relations nor to our power of becoming conscious of the obligations which they involve; so it is manifest that no limit can be conceived to the progress of man's capacity for virtue. It evidently contains within itself elements adapted to infinite improvement in any state in which we may exist.

3. And the same may be said of vice. As our obligations must, from what we already know, continue to increase, and our power for recognizing them must also continue to increase; if we perpetually violate them we become more and more capable of wrong; and thus also become more and more intensely vicious. And thus the very elements of a moral constitution seem to involve the necessity of illimitable progress, either in virtue or in vice, so long as we exist.

4. And as, on the one hand, we can have no conception of the amount of attainment, both in virtue and vice, of which man is capable, so, on the other hand, we can have no conception of the delicacy of that moral tinge by which his character is first designated. We *detect* moral character at a very early age; but this by no means proves that *it did not exist long before* we detected it. Hence as it may thus have existed before we were able to detect it, it is manifest that we have no elements by which to determine the time of its commencement. That is to say, in general we are capable of observing moral qualities within certain limits, as from childhood to old age; but this is no manner of indication that these qualities may not exist in the being both before and afterwards in degrees greatly below and infinitely above anything which we are capable of observing.

Section II · Of Virtue in Imperfect Beings

Let us now consider this subject in relation to a being whose moral constitution has become disordered.

Now this disorder might be of two kinds:

1. He might not perceive all the relations in which he stood, and which gave rise to moral obligations, and, of course, would be unconscious of the corresponding obligations.

2. He might perceive the relation, but his conscience might be so disordered as not to feel all the obligation which corresponded to it.

What shall we say concerning the actions of such a being?

1. The relations under which he is constituted are the same, and the obligations arising out of these relations are the same, as though his moral constitution had not become disordered.

2. His actions would all be comprehended under two classes;

1. Those which came, if I may so express it, within the limit of his conscience; that is, those in which his conscience did correctly intimate to him his obligation; and,

2. Those in which it did not so intimate it.

Now of the first class of actions it is manifest that where conscience did correctly intimate to him his obligations, the doing of right and obedience to conscience would, as in the last section, be equivalent terms.

But what shall we say of those without this limit; that is, of those which he, from the conditions of his being, is under obligation to perform, but of which, from the derangement of his moral nature, he does not perceive the obligation?

1. Suppose him to perform these very actions, there could be in them no virtue; for the man perceiving in them no moral quality and having towards them no moral impulsion, moral obligation could be no motive for performing them. He might act from passion or from self-love; but under such circumstances, as there is no moral motive, there could be no praiseworthiness. Thus for a judge to do justice to a poor widow is manifestly right; but a man may do this without any moral desert; for hear what the unjust judge saith:

"Though *I fear not God,* nor *regard man,* yet, because *this widow troubleth me,* I will avenge her, lest, by her continual coming, she weary me."

It does not, however, follow that the performing of an action in this manner is innocent. The relation in which a being stands to other beings involves the obligation to certain feelings, as well as to the acts correspondent to those feelings. If the act be performed and the feeling be wanting, the obligation is not fulfilled, and the man *may be guilty.* How far he is guilty will be seen below.

2. But secondly, suppose him *not* to perform those actions which are, as we have said, without the limit of his conscience. In how far is the omission of these actions, or the doing of the contrary, innocent? That is to say, is the impulse of conscience in an imperfectly constituted moral being the limit of moral obligation?

This will, I suppose, depend upon the following considerations:

1. His knowledge of the relations in which he stands.

If he know not the relations in which he stands to others and *have not the means of knowing them,* he is guiltless. If *he know them* or *have the means of knowing them,* and *have not improved these means,* he is guilty. This is, I think, the principle asserted by the Apostle Paul in his Epistle to the Romans. He asserts that the heathen are guilty in sinning against God because His attributes may be known by the light of nature. He also asserts that there will be a difference between the condemnation of the Jews and that of the heathen, on the ground that the Jews were informed of many points of moral obligation which the heathen could not have ascertained without a revelation: "Those that sin without law, shall perish without law; and those that have sinned in the law, shall be judged by the law."

2. His guilt will depend, secondly, on the *cause* of this imperfection of his conscience.

Were this imperfection of conscience not the result of his own act, he would be guiltless. But in just so far as it is the *result of his own conduct,* he is responsible. And inasmuch as imperfection of conscience, or diminution of moral capacity, can result from nothing but voluntary transgression, I suppose that he must be answerable for the whole amount of that imperfection. We have already seen that conscience may be improved by use and injured by disuse or by abuse. Now as a man is entitled to all the benefits which accrue from the faithful improvement of his conscience, so he is responsible for all the injury that results from the abuse of it.

That this is the fact is, I think, evident from obvious considerations:

1. It is well known that the repetition of wickedness produces great stupidity of conscience, or, as it is frequently termed, hardness of heart. But no one ever considers this stupidity as in any manner an excuse. It is, on the contrary, always held to be an aggravation of crime. Thus we term a man who has become so accustomed to crime that he will commit murder without feeling and without regret, a *remorseless* murderer, a *cold-blooded* assassin; and everyone knows that by these epithets we mean to designate a special and additional element of guiltiness. This I take to be the universal sentiment of man.

2. The assertion of the contrary would lead to results manifestly erroneous.

Suppose two men of precisely the same moral attainments, today, to commence, at the same time, two courses of conduct diametrically opposed to each other. The first, by the scrupulous doing of right, cultivates to the utmost his moral nature, and increases, with every day, his capacity for virtue. The sphere of his benevolent affections enlarges and the play of his moral feelings becomes more and more intense, until he is filled with the most ardent desire to promote the welfare of every fellow creature and to do the will of God with his whole heart. The other, by a continued course of crime, gradually destroys the susceptibility of his conscience and lessens his capacity for virtue until his soul is filled with hatred to God, and no other feeling of obligation remains except that of fidelity to his copartners in guilt.

Now at the expiration of this period, if both of these men should act according to what each felt to be the dictate of conscience, they would act very differently. But if a man can be under obligation to do and to leave undone nothing but what his conscience at a particular moment indicates, I do not see but that these men would be, in the actions of that moment, equally innocent. The only difference between them, so far as the actions of a particular moment were concerned, would be the difference between a virtuous man and a virtuous child.

From these facts we are easily led to the distinction between *right and wrong,* and *innocence and guilt. Right and wrong* depend upon the relations under which beings are created; and hence the obligations resulting from these relations are, in their nature, fixed and unchangeable. *Guilt and innocence* depend upon the knowledge of these relations [6] and of the obligations arising from them. As these are manifestly susceptible of variation, while right and wrong are invariable, the two notions may manifestly not always correspond to each other.

Thus, for example, an action may be wrong; but if the actor have no means of knowing it to be wrong, he is held morally guiltless in the doing of it. Or again, a man may have a consciousness of obligation and a sincere desire to act in conformity to it; and may, from ignorance of the way in which that obligation is to be discharged, perform an act in its nature wrong; yet if he have acted according to the *best of his possible knowledge,* he may not only be held guiltless, but even virtuous. And on the contrary, if a man do what is actually right, but without a desire to fulfill the obligation of which he is conscious, he is held to be guilty; for he has not manifested a desire to act in obedience to the obligations under which he knew himself to be created. Illustrations of these remarks may be easily drawn from the ordinary affairs of life or from the Scriptures.

And hence we also arrive at another principle of importance in our moral judgments, namely, that our own consciousness of innocence or our not being conscious of guilt is by no means a sufficient proof of our innocence. A man may never have reflected on the relations in which he stands to other men or to God; and hence may be conscious of no feeling of obligation toward either, in any or in

[6] The 1835 edition: "relations, and are moreover, affected by the degree in which the imperfection of conscience was the result of the voluntary agency of the individual himself."

particular respects. This may be the fact; but his innocence would not be established unless he can also show that he has faithfully and impartially used all the powers which God has given him to obtain a knowledge of these relations. Or again, he may understand the relation and have no corresponding sensibility. This may be the fact; but his innocency would not be established unless he can also show that he has always faithfully and honestly obeyed his conscience, so that his moral insensibility is in no manner attributable to his own acts. Until these things can be shown the want of consciousness of guilt will be no proof of innocence. To this principle, if I mistake not, the Apostle Paul alludes, in 1 *Cor.* iv. 3, 4: "But with me, it is a very small thing to be judged of you, or of man's judgment: yea, I judge not my ownself, for I know nothing of my ownself (or, rather, I am conscious of nothing wrong in myself; that is, of no unfaithfulness in office); yet, *am I not hereby justified:* but he that judgeth me is the Lord." And thus a man may do great wrong, and be deeply guilty in respect to a whole class of obligations, without being, in any painful degree, sensible of it. Such I think to be the moral state in which men in general are, in respect to their obligations to God. Thus saith our Saviour to the Jews: "I know you, *that ye have not the love of God in you;"* while they were supposing themselves to be the special favorites of Heaven.

From these remarks we may also learn the relation in which beings, created as we are, stand to moral law.

Man is created with moral and intellectual powers, capable of progressive improvement. Hence if he use his faculties as he ought, he will progressively improve; that is, become more and more capable of virtue. He is assured of enjoying all the benefits which can result from such improvement. If he use these faculties as he ought not, and become less and less capable of virtue, he is hence held responsible for all the consequences of his misimprovement.

Now as this misimprovement is his own act, for which he is responsible, it manifestly does not affect the relations under which he is created nor the obligations resulting from these relations; that is, he stands, in respect to the moral requirements under which he is created, precisely in the same condition as if he had always used his moral powers correctly. That is to say, under the present moral constitution every man is justly held responsible, at every period of his existence, for that degree of virtue of which he would have been capable had he from the first moment of his existence improved his moral nature in every respect, just as he ought to have done. In other words, suppose some human being to have always lived thus (Jesus Christ, for instance), every man, supposing him to have the same means of knowing his duty, would, at every successive period of his existence, be held responsible for the same degree of virtue as such a perfect being attained to at the corresponding periods of his existence. Such I think evidently to be the nature of the obligation which must rest upon such beings throughout the whole extent of their duration.

In order to meet this increasing responsibility in such a manner as to fulfill the requirements of moral law, a being under such a constitution must, at every moment of his existence, possess a moral faculty which, by perfect previous cultivation, is adapted to the responsibilities of that particular moment. But suppose this not to have been the case; and that, on the contrary, his moral faculty, by once doing wrong, has become impaired so that it either does not admonish him correctly of his obligations or that he has become indisposed to obey its monitions. This must, at the next moment, terminate in action more at variance with rectitude than before. The adjustment between conscience and the passions must become deranged; and thus the tendency, at every successive moment, must be to involve him deeper and deeper in guilt. And unless some other moral force be exerted in the case, such must be the tendency forever.

And suppose some such force to be exerted and, at any period of his existence, the being to begin to obey his conscience in every one of its *present monitions*. It is manifest that he would now need some other and more perfect guide in order to inform him perfectly of his obligations and of the mode in which they were to be fulfilled. And supposing this to be done: as he is at this moment responsible for *such a capacity for virtue* as would have been attained by a *previously perfect rectitude;* and as his capacity is inferior to this; and as no reason can be suggested why *his* progress in virtue should, under these circumstances, be more rapid than that of a perfect being, but the contrary; it is manifest that he must ever fall short of what is justly required of him—nay, that he must be continually falling farther and farther behind it.

And hence the present constitution tends to show us the remediless nature of moral evil under the government of God, unless some other principle than that of *law* be admitted into the case. These conditions of being having been violated, unless man be placed under *some other conditions,* natural religion would lead us to believe that he must suffer the penalty, whatever it be, of wrong. Penitence could in no manner alter his situation; for it is merely a temper justly demanded in consequence of his sin. But this could not replace him in his original relation to the law which had been violated. Such seems to be the teachings of the Holy Scriptures; and they seem to me to declare, moreover, that this change in the conditions of our being has been accomplished by the mediation of a Redeemer, by which change of conditions we may, through the obedience of another, be justified (that is, treated as though just), although we are, by confession, guilty.

And hence although it were shown that a man was, at any particular period of his being, incapable of that degree of virtue which the law of God required, it would neither follow that he was not under obligation to exercise it nor that he was not responsible for the whole amount of that exercise of it; since if he have dwarfed his own powers, he is responsible for the result. And, conversely, if God require this whole amount of virtue, it will not prove that man is now capable of exercising it; but only that he is either thus capable or that he would have been so if he had used correctly the powers which God gave him.

A few suggestions respecting the moral relations of habit will close this discussion.

Some of the most important facts respecting habit are the following:

It is found to be the fact that the repetition of any physical act at stated periods, and especially after brief intervals, renders the performance of the act easier; it is accomplished in less time, with less effort, with less expense of nervous power and of mental energy. This is exemplified every day in the acquisition of the mechanical arts and in learning the rudiments of music. And whoever will remark may easily be convinced that a great part of our education, physical and intellectual, insofar as it is valuable, consists in the formation of habits.

The same remarks apply, to a very considerable extent, to moral habits.

The repetition of a virtuous act produces a *tendency* to continued repetition; the force of opposing motives is lessened; the power of the will over passion is more decided; and the act is accomplished with less moral effort. Perhaps we should express the fact truly by saying that by the repetition of virtuous acts, moral power is gained; while for the performance of the same acts less moral power is required.

On the contrary, by the repetition of vicious acts a *tendency* is created towards such repetition; the power of the passions is increased; the power of opposing forces is diminished; and the resistance to passion requires a greater moral effort; or, as in the contrary of the preceding case, a greater moral effort is required to resist our passions, while the moral power to resist them is diminished.

Now the obvious nature of such a tendency is to arrive at a fixed and unalterable moral state. Be the fact accounted for as it may, I think that habit has an effect upon the will such as to establish *a tendency toward the impossibility to resist it*. Thus the practice of virtue seems *to tend* toward rendering a man incapable of vice, and the practice of vice toward rendering a man incapable of virtue. It is common to speak of a man as *incapable* of meanness; and I think we see men as often, in the same sense, incapable of virtue. And if I mistake not we always speak of the one incapacity as an object of praise, and of the other as an object of blame.

If we inquire what are the moral effects of such a condition of our being, I think we shall find them to be as follows:

1. Habit cannot alter the nature of an action as right or wrong. It can alter neither our relations to our fellow creatures nor to God,

nor the obligations consequent upon those relations. Hence the character of the action must remain unaffected.

2. Nor can it alter the guilt or innocence of the action. As he who acts virtuously is entitled to the benefit of virtuous action, among which the tendency to virtuous action is included; so he who acts viciously is responsible for all the consequences of vicious action, the correspondent tendency to vicious action also included. The conditions being equal and he being left to his own free choice, the consequences of either course rest justly upon himself.

The *final causes* of such a constitution are also apparent.

1. It is manifestly and precisely adapted to our present state when considered as probationary and capable of moral changes, and terminating in one where moral change is impossible. The constitution under which we are placed presents us with the apparent paradox of a state of incessant moral change in which every individual change has a *tendency* to produce a state that is unchangeable.

2. The fact of such a constitution is manifestly intended to present the strongest possible incentives to virtue and monitions against vice. It teaches us that consequences are attached to every act of both, not only present but future, and, so far as we can see, interminable. As everyone can easily estimate the pleasures of vice and the pains of virtue both in extent and duration; but as no one, taking into consideration the results of the tendency which each will produce, can estimate the interminable consequences which must arise from either —there is, therefore, hence derived the strongest possible reason why we should always do right, and never do wrong.

3. And again. It is evident that our capacity for increase in virtue depends greatly upon the present constitution in respect to habit. I have remarked that the effect of the repetition of virtuous action was to give us greater moral power, while the given action itself required less moral effort. There hence arises, if I may so say, a surplus of moral power, which may be applied to the accomplishment of greater moral achievements. He who has overcome one evil temper has acquired moral power to overcome another; and that which was first subdued is kept in subjection without a struggle. He

who has formed one habit of virtue practices it without effort as a matter of course or of original impulse; and the power thus acquired may be applied to the attainment of other and more difficult habits and the accomplishment of higher and more arduous moral enterprises. He who desires to see the influence of habit illustrated with great beauty and accuracy will be gratified by the perusal of "The Hermit of Teneriffe," one of the most delightful allegories to be found in the English language.

The relation between the moral and the intellectual powers in the moral conditions of our being, may be thus briefly stated:

1. We are created under certain relations to our Creator and to our fellow creatures.

2. We are created under certain obligations to our Creator and our fellow creatures in consequence of these relations—obligations to exercise certain affections and to maintain courses of action correspondent to those affections.

3. By means of our intellectual powers, we perceive these relations.

4 By means of our moral powers, we become conscious of these obligations.

5. The consciousness of these obligations alone would not always teach us how they were to be discharged; as, for example, the consciousness of our obligations to God would not teach us how God should be worshipped, and so in various other cases. It is by the use of the powers of our intellect that we learn how these moral affections are to be carried into action. The use of the intellect is, therefore, twofold. First, to discover to us our relations. Secondly, to discover in what manner our obligations are to be discharged.

WE have already on several occasions alluded to the fact that God has created everything double; a world without us, and a correspondent world within us. He has made light without, and the eye within; beauty without, and taste within; moral qualities in actions, and conscience to judge of them; and so of every other case. By means of this correspondence, our communication with the external world exists.

These internal powers are called into exercise by the presence of their correspondent external objects. Thus the organ of vision is excited by the presence of light, the sense of smell by odors, the faculty of taste by beauty or by deformity, and so of the rest.

The first effect of this exercise of these faculties is that we are conscious of the existence and qualities of surrounding objects. Thus by sight we become conscious of the existence and colors of visible objects; by hearing, of the existence and sound of audible objects, &c.

But it is manifest that this knowledge of the existence and qualities of external objects is far from being all the intercourse which we are capable of holding with them. This knowledge of their existence and qualities is most frequently attended with pleasure or pain, desire or aversion. Sometimes the mere perception itself is immediately pleasing; in other cases it is merely the sign of some other quality which has the power of pleasing us. In the first case, the perception produces gratification; in the other, it awakens desire.

That is, we stand in such relations to the external world that certain objects, besides being capable of being perceived, are also capable of giving us pleasure; and certain other objects, besides being perceived, are capable of giving us pain. Or, to state the same truth in the other form, we are so made as to be capable not only of perceiving, but also of being pleased with or pained by the various objects by which we are surrounded.

This general power of being pleased or pained may be, and I think frequently is, termed sensitiveness.

This sensitiveness, or the power of being made happy by surrounding objects, is intimately connected with the *exercise* of our various faculties. Thus the pleasure of vision cannot be enjoyed in any other manner than by the *exercise* of the faculty of sight. The pleasure of knowledge can be enjoyed in no other way than by the exercise of the intellectual powers. The pleasure of beauty can be enjoyed in no other manner than by the exercise of the faculty of taste, and of the other subordinate faculties on which this faculty depends. And thus, in general, our sensitiveness derives pleasure from the *exercise of those powers which are made necessary for our existence and well-being* in our present state.

Now I think that we can have no other idea of happiness than the exercise of this sensitiveness upon its corresponding objects and qualities. It is the gratification of desire, the enjoyment of what we love; or as Dr. Johnson remarks, "Happiness consists in the multiplication of agreeable consciousness."

It seems, moreover, evident that this very constitution is to us an indication of the will of our Creator; that is, inasmuch as he has created us with these capacities for happiness and has also created objects around us precisely adapted to these capacities, he meant that the one should be exercised upon the other; that is, that we should be made happy in this manner.

And this is more evident from considering that this happiness is intimately connected with the exercise of those faculties the employment of which is necessary to our existence and our well-being. It thus becomes the incitement to or the reward of certain courses of conduct which it is necessary, to our own welfare or to that of society, that we should pursue.

And thus we arrive at the general principle that our desire for a particular object, and the existence of the object adapted to this desire is, in itself, a reason why we should enjoy that object, in the same manner as our aversion to another object is a reason why we should avoid it. There may sometimes be, it is true, other reasons to the contrary, more authoritative than that emanating from this desire or aversion, and these may and ought to control it; but this does not show that this desire is not *a reason,* and a sufficient one, if no better reason can be shown to the contrary.

But if we consider the subject a little more minutely, we shall find that the simple gratification of desire, in the manner above stated, is not the only condition on which our happiness depends.

We find, by experience, that a desire or appetite may be so gratified as forever afterwards to destroy its power of producing happiness. Thus a certain kind of food is pleasant to me; this is a reason why I should partake of it. But I may eat of it to excess, so as to loathe it forever afterwards and thus annihilate in my constitution this mode of gratification. Now the same reasoning which proves that God intended me to *partake* of this food, namely because it will promote my happiness, also proves that he did not intend me to partake of it *after this manner,* for by so doing I have diminished, by this whole amount, my capacity for happiness, and thus defeated, insofar, the very end of my constitution. Or again, though I may not destroy my desire for a particular kind of food by a particular manner of gratification, yet I may so derange my system that the eating of it shall produce pain and distress, so that it ceases to be to me a source of happiness *upon the whole*. In this case I equally defeat the design of my constitution. The result equally shows that, although the Creator means that I should eat it, he does not mean that I should eat it in this manner.

Again, every man is created with various and dissimilar forms of desire, correspondent to the different external objects designed to promote his happiness. Now it is found that one form of desire may be gratified in such a manner as to destroy the power of receiving happiness from another; or, on the contrary, the first may be so gratified as to leave the other powers of receiving happiness unimpaired. Since, then, it is granted that these were all given us for the same end, namely to promote our happiness, if by the first manner of gratification we destroy another power of gratification, while by the second manner of gratification we leave the other power of gratification uninjured, it is evidently the design of our Creator that we should limit ourselves to this second mode of gratification.

Thus I am so formed that food is pleasant to me. This, even if there were no necessity for eating, is a reason why I should eat it. But I am also formed with a desire for knowledge. This is a reason why I should study in order to obtain it. That is, God intended me to derive happiness from both of these sources of gratification. If, then, I eat in such a manner that I cannot study, or study in such a manner that I cannot eat, in either case I defeat his design concerning me by destroying those sources of happiness with which he has created me. The same principle might be illustrated in various other instances.

Again, we find that the indulgence of any one form of gratification in such manner as to destroy the power of another form of gratification, also in the end diminishes, and frequently destroys, the power of deriving happiness, even from that which is indulged. Thus he who eats so as to injure his power of intellectual gratification, injures also his digestive organs, and produces disease, so that his pleasure from eating is diminished. Or he who studies so as to destroy his appetite, in the end destroys also his power of study. This is another and distinct reason to show that while I am designed to be happy by the gratification of my desires, I am also designed to be happy by gratifying them within a limit. The limit to gratification enters into my constitution as a being designed for happiness, just as much as the power of gratification itself.

And again, our Creator has endowed us with an additional and superior power by which we can contemplate these two courses of conduct; by which we can approve of the one and disapprove of the other; and by which the one becomes a source of pleasure and the other a source of pain; both being separate and distinct from the sources of pain and pleasure mentioned above. And, moreover, he has so constituted us that this very habit of regulating and limiting our desires is absolutely essential to our success in every undertaking. Both of these are, therefore, additional and distinct reasons for believing that the restriction of our desires within certain limits is made by our Creator as clearly necessary to our happiness as the indulgence of them.

All this is true if we consider the happiness of man merely as an individual. But the case is rendered still stronger if we look upon man as a society. It is manifest that the *universal* gratification of any *single* appetite or passion without limit, not to say the gratification of all, would, in a very few years, not only destroy society, but absolutely put an end to the whole human race. And hence we see that the limitation of our desires is not only necessary to our happiness, but also to our existence.

Hence while it is *the truth* that human happiness consists in the gratification of our desires, it is not *the whole truth*. It consists in the *gratification of our desires within the limits assigned to them by our Creator*. And the happiness of that man will be the most perfect who regulates his desires most perfectly in accordance with the laws under which he has been created. And hence the greatest happiness of which man is, in his present state, capable, is to be attained by conforming his whole conduct to the laws of virtue, that is, to the will of God.

By the term sensitiveness I have designated the capacity of our nature to derive happiness from the various objects and qualities of the world around us. Though intimately associated with those powers by which we obtain a knowledge of external objects, it differs from them. When a desire for gratification is excited by its appropriate objects, it is termed appetite, passion, &c.

As our means of gratification are various and are also attended by different effects, there is evidently an opportunity for a choice between them. By declining a gratification at present, we may secure one of greater value at some future time. That which is at present agreeable may be of necessity followed by pain; and that which is at present painful may be rewarded by pleasure which shall far overbalance it.

Now it must be evident to everyone who will reflect that my happiness at any one period of my existence is just as valuable as my happiness at the present period. No one can conceive of any reason why the present moment should take the precedence, in any respect, of any other moment of my being. Every moment of my past life was once present and seemed of special value; but in the retrospect all seem, so far as the happiness of each is concerned, of equal value. Each of those to come may, in its turn, claim some pre-eminence; though now, we plainly discover in anticipation that no one is more than another entitled to it. Nay, if there be any difference, it is manifestly in favor of the most distant future in comparison with the present. The longer we exist, the greater is our capacity for virtue and happiness and the wider is our sphere of existence. To postpone the present for the future seems, therefore, to be the dictate of wisdom if we calmly consider the condition of our being.[7]

But it is of the nature of passion to seize upon the present gratification, utterly irrespective of consequences, and utterly regardless of other or more excellent gratifications which may be obtained by self-denial. He whose passions are inflamed looks at nothing beyond the

[7] See Appendix (c) for quotation inserted in the 1865 edition.

present gratification. Hence he is liable to seize upon a present enjoyment to the exclusion of a much more valuable one in future, and even in such a manner as to entail upon himself poignant and remediless misery. And hence in order to be enabled to enjoy all the happiness of which his present state is capable, the sensitive part of man needs to be combined with another which, upon a comparison of the present with the future, shall impel him towards that mode either of gratification or of self-denial which shall most promote his happiness upon the whole.

Such is self-love. We give this name to that part of our constitution by which we are incited to do or to forbear, to gratify or to deny our desires simply on the ground of obtaining the greatest amount of happiness for ourselves, taking into view a limited future or else our entire future existence. When we act from simple respect to present gratification, we act from passion. When we act from a respect to our whole individual happiness without regard to the present, only as it is a part of the whole, and without any regard to the happiness of others, only as it will contribute to our own, we are then said to act from self-love.

The difference between these two modes of impulsion may be easily illustrated.

Suppose a man destitute of self-love and actuated only by passion. He would seize without reflection and enjoy without limit every object of gratification which the present moment might offer, without regard to its value in comparison with others which might be secured by self-denial, and without any regard to the consequences which might follow present pleasure, be they ever so disastrous.

On the contrary, we may imagine a being destitute of passions and impelled only by self-love; that is, by a desire for his own happiness on the whole. In this case, so far as I see, he would never act at all. Having no desires to gratify, there could be no gratification; and hence there could be no happiness. Happiness is the result of the exercise of our sensitiveness upon its corresponding objects. But we have no sensitiveness which corresponds to any object in ourselves; nor do ourselves present any object to correspond to such sensitiveness. Hence the condition of a being destitute of passions and actuated only by self-love, would be an indefinite and most painful long-ing after happiness, without the consciousness of any relation to ex-ternal objects which could gratify it. Nor is this an entirely imaginary condition. In cases of deep melancholy and of fixed hypochondria tending to derangement, I think everyone must have observed in others, and he is happy if he have not experienced in himself, the tendencies to precisely such a state. The very power of affection, or sensitiveness, seems paralyzed. This state of mind has, I think, been ascribed to Hamlet by Shakespeare in the following passage:

"I have, of late (but wherefore I know not), lost all my mirth, foregone all custom of exercises; and, indeed, it goes so heavily with my dispositions, that this goodly frame, the earth, seems to me a sterile promontory; this most excellent canopy, the air—look you—this brave overhanging firmament; this majestical roof, fretted with golden fire; why, it appears no other thing to me, than a foul and pestilent congregation of vapors. Man delights me not, nor woman neither, though by your smiling you seem to say so."—*Hamlet,* Act ii, Sc. 2.

It would seem, therefore, that self-love is not in itself a faculty, or part of our constitution, in itself productive of happiness; but rather an impulse, which, out of several forms of gratification which may be presented, inclines us to select that which will be the most for our happiness, considered as a whole. This seems the more evident from the obvious fact that a man actuated by the most zealous self-love, derives no more happiness from a given gratification than any other man. His pleasure, in any one act of enjoyment, is not in the ratio of his self-love, but of his sensitiveness.

From these remarks we can easily determine the *rank* to which self-love is entitled.

1. Its rank is superior to that of *passion.* As our happiness as a whole is of more consequence than the happiness of any separate moment, so the faculty which impels us toward our happiness upon the whole was manifestly intended to control that which impels toward our happiness for a moment. If happiness be desirable, the greatest amount of it is most desirable; and as we are provided with a constitution by which we are forewarned of the difference and

impelled to a correct choice, it is the design of our Creator that we should obey it.

2. Its rank is inferior to that of *conscience*. We are made not only sensitive beings, that is, beings capable of happiness, but also moral beings, that is, beings capable of virtue. The latter is manifestly the most important object of our being, even insofar as our own happiness is concerned; for by the practice of virtue without respect to our own temporal happiness, we secure our moral happiness, the most valuable of any of which even at the present we are capable; while by acting for [our] own happiness when these seem to come into competition, we lose that which is most valuable, and can be by no means certain of obtaining the other. That is to say, when our own happiness and our duty seem to come into collision, we are bound to discard the consideration of our own happiness, and to do what we believe to be right.

This may be illustrated by an example.

Suppose that two courses of action are presented to our choice. The one, so far as we can see, will promote our individual happiness; the other will fulfill a moral obligation. Now in this case we may act in either of these ways:

1. We may seek our own happiness, and violate our obligations. In this case we certainly lose the pleasure of virtue and suffer the pain of remorse, while we must be uncertain whether we shall obtain the object of our desires.

2. We may perform the act which conscience indicates, but from our self-love as a motive. Here we shall gain whatever reward, by the constitution under which we are placed, belongs to the action; but we lose the pleasure of virtue.

3. We may perform the act indicated by conscience, and from the simple impulse of duty. In this case we obtain every reward which could be obtained in the preceding case, and, in addition, are blessed with the approbation of conscience. Thus suppose I deliberate whether I shall spend a sum of money in self-gratification, or else in an act of benevolence which is plainly my duty. If I pursue the former course it is very uncertain whether I actually secure the gratification which I seek, while I lose the pleasure of rectitude and

am saddened by the pains of remorse. The pleasure of gratification is soon over, but the pain of guilt is enduring. Or again, I may perform the act of benevolence from love of applause or some modification of self-love. I here obtain with more certainty the reputation which I seek, but lose the reward of conscious virtue. Or thirdly, if I do the act without any regard to my own happiness, and simply from love to God and man, I obtain all the rewards which attach to the action by the constitution under which I am placed and also enjoy the higher rewards of conscious rectitude.

This subordination of motives seems clearly to be referred to by our Saviour: "There is no man, that hath left house, or brethren, or sisters, or father, or mother, or wife, or children, or lands, *for my sake and the gospel's,* but he shall receive an hundred fold now, in this time, and, in the world to come, life everlasting." That is to say, a man does not obtain the reward of virtue, even in self-denial, unless he disregard the consideration of himself and act from simple love to God. To the same purport is the often repeated observation of our Saviour: "Whosoever will save his life shall lose it; and whosoever will lose his life, *for my sake,* shall find it." There are many passages of Scripture which seem to assert that the very turning point of moral character, so far as our relations to God are concerned, consists in yielding up the consideration of our own happiness as a controlling motive, and subjecting it without reserve to the higher motive, the simple will of God.

If these remarks be true we see,

1. That when conscience speaks the voice of self-love must be silent. That is to say, we have no right to seek our own happiness in any manner at variance with moral obligation. Nevertheless, from several courses of action, either of which is innocent, we are at liberty to choose that which will most conduce to our own happiness. In such a case the consideration of our happiness is justly ultimate.

2. The preceding chapter has shown us that man was designed to be made happy by the gratification of his desires. The present chapter teaches us that when the gratification of desire is at variance with virtue, a greater happiness is to be obtained by self-denial. Or, in other words, our *greatest* happiness is to be obtained, not by the

various modes of self-gratification, but by simply seeking the good of others, and in doing the will of God from the heart.

3. And hence we may arrive at the general principle that every impulse or desire is supreme *within its own assigned limits;* but that when a lower comes into competition with a higher impulsion, the inferior accomplishes its own object most perfectly by being wholly subject to the superior. Thus desire, or the love of present gratification, may, within its own limits, be indulged. But when this present gratification comes into competition with self-love, even passion accomplishes its own object best; that is, a man actually attains to more enjoyment by submitting present desire implicitly to self-love. And so self-love is ultimate within its proper limits; but when it comes into competition with conscience, it actually accomplishes its own object best by being entirely subject to that which the Creator has constituted its superior.

4. The difference between self-love, as an innocent part of our constitution, and selfishness, a vicious disposition, may be easily seen. Self-love properly directs our choice of objects where both are equally innocent. Selfishness is a similar disposition to promote our own happiness upon the whole: but it disposes us to seek it in objects over which we have no just control; that is, which are not innocent, and which we could not enjoy without violating our duties either to God or to our neighbor.

CHAPTER SIXTH

IT has been already remarked that a distinction may be very clearly observed between right and wrong, and guilt and innocence. Right and wrong depend upon the relations under which we are created and the obligations resulting from them, and are in their nature immutable. Guilt and innocence have respect to the individual and are modified, moreover, by the amount of his knowledge of his duty, and are not decided solely by the fact that the action was or was not performed.

It is, moreover, to be observed that the results of these two attributes of actions may be seen to differ. Thus every right action is followed, in some way, with pleasure or benefit to the individual; and every wrong one by pain or discomfort, irrespective of the guilt or innocence of the author of the act. Thus in the present constitution of things, it is evident that a nation which had no knowledge of the wickedness of murder, revenge, uncleanness, or theft would, if it violated the moral law in these respects, suffer the consequences which are attached to these actions by our Creator. And, on the contrary, a nation which practiced forgiveness, mercy, honesty, and purity, without knowing them to be right, would enjoy the benefits which are connected with such actions.

Now whatever be the object of this constitution by which happiness or misery are consequent upon actions as right or wrong, whether it be as a monition or to inform us of the will of God concerning us, one thing seems evident—it is not to punish actions as *innocent or guilty;* for the happiness or misery of which we speak affect men simply in consequence of the *action,* and without any regard to the innocence or guilt of the actor.

Let us now add another element. Suppose a man to know the obligations which bind him to his Creator, and also what is his Creator's will respecting a certain action, and that he then deliberately violates this obligation. Every man feels that this violation of obligation deserves punishment on its own account, and also punishment in proportion to the greatness of the obligation violated. Hence the consequences of any action are to be considered in a twofold light: first, the consequences depending upon the present constitution of things; and secondly, those which follow the action as innocent or guilty; that is, as violating or not violating our obligations to our Creator.

These two things are plainly to be considered distinct from each other. Of the one, we can form some estimate; of the other, none whatever. Thus whatever be the design of the constitution by which pain should be consequent upon wrong actions, irrespective of guilt, whether it be to admonish us of dangers or to intimate to us the will of our Creator, we can have some conception how great it would probably be. But if we consider the action as guilty, that is, as violating the known will of our Creator, no one can conceive how great the punishment of such an act ought to be, for no one can conceive how vast is the obligation which binds a creature to his God: nor, on the other hand, can anyone conceive how vast would be the reward if this obligation were perfectly fulfilled.

As, then, every moral act is attended with pleasure or pain, and as every one also exposes us to the punishments or rewards of guilt or innocence, both of which manifestly transcend our power of conception; and if such be our constitution that every moment is rendering our moral condition either better or worse; specially if this world be a state of probation, tending to a state where change is impossible; it is manifestly of the greatest possible importance that we should both know our duty and be furnished with all suitable impulsions to perform it. The constitution under which man is formed in this respect has been explained at the close of the chapter on virtue. And were the intellect and conscience of man to be in a perfect state, and were he in entire harmony with the universe around him, there can be no doubt that his happiness, in the present state, would be perfectly secured.

It would not, however, be certain that with intellectual and moral powers suited to his station, man would be in no need of farther communication from his Maker. Although his feeling of obligation and his desire to discharge it might be perfect, yet he might not be fully aware of the *manner* in which his obligation should be discharged. Thus though our first parents were endowed with a perfect moral constitution, yet it was necessary that God should make to them a special revelation respecting some portion of his will. Such might also be the case in any other instance of a perfect moral constitution in a being of limited capacity.

How much more evidently is additional light necessary when it is remembered that the moral constitution of man seems manifestly to be imperfect? This may be observed in several respects:

1. There are many obligations under which man is created, both to his fellow creatures and to God, which his unassisted conscience does not discover. Such are the obligations to *universal* forgiveness, to repentance, and many others.

2. When the obligations are acknowledged, man frequently errs in respect to the mode in which they are to be discharged. Thus a man may acknowledge his obligations to God, but may suppose that God will be pleased with a human sacrifice. A man may acknowledge his obligation to love his children, but may believe that this obligation may best be discharged by putting them to death. Now it is manifest that in both these cases a man must suffer all the present evils resulting from such a course, just as much as though he *knowingly* violated these obligations.

3. When men both know the obligations under which they are created and the mode in which they are to be discharged, they willfully disobey the monitions of conscience. We act according to the impulsions of blind, headlong passion, regardless of our own best good and of the welfare of others, in despite of what we know to be the will of our Maker. It is the melancholy fact that men do deliberately violate the commands of God, for the sake of the most transient and trifling gratification. Hence the hackneyed confession:

> Video, proboque meliora;
> Deteriora sequor.

And hence it is evident that not only are men exposing themselves to the pains attendant upon wrong actions during the present life;

but they are also exposing themselves to the punishments, how great and awful soever these may be, which are incurred by violating our obligations to our Creator and our Judge. The state of human nature in these respects I suppose to be vividly set forth by St. Paul in the *Epistle to the Romans,* ch. vii, v. 7–25.

If such be our state, it is manifest that under such a moral constitution as we have above described, our condition must be sufficiently hopeless. Unless something be done, it would seem that we must all fail of a large portion of the happiness to which we might otherwise in the present life attain; and still more, must be exposed to a condemnation greater than we are capable of conceiving.

Under such circumstances, it surely is not improbable that a benevolent Deity should make use of some additional means to inform us of our duty and thus warn us of the evils which we were bringing upon ourselves. Still less is it improbable that a God delighting in right should take some means to deliver us from the guilty habits which we have formed, and restore us to that love and practice of virtue which can alone render us pleasing to him. That God was under any *obligation* to do this, is not asserted; but that a being of infinite compassion and benevolence should do it, though not under any obligation, is surely not improbable.

Should a revelation be made to remedy the defects of man's moral state, we can form some conceptions of what might be expected in order to accomplish such a result.

1. Our defective knowledge of moral obligation might be remedied by a clear view of the attributes of God and of the various relations which we sustain to him.

2. Our ignorance of the mode in which our obligations should be discharged might be dispelled either by a more expanded view of the consequences of actions, or by direct precept.

3. In order to overcome our temper of disobedience, I know not what means might be employed. A reasonable one would seem to be a manifestation of the character of the Deity to us in some new relation, creating some new obligations, and thus opening a new source of moral motives within the soul of man.

The first and second of these objects are accomplished, as I suppose, by the discoveries of natural religion and by the promulgation of the moral law under the Old Testament dispensation. The third is accomplished by the revelation of the facts of the New Testament, and specially by the revelation of God as the author of a new and a remedial dispensation.

Hence we see that the sources of moral light, irrespective of conscience, are,

1. The precepts of natural religion.
2. The precepts and motives of the sacred Scriptures.

From what has been remarked in the present chapter a few inferences naturally arise, which I will insert in this place.

It is mentioned above that the evil consequences of doing wrong are manifestly of two kinds. First, those connected with an *action as right or wrong* and arising from the present constitution of things; and, secondly, those resulting from the action as *innocent or guilty;* that is, as willfully violating, or not, the obligations due to our Maker.

Now from this plain distinction we see,

1. That no sin can be of trifling consequence. The least as well as the greatest, being a violation of an obligation more sacred and awful than we can conceive, must expose us to punishment more dreadful than we can comprehend. If it be said, the thing in itself is a trifle, the answer is obvious: How wicked must it be, for the sake of a trifle, to violate so sacred and solemn an obligation as that which binds us to our Creator!

2. Hence we see how unfounded is the assertion sometimes made that God could not, for the momentary actions of this short life, justly inflict upon us any severe or long enduring punishment. If an act, whether long or short, be a violation of our obligations to God; if ill desert be according to the greatness of the obligation violated; and if no one can pretend to comprehend the vastness of the obligations which bind the creature to the Creator; then no one can *a priori* pretend to decide what is the punishment justly due to every act of willful wickedness.[8] It is evident that no one can decide

---

[8] The 1865 edition: "wickedness—especially when it is remembered that a single act of sin transforms man's nature, and renders him permanently a rebel against God."

this question but he who fully knows the relation between the parties; that is, the Creator himself.

3. Since every impure, revengeful, deceitful, or envious thought is a violation of our obligations to our Maker, and much more the words and actions to which these thoughts give rise; and since even the imperfect conscience of every individual accuses him of countless instances, if not of habits, of such violation: if the preceding observations be just, it is manifest that our present moral condition involves the elements of much that is alarming. It surely must be the duty of every reasonable man to inquire with the deepest solicitude, whether any way of escape from punishment and of moral renovation have been revealed by the Being against whom we have sinned; and if any such revelation have been made, it must be our most solemn duty to conform our lives to such principles as shall enable us to avail ourselves of its provisions.

4. The importance of this duty will be still more clearly evident if we consider that the present is a state of probation in which alone moral change is possible; and which must speedily terminate in a state by necessity unchangeable; for which, also, the present state therefore offers us the only opportunity of preparation. To neglect either to possess ourselves of all the knowledge in our power on this subject, or to neglect to obey any reasonable precepts which afford the least probability of improving our condition for the future, seems a degree of folly for which it is really impossible to find an adequate epithet.

5. Nor does it render this folly the less reprehensible for a man gravely to assert that we do not know anything about the future world, and therefore it is needless to inquire respecting it. This is to assert, *without* inquiry, what could only be reasonably asserted after the most *full and persevering inquiry*. No man can reasonably assert that we know nothing respecting the other world until he has examined every system of religion within his knowledge, and by the fair and legitimate use of his understanding shown conclusively that none of them throw any light upon the subject. By what right, therefore, can a man utter such an assertion who, at the outset, declares

that he will examine none of them? What should we think of the man who declared that he would not study astronomy for that no one knew more about the heavens than he did himself? Yet many men neglect to inform themselves on the subject of religion for no better reason. It is very remarkable that men do not perceive the absurdity of an assertion respecting *religion* which they would immediately perceive if uttered respecting *anything else*.

CHAPTER SEVENTH
OF NATURAL RELIGION

In the preceding chapter I have endeavored to illustrate the nature of our moral constitution, and to show that, in our present state, conscience, unassisted, manifestly fails to produce the results which seem to have been intended; and which are necessary to our attaining the happiness which is put within our power; and to our avoiding the misery to which we are exposed. That some additional light will be granted to us and that some additional moral power will be imparted seems clearly not improbable. This I suppose to have been done by the truths of natural and revealed religion. In the present chapter I shall treat of natural religion under the following heads:

1. The manner in which we may learn our duty by the light of nature.

2. The extent to which our knowledge of duty can be carried by this mode of teaching.

3. The defects of the system of natural religion.

Section I · Of the Manner in Which We May Learn Our Duty by the Light of Nature

In treating upon this subject it is taken for granted,

1. That there is an intelligent and universal First Cause who made us as we are and made all things around us capable of affecting us, both as individuals and as societies, as they do.

2. That He had a design in so making us and in constituting the relations around us as they are constituted; and that a part of that design was to intimate to us his will concerning us.

3. That we are capable of observing these relations and of knowing how various actions affect us and affect others.

4. And that we are capable of learning the design with which these various relations were constituted; and, specially, that part of the design which was to intimate to us the will of our Creator.

The application of these self-evident principles to the subject of duty is easy. We know that we are so made as to derive happiness from some courses of conduct, and to suffer unhappiness from others. Now no one can doubt that the intention of our Creator in these cases was that we should pursue the one course and avoid the other. Or again, we are so made that we are rendered unhappy, on the whole, by pursuing a course of conduct in some particular manner or beyond a certain degree. This is an intimation of our Creator respecting the manner and the degree in which he designs us to pursue that course of conduct.

Again, as has been said before, society is necessary not merely to the happiness, but to the actual existence of the race of man. Hence it is necessary, in estimating the tendency of actions upon our own happiness, to extend our view beyond the direct effect of an action upon ourselves. Thus if we cannot perceive that any evil would result to ourselves from a particular course of action, yet if it would tend to injure society, specially if it would tend to destroy society altogether, we may hence arrive at a clear indication of the will of our Creator concerning it. As the destruction of society would be the destruction of the individual, it is as evident that God does not intend us to do what would injure society as that He does not intend us to do what would injure our own bodies or diminish our individual happiness. And the principle of limitation suggested above applies in the same manner here: that is, if a course of conduct, pursued in a certain manner or to a certain extent, be beneficial to society; and if pursued in another manner or beyond a certain extent, is injurious to it, the indication is, in this respect, clear as to the will of our Maker respecting us.

To apply this to particular cases. Suppose a man were in doubt whether or not drunkenness were agreeable to the will of his Maker. Let us suppose that intemperate drinking produces present pleasure, but that it also produces subsequent pain; and that by continuance in the habit the pleasure becomes less and the pain greater; and that the pain affects various powers of the mind and different organs of the body. Let a man look around him and survey the crime, the vice, the disease, and the poverty which God has set over against the momentary gratification of the palate and the subsequent excitement which it produces. Now whoever will look at these results, and will consider that God had a design in creating things to affect us as they do, must be as fully convinced that by these results He intended to forbid intemperance as though He had said so by a voice from heaven. The same principle may be applied to gluttony, libertinism, or any other vice.

Another example may be taken from the case of revenge. Revenge is that disposition which prompts us to inflict pain upon another for the sake of alleviating the feeling of personal degradation consequent upon an injury. Now suppose a man, inflamed and excited by this feeling of injury, should inflict upon the other party, pain, until his excited feeling was gratified: the injured party would then manifestly become the injurer; and thus the original injurer would be, by the same rule, entitled to retaliate. Thus revenge and retaliation would go on increasing until the death of one of the parties. The duty of vengeance would then devolve upon the surviving friends and relatives of the deceased and the circle would widen until it involved whole tribes or nations. Thus the indulgence of this one evil passion would in a few generations render the thronged city an unpeopled solitude. Nor is this a mere imaginary case. The Indians of North America are known to have considered the indulgence of revenge not merely as innocent, but also as glorious and in some sense obligatory. The result was that at the time of the discovery of this continent, they were universally engaged in wars; and according to the testimony of their oldest and wisest chiefs, their numbers were rapidly diminishing. And hence he who observes the effects of revenge upon society must be convinced that he who formed the constitution under which we live must have intended, by these effects, to have forbidden it, as clearly as though he had made it known by language. He has given us an understanding by the simplest exercise of which we arrive at this conclusion.

It is still further to be observed that whenever a course of conduct produces individual, it also produces social misery; and whenever a course of conduct violates the social laws of our being, it of necessity produces individual misery. And hence we see that both of these indications are combined to teach us the same lesson; that is, to intimate to us what is, and what is not, the will of God respecting our conduct.

Hence we see that two views may be taken of an action when it is contemplated in the light of nature: first, as affecting ourselves; and secondly, as affecting both ourselves and society, but specially the latter. It is in this latter view that we introduce the doctrine of general consequences. We ask in order to determine what is our duty, What would be the result if this or that action were universally practised among men? Or, how would it affect the happiness of individuals and of the whole? By the answer to these questions, we ascertain what is the will of God in respect to that action or that course of action. When once the will of God is ascertained, conscience, as we have shown, teaches us that we are under the highest obligation to obey it. Thus from the consideration of the greatest amount of happiness, we arrive at the knowledge of our duty, not directly, but indirectly. The feeling of moral obligation does not arise from the *simple fact that such a course of conduct will or will not produce the greatest amount of happiness;* but from the fact that *this tendency shows us what is the will of our Creator;* and we are, by the principles of our nature, under the highest possible obligation to obey that will.

It must be evident that a careful observation of the results and tendencies of actions and of different courses of conduct will teach us, in very many respects, the laws of our moral nature; that is, what, in these respects, is the will of our Creator. Now these laws, thus arrived at, and reduced to order and arrangement, form the system of natural religion. So far as it goes, everyone must confess such a system to be valuable; and it, moreover, rests upon as sure and certain a basis as any system of laws whatever.

To all this, however, I know but of one objection that can be urged. It is that pain is not of necessity punitive or prohibitory; and that it may be merely monitory or advisory.[9] Thus if I put my hand incautiously too near the fire, I am admonished by the pain which I feel to withdraw it. Now this pain is manifestly only monitory and

[9] See Appendix (D) for text of the 1865 edition here shown between nn. 9 and 10.

intended merely to warn me of danger. It is not of necessity prohibitory; for I may hold my hand so near to the fire as to produce
great pain for some necessary purpose—as, for instance, for the sake
of curing disease—and yet not violate my obligations to my Creator
nor in any measure incur his displeasure.

Now the fact thus stated may be fully admitted, without in the
least affecting the argument. It is evident that many of the pains
to which we are at present exposed are, in their nature, intended to
warn us of approaching harm, as in the instance just mentioned;
or they may be intimations of mischief actually commenced of which
we could not be otherwise aware—as in the case of internal diseases.
And it is manifest that such being their nature and design they
must be intimately connected with, and either accompany or precede, that injury of which they are intended to forewarn or to inform
us; and it is natural to expect that they would *cease* or *tend to cessation* as soon as they have accomplished the object for which they
were intended. And such, I think, will in general be found to be the
fact with respect to those pains which are in their nature monitory.

But I think it will be evident, to everyone who will observe, that
many of the pains endured under the present constitution are not
of this kind.

Thus for example:

1. There are many pains which are inflicted in consequence of
actions of which we were forewarned by conscience. It would seem
that the design of *these* pains could not be monitory, inasmuch as
monition is performed by another faculty.

2. There are many pains which, from the nature of our constitution, are not inflicted until after the act has been performed and the
evil accomplished. This is the case with drunkenness and many other
vices. Here the pain cannot be intended as a premonition; for it is
not inflicted in its severity until after the injury has actually been
done.

3. Not only does the pain in many cases occur afterwards; it
frequently does not occur until a long time after the offense. Months,
and even years, may elapse before the punishment overtakes the
criminal. This is very frequently the case with youthful crimes,

which ordinarily exhibit their result not until manhood or even old age. Now pain must here be intended to signify something else besides warning.

4. We find that the punishment in many cases bears no sort of proportion either to the benefit obtained by the individual, or even to the injury in the particular instance inflicted upon society. This is manifest in very many instances of lying, forgery, small theft, and the like, in which, by a single act of wrong, a person ruins a reputation which it had taken a whole life to establish. Now in such a case as this, it is evident that the purpose of warning could not be intended; for this end could be accomplished, at vastly less expense of happiness, in some other way.

5. We find that the tendency of many instances of punishment is not to leave the offender in the same state as before, but rather in a worse state. His propensities to do wrong are rendered stronger, and his inducement to do well weaker; and thus he is exposing himself to greater and greater punishments. The tendency, therefore, is not to recovery, but to more fatal moral disease.

6. Although a man, by reformation, may frequently regain the standing which he has lost, yet there are manifest indications in the present constitution that, after a given amount of trial has been granted, a decisive punishment is inflicted which extinguishes forever all hope, if not all possibility, of recovery. A man may waste part of his youth in idleness, and may by diligence regain the time which he had lost. But he soon arrives at a point beyond which such opportunity is impossible. Thus also in morals, a man may sometimes do wrong and return to virtue and escape present punishment; but every instance of crime renders the probability of escape less; and he at last arrives at a point beyond which nothing can avert the infliction of the merited and decisive calamity.

7. We find that some actions produce misery which extends to other beings besides those who are actually concerned in committing them.

This takes place sometimes by example, and at other times the pain is inflicted upon those who could not be infected by the example. Illustrations of this are seen in cases of disease propagated by hereditary descent, in misery arising from the misconduct of rulers, in the suffering of men from flagitious crimes of relatives and acquaintances. And in consequence of the constitution under which we exist these miseries are frequently transmitted down beyond any assignable limit. Thus the condition of the Jews is by themselves and others frequently believed to be the result of some crime committed by their forefathers, either at or before the time of Christ. The sad effects of the persecution of Protestantism in Spain and Portugal at the time of the Reformation can be clearly traced in all the subsequent history of these countries.

Now all these considerations seem clearly to indicate that there are pains inflicted upon man for other purposes except warning; and that they are of the nature of punishment; that is, of pain inflicted after crime has been voluntarily committed in spite of sufficient warning, and inflicted by way of desert as what the offense really merits, and what it behooves a righteous governor to award transgression.

Nor will it avail to object that these inflictions are intended to be warnings to others. This is granted; but this by no means prevents their being also punishments in the sense in which we have considered them. Such is the case in all punishments inflicted by society. They are intended to be a warning to others; but this hinders not their being also in the strictest sense punishments; that is, inflictions of pain as the just desert of crime and as clear indications of the will of society respecting the action of which they are the result.[10]

From what has been said I think we may safely conclude:

1. That God has given to man a moral and an intellectual constitution by which he may be admonished of his duty.

2. That He allows man to act freely and to do either right or wrong as he chooses.

3. That He, in the present life, has connected rewards with the doing of right, and punishments with the doing of wrong; and that these rewards and punishments affect both the individual and society.

4. And hence that from an attentive observation of the results of

[10] Concludes material shown in Appendix (D).

actions upon individuals, and upon society, we may ascertain what is the will of God concerning us.

5. And for all the opportunities of thus ascertaining his will by his dealings with men—that is, by the light of nature—God holds all his creatures responsible.

Section II · How Far We May Discover Our Duty by the Light of Nature

It has been shown that we may, by observing the results of our actions upon individuals and upon society, ascertain what is the will of our Creator concerning us. In this manner we may discover much moral truth which would be unknown, were we left to the guidance of conscience unassisted; and we may derive many motives to virtue which would otherwise be inoperative.

I. By the light of nature we discover much moral truth which could never be discovered by conscience unassisted.

1. Conscience indicates to us our obligations to others when our relations to them are discovered; and impels us toward that course of conduct which the understanding points out as corresponding with these obligations. But there are many obligations which conscience seems not to point out to men, and many ways of fulfilling these obligations which the understanding does not clearly indicate. In these respects, we may be greatly assisted by natural religion.

Thus I doubt whether the unassisted conscience would teach the wrong of polygamy or of divorce. The Jews, even at the time of our Saviour, had no conception that a marriage contract was obligatory for life. But anyone who will observe the effects of polygamy upon families and societies can have no doubt that the precept of the gospel on this subject is the moral law of the system under which we are. So I do not know that unassisted conscience would remonstrate against what might be called reasonable revenge, or the operation of the Lex Talionis. But he who will observe the consequences of revenge, and those of forgiveness of injuries, will have no difficulty in deciding which course of conduct has been indicated as his duty by his Maker.

2. The *extent* of obligations previously known to exist is made known more clearly by the light of nature. Conscience might teach us the obligations to love our friends or our countrymen, but it might not go farther. The results of different courses of conduct would clearly show that our Creator intended us to love all men, of every nation, and even our enemies.

3. It is by observing the results of our actions that we learn the *limitations* which our Creator has affixed to our desires, as we have shown in the chapter on happiness. The simple fact that gratification of our desires beyond a certain limit will produce more misery than happiness, addresses itself to our *self-love* and forms a reason why that limit should not be transgressed. The fact that this limit was fixed by our Creator and that he has thus intimated to us his will, addresses itself to our *conscience* and places us under obligation to act as he has commanded on pain of his displeasure.

4. In many cases where the obligation is acknowledged, we might not be able, without the light of natural religion, to decide in what manner it could best be discharged. Thus a man who felt conscious of his obligations as a parent and wished to discharge them would derive much valuable information by observing what mode of exhibiting paternal love had produced the happiest results. He would hence be able the better to decide what was required of him.

In this manner it cannot be doubted that much valuable knowledge of moral truth might be acquired beyond what is attainable by unassisted conscience. But this is not all.

II. Natural religion *presents additional motives* to the practice of virtue.

1. It does this, in the first place, by more clearly setting before us the rewards of virtue and the punishments of vice. Conscience forewarns us against crime and inflicts its own peculiar punishment upon guilt; but natural religion informs us of the additional consequences, independent of ourselves, which attach to moral action according to the constitution under which we are created. Thus conscience might forewarn a man against dishonesty, and might inflict upon him the pains of remorse if he had stolen; but her monition would surely derive additional power from an observation of

the effect which must be produced upon individuals and societies by the practice of this immorality; and also by the contrary effects which must arise from the opposite virtue.

2. Still further. Natural religion presents us with more distinct and affecting views of the character of God than could be obtained without it. One of the first aspirations of a human soul is after an Intelligent First Cause; and the most universal dictate of conscience is that this First Cause ought to be obeyed. Hence every nation, how rude soever it be, has its gods and its religious services. But such a notion of the Deity is cold and inoperative when compared with that which may be derived from an intelligent observation of the laws of nature, physical and moral, which we see pervading the universe around us. In every moral law which has been written on the page of this world's history, we discover a new lineament of the character of the Deity. Every moral attribute of God which we discover, imposes upon us a new obligation and presents an additional motive why we should love and serve Him. Hence we see that the knowledge of God derived from the study of nature is adapted to add greatly to the impulsive power of conscience.

We see, then, how large a field of moral knowledge is spread open before us if we only, in a suitable manner, apply our understandings to the works of God around us. He has arranged all things for the purpose of teaching us these lessons, and He has created our intellectual and moral nature expressly for the purpose of learning them. If, then, we do not use the powers which He has given us for the purpose for which He has given them, He holds us responsible for the result. Thus said the prophet: "Because they *regard not* the works of the Lord, neither consider the operation of His hands, *therefore,* He shall destroy them, and not build them up." Thus the Scriptures elsewhere declare all men to be responsible for the correct use of all the knowledge of duty which God had set before them. St. Paul, *Rom.* i, 19, 20, asserts, "That which may be known of God, is manifest in (or to) them, for God hath showed it to them: so that (or therefore) they are without excuse." Thus he also declares, "They that sin without law (that is, without a written revelation), shall perish without law." And thus we come to the general conclusion that natural religion presents to all men a distinct and important means of knowing the character and will of God, and the obligations and duties of man; and that for this knowledge all men are justly held responsible.

Section III · Defects of the System of Natural Religion

I. Without any argument on the subject, the insufficiency of natural religion as a means of human reformation might be readily made manifest by *facts*.

1. *The facts* on which natural religion rests and *the intellectual power* to derive the moral laws from the facts have been in the possession of man from the beginning. Yet the whole history of man has exhibited a constant tendency to moral deterioration. This is proved by the fact that every people not enlightened by revelation consider the earliest period of their history as the period of their greatest moral purity. Then the gods and men held frequent intercourse; this intercourse, in consequence of the sins of men, has since been discontinued. That was the golden age; the subsequent ages have been of brass or of iron. The political history of men seems to teach the same lesson. In the early ages of national existence, sparseness of population, mutual fear, and universal poverty have obliged men to lay the foundations of society in principles of justice in order to secure national existence. But as soon as, under such a constitution, wealth was increased, population become dense, and progress in arts and arms have rendered a nation fearless, the antisocial tendencies of vice have shown themselves too powerful for the moral forces by which they have been opposed. The bonds of society have been gradually dissolved, and a nation rich in the spoils of a hundred triumphs becomes the prey of some warlike and more virtuous horde, which takes possession of the spoil merely to pursue the same career to a more speedy termination.

2. The systems of religion of the heathen may be fairly considered as the legitimate result of all the moral forces which are in operation upon man, irrespective of revelation. They show us, not what man might have learned by the proper use of his faculties in the study

of duty, but what he has always actually learned. Now these systems, so far from having any tendency to make man better, have a manifest tendency to make him worse. Their gods were of the most profligate and demoralizing character. Had natural religion succeeded in instilling into the minds of men true ideas of virtue and duty, their imaginations, in forming conceptions of deities, would have invested them with far different attributes.

3. The ethical systems of philosophers, it is true, not unfrequently presented sublime and pure conceptions of Deity. But as instruments of moral reformation, they were clearly inoperative. They were extremely imperfect in everything which relates to our duties to man, and specially in everything which relates to our duty to God; they offered no sufficient motives to obedience; they were established on subtle reasonings which could not be comprehended by the common people; and they imposed no obligation upon their disciples to disseminate them among others. Hence, they were never extensively known beyond the small circle of meditative students; and by these, they were considered rather as matters of doubtful speculation than of practical benefit; adapted rather to the cultivation of intellectual acuteness than to the reformation of moral conduct. I think that anyone, on reading the ethical disquisitions of the ancients, must be struck with the fact that honest, simple, and ardent love of truth seems to have furnished no motive whatever to their investigations; and that its place was supplied by mere curiosity or love of the new, the refined, and even the paradoxical.

And hence as might be expected, these ethical systems made no converts from vice to virtue. From the era of which of the systems of ancient ethics can any reformation be dated? Where are their effects recorded in the moral history of man? Facts have abundantly proved them to be utterly destitute of any power over the conscience or of any practical influence over the conduct.

4. Nor can this failure be attributed to any want of intellectual cultivation. During a large portion of the period of which we have spoken, the human mind had in many respects attained to as high a state of perfection as it has attained at any subsequent age. Elo-

quence, poetry, rhetoric, nay, some of the severer sciences were studied with a success which has never since been surpassed. This is universally confessed. Yet what progress did the classic ages make in morals? And hence, we think, it must be admitted that the human mind even under the most favorable circumstances has never, when unassisted by revelation, deduced from the course of things around us any such principles of duty or motives to the performance of it, as were sufficient to produce any decided effect upon the moral character of man.

And hence were we unable to assign the cause of this failure; yet the fact of the failure alone is sufficient to prove the necessity of some other means for arriving at a knowledge of duty than is afforded by the light of nature.

II. But secondly, the causes of this insufficiency may, in many respects, be pointed out. Among them are obviously the following:

1. The mode of teaching natural religion is by experience. We can form no opinion respecting the results of two opposite courses of action until they be both before us. Hence we cannot certainly know what the law is, except by breaking it. Hence the habit of violation must, in some sense, be formed, before we know what the law is which we violate. Consequently, from the nature of the case, natural religion must always be much behind the age and must always utter its precepts to men who are in some manner fixed in the habit of violating them.

2. There are many moral laws in which the connection between the transgression and the punishment cannot be shown except in the more advanced periods of society. Such is the fact in respect to those laws which can be ascertained only by extended and minute observation; and, of course, a state of society in which knowledge is widely disseminated, and the experience of a large surface, and for a long period, may be necessary to establish the fact of the connection between this particular violation and this particular result. In the meantime, mankind will be suffering all the consequences of vice; and the courses of conduct which are the causes of misery will be interweaving themselves with the whole customs and habits

and interests of every class of society. Thus it too often happens that the knowledge is with great difficulty acquired, and when acquired, unfortunately comes too late to effect a remedy.

3. A still more radical deficiency, however, in natural religion is that it is, from its nature, incapable of teaching *facts*. It can teach only laws and tendencies. From observing *what* has been done and *how* it has been done, it can infer that if the same thing were done again it would be done in the same manner and would be attended, in all places, and at all times, if under the same conditions, with the same results. But as to *a fact,* that is, whether an action were actually performed at some other place or time or whether it ever would be, natural religion can give us no information. Thus we know by experience that if a man fall from a precipice, he will be destroyed; but whether a man ever did so fall, much less whether A or B did fall from it, we can never be informed by general principles. Thus from the fact that we see guilt punished in this world, we infer, from natural religion, that it will always be punished in this world; we infer, though not so certainly, that it will also be punished in another world, if there be another world; but of the fact whether there be another world, natural religion can give us no certain information; much less can it give us any information respecting the question whether God has actually done anything to remedy the evils of sin and vary those sequences which, without a remedy, experience shows us to be inevitable.

4. Hence natural religion must derive all its *certain* motives from the present world. Those from the other world are, so far as it is concerned, in their nature contingent and uncertain. And hence it loses all that power over man which would be derived from the certain knowledge of our existence after death, of the nature of that existence, and of what God has done for our restoration to virtue and happiness. All these being *facts,* can never be known except by language, that is, by revelation. They must always remain in utter incertitude so long as we are left to the teachings of natural religion.

We see, then, that natural religion is obliged to meet the impulsions from this world solely by impulsions from this world. Nay, more, she is obliged to resist the power of the present, of passion strengthened and confirmed by habit, by considerations drawn from the distant, the future, and what may seem to be the uncertain. Hence its success must be at best but dubious even when its power is exerted upon those least exposed to the allurements of vice. Who does not see that it is utterly vain to hope for success from such a source in our attempts to reform men in general? Everyone who is at all acquainted with the history of man must be convinced that nothing less powerful than the whole amount of motive derived from the knowledge of an endless existence, has ever been found a sufficient antagonist force to the downward and headlong tendencies of appetite and passion.

And hence from the fact of the recorded failure of natural religion as a means of reformation, and from the defects inherent in its very nature as a means of moral improvement, there seems clearly to exist a great need of some additional moral force to correct the moral evils of our nature. It is surely not improbable that some additional means of instruction and improvement may have been granted to our race by a merciful Creator.

IF what we have said be true, the defects of natural religion would lead us to expect that some other means of moral instruction would be afforded us. And indeed, this is the conclusion at which some of the wisest of the heathen philosophers arrived, from a consideration of that utter ignorance of futurity in which they were of necessity plunged, by the most attentive study of natural religion. They felt convinced that the Deity would not have constructed a system of moral teaching which led to impervious darkness, unless He intended, out of that very darkness, at some period or other, to manifest light.

But still more, I think that an attentive observation of what natural religion teaches, and of its necessary and inherent defects, would afford us some grounds of expectation respecting the nature of that revelation which should be made. If we can discover the moral necessities of our race and can also discover in what respects, and for what reason, the means thus far employed have failed to relieve them, we may with certainty predict some of the characteristics which must mark any system which should be devised to accomplish a decided remedy.

For example:

1. It is granted that natural religion does teach us some unquestionable truths. Now no truth can be inconsistent with itself. And hence it might be expected that whenever natural and revealed religion treated upon the same subjects, they would teach in perfect harmony. The second instructor may teach more than the first; but so far as they give instruction on the same subjects, if both teach the truth they must both teach the same lesson.

2. It is natural to expect that a revelation would give us much information upon the subject of duty which could not be learned by the light of nature. Thus it might be expected to make known more clearly to us than we could otherwise learn them, the obligations by which we are bound to our fellow men and to God; and also the manner in which those obligations are to be discharged.

3. That it would present us with motives to virtue in addition to those made known by the light of nature. We have seen that the motives of natural religion are derived from this world and are in their nature insufficient. We should expect that those in a revelation would be drawn from some other source. And still more, as natural religion may be considered to have exhausted the motives of this world, it is surely not unreasonable to expect that a *revelation* leaving this world would draw its motives principally, if not entirely, from another, if it revealed to us the fact that another world existed.

4. We should not expect that the Deity would employ a second and additional means to accomplish what could be done by any modification of the means first employed. Hence if a revelation were made to men, we might reasonably expect that it would make known to us such truths as could not, in the nature of the case, be communicated by natural religion.

These are, I think, just anticipations. At any rate, I think it must be admitted that if a system of religion purporting to be a revelation from heaven met all these expectations, its relations to natural religion not only would present no argument against its truth, but would create a strong *a priori* presumption in its favor.

Now these expectations are all fully realized in the system of religion contained in the Scriptures of the Old and New Testaments.

1. The truths of revealed religion *harmonize* perfectly with those of natural religion. The difference between them consists in this— that the one teaches plainly what the other teaches by inference; the one takes up the lesson where the other leaves it, and adds to it other and vitally important precepts. Nay, so perfect is the harmony between them that it may safely be asserted that not a single precept of natural religion exists which is not also found in the Bible, and still more, that the Bible is every day directing us to new lessons taught us by nature, which, but for its information, would never have been discovered. So complete is this coincidence as to afford irrefragable proof that the Bible contains the moral laws of the universe; and hence that the Author of the universe—that is, of natural religion—is also the Author of the Scriptures.

2. The Holy Scriptures, as has just been intimated, give us much

information on questions of duty which could not be obtained by the light of nature. Under this remark may be classed the scriptural precepts respecting the domestic relations; respecting our duties to enemies and to men in general; and especially respecting our obligations to God, and the manner in which He may most acceptably be worshipped.

3. The Scriptures present motives to the practice of virtue, additional, generically different from those of natural religion, and of infinitely greater power.

1. The motives to virtue from consequences in this world are strengthened by a clearer development of the indissoluble connection between moral cause and effect than is made known by natural religion.

2. In addition to these motives, we are assured of our existence after death; and eternal happiness and eternal misery are set forth as the desert of virtue and vice.

3. The Scriptures reveal to us the Deity as assuming new relations to us and devising a most merciful way for our redemption: by virtue of this new relation, establishing a new ground of moral obligation between the race of man and himself and thus adding a power to the impulsion of conscience of which natural religion must, in the nature of the case, be destitute.

4. It is manifest that much of the above knowledge which the Scriptures reveal is of the nature of *fact;* and therefore could not be communicated to us by experience or in the way of general laws, but must be made known by language, that is, by revelation.

Thus the existence of a state of being after death, the doctrine of the resurrection, of a universal and impartial judgment, of an endless state of rewards and punishments, of a remedial dispensation by which the connection between guilt and punishment may be conditionally severed; the doctrine of the atonement and the way in which a man may avail himself of the benefits of this remedial dispensation—all these are manifestly of great practical importance in a scheme of moral reformation; and yet, all of them being of the nature of facts, they could be made known to man in no other way than by language.

Now as these seem clearly to be just anticipations respecting any system which should be designed to supply the evident defects of natural religion, and as all these anticipations are realized in the system of religion contained in the Scriptures, each one of these anticipations thus realized furnishes a distinct *a priori* presumption in favor of the truth of revealed religion. We do not pretend that any, or that all of these considerations, prove the Scriptures to be a revelation from God. This proof is derived from other sources. What we would say is this: that from what we know of God's moral government by the light of nature, it is manifestly probable that he would give us some additional instruction, and that that instruction would be, in various important respects, analogous to that contained in the Holy Scriptures. And we hence conclude that although it were granted—which, however, need not be granted—that, were *there no antecedent facts* in the case, it might seem unlikely that God would condescend to make a special revelation of his will to men; yet *when the antecedent facts are properly considered,* this presumption, if it ever could be maintained, is now *precisely reversed,* and that there *now* exists *a fair presumption* that such a revelation *would actually be made.* And hence we conclude, that a revelation of the will of God by language is not, as many persons suppose, an event so unlikely that no evidence can be conceived sufficiently strong to render it credible; but that it is, on the contrary, an event, from all that we know of God already, essentially probable; and that it is, to say the least of it, as fairly within the limits of evidence as any other event, and when proved on the ordinary principles of evidence, is as much entitled to belief as any other event. And hence we conceive that when men demand, in support of the truth of revealed religion, evidence unlike to that which is demanded in support of any other event—that is, evidence of which they themselves cannot define the nature—they demand what is manifestly unreasonable, and proceed upon a presumption wholly at variance with all the known facts in the case.

THIS would seem to be the place in which to present the proof of the authenticity of the Holy Scriptures as a revelation from God. This, however, being only a particular exemplification of the general laws of evidence, it belongs to the course of instruction in Intellectual Philosophy. It must therefore be here omitted. We shall, in the remainder of these remarks, take it for granted that the Scriptures of the Old and New Testament contain a revelation from God to man, and that these books contain all that God has been pleased to reveal unto us by language; and, therefore, all which is recorded in language that is ultimate in morals and that is, by its own authority, binding upon the conscience. Taking this for granted, we shall in the present chapter consider, 1st, what the Scriptures contain; and, 2d, how we may ascertain our duty from the Scriptures.

Section I · A View of the Holy Scriptures

The Holy Scriptures are contained in two separate volumes, entitled the Old and the New Testament. These volumes have each a distinct object, and yet their objects are in perfect harmony; and together they contain all that could be desired in a revelation to the human race.

The design of the Old Testament mainly is to reveal a system of simple law; to exhibit the results of such a system upon the human race, and to direct the minds of men to the remedial dispensation which was to follow. In accomplishing this design, it contains several distinct parts.[11]

1. An account of the creation of the world, of the creation and fall of man, and a brief history of the race of man until the deluge. The cause of this deluge is stated to be the universal and intense wickedness of man.

2. The account of the separation of a particular family, the germ of a nation, designed to be the depositaries of the revealed will of

[11] See Appendix (E) for paragraph inserted in the 1865 edition.

God; and the history of this nation from the call of Abraham until the return from the captivity in Babylon, a period of about fifteen hundred years.

3. The system of laws which God gave to this nation. These laws may be comprehended under three classes:

Moral laws, or those which arise from the immutable relations existing between God and man.

Civil laws, or those enacted for the government of civil society; adapted specially to the Jewish Theocracy, or that form of government in which God was specially recognised as King.

Ceremonial laws. These were of two kinds: First, those which were intended to keep this nation separate from other nations; and second, those intended to prefigure events which were to occur under the second or new dispensation.

4. Various events in their history, discourses of prophets and inspired teachers, prayers, odes of pious men; all tending to illustrate what are the effects of a system of moral law upon human nature, even when placed under the most favorable circumstances; and also to exhibit the effects of the religious principle upon the soul of man under every variety of time and condition.

The result of all this series of moral means seems to be this. God, in various modes suited to their condition, made known his will to the whole human race. They all, with the exception of a single family, became so corrupt that he destroyed them by a general deluge. He then selected a single family and gave them his written law, and by peculiar enactments secluded them from all other nations, that the experiment might be made under the most favorable circumstances. At the same time, the effects of natural religion were tried among the heathen nations that surrounded them. The result was a clear demonstration that under the conditions of being in which man was created, any reformation was hopeless, and that unless some other conditions were revealed, the race would perish by its own vicious and antisocial tendencies and enter the other world to reap the reward of its guilt forever. While this is said to be the main design of the Old Testament, it is not to be understood that this is its whole design. It was intended to be introductory to the new dispensation, and also to teach those to whom it was addressed, the way of salvation. Hence allusions to the principal events in the new dispensation are everywhere to be met with. Hence also, assurances of pardon are made to the penitent, and God is represented as ready to forgive; though the procuring cause of our pardon is not explicitly stated; but only alluded to in terms which could not be fully understood until the remedial dispensation was accomplished.

The design of the New Testament is to reveal to the race of man the new conditions of being under which it is placed by virtue of a remedial dispensation.

In pursuance of this design the New Testament contains—

1. A narrative of the life and death, resurrection and ascension, the acts and conversations of Jesus of Nazareth; a Being in whom the divine and human natures were mysteriously united; who appeared on earth to teach us whatever was necessary to be known of our relations to God, and by his obedience to the law and voluntary sufferings and death, to remove the obstacles to our pardon, which, under the former dispensation, existed in consequence of the holiness of God.

2. A brief narrative of the facts relating to the progress of the Christian religion for several years after the ascension of Jesus of Nazareth.

3. The instructions which his immediate followers, or apostles, by divine inspiration gave to the men of their own time, and which were rendered necessary in consequence of their ignorance of the principles of religion, or the weakness of their virtue, and the imperfection of their faith.

The whole of this volume taken together teaches us the precepts, the sanctions, and the rewards of the law of God with as great distinctness as we could desire; and also a way of salvation on different grounds from that revealed both by natural religion and by the Old Testament; a way of depending for *merit* upon the doings and sufferings of another, but yet *available* to us on no other conditions than those of supreme, strenuous, and universal moral effort after perfect purity of thought and word and action.

This, being a remedial dispensation, is in its nature fixed. We have no reason to expect any other; nay, the idea of another would be at variance with the belief of the truth of this. And hence the Scriptures of the Old and New Testaments contain all that God has revealed to us by language respecting his will. What is contained here alone is binding upon the conscience. Or in the words of Chillingworth, "THE BIBLE, THE BIBLE, THE RELIGION OF PROTESTANTS."

Section II · In What Manner Are We to Ascertain Our Duty from the Holy Scriptures?

Taking it for granted that the Bible contains a revelation of the will of God such as is stated in the preceding section, it will still be of importance for us to decide how we may ascertain from the study of it what God really requires of us. Much of it is mere history, containing an unvarnished narration of the actions of good and of bad men. Much of it has reference to a less enlightened age, and to a particular people, set apart from other people for a special and peculiar purpose. Much of it consists of exhortations and reproofs addressed to this people in reference to the laws then existing, but which have been since abrogated. Now amidst this variety of instructions, given to men at different times and of different nations, it is desirable that the principles be settled by which we may decide what portion of this mass of instruction is binding upon the conscience at the present moment. My object in the present section is to ascertain as far as possible, the principles by which we are to be guided in such a decision.

When a revelation is made to us by language, it is taken for granted that whatever is our duty will be signified to us by a command; and hence what is not commanded is not to be considered by us as obligatory. Did we not establish this limitation, everything recorded, as, for instance, all the actions both of good and of bad men, might be regarded as authority; and thus a revelation given for the purpose of teaching us our duty, might be used as an instrument to confound all distinction between right and wrong.

The ground of moral obligation as derived from a revelation must, therefore, be a *command of God*.

Now a command seems to involve three ideas:

1. *That an act be designated.* This may be by the designation of the *act* itself, as, for instance, giving bread to the hungry; or else by the designation of a *temper of mind,* as that of universal love, under which the above act and various other acts are clearly comprehended.

2. That it be somehow signified to be *the will of God that this act be performed.* Without this intimation, every act that is described or even held up for our reprobation might be quoted as obligatory.

3. That it be signified that *we are included* within the number to whom the command is addressed. Otherwise all the commandments to the patriarchs and prophets, whether ceremonial, symbolical, or individual, would be binding upon everyone who might read them. And hence, in general, whosoever urges upon us any duty as the command of God revealed in the Bible, must show that God has somewhere *commanded that action* to be done and that he has *commanded us to do it.*

This principle will *exclude—*

1. Everything which is *merely* history. Much of the Bible contains a mere narrative of facts. For the truth of this narrative, the veracity of the Deity is pledged. We may derive from the account of God's dealings, lessons of instruction to guide us in particular cases; and from the evil conduct of men, matter of warning. But *the mere fact that anything has been done, and recorded in the Scripture,* by no means places us under obligation to do it.

2. It excludes from being obligatory upon *all,* what has been commanded but which can be shown to have been intended only for individuals or for nations, and *not for the whole human race.* Thus many commands are recorded in the Scriptures as having been given to *individuals.* Such was the command to Abraham to offer up his son; to Moses to stand before Pharaoh; to Samuel to anoint Saul and David; and a thousand others. Here, evidently, the Divine direction was exclusively intended for the individual to whom it was given. No one can pretend that he is commanded to offer up his son because Abraham was so commanded.

Thus also many of the commands of God in the Old Testament

were addressed to *nations*. Such were the directions to the Israelites to take possession of Canaan; to make a war upon surrounding nations; to keep the ceremonial law; and so of various other instances. Now of such precepts it is to be observed, 1. They are to be obeyed only *at the time* and *in the manner* in which they were commanded. Thus the Jews at present would have no right, in virtue of the original command, to expel the Mohammedans from Palestine; though the command to Joshua was a sufficient warrant for expelling the Canaanites at the time in which it was given. 2. They are of force only *to those to whom they were given*. Thus supposing the ceremonial law was not abolished; as it was given specially to Jews and to no one else, it would bind no one but Jews now. Supposing it to be abolished, it of course now binds no one. For if when in force it was obligatory on *no one but the Jews,* and was *nothing to anyone else;* when it is abolished *as to them,* it is *nothing to anyone*. Such is the teaching of St. Paul on this subject.

3. It would exclude whatever was done by inspired men if it was done without the addition of being somehow commanded. Thus the New Testament was manifestly intended for the whole human race and at all times; and it was written by men who were inspired by God to teach us His will. But still, their example is not binding *per se;* that is, we are not under obligation to perform an act *simply because they have done it*. Thus Paul and the other apostles kept the Feast of Pentecost; but this imposes no such obligation upon us. Paul circumcised Timothy; but this imposes no obligation upon us to do likewise: for upon another occasion he did not circumcise Titus. The examples of inspired men in the New Testament would, unless exception be made, prove the *lawfulness* of an act, but it could by no means establish its *obligatoriness*.

This principle will *include* as obligatory—

1. Whatever has been enjoined as the will of God upon man *as man,* in distinction from what has been enjoined upon men *as individuals* or *as nations*. The command may be given us, 1. By God himself, as when he proclaimed his law from Mount Sinai; or, 2. By the Mediator Christ Jesus; or, 3. By any persons divinely commissioned to instruct us in the will of God; as prophets, apostles, or

evangelists. This includes as obligatory on the conscience simply what is proved to be intended according to the *established principles of interpretation*. But it by no means includes anything which man may infer from what is thus intended. Any idea which man adds to the idea given in the Scriptures is the idea of man, and has no more obligation on the conscience of his fellow men than any other idea of man.

But it may be asked, granting that nothing but a Divine command is obligatory on the conscience, yet as general and particular commandments in the Scriptures are frequently in a considerable degree blended together, how may we learn to distinguish that part which is obligatory upon us from that which is in its nature local and peculiar? In attempting to answer this question I would suggest,

That the distinction of nations or individuals is nowhere adverted to in the New Testament. Its instructions are clearly intended for men of all ages and nations; and hence they never involve anything either local or peculiar, but are universally binding upon all. The question must therefore refer to the Old Testament.

If we confine ourselves, then, to the Old Testament, this question may be decided on the following principles:

1. In by far the greater number of cases, we shall be able to decide by reference to the nature of the Jewish commonwealth; a temporary or preparatory dispensation which was to cease when that to which it was preparatory had appeared.

2. The New Testament, being thus intended for the whole human race, and being a final revelation of the will of God to man, may be supposed to contain all the moral precepts both of natural religion and of the Old Testament, together with whatever else it was important to our salvation that we should know. If, then, a revelation has been made in the Old Testament which is repeated in the New Testament, we shall be safe in making the later revelation the criterion by which we shall judge respecting the precepts of the earlier. That is to say, no precept of the Old Testament which is not either given to man as man, or which is not either repeated or its obligations acknowledged under the new dispensation, is binding upon us at the present day. This principle is, I think, avowed, in

substance, by the Apostle Paul in various places in his Epistles. While he repeatedly urges the moral precepts of the Old Testament as of unchanging obligation, he speaks of everything else, so far as moral obligation is concerned, as utterly annihilated.

Such, then, are the means afforded to us by our Creator for acquiring a knowledge of our duty. They are, first, natural religion; second, the Old Testament or a dispensation of law; third, the Gospel, a remedial dispensation or a dispensation of grace.

The relation existing between our moral power, and these means of moral cultivation may, I suppose, be stated somewhat as follows:

1. By conscience, we attain a feeling of moral obligation towards the various beings to whom we are related. The elements of this feeling are developed as soon as we come to the knowledge of the existence and attributes of those beings and the relation in which we stand to them. Such elements are the feeling of obligation of reciprocity to man and of universal love and obedience to our Creator.

2. In order to illustrate the relations in which we stand to other beings, created and uncreated, as well as to teach us His character and His will concerning us, God has given us other means of instruction.

1. He has so arranged and governed all the events of this world as to illustrate His character by His dealings with men; and He has given us powers by which we may, if we will, acquire the knowledge thus set before us. The fact that we may acquire this knowledge of the will of God, and that we are so constituted as to feel that we ought to do the will of God, renders us responsible for obedience to all the light which we may acquire.

2. In the utter failure of this mode of instruction to reclaim men, God has seen fit to reveal His will to us by language. Here the truth is spread before us without the necessity of induction from a long and previous train of reasoning. This knowledge of the will of God, thus obtained, renders man responsible for the additional light thus communicated.

In the same manner, when this means failed to produce any important moral result, a revelation has been made, instructing us still farther concerning our duties to God, His character and will;

and above all informing us of a new relation in which the Deity stands to us and of those new conditions of being under which we are placed. And we are, in consequence of our moral constitution, rendered responsible for a conduct corresponding to all this additional moral light and consequent moral obligation.[12]

Now if it be remembered that we are under obligations, greater than we can estimate, to obey the will of God by what manner soever signified, and that we are under obligation, therefore, to obey Him if he had given us no other intimation of His will than merely the monition of conscience, unassisted by natural or revealed religion, how greatly must that obligation be increased when these additional means of information are taken into account! And if the guilt of our disobedience be in proportion to the knowledge of our duty, and if that knowledge of our duty be so great that we cannot readily conceive how, consistently with the conditions of our being, it could have been greater, we may judge how utterly inexcusable must be every one of our transgressions. Such does the Bible represent to be the actual condition of man; and hence it everywhere treats him as under a just and awful condemnation; a condemnation from which there is no hope of escape but by means of the special provisions of a remedial dispensation.

It belongs to theology to treat of the nature of this remedial dispensation. We shall, therefore, attempt no exhibition either of its character or its provisions, beyond a simple passing remark to show its connections with our present subject.

The *law of God,* as revealed in the Scriptures, represents our eternal happiness as attainable upon the simple ground of perfect obedience, and perfect obedience upon the principles already explained. But this, in our present state, is manifestly unattainable. A single sin, both on the ground of its violation of the conditions on which our future happiness was suspended, as well as by the effects which it produces upon our whole subsequent moral character, and our capacity for virtue, renders our loss of happiness inevitable. Even after reformation, our moral attainment must fall short of the requirements of the law of God and thus present no claim to the

---

[12] See Appendix (F) for paragraph inserted in the 1865 edition.

Divine favor. For this reason our salvation is made to depend upon the obedience and merits of another. But we are entitled to hope for salvation upon the ground of the merit of Christ, solely upon the condition of yielding ourselves up in entire obedience to the whole law of God. "He that saith, I know Him, and keepeth not His commandments, is a liar, and the truth is not in him." *John* ii. 4. And hence a knowledge of the law of God is of just as great importance to us under a remedial dispensation as under a dispensation of law; not on the ground that we are to be saved by keeping it without sin; but on the ground that unless the will of God be the habitually controlling motive of all our conduct, we are destitute of the elements of that character to which the blessings of the remedial dispensation are promised. Hence under the one dispensation as well as under the other, though on different grounds, the knowledge of the law of God is necessary to our happiness both here and hereafter.

BOOK SECOND
PRACTICAL ETHICS

In the preceding pages it has been my design to illustrate the moral constitution of man, and to point out the sources from which that truth emanates which is addressed to his moral constitution. My design in the present book is to classify and explain some of the principal moral laws under which God has placed us in our present state. We shall derive these laws from natural or from revealed religion or from both, as may be most convenient for our purpose.

The Scriptures declare that the whole moral law is contained in the single word LOVE.

The beings to whom man is related in his present state are, so far as this subject is concerned, God his Creator and man his fellow creature. Hence the moral obligations of men are of two kinds; first, LOVE TO GOD, or PIETY; second, LOVE TO MAN, or MORALITY.

This book will, therefore, be divided into two parts, in which those two subjects will be treated of in their order.

CHAPTER FIRST

THE GENERAL OBLIGATION TO SUPREME LOVE TO GOD

THE scriptural precept on this subject may be found recorded in various passages. It is in these words: "Thou shalt love the Lord thy God with all thy heart, and with all thy soul, and with all thy mind, and with all thy strength." See *Matthew* xxii, 37; *Mark* xii, 30; *Luke* x, 27.

In order to illustrate this precept I shall consider, *first,* the relation which exists between us and the Deity; *secondly,* the rights and obligations which that relation imposes; and *thirdly,* the facts in our constitution which show that these are manifestly the law of our being.

I. The relation which exists between God and us.

1. He is our Creator and Preserver. A few years since, and we had no existence. Within a few more years, and this whole system of which we form a part had no existence. Over our own existence, neither we nor any created thing has any more than the semblance of power. We are upheld in being by the continued act of Omnipotence. Not only we ourselves, but every faculty which we and which all creatures enjoy, was created and is continually upheld by the same Creator. Nor this alone; all the circumstances by which we are surrounded and all the modifications of external nature, of what sort soever they may be, whether physical, intellectual, social, or moral, are equally created and sustained by God and derive their powers to render us happy or wise or good purely from his provident care and from the exertion of his omnipotent and omnipresent goodness. The relation, therefore, existing between the Deity and us is that of dependence, more profound, universal, and absolute than we are able adequately to comprehend, upon a Being absolutely and essentially independent, omniscient, omnipotent, and all-providing.

2. The Deity has revealed himself to us as a Being in whom are united, by the necessity of his existence, every perfection of which the human mind can conceive, and every perfection that can possibly exist, how much soever they may transcend the powers of our conception. To Him belong, from the necessity of His being, almighty power, omniscient wisdom, unchanging veracity, inflexible justice, transcendent purity, illimitable benevolence, and universal love. Not only does He treasure up within Himself all that can be conceived of every perfection, but He is the exhaustless fountain, from which emanates all of these attributes, that exists throughout this wide creation. As every object that we see in nature is seen only by its reflecting rays of the sun, so every exhibition of goodness which we behold in creatures is nothing but the reflection of the perfections of Him who is the Father of Lights, with whom is neither variableness nor the shadow of a turning. The relation, therefore, in this respect, which exists between us and the Creator is that which exists between beings whom He has formed to admire and love all these perfections and the Uncreated Being in whom they all exist in a degree infinitely surpassing all that it is in our power to conceive.

3. This creative power, and this incomprehensible wisdom, have been exerted in obedience to all these transcendent moral perfections for the production of our best good, our highest temporal and eternal happiness; nay, they have been as fully exerted in behalf of our race as though there were no other race in existence; and in behalf of each one of us as though each individual were the only being created within this illimitable universe. And upon all this exertion of goodness towards us, we have not the semblance of a claim; for God was under no manner of obligation to create us, much less to create us capable of that happiness which we enjoy. The relation, therefore, in this respect, existing between us and the Deity is that between beings who, without any claim whatever, are at every moment receiving the results of the exercise of every conceivable perfection, from a Being who is moved thus to conduct toward them by nothing but His own independent goodness.

II. From these relations existing between *creatures and the Cre-*

ator, there arise various *rights* of the Creator and various *obligations* of the creature.

Everyone who will reflect upon this subject must be convinced that, inasmuch as these relations are entirely beyond the range of human analogies and also manifestly beyond the grasp of finite conception, they must involve obligations in their very nature more profound and universal than we can adequately comprehend; and that, therefore, no conception of ours can possibly transcend their solemnity and awfulness. As in our present state we are so little able to understand them or even to inquire after them, we see the need of instruction concerning them from Him who alone, of all beings that exist, can fathom their depth or measure their immensity. Let us, therefore, inquire, What are the claims which, in his revealed word, God asserts over us, and what are the obligations which in his sight bind us to Him?

1. By virtue of his relation to us as *Creator,* he asserts over us the right of *unlimited possession.* Inasmuch as we are *his creatures,* we are *his* in the highest and most extensive sense in which we can conceive of the idea of possession. Neither we ourselves, nor anything which we seem to possess, are our own. Even our wills are not our own, but he claims that we shall only *will* precisely what *He wills.* Our faculties, of what sort soever, are not our own. He claims that from the commencement of our existence they be used precisely in the manner, for the purposes, and within the limits, that He shall direct. Not only does God assert this right in his word, but we find that he actually exercises it. Without regard to what we will, He does his pleasure in the armies of heaven and among the inhabitants of the earth. He takes from us health, possessions, friends, faculties, life, and *He giveth not account of any of his matters.* That is, he manifestly acts upon the principle that He is the Sovereign and rightful Proprietor both of ourselves and of all that we seem to ourselves to possess.

And thus, on the other hand, God asserts that we are all under obligations, greater and more solemn than we can possibly conceive, to render to Him that entire obedience and submission which his essential right over us renders manifestly his due.

This right, and the correspondent obligation, have respect to two classes of duties. The first class is that which respects simply our *relations to him,* and which would be obligatory upon us although each one of us were the only created being in the universe. The second class of duties respects our fellow creatures. If we could suppose moral creatures to exist without a Creator, there would yet be duties which, from their *constitution as moral creatures,* they would owe to each other. But inasmuch as *every creature is the creature of God,* He has made the duties which they owe to each other a part of their duty to Him. That is to say, he requires us, who are his creatures, and who are under universal obligations to him, to treat our fellow creatures, who are also his creatures and under his protection, in such a manner as he shall direct. He is the Father of us all and he requires that every one of his children conduct himself toward others, who are also his children, as he shall appoint. And hence the duties which are required of us to our fellow creatures are required of us under a twofold obligation. First, that arising from our relation to God, and secondly, that arising from our relation to our fellows. And hence there is not a single act which we are under obligation to perform, which we are not also under obligation to perform from the principle of obedience to our Creator. Thus the obligation *to act religiously,* or piously, extends to the minutest action of our lives, and no action of any sort whatever can be, *in the full acceptation of the term,* virtuous, that is, be entitled to the praise of God, which does not involve in its motives the temper of filial obedience to the Deity. And still more, as this obligation is infinitely superior to any other that can be conceived, an action performed from the conviction of any other obligation, if this obligation be excluded, fails in infinitely the most important respect; and must, by the whole amount of this deficiency, expose us to the condemnation of the law of God, whatever that condemnation may be.

And once more, we are taught in the Scriptures that the relation in which we stand to the Deity places us under such obligations that, while our whole and uninterrupted service is thus due to God, we can, after it is all performed, in no manner bring him under any obligation to us. This I suppose to be the meaning intended by our

Saviour in the parable, *Luke* xvii, 7—10: "But which of you, having a servant (a slave), ploughing or feeding cattle, will say unto him, by and by, when he is come from the field, Go and sit down to meat; and will not rather say unto him, Make ready wherewith I may sup, and gird thyself and serve me, until I have eaten and drunken; and afterwards thou shalt eat and drink? Doth he *thank* that servant because *he hath done the things that were commanded him?* I suppose not. So, likewise ye, when ye have done all the things which are commanded you, say, We are unprofitable servants, we have done that which was our duty to do." That is, the obligation of the servant is not fulfilled by *doing any one thing,* but only by *occupying his whole time* and exerting his whole power to its full extent in doing whatever is commanded him. And when all this is done, such is the relation between the parties, that he has placed the Master, God, under no obligation; he has only discharged a duty; he has merely paid a debt; nor is it possible, from the nature of the relation, that he should ever do anything more. Such, I think, everyone will acknowledge, upon reflection, to be the relation existing between us and our Creator.

And hence we see that a failure in duty to God on the part of the creature must be remediless. At every moment he is under obligation to the full amount of his ability; and when this whole amount of obligation is discharged he has then simply fulfilled his duty. Hence no act can have any retrospective effect; that is, it cannot supply the deficiencies of any other act. This would be the case even if his moral powers were not injured by sin. But if we add this other element, and reflect that by sin our moral powers are permanently injured; that is, our capacity for virtue is diminished according to the laws of our constitution; by how much more is it evident that under a system of mere law, a single failure in our duty to God must be of necessity fatal! What shall we then say of a life of which every act is, when strictly considered, by confession a moral failure?

2. God has revealed himself to us as a Being endowed with every attribute of *natural and moral excellence;* and in virtue of the *relation which on this account* he sustains to us, a new form of obligation is imposed upon us.

We are evidently formed to love whatever is beautiful and to admire whatever is great in power or excellent in wisdom. This is too evident to need illustration. But we are so made as to love and admire still more *the cause* from which all these emanate. We admire the tragedies of Shakespeare and the epic of Milton, but how much more the minds in which these works were conceived and by which they were executed. Now all that we see in creation, whether of beauty or loveliness or grandeur, is the work of the Creator. It all existed in His conceptions before it existed in fact. Nor this alone. The powers by which we perceive and are affected by, these exhibitions all proceed from Him, and both the external qualities and the internal susceptibilities are upheld by his all-sustaining energy. Thus every feeling of love or of admiration which we exercise involves, from the constitution of our nature, the obligation to exercise these feelings in a higher degree towards Him who is the author of all. But as He is the author not only of whatever is lovely or glorious that we see, but of all that we have ever seen; not only of all that *we* have ever seen, but of all that has ever existed; not only of all that has ever existed, but of all that ever can exist; by how much are we under obligation to love Him better than all things else that we know! and by how much more than any individual form of excellence with which it is possible for us ever to become acquainted.

Again, God reveals himself to us as the possessor of every *moral* attribute in infinite perfection. In him are united infinitely more than we or other created beings can conceive, of justice, holiness, mercy, compassion, goodness, and truth. Now we are manifestly formed to love and admire actions emanating from such attributes as they are exhibited on earth, and specially the moral characters of those by whom such actions are performed. We are not only formed to do this, but we are *specially* formed to do it. We are created with an impulsion to exercise these affections and we are conscious that it is the highest impulsion of our nature. Now whatever we see of moral excellence on earth springs from Him as its first and original cause. He created the circumstances under which it exists, and created, with all its powers, the being by whom it is displayed. Nor this alone. He possesses, essentially, and in an infinite degree, and without the possibility of imperfection, every moral attribute. If, then, the highest impulsion of our nature teaches us to love and venerate these attributes even as they are displayed in their imperfection on earth, by how much more are we under obligation to love these attributes as they are possessed by our Father who is in heaven! If a single act of justice deserves our veneration, how much more should we venerate that justice which has governed this universe without the shadow of a spot, from eternity! If a single act of purity deserves our regard, with what awe should we adore the holiness of Him in whose sight the heavens are unclean! If a single act of benevolence deserve our love, with what affection should we bow before Him who, from eternity, has been pouring abroad a ceaseless flood of blessedness over the boundless universe by which He is surrounded!

And yet more, I think it is manifest that we are so constituted as to be under obligations to love such attributes as I have mentioned, entirely aside from the consideration of their connection with ourselves. We admire justice and benevolence in men who existed ages ago and in countries with which we have no interests in common. And thus these obligations to love and adore these attributes in the Deity would exist in full force, irrespective of the fact of our receiving any benefit from them. And our Creator might, and justly would, require of us all these affections of which I have spoken, did these moral attributes exist in some other being besides himself. The obligation is sustained upon the simple consideration that we are constituted such moral beings as we are, and that another Being exists, endowed with attributes in this particular manner corresponding to our moral constitution. By how much is this obligation increased by the consideration that He in whom these attributes exist, stands to us in the relation of Creator!

3. As by the constitution of our moral nature we are under obligation to love whatever is morally excellent, irrespective of any benefit which we may derive from it ourselves, so when this moral excellence is intentionally the source of happiness to us, we are under the additional obligation to *gratitude,* or a desire to do something which shall please Him from whom our happiness has proceeded. This obligation is so manifestly recognized as one of the instinctive

impulses of our nature that, whilst we merely esteem him who acts in obedience to it, the neglect of it, without the exhibition of the positively opposite temper, is always met by the feeling of intense moral reprobation.

Now since whatever of favor we receive from others is derived from them merely as second causes, it all originates, essentially, from the First and All-Pervading Cause. Whatever gratitude we feel, therefore, toward creatures is really, and in the highest possible sense, due to God, from whom it all really emanates.

But how small is that portion of the happiness which we enjoy which is conferred by the *favor of our fellows!* Immeasurably the greater part is the direct gift of our Creator. The obligation to gratitude is in proportion to the amount of benefits conferred and the disinterestedness of the goodness from which they have proceeded. By these elements let us estimate the amount of obligation of *gratitude* to God.

As the Deity is essentially independent of all his creatures, and as He has created us from nothing, and as He has created also all the circumstances under which we exist, He can be under no sort of obligation to us, nor can our relation to Him ever be of any other sort than that of the recipients of favor which we can by no possibility merit.

Under such circumstances, a sensation of happiness for a single moment, even if it terminated with that single moment, would be a cause for gratitude so long as it could be remembered. How much more if this form of happiness continued throughout our whole extent of being! The enjoyment of one form of happiness, say of that derived from a single sense, would deserve our gratitude; how much more that derived from all our senses, and specially that derived from the combination of them all! The enjoyment of ever so transient a sensation of intellectual happiness would deserve our gratitude; how much more that of a permanent constitution which was a source of perpetual intellectual happiness, and specially a constitution involving a great variety of forms of intellectual happiness! Thus also, a single emotion of moral happiness would deserve our gratitude; how much more a constitution formed for perpetual moral happiness! And yet more, if these forms of happiness taken singly would be each a cause of perpetual and increasing gratitude, how much more a constitution by which the very relations which they sustain to each other become a source of additional and increased happiness! Add to this that the external world is itself adjusted to all these powers and susceptibilities of man and each adjustment is manifestly intended for our best good. And add to this that such are the conditions of being under which we are placed that, if we only use these powers according to the will of God and to the nature which He has given us, that is, in such a way as to promote our highest happiness here, we shall be advanced to a state of happiness more excellent and glorious than any of which we can conceive; and we shall be fixed in it unchangeably and forever. Now if a single act of disinterested goodness and undeserved favor deserve our gratitude forever, what limits can be set to the intensity of that grateful adoration which should, throughout our whole being, pervade our bosoms toward Him from whom every blessing is perpetually flowing in so exhaustless a flood of unfathomable goodness!

Such, then, are the obligations to love and gratitude which, in addition to that of obedience, we owe to our Creator. But it deserves to be remarked that these forms of obligation reciprocally involve each other. For if we possess that temper of entire obedience which springs from a recognition of the universal right of the Creator over us, we shall dedicate our *affections* to Him as entirely as our *will;* that is, we shall love only what he commands, and just as he has commanded; that is, we shall not only do his will, but we shall love to do it, not only on account of what he is *in himself,* but also on account of what he is and always has been *to us.* And on the other hand, if we love his character and attributes as they deserve, we shall love to perform actions which are in harmony with those attributes; that is, which spring from the same dispositions in ourselves. In other words, we shall love to act in perfect accordance with the will of God. And still more, if we are penetrated with a proper conviction of the obligations of gratitude under which we are placed, we shall love to please our Supreme Benefactor; and the only way in which we can do this is by implicitly obeying his commands.

It was remarked in a former part of this work that happiness consists in the exercise of our sensitiveness upon its appropriate objects.
Now that man has moral sentiments, that is, that he is formed to
derive happiness from the contemplation of moral qualities and specially from the love of those beings in whom these moral qualities
reside, is too evident to need argument. It is also evident that this
is the highest and most exalted form of happiness of which he is
susceptible. But created beings and the moral qualities of created
beings are not the objects adapted to his moral sensitiveness. This
power of our being finds its appropriate object in nothing less than
in supreme and unlimited and infinite moral perfection. And yet
more, the moral susceptibility of happiness expands by exercise, and
the uncreated object to which it is directed is, by necessity, unchangeable, eternal, and infinite. A provision is thus made for the happiness of man, eternal and illimitable; that is to say, not only is it
evident from the constitution of man that he is made to love God,
but also that he is made to love Him infinitely more than anything
else; to be happier from loving Him than from loving anything else;
and also, to be more and more intensely happy from loving Him,
throughout eternity.

Thus in general, from the relations which we sustain to God, we
are under more imperative obligations than we are able to conceive
to exercise toward him that temper of heart which is, perhaps, in
the language of men best expressed by the term *a filial disposition;*
that is, a disposition to universal obedience pervaded by the spirit
of supreme and grateful affection. This temper of heart is that generically denominated in the Scriptures *faith.* In the New Testament
it is somewhat modified by the relations in which we stand to God in
consequence of the provisions of the remedial dispensation.

Now all these dispositions would be required of us if we were
sinless beings, and possibly no others would be required. The same
are manifestly our duty after we have sinned; for our sin changes
neither the character of God nor His claim upon our obedience and
affection. A child who has done wrong is not under any the less
imperative obligation to exercise a filial disposition towards a parent.
But suppose a creature to have sinned, it is manifest that he would

be under obligations to exercise another moral disposition. He ought to regret his fault, not on account of its consequences to himself, but on account of the violation of moral obligation, which is the essence of its guiltiness. Acknowledging its utter wrongfulness, justifying God, and taking all the blame of his act upon himself, he ought to hate his own act, and from such feelings to the act as well as from the temper of filial obedience to God, commence a life of moral purity. Such is *repentance*. This is the temper of heart which the Scriptures teach us that God requires of us as *sinners*.

III. Such, then, is the obligation under which, by our creation, we stand to God. It would be easy to show that this is the only principle of action suited to our nature under the present constitution.

For, 1. As we live under a constitution of law, that is, under which every action is amenable to law, and since to every action is affixed, by omnipotent power and unsearchable wisdom, rewards or punishments, both in this life and also in the other, and as these consequences can by no power of ours be severed from the action, it is manifest that we can attain to happiness and escape from misery only by perfectly obeying the will of our Creator. And yet more, since we are creatures endowed with will and the power of choice, we never can be completely happy unless we act as we choose; that is, unless we obey because we love to obey. Hence from the elements of our constitution it is evident, we can be happy on no other principles than those of perfect obedience to God, and obedience emanating from, and pervaded by, love.

2. The same truth is evident from a consideration of the relations which every individual sustains to the whole race of man. It manifestly enters into the constitution under which we exist that every individual shall have a power over society, both for good and for evil, so far as we can see, in its nature illimitable. That such is the fact will be evident to everyone who will reflect for a moment upon the results emanating from the lives of St. Paul, Luther, Howard, Clarkson, or Wilberforce; and of Alexander, Julius Cæsar, Voltaire, Lord Byron, or Napoleon. Now it is only necessary to recollect that the being possessed of this power is by nature utterly ignorant of the future, wholly incapable even during life, and much more after death,

of controlling and directing the consequences of his actions; and still more, that he is fallible—that is, liable not only to err from ignorance, but also from a wrong moral bias; and we must be convinced that the exercise of this power could never be safe for his fellows unless it were under the supreme direction of a Being who knew the end from the beginning, and who was by his very nature incapable of wrong.

From what has been said it will follow that our duty to God forbids—

1. Idolatry—that is, rendering divine homage to any other being than the Deity.

2. Rendering obedience to any creature in opposition to the will of the Creator.

3. Yielding obedience to our own will or gratifying our own desires in opposition to His will.

4. Loving anything which He has forbidden.

5. Loving anything which He has allowed us to love, in a manner and to a degree that He has forbidden.

6. Loving anything created in preference to Him.

Each of these topics is susceptible of extended illustration. As, however, they are discussed in full in works on theology, to which science they more particularly belong, we shall leave them with this simple enumeration.

In treating of the remainder of this subject we shall, therefore, consider only the means by which the love of God, or piety, may be cultivated. These are three: 1st. A spirit of devotion. 2d. Prayer. 3d. The observance of the Sabbath.

CHAPTER SECOND
THE CULTIVATION OF A DEVOTIONAL SPIRIT

FROM what has already been said, it will be seen that the relation which we sustain to God imposes upon us the obligation of maintaining such an habitual temper toward *Him* as shall continually incite us to do whatever will please Him. It is natural to suppose that our Creator would have placed us under such circumstances as would, from their nature, cultivate in us such a temper. Such we find to be the fact. We are surrounded by objects of knowledge which not merely by their existence, but also by their ceaseless changes, remind us of the attributes of God and of the obligations under which we are placed to Him. A devotional spirit consists in making the moral use which is intended, of all the objects of intellection that come within our experience or our observation.

1. Our existence is dependent on a succession of changes which are taking place at every moment in ourselves, over which we have no power whatever, but of which each one involves the necessity of the existence and the superintending power of the Deity. The existence of the whole material universe is of the same nature. Now each of these changes is with infinite skill adapted to the relative conditions of all the beings whom they affect; and they are subjected to laws which are most evident expressions of almighty power, of unsearchable wisdom, and of exhaustless goodness. Now were we merely intellectual beings, it would not be possible for us to consider anything more than these laws themselves; but inasmuch as we are intellectual and also *moral* beings, we are capable not only of considering the laws, but also the attributes of the Creator from whom such laws are the emanations. As everything which we can know teaches a lesson concerning God, if we connect that lesson with everything which we learn, everything will be resplendent with the attributes of Deity. By using in this manner the knowledge which is everywhere spread before us, we shall habitually cultivate a devout temper of mind. Thus "the heavens will declare unto us the glory of God, and the firmament will show his handy-work;

thus day unto day will utter speech, and night unto night show forth *knowledge of Him."*

2. Nor is this true of *physical* nature alone. The whole history of the human race teaches us the same lesson. The rewards of virtue and the punishments of vice, as they are beheld in the events which befall both individuals and nations, all exhibit the attributes of the Deity. It is He that "stilleth the noise of the seas, the noise of their waves, and the tumult of the people." "The Lord reigneth, let the earth rejoice; let the multitude of isles be glad thereof. Clouds and darkness are round about him; righteousness and judgment are the habitation of his throne." His forbearance and long-suffering, and at the same time His inflexible justice, His love of right and His hatred of wrong, are legibly written in every page of individual and national history. And hence it is that every fact which we witness in the government of moral beings has a twofold chain of connections and relations. To the mere political economist or the statesman, it teaches the law by which *cause and effect are connected.* To the pious man it also teaches the *attributes of that Being who has so connected cause and effect;* and who, amidst all the intricate mazes of human motive and social organization, carries forward His laws with unchanging certainty and unerring righteousness. Now it is by observing not merely the *law,* but the *moral lesson derived from the law;* it is by observing not merely the connections of events with each other, but also their connection with the Great First Cause, that a devotional spirit is to be cultivated.

And hence we see that knowledge of every kind, if suitably improved, has in its very nature a tendency to devotion. If we do not thus use it, we sever it from its most important connections. We act simply as intellectual, and not as moral beings. We act contrary to the highest and most noble principles of our constitution. And hence we see how progress in knowledge really places us under progressive obligations to improvement in piety. This should be borne in mind by every man and specially by every educated man. For this improvement of our knowledge, God holds us accountable. "Because they regard not the works of the Lord, nor *consider* the operations of his hand, therefore will He destroy them."

3. But if such are the obligations resting upon us from our relation to the works of Nature and Providence, how much are these obligations increased by our knowledge of God as it is presented to us by revelation! I suppose that a person acquainted with the laws of optics, who had always stood with his back to the sun, might acquire much important knowledge of the nature of light and of the path of the sun through the heavens, by reasoning from the reflection of that light observed in the surrounding creation. But how uncertain would be this knowledge, compared with that which he would acquire by looking directly upon the sun and tracing his path by his own immediate observation! So of revelation. Here we are taught by language that truth which we otherwise could learn only by long and careful induction. God has here made known to us His attributes and character; here He has recorded His law; here He has written a portion of the history of our race as a specimen of His providential dealings with men; and here He has, more than all, revealed to us a remedial dispensation by which our sins may be forgiven and we be raised to higher and more glorious happiness than that which we have lost. It surely becomes us, then, specially to study the Bible, not merely as a book of antiquities or a choice collection of poetry or an inexhaustible storehouse of wisdom; but for the more important purpose of ascertaining the character of God and our relations to Him, and of thus cultivating towards Him those feelings of filial and reverential homage which are so manifestly our duty, and which such contemplations are in their nature so adapted to foster and improve.

4. A devout temper is also cultivated by the exercise of devotion. The more we exercise the feeling of veneration, of love, of gratitude, and of submission towards God, the more profound, and pervading, and intense, and habitual, will these feelings become. And unless the feelings themselves be called into exercise, it will be in vain that we are persuaded that we ought to exercise them. It is one thing to be an admirer of devotion, and another thing to be really devout. It becomes us, therefore, to cultivate these feelings by actually exercising towards God the very tempers of mind indicated by our cir-

cumstances and our progressive knowledge. Thus submission to His will, thankfulness for His mercies, trust in His providence, reliance on His power, and sorrow for our sins should be, not the occasional exercise, but the habit of our souls.

5. By the constitution of our nature a most intimate connection exists between action and motive; between the performance of an action and the principle from which it emanates. The one cannot long exist without the other. True charity cannot long exist in the temper unless we perform acts of charity. Meditation upon goodness will soon become effete unless it be strengthened by good works. So the temper of devotion will be useless; nay, the profession of it must, of necessity, be hypocritical unless it produce obedience to God. By this alone is its existence known; by this alone can it be successfully cultivated. The more perfectly our wills are subjected to the will of God and our whole course of conduct regulated by His commands, the more ardent will be our devotion and the more filial the temper from which our actions proceed.

6. It is scarcely necessary to observe that as penitence is a feeling resulting from a conviction of violated obligation, it is to be cultivated, not merely by considering the character of God, but also our conduct towards Him. The contrast between His goodness and compassion, and our ingratitude and rebellion, is specially adapted to fill us with humility and self-abasement and also with sorrow for all our past transgressions. Thus said the prophet: "Wo is me, for I am a man of unclean lips; and I dwell in the midst of a people of unclean lips; *for mine eyes have seen the King, the Lord of Hosts!*"

Lastly. It is surely unnecessary to remark that such a life as this is alone suited to the character of man. If God have made us capable of deriving our highest happiness from Him, and have so constituted the universe around us as perpetually to lead us to this source of happiness, the most unreasonable, ungrateful, and degrading, not to say the most guilty, course of conduct which we can pursue must be to neglect and abuse this, the most noble part of our constitution, and to use the knowledge of the world around us for every other purpose than that for which it was created. Let every frivolous, thoughtless human being reflect what must be his condition when he, whose thoughts are limited by created things, shall stand in the presence of Him, "before whose face the heavens and the earth shall flee away, and there be no place left for them!"

In the present chapter we shall treat of the *nature,* the *obligation,* and the *utility* of prayer.

I. *The nature of prayer.*

Prayer is the direct intercourse of the spirit of man with the spiritual and unseen Creator. "God is a spirit, and those that worship Him, must worship Him in spirit and in truth."

It consists in the expression of our adoration, the acknowledgment of our obligations, the offering up of our thanksgivings, the confession of our sins, and in supplication for the favors, as well temporal as spiritual, which we need; being always accompanied with a suitable temper of mind.

This temper of mind presupposes—

1. A solemn conviction of the character and attributes of God and of the relations which He sustains to us.

2. A conviction of the relations which we sustain to Him and of our obligations to Him.

3. An affecting view of our sinfulness, helplessness, and misery.

4. Sincere gratitude for all the favors which we have received.

5. A fixed and undissembled resolution to obey the commands of God in future.

6. Unreserved submission to all His will.

7. Unshaken confidence in His veracity.

8. Importunate desires that our petitions, specially for spiritual blessings, should be granted.

9. A soul at peace with all mankind.

Illustrations of all these dispositions from the prayers recorded in the Holy Scriptures, as well as the precepts by which they are enforced, might be easily adduced. I presume, however, they are unnecessary. I will only remark that it is not asserted that all these dispositions are always to be in exercise at the same time, but only such of them as specially belong to the nature of our supplications.

Inasmuch as we are dependent on God, not only for all the blessings which we derive directly from His hands, but also for all those which arise from our relations to each other, it is manifestly proper that we confess our sins and supplicate His favor, not only as individuals, but as societies. Hence prayer may be divided into individual, domestic, and social.

Individual Prayer. As the design of this institution is to bring us, as *individuals,* into direct communion with God, to confess our personal infirmities, and to cultivate personal piety, it should be strictly in private. We are commanded to pray to our Father *in secret.* It should, moreover, be solemn, unreserved, and, in general, accompanied with the reading of the Holy Scriptures. As, moreover, this direct communion with the unseen Creator is intended to be the great antagonist force to the constant pressure of the things seen and temporal, it should be habitual and frequent.

Domestic Prayer. As the relation sustained by parents and children is the source of many and peculiar blessings; as the relation involves peculiar responsibilities, in the fulfillment of which we all need special guidance and direction, there is a peculiar propriety in the acknowledgment of God in connection with this relation. The importance of this duty is specially urged upon us by its effect upon the young. It associates with religion all the recollections of childhood and all the sympathies of home. It gives to parental advice the sanction of religion and, in afterlife, recalls the mind to a conviction of duty to God, with all the motives drawn from a father's care and a mother's tenderness.

Social Prayer. Inasmuch as all our social and civil blessings are the gift of God, it is meet that we should, as societies, meet to acknowledge them. This is one of the most important duties of the Sabbath day. It will, therefore, be more fully treated of under that branch of the subject.

Since prayer is the offering up of our desires, &c., with a suitable temper of heart, it is manifest that the question whether a form of prayer, or extemporary prayer, should be used, is merely one of expediency and has no connection with morals. We are under obligation to use that which is of the greatest spiritual benefit to the individual. Private prayer should, however, I think, be expressed in the words of the supplicant himself.

II. *The duty of prayer.*

The duty of prayer may be seen from *the conditions of our being* and *from the Holy Scriptures.*

I. The conditions of our being.

1. We are utterly powerless, ignorant of the future, essentially dependent at the present and for the future, and are miserably sinful. We need support, direction, happiness, pardon, and purification. These can come from no other being than God, who is under no obligation to confer them upon us. What can be more manifestly proper than that we should supplicate the Father of the universe for those blessings which are necessary, not only for our happiness, but for our existence, and that we should receive every favor with a devout acknowledgment of the terms on which it is bestowed?

2. Inasmuch as we are sinners and have forfeited the blessings which we daily receive, what can be more suitable than that we should humbly thank that Almighty power, from whom comes such an inexhaustible supply of goodness to us so utterly undeserving? and what more obligatory than to ask the pardon of our Creator for those sins of omission and of commission with which we are every hour justly chargeable?

3. Specially is this our duty, when we reflect that this very exercise of habitual reliance upon God is necessary to our happiness in our present state, and that the temper which it presupposes is essential to our progress in virtue.

That such is the dictate of our moral constitution is evident from the fact that all men who have any notion of a Supreme Being, under any circumstances, acknowledge it as a duty and, in some form or other, profess to practice it. And besides this, all men, even the most abandoned and profligate, when in danger, pray most eagerly. This has been the case with men who, in health and safety, scoff at religion and ridicule the idea of moral obligation. But it is evident that it can be neither more proper nor more suitable to pray when we are in danger than to pray at any other time; for our relations to God are always the same and we are always essentially dependent upon him for everything, both temporal and spiritual, that we enjoy at the present or hope for in the future. It is surely as proper to thank God for those *mercies which we receive every mo-ment* as to deprecate those *judgments by which we are occasionally alarmed.*

II. The duty of prayer, as taught in the Scriptures.

The Scriptures treat of prayer as a duty arising so immediately out of our relations to God and our obligations to Him, as scarcely to need a positive precept. Every disposition of heart which we are commanded to exercise towards God presupposes it. Hence it is generally referred to incidentally, as one of which the obligation is already taken for granted. Precepts, however, are not wanting in respect to it. I here only speak of the general tendency of the Scrip-ture instructions:

1. It is expressly commanded: "Pray *without ceasing.*" "*In every thing* giving thanks, for this is the will of God, in Christ Jesus, concerning you." "*In all things,* by prayer and supplication, let your request be made known unto God." *Phil.* iv, 6. "I exhort that sup-plications and prayers, intercessions and giving of thanks, be *made for all men;* for this is *good and acceptable* in the sight of God, our Saviour." 1 *Tim.* ii, 1–3.

2. God declares it to be a principal condition on which He will bestow favors. "If any man lack wisdom, let *him ask* of God, who giveth to all men liberally, and upbraideth not, and *it shall be given him.*" *James* i, 5. "Ask, and it shall be given you; seek, and ye shall find; knock, and it shall be opened unto you: for every one that asketh receiveth, and he that seeketh findeth, and to him that knocketh it shall be opened. Or, what man is there of you, whom, if his son ask bread, will he give him a stone, or, if he ask a fish, will he give him a serpent? If ye, then, being evil, know how to give good gifts to your children, how much more shall your Fa-ther, that is in heaven, give good things *to them that ask him!*" *Matthew* vii, 7–11. Now it is too obvious to need a remark that God would not have connected so important consequences with prayer unless He meant to inculcate it as a universal duty.

3. The Scriptures make the habit of prayer the mark of distinc-tion between the righteous and the wicked; between the enemies and the friends of God. Thus the wicked say: "What is the Almighty,

that we should serve Him? or, what profit shall we have, if we call upon Him?" *Job* xxi, 15. "The wicked, through *the pride of his countenance,* will not seek after God. God is not in all his thoughts." *Psalms* x, 4. On the contrary, righteous persons, those whom God approves, are specially designated as *those who call upon Him.*

4. Examples of the prayers of good men are, in the Scriptures, very abundant. In fact, a large portion of the Bible is made up of the prayers and praises of those whom God has held up for our imitation. To transcribe these would be to transcribe a large portion of the sacred books.

5. The Bible abounds with examples recorded by God of special answers to prayer of every kind that can be conceived. There are examples of the successful prayer of individuals for temporal and for spiritual blessings, both for themselves and for others; of individual prayers for nations, and of nations for themselves; of individuals for societies, and of societies for individuals; and, indeed, of men in all the circumstances in which they can be placed, for every blessing, and under every variety of relation. Now what God has at so great length, and in so great a variety of ways, encouraged us to do, must be not only a privilege but a duty.

In a word, the Bible teaches us on this subject that our relation to God is infinitely nearer, and more universal, than that in which we can possibly stand to any other being. He allows us, with the simplicity and confidence of children, to unbosom all our cares, to make known all our wants, and express all our thanks, with unreserved freedom to Him. He assures us that this exercise and the temper from which it springs, and which it cultivates, is most acceptable to Him. And having thus condescended to humble Himself to our situation, He holds us as most ungrateful, proud, insolent, and sinful if we venture to undertake any business or receive any favor, without holding direct and childlike communion with Him.

6. Under the remedial dispensation, a special encouragement is given to prayer. We are there taught that though we are unworthy of the blessings which we need, yet we may ask and receive, for the sake of the Mediator. "Whatsoever ye shall ask the Father in my name, He will give it you." The death of Christ is also held forth

as our special ground of confidence in prayer: "He that spared not His own Son, but gave Him up for us all, how shall He not, with Him, freely give us all things?" And yet more, we are informed that it is the special office of the exalted Mediator to intercede for us before the throne of God. Greater encouragements than these, to prayer, could not possibly be conceived.

III. *The utility of prayer.*

This may be shown—

1. From the nature and attributes of God: He would not require anything of us which was not for our good.

2. The utility of prayer is seen from the tempers of mind which it presupposes. We have already shown what these tempers of mind are. Now it must be evident to everyone that the habitual exercise of these dispositions must be, in the nature of the case, in the highest degree beneficial to such creatures as we.

3. The utility of prayer is also evident from its connection with our reception of favors from God.

1. In the government of this world God establishes such connections between cause and effect, or antecedent and consequent, as he pleases. He has a perfect right to do so. The fact that one event is the antecedent of another involves not the supposition of any essential power in the antecedent, but merely the supposition that God has placed it in that relation to something that is to follow.

2. The bestowment of favors is one event. God has a right to ordain whatever antecedent to this event he chooses. We are not competent to say *of any event* that *it* cannot be the antecedent to the bestowment of favors any more than that rain cannot be the antecedent to the growth of vegetation.

3. Since, then, any event whatever may be the antecedent to any other event whatever, we are surely not competent to say that *prayer cannot be* the antecedent to the *bestowment of* favors, any more than to say this of anything else. It is surely, to say the least of it, *as good as any other antecedent,* if God saw fit so to ordain.

4. But since God is a *moral* Governor and must, therefore, delight in and reward virtuous tempers, there is a manifest moral propriety in his making these tempers the antecedent to his bestow-

ment of blessings. Nay, we cannot conceive how he would be a righteous moral Governor unless he did do so. And hence we see that the supposition that God bestows blessings in answer to prayer which he would not bestow on any other condition, is not only not at variance with any of his natural attributes, but that it is even demanded by his moral attributes.

5. But inasmuch as God has revealed to us the fact that this is the condition on which he bestows the most valuable of his gifts, and as he has bound himself, by his promise, to reward abundantly all who call upon him, the utility of prayer to creatures situated as we are is as manifest as our necessities are urgent, both for time and for eternity.

4. And finally, there can be no clearer evidence of the goodness of God than just such a constitution as this. God promises favors in answer to prayer; but prayer, as we have seen, is one of the most efficient means of promoting our moral perfection; that is, our highest happiness; that is to say, God promises us favors on conditions which in themselves involve the greatest blessings which we could possibly desire. Bishop Wilson beautifully remarks, "How good is God, who will not only give us what we pray for, but will *reward us for going to him,* and laying our wants before him!"

That a man will, however, receive everything he asks for, and just as he asks for it, is by no means asserted, in an unlimited sense; but only that which he prays for, in a strict sense. *True* prayer is the offering up of our desires, in entire subjection to the will of God; that is, desiring that he will do what we ask if He, in His infinite wisdom and goodness, sees that it will be best. Now if we ask *thus,* our prayer will be granted, for thus He has promised to do for us. Hence our prayers respecting temporal blessings are answered only contingently; that is, under this condition; but our prayers respecting spiritual blessings are answered absolutely; for God has positively promised to give His Holy Spirit to them that ask Him.

If God have allowed us thus to hold the most intimate and unreserved communion with Him; and if He have promised, on this condition, to support us by His power, to teach us by His wisdom, to purify us by His Spirit, and to work in us all those tempers which

He sees will best prepare us for the highest state of future felicity, what can be more ennobling and more lovely than a prayerful life? and what more ungrateful and sinful than a life of thoughtless irreverence and impiety? Is not the single fact of living without habitual prayer a conclusive evidence that we have not the love of God in us; that we are living in habitual violation of every obligation that binds us to our Maker; and that we are, therefore, under the solemn condemnation of His most holy law?

THIS is the second special means appointed by our Creator for the purpose of cultivating in us suitable moral dispositions. We shall treat first *of the original institution of the Sabbath;* secondly, *of the Mosaic Sabbath,* thirdly, *of the Christian Sabbath.*

Although the Sabbath is a positive institution and, therefore, the proof its obligation is to be sought for entirely from revelation, yet there are indications in the present constitution that periods of rest are necessary, both for man and for beast. The recurrence of night and the necessity of repose show that the principle of rest enters into the present system as much as that of labor. And besides, it is found that animals which are allowed one day in seven for rest live longer and enjoy better health than those which are worked without intermission. The same may, to a considerable degree, be said of man. The late Mr. Wilberforce attributed his length of life and the superiority of health which he enjoyed over his political contemporaries, mainly to his resolute and invariable observance of the Sabbath day; a duty which, unfortunately, they too frequently neglected.

I shall not go into the argument on this subject in detail, as the limits of the present work will not admit of it, but shall merely give what seem to me the results. To those who wish to examine the question of the obligation of the Sabbath at large, I would recommend the valuable treatise of Mr. J. J. Gurney, on the history, authority, and use of the Sabbath; from which much of the present article is merely an abridgment.

I. *Of the original institution of the Sabbath.*

First. The Divine authority for the institution of the Sabbath is found in *Genesis* ii, 1–3. "Thus, the heavens and the earth were finished, and all the hosts of them; and on the seventh day, God ended his work which He had made, and He rested on the seventh day from all his works which He had made. And God blessed the seventh day, and sanctified it; because that in it He had rested from all his work which God had created and made."

Now, concerning this passage, we remark

1. It was given to our first parents; that is, to the *whole human race.*

2. God *blessed* it; that is, bestowed upon it a peculiar blessing, or made it a source of peculiar blessings to man. Such, surely, must be that day which is given in order to cultivate in ourselves moral excellence and prepare us for the happiness of heaven. He *sanctified* it; that is, set it apart from a common to a sacred and religious use.

3. The *reason* is a general one: *God rested.* This has no reference to any peculiar people, but seems in the light of an example from God for all the human race.

4. The *nature* of the ordinance is general. God sanctified *it;* that is, the day. The act refers not to any particular people, but to the day itself.

5. The *object to be accomplished* is general, and can apply to no one people more than to another. If it be rest, all men equally need it. If it be moral cultivation, surely no people has ever existed who did not require such a means to render them better.

Secondly. There are indications that the hebdomadal division of time was observed by the patriarchs before the time of Moses, and that the Sabbath was regarded as the day for religious worship.

1. *Genesis* iv, 3. "And in process of time, it came to pass that Cain brought of the fruit of the ground an offering to the Lord." The words rendered "in process of time," literally signify "at the end of days;" or, "at the cutting off of days;" that is, as I think probable, at the close, as we should say, of a section of days; a very natural expression for the end of a week. If this be the meaning, it would seem to refer to the division of time just previously mentioned, and also to the use of this day for religious worship.

2. Noah seems to have observed the same hebdomadal division of time. The command to enter into the ark was given *seven* days before the flood came. *Genesis* vii, 4–10. So he allowed *seven* days to elapse between the times of sending forth the dove. *Genesis* viii, 10–12. Now I think that these intimations show that this division of time was observed according to the original command; and we may well suppose that with it was connected the special time for re-

ligious worship. Thus also, Joseph devoted *seven* days, or a whole week, to the mourning for his father.

3. The next mention of the Sabbath is shortly after the Israelites had left Egypt, and were fed with manna in the wilderness. *Exodus* xvi, 22–30. As the passage is of considerable length, I need not quote it. I would, however, remark—

1. It occurs before the giving of the law; and, therefore, the obligatoriness of the Sabbath is hereby acknowledged, irrespective of the Mosaic law.

2. When first alluded to, it is spoken of as a thing known. God first, without referring to the Sabbath, informs Moses that on the sixth day the Israelites should gather twice as much manna as on any other day. From this it seems that the division of time by weeks was known and that it was taken for granted that they would know the reason for the making of this distinction. In the whole of the narration there is no precept given for the keeping of the day; but they are reproved for not suitably keeping it, as though it were an institution *with which they ought to have been* familiar.

Besides these, there are many indications in the earliest classics that the Greeks and Romans observed the hebdomadal division of time; and also that the seventh day was considered peculiarly sacred. This seems to have been the case in the time of Hesiod. The same is supposed to have been the fact in regard to the northern nations of Europe, from which we are immediately descended. The inference which seems naturally to arise from these facts is that this institution was originally observed by the whole human race; and that it was transmitted, with different degrees of care, by different nations, until the period of the commencement of our various historical records.

From the above facts, I think we are warranted in the conclusion that the seventh day, or perhaps generally, the seventh part of time, was originally set apart for a religious purpose by our Creator for the whole human race; that it was so observed by the Hebrews, previously to the giving of the law; and that, probably, the observance was, in the infancy of our race, universal.

II. *The Mosaic Sabbath.*

The precept for the observance of the Sabbath at the giving of the law is in these words: "Remember the Sabbath day, to keep it holy. Six days shalt thou labor, and do all thy work; but the seventh is the Sabbath of the Lord thy God; in it, thou shalt not do any work, thou, nor thy son, nor thy daughter, nor thy man-servant, nor thy maid-servant, nor thy cattle, nor thy stranger that is within thy gates; for in six days the Lord made heaven and earth, the sea, and all that in them is, and rested the seventh day. Wherefore the Lord blessed the seventh day, and hallowed it." *Exodus* xx, 11.

Now concerning this precept there are several things worthy of remark:

1. It is found in the law of the *ten commandments,* which is always referred to in the Scriptures as containing the sum of the moral precepts of God to man. Our Saviour and the Apostles, who made the most decided distinction between moral and ceremonial observances, never allude to the law of the ten commandments in any other manner than as of permanent and universal obligation. Now I know of no reason which can be assigned, why this precept should be detached from all the rest and considered as *ceremonial,* when the whole of these, taken together, are allowed by universal consent to have been quoted as moral precepts by Christ and his Apostles. Besides, our Saviour expressly declares that *"the Sabbath was made for* MAN*,"* that is, for man in general, for the whole human race; and consequently, that it is binding upon the whole race, that is, that it is a precept of universal obligation.

2. The reasons given for observing it are the same as those given at the time of its first institution. Inasmuch as these reasons are in their nature general, we should naturally conclude that the obligation which it imposes is universal.

3. This commandment is frequently referred to by the prophets as one of high moral obligation; the most solemn threatenings are uttered against those who profane it; and the greatest rewards promised to those who keep it. See *Isaiah* lvi, 2–6; *Jeremiah* xvii, 24, 25; *Nehemiah* xiii, 15–21.

4. In addition to rest from labor, the meeting together for wor-

ship and the reading of the Scriptures was made a part of the duty of the Sabbath day. Six days shall work be done; but the seventh is the Sabbath of rest; *a holy convocation. Leviticus* xxiii, 3. Thus also, Moses, of old time, hath, in every city, them that *preach him, being read in the synagogues every Sabbath day. Acts* xv, 21.

Besides this re-enaction of the Sabbath day in the Mosaic law, there were special additions made to its observance which belong to the Jews alone, and which were a part of their civil or ceremonial law. With this view other reasons were given for observing it and other rites were added. Thus for instance—

1. It was intended to distinguish them from the surrounding idolatrous nations. *Exodus* xxxi, 12–17.

2. It was a memorial of their deliverance from Egypt. *Deuteronomy* v, 15.

3. And with these views, the principle of devoting the seventh part of time was extended also to years; every seventh year being a year of rest.

4. The violation of the Sabbath was punished with death by the civil magistrate.

Now whatever is in its nature local, and designed for a particular purpose, ceases whenever that purpose is accomplished. Hence these civil and ceremonial observances cease with the termination of the Jewish polity; while that which is moral and universal, that which "was made for man" and not specially for the Jews, remains as though the ceremonial observances had never existed. I think that this view of the subject is also confirmed by the example and precept of Christ, who gave directions concerning the manner in which the Sabbath was to be kept and also was himself accustomed to observe the day for the purposes of religious worship. *"As his custom was,* he went into the synagogue on the Sabbath day, and *stood up to read." Luke* iv, 16. See also *Matthew* xii, 2–13. When our Lord also, in teaching the mode in which the Sabbath is to be kept, specifies what things it is *lawful* to do on the Sabbath day, he clearly proceeds upon the principle that it was lawful to do things on *other days* which it would not be lawful to do on *the Sabbath day*.

III. *The Christian Sabbath.*

We shall consider here 1st, The day on which the Christian Sabbath is to be kept; 2d, The manner in which it is to be kept.

FIRST. The day on which the Christian Sabbath is to be kept.

First. There are indications from the facts which transpired on that day, that it was to be specially honored under the new dispensation.

1. Our Saviour arose on that day from the dead, having accomplished the work of man's redemption.

2. On this day he appeared to his Apostles, a week from his resurrection, at which time he had his conversation with Thomas.

3. On this day also, occurred the feast of Pentecost, when the Spirit was in so remarkable a manner poured out, and when the new dispensation emphatically commenced.

Second. That the primitive Christians, in the days of the Apostles, were accustomed to observe this day as their day of weekly worship, is evident from several passages in the New Testament and also from the earliest ecclesiastical records.

1. That the early disciples, in all places, were accustomed to meet statedly to worship and celebrate the Lord's Supper is evident from 1 *Corinthians* xi, 1, 14, 20, 23, 40. And that these meetings were on the first day of the week may be gathered from 1 *Corinthians* xvi, 1, 2.

2. That these meetings were held on the first day of the week is also further evident from *Acts* xx, 6–11; where we are informed that in Troas the Christians met on the first day of the week to break bread (that is, to celebrate the Lord's Supper), and to receive religious instruction. From these passages we see that this custom had already become universal not merely in the neighborhood of Jerusalem but throughout the regions in which the Christian religion was promulgated.

3. Again (*Revelations* i, 10), it is observed by John, "I was in the Spirit *on the Lord's day.*" From this remark it is probable that John kept this day with peculiar solemnity. It is certain that the day had already obtained a particular name; *a name* by which it has continued to be distinguished in every subsequent age.

Besides these allusions to the day from the New Testament, there are various facts bearing upon the subject from uninspired historians.

1. The early fathers frequently refer to this day as the day set apart for religious worship; and allude to the difference between keeping this day and keeping the seventh, or Jewish Sabbath, specially on the ground of its being the day of our Saviour's resurrection.

2. Pliny, in his letter to Trajan, remarks that the Christians "were accustomed, on a *stated day,* to meet before day-light, and to repeat among themselves a hymn to Christ, as to a God, and to bind themselves, by a sacred obligation, not to commit any wickedness, but, on the contrary, to abstain from thefts, robberies and adulteries; also, not to violate their promise, or deny a pledge; after which, it was their custom to separate, and meet again at a promiscuous and harmless meal." It is needless here to remark the exact coincidence between this account from the pen of a heathen magistrate with the account given of the keeping of the day in the passages where it is mentioned in the New Testament.

3. That this stated day was the first day of the week, or the Lord's day, is evident from another testimony. So well known was the custom of the early Christians on this subject that the ordinary question put by their persecutors to the Christian martyrs was, "Hast thou kept the Lord's day?" *Dominicum servasti?* To which the usual answer was, "I am a Christian: I cannot omit it." *Christianus sum: intermittere non possum.*

4. It is, however, manifest that the Jews, who were strongly inclined to blend the rites of Moses with the Christian religion, at first kept the seventh day; or, what is very probable, at first kept both days. The Apostles declared that the disciples of Jesus were not under obligation to observe the seventh day. See *Colossians* ii, 16, 17. Now as the observance of the Sabbath is a precept given to the whole human race; as it is repeated in the Mosaic law as a moral precept; as the authority of this precept is recognized both by the teaching and example of Christ and his Apostles; as the Apostles teach that the keeping of the *seventh day is not obligatory;* and as they did keep

the *first day* as a day of *religious worship;* it seems reasonable to conclude that they intended to teach that the first day was that which we are, as Christians, to observe.

5. From these considerations, we feel warranted to conclude that the first day of the week *was actually kept* by the inspired Apostles as the Christian Sabbath. Their example is sufficient to teach us that the keeping of *this* day is acceptable to God; and we are, on this ground, at *liberty to keep it* as the Sabbath. If, however, any other person be dissatisfied with these reasons and feel under obligation to observe the seventh day, I see no precept in the word of God to forbid him.

6. If, however, as seems to me to be the case, both days are allowable; that is, if I have sufficient reason to believe that either is acceptable to God; but if by observing the first day, I can enjoy more perfect leisure and suffer less interruption and thus better accomplish the object of the day; and if, besides, I have the example of inspired Apostles in favor of this observance; I should decidedly prefer to observe the first day. Nay, I should consider the choice of that day as obligatory. For if I am allowed to devote either day to the worship of God, it is surely obligatory on me to worship God on that day on which I can best accomplish the very object for which the day was set apart.

If it be asked when this day is to begin, I answer that I presume we are at liberty to commence this day at the same time that we commence other days; for the obvious reason that thus we can generally enjoy the quiet of the Sabbath with less interruption.

SECONDLY. Of the *manner in which the Christian Sabbath is to be observed.*

The design for which the Sabbath was instituted I suppose to be, to set apart a portion of our time for the uninterrupted worship of God and the preparation of our souls for eternity; and also to secure to man and beast one day in seven as a season of rest from labor.

Hence the law of the Sabbath forbids,

1. All *labor* of body or mind of which the immediate object is not the worship of God or our own religious improvement. The only exceptions to this rule are works of necessity or of mercy. The

necessity, however, must be one which is imposed by the providence of God, and not by our own will. Thus a ship, when on a voyage, may sail on the Sabbath as well as on any other day without violating the rule. The rule, however, would be violated by *commencing* the voyage on the Sabbath, because here a choice of days is in the power of the master.

2. The pursuit *of pleasure,* or of any animal, or merely intellectual gratification. Hence the indulgence of our appetites in such manner as to prevent us from free and buoyant spiritual contemplation, riding or journeying for amusement, the merely social pleasure of visiting, the reading of books designed for the gratification of the taste or of the imagination, are all, by the principles of the command, forbidden.

3. The labor of those committed to our charge.

1. The labor of *servants.* Their souls are of as much value as our own and they need the benefit of this law as much as ourselves. Besides, if this portion of their time be claimed by our Creator, we have no right to purchase it, nor have they a right to negotiate it away. Works of necessity must, of course, be performed; but these should be restricted within the limits prescribed by a conscientious regard to the object and design of the day.

2. *Brutes* are, by the fourth commandment, included in the law which ordains rest to all the animate creation. They need the repose which it grants and they are entitled to their portion of it.

On the contrary, the law of the Sabbath enjoins *the employment of the day in the more solemn and immediate duties of religion.*

1. Reading the Scriptures, religious meditation, prayer in private, and also the special instruction in religion of those committed to our charge. And hence it enjoins such domestic arrangements as are consistent with these duties.

2. Social worship. Under the Mosaic and Christian dispensation this was an important part of the duties of the day. As the setting apart of a particular day to be universally observed involves the idea of social as well as personal religion, one of the most obvious duties which it imposes is that of social worship; that is, of meeting together in societies to return thanks for our social mercies, to implore

the pardon of God for our social sins, and beseech His favor for those blessings which we need as societies no less than as individuals.

The importance of the religious observance of the Sabbath is seldom sufficiently estimated. Every attentive observer has remarked that the violation of this command by the young is one of the most decided marks of incipient moral degeneracy. Religious restraint is fast losing its hold upon that young man who, having been educated in the fear of God, begins to spend the Sabbath in idleness or in amusement. And so also of communities. The desecration of the Sabbath is one of those evident indications of that criminal reckless-ness, that insane love of pleasure, and that subjection to the govern-ment of appetite and passion which forebodes that the "beginning of the end" of social happiness and of true national prosperity has arrived.

Hence we see how imperative is the duty of parents and of legislators on this subject. The head of every family is obliged, by the command of God, not only to honor this day himself, but to use all the means in his power to secure the observance of it by all those committed to his charge. He is thus promoting not only his own but also his children's happiness; for nothing is a more sure antago-nist force to all the allurements of vice, as nothing tends more strongly to fix in the minds of the young a conviction of the existence and attributes of God than the solemn keeping of this day. And hence also, legislators are false to their trust who, either by the enact-ment of laws, or by their example, diminish in the least degree in the minds of a people the reverence due to that day which God has set apart for Himself.

The only question which remains is the following:

Is it the duty of the civil magistrate to enforce the observance of the Sabbath?

We are inclined to think not, and for the following reasons:

1. The duty arises solely from our relations to God, and not from our relations to man. Now our duties to God are never to be placed within the control of human legislation.

2. If the civil magistrate has a right to take cognizance of this duty to God, he has a right to take cognizance of every other. And if

he have a right to take cognizance of the duty, he has a right to prescribe in what manner it shall be discharged; or, if he sees fit, to forbid the observance of it altogether. The concession of this right would, therefore, lead to direct interference with liberty of conscience.

3. The keeping of the Sabbath is a *moral* duty. Hence if it be acceptably observed, it must be a voluntary service. But the civil magistrate can never do anything more than produce obedience to the external precept; which, in the sight of God, would not be the keeping of the Sabbath at all. Hence to allow the civil magistrate to enforce the observance of the Sabbath would be to surrender to him the control over the conscience, without attaining even the object for which the surrender was made.

4. It is, however, the duty of the civil magistrate to protect every individual in the undisturbed right of worshipping God as he pleases. This protection every individual has a right to claim, and society is under obligation to extend it. And also, as this is a leisure day, and is liable to various abuses, the magistrate has a right to prevent any modes of gratification which would tend to disturb the peace of society. This right is acknowledged in regulations respecting other days of leisure or rejoicing; and there can be no reason why it should not be exercised in respect to the Sabbath.

5. And lastly, the law of the Sabbath applies equally to societies and to individuals. An individual is forbidden to labor on the Sabbath or to *employ another person to labor for him*. The rule is the same when applied to any number of individuals; that is, to a society. Hence a society has no right to employ persons to labor for them. The contract is a violation of the Sabbatical law. It is on this ground that I consider the carrying of the mail on this day a social violation of the Christian Sabbath.

IT has been already observed that our duties, to both God and man, are all enforced by the obligation of love to God. By this we mean that in consequence of our moral constitution, we are under obligation to love our fellow men, because they are our fellow men; and we are also under obligation to love them because we have been commanded to love them by our Father who is in heaven. The nature of this obligation may be illustrated by a familiar example. Every child in a family is under obligation to love its parent. And every child is bound to love its brother both because *he is its brother,* and also, because this love is a duty enforced by the relation in *which they both stand to their common parent.*

The relation in which men stand to each other is essentially the relation of *equality; not equality of condition,* but *equality of right.*

Every human being is a distinct and separately accountable individual. To each one God has given just such means of happiness and placed him under just such circumstances for improving those means of happiness, as it has pleased him. To one he has given wealth; to another, intellect; to another, physical strength; to another, health; and to all in different degrees. In all these respects, the human race presents a scene of the greatest possible diversity. So far as natural advantages are concerned, we can scarcely find two individuals who are not created under circumstances widely dissimilar.

But viewed in another light, all men are placed under circumstances of *perfect equality.* Each separate individual is created with precisely *the same right to use* the advantages with which God has endowed him as every other individual. This proposition seems to me in its nature so self-evident as almost to preclude the possibility of argument.[13] The only reason that I can conceive on which anyone could found a plea for *inequality of* [14] *right,* must be *inequality of condition.* But this can manifestly create no diversity of *right.* I may have been endowed with better eyesight than my neighbor; but this evidently gives me no right to put out his eyes or to interfere with his right to derive from them whatever of happiness the Creator has placed within his power. I may have greater muscular strength than my neighbor; but this gives me no right to break his arms or to diminish in any manner his ability to use them for the production of his own happiness. Besides, this supposition involves direct and manifest contradiction. For the principle asserted is that superiority of condition confers superiority of right. But if this be true, then every kind of superiority of condition must confer correspondent superiority of right. Superiority in muscular strength must confer it as much as superiority of intellect or of wealth; and must confer it in the ratio of that superiority. In that case, if A, on the ground of intellectual superiority, have a right to improve his own means of happiness by diminishing those which the Creator has given to B, B would have the same right over A, on the ground of superiority of muscular strength; while C would have a correspondent right over them both, on the ground of superiority of wealth; and so on indefinitely; and these rights would change every day, according to the relative situation of the respective parties. That is to say, as right is, in its nature, exclusive, all the men in the universe have an exclusive right to the same thing; while the right of every one absolutely annihilates that of every other. What is the meaning of such an assertion, I leave it for others to determine.

But let us look at man in another point of light.

1. We find all men possessed of the same appetites and passions, that is, of the same desire for external objects and the same capacity for receiving happiness from the gratification of these desires. We do not say that all men possess them all in an equal degree; but

---

[13] The 1865 edition has the following inserted sentences: "The truth that every man has a right to himself can hardly be rendered more evident by argument. It is of the nature of a moral maxim."

[14] The 1865 edition: "right—that is, for a right in one man to appropriate the faculties and means of happiness of another—must"

only that all men actually possess them all and that their happiness depends upon the gratification of them.

2. These appetites and passions are created, so far as they themselves are exclusively concerned, without limit. Gratification generally renders them both more intense and more numerous. Such is the case with the love of wealth, the love of power, the love of sensual pleasure, or with any of the others.

3. These desires *may be* gratified in such a manner as *not to interfere* with the right which every other man has over his own means of happiness. Thus I may gratify my love of wealth by industry and frugality while I conduct myself towards every other man with entire honesty. I may gratify my love of science without diminishing in any respect the means of knowledge possessed by another. And, on the other hand, I am created with the *physical power* to gratify my desires in such a *manner as to interfere* with the right which another has over the means of happiness which God has given him. Thus I have a physical power to gratify my love of property by stealing the property of another, as well as to gratify it by earning property for myself. I have, by the gift of speech, the physical power to ruin the reputation of another for the sake of gratifying my own love of approbation. I have the physical power to murder a man for the sake of using his body to gratify my love of anatomical knowledge. And so of a thousand cases.

4. And hence we see that the relation in which human beings stand to each other is the following: Every individual is created with a desire to use the means of happiness which God has given him in such a manner as he thinks will best promote that happiness; and of this manner he is the sole judge. Every individual is endowed with the same desires, which he *may gratify* in such a manner as will *not* interfere with his neighbor's means of happiness: but each individual has, also, the *physical power* of so gratifying his desires as *will* interfere with the means of happiness which God has granted to his neighbor.

5. From this relation it is manifest that every man is under obligation to pursue his own happiness in such a manner *only* as will leave his neighbor in the undisturbed exercise of that common right

which the Creator has equally conferred upon both, that is, to restrain his physical power of gratifying his desires within such limits that he shall interfere with the rights of no other being, because in no other manner can the evident design of the Creator, the common happiness of all, be promoted.

That this is the law of our being may be shown from several considerations:

1. By violating it, the happiness of the aggressor is not increased, while that of the sufferer is diminished; while by obeying it, the greatest amount of happiness of which our condition is susceptible is secured; because by obeying it, everyone derives the greatest possible advantage from the gifts bestowed upon him by the Creator.

2. Suppose any other rule of obligation; that is, that a man is not under obligation to observe, with this exactitude, the rights of his neighbor. Where shall the limit be fixed? If violation be allowed in a small degree, why not in a great degree? and if he may interfere with one right, why not with all? And as all men come under the same law this principle would lead to the same absurdity as that of which we have before spoken; that is, it would abolish the very idea of right and, as everyone has an equal liberty of violation, would surrender the whole race to the dominion of unrestrained desire.

3. If it be said that one class of men is not under the obligation to observe this rule in its conduct towards another class of men, then it will be necessary to show that the second class are not men, that is, human beings; for these principles apply to men, as men; and the simple fact that a being is a man places him within reach of these obligations and of their protection. Nay, more, suppose the inferior class of beings were not *truly men;* if they were intelligent moral agents I suppose that we should be under the same obligation to conduct ourselves towards them upon the principle of reciprocity. I see no reason why an angel would have a right by virtue of his superior nature to interfere with the means of happiness which God has conferred upon man. By parity of reasoning, therefore, superiority of rank would give to man no such power over an inferior species of moral and intelligent beings.

And lastly, if it be true that the Creator has given to every separate individual, control over those means of happiness which He has bestowed upon him, then the simple question is, Which is of the highest authority, this grant of the Creator, or the desires and passions of the creature? for these are really the notions which are brought into collision. That is to say, ought the grant of God and the will of God, to limit my desires; or ought my desires to vitiate the grant and set at defiance the will of God? On this question a moral and intelligent creature can entertain but one opinion.

Secondly. Let us examine the teaching of the Holy Scriptures on this subject.

The precept in the Bible is in these words: "Thou shalt love thy neighbor as thyself."

Two questions are here to be considered. First, To whom does this command apply; or in other words, Who is my neighbor? and secondly, What is implied in the precept?

1. The first of these questions is answered by our Saviour himself in the parable of the good Samaritan. *Luke* x, 25–37. He there teaches us that we are to consider as our neighbor, not our kinsman or our fellow citizen or those to whom we are bound by the reception of previous kindness, but the stranger, the alien, the hereditary national enemy; that is, *man as man;* any human being to whom we may in any manner do good. Every *man* is our *neighbor* and therefore we are under obligation to *love every man as ourselves.*

2. What is the import of the command to love such a one as ourselves?

The very lowest meaning that we can assign to this precept is as follows. I have already stated that God has bestowed upon every man such means of happiness as in his own sovereign pleasure he saw fit; and that he has given to every man an equal right to use those means of happiness as each one supposes will best promote his own well-being. Besides this, everyone has an instinctive desire thus to use them. He cannot be happy unless this desire be gratified and he is painfully conscious of injury if this right be interfered with. In this manner, he loves himself. Now in the same manner he is commanded to love his neighbor. That is, he is by this precept obliged to have the same desire that his neighbor should enjoy, unmolested, the control over whatever God has bestowed upon him, as he has to enjoy, unmolested, the same control himself; and to feel the same consciousness of injury when another man's rights are invaded as when his own rights are invaded. With these sentiments he would be just as unwilling to violate the rights of another as he would be to suffer a violation of his own. That this view of the subject exhausts the command we by no means assert; but we think it evident that the language is capable of a *no less comprehensive* meaning.

The same precept is expressed in other places under another form of language: "All things whatsoever ye would that men should do unto you, do ye even so unto them; for this is the law and the prophets." *Matthew* vii, 12.

The words here, as in the former case, are used to denote a principle of universal obligation: "*All things whatsoever* ye would that men should do unto you, *do ye even so* unto them.*"

The precept itself teaches us to estimate the rights of others by the consciousness of individual right in our own bosoms. Would we wish to know how delicate a regard we are bound to entertain toward the control which God has given to others over the means of happiness which He has granted to them, let us decide the question by asking how tender and delicate is the regard which we would wish them to entertain toward us under similar circumstances. The decision of the one question will always be the decision of the other. And this precept goes a step farther. It renders it obligatory on every man to *commence* such a course of conduct irrespectively of whatever may be the conduct of others to himself. It forbids us to demand more than the law of reciprocity allows; it commands us always to render it; and still more, if we complain to another of his violation of the law, it renders it imperative on us, while we urge upon him a change of conduct, to commence by setting him the example. And it really, if carried out to the utmost, would preclude our claim upon him until we had ourselves first manifested toward him the very disposition which we demand toward ourselves. The moral beauty of this precept will be at once seen by anyone who will take the trouble, honestly, to generalize it. He will immediately perceive that it would always avert injury at the very outset; and by rendering both parties more virtuous would tend directly to banish injury and violence and wrong from the earth.

Thirdly. This law of universal reciprocity applies with the same force to communities as to individuals.

Communities are composed of individuals and can have *in respect to each other* no other rights than those of the individuals who constitute them. If it be wrong for one man to injure another man it must be equally wrong for two men to injure two other men; and so of any other number. And moreover, the grant of the Creator is in both cases under the same circumstances. God has bestowed upon nations physical and intellectual advantages in every possible degree of diversity. But He has granted to them all an equal right to use those advantages in such manner as each one may suppose will best conduce to the promotion of his own happiness.

Hence it will follow—

1. That the precept applies as *universally* to nations as to individuals. Whenever societies of men treat with each other; whether powerful with weak or polite with rude, civilized with savage or intelligent with ignorant; whichever, friends with friends or enemies with enemies; *all* are bound by the law of reciprocity to love each other as themselves and to do unto others *in all things* whatsoever they would desire others to do unto them.

2. And hence also, *the precept itself* is as obligatory upon nations as upon individuals. Every nation is bound to exhibit as sensitive a regard for the preservation inviolate of the rights of another nation as it exhibits for the preservation inviolate of its own rights. And still more, every nation is under the same obligation as every individual to measure the respect and moderation which it displays to others by the respect and moderation which it demands for itself; and is also, if it complain of violation of right, to set the first example of entire and perfect reciprocity and fidelity. Were this course pursued by individuals and nations, the causes of collision would manifestly cease and the appeal to arms would soon be remembered only as one of the strange infatuations of bygone, barbarous, and bloodthirsty ages. Chicanery and intrigue and overreaching are as wicked

and as disgraceful in the intercourse of nations and societies as in that of individuals; and the tool of a nation or of a party is as truly contemptible as the tool of an individual. The only distinction which I perceive is that in the one case, the instrument of dishonesty is ashamed of his act and dare not wear the badge of his infamy; while in the other case, even the ambiguous virtue of shame has been lost, and the man glories in the brand which marks him for a villain.

CLASSIFICATION OF THE DUTIES ARISING FROM THE LAW OF RECIPROCITY

The duties of reciprocity may be divided into three classes:

Class 1. DUTIES TO MEN AS MEN.

Class 2. DUTIES ARISING FROM THE CONSTITUTION OF THE SEXES.

Class 3. DUTIES ARISING FROM THE CONSTITUTION OF CIVIL SOCIETY.

Class 1. DUTIES TO MEN AS MEN.

This includes Justice and Veracity.

I. *Justice* as it regards, 1. Liberty.
2. Property.
3. Character.
4. Reputation.

II. *Veracity*. 1. Of the past and present.
2. Of the future.

Class 2. DUTIES ARISING FROM THE CONSTITUTION OF THE SEXES.

Including, 1. General duty of chastity.
2. The law of marriage.
3. The duties and rights of parents.
4. The duties and rights of children.

Class 3. DUTIES ARISING FROM THE CONSTITUTION OF CIVIL SOCIETY.

1. The nature of civil society.
2. The mode in which the authority of civil society is maintained.
3. Of forms of government.
4. Duties of magistrates.
5. Duties of citizens.

Justice, when used in a judicial sense, signifies that temper of mind which disposes a man to administer rewards and punishments according to the character and actions of the object.

It is also used to designate the act by which this administration is effected. Thus we speak of a judge, who administers justice.

In the present case, however, it is used in a more extensive signification. It is here intended to designate that temper of mind which disposes us to leave every other being in the unmolested enjoyment of those means of happiness bestowed upon him by his Creator. It is also frequently used for the exhibition of this conduct in outward act. Thus when a man manifests a proper respect for the rights of others, we say he acts justly; when he in any manner violates these rights, we say he acts unjustly.

The most important means of happiness which God has placed in the power of the individual are, first, HIS OWN PERSON; second, PROPERTY; third, CHARACTER; fourth, REPUTATION.

CHAPTER FIRST

PERSONAL LIBERTY

Section I · Of the Nature of Personal Liberty

EVERY human being is, by his constitution, a separate and distinct and complete system, adapted to all the purposes of self-government and responsible, separately, to God for the manner in which his powers are employed. Thus every individual possesses a body, by which he is connected with the physical universe, and by which that universe is modified for the supply of his wants; an understanding, by which truth is discovered, and by which means are adapted to their appropriate ends; passions and desires, by which he is excited to action, and in the gratification of which his happiness consists; conscience, to point out the limit within which these desires may be rightfully gratified; and a will, which determines him to action.

The possession of these is necessary to a human nature and it also renders every being so constituted a distinct and independent individual. He may need society, but every *one* needs it equally with *every other one;* and hence all enter into it upon terms of strict and evident reciprocity. If the individual use these powers according to the laws imposed by his Creator, his Creator holds him guiltless. If he use them in such manner as not to interfere with the use of the same powers which God has bestowed upon his neighbor, he is as it respects his neighbor, whether that neighbor be an individual or the community, to be held guiltless. So long as he uses them within this limit he has a right, so far as his fellow men are concerned, to use them in the most unlimited sense, *suo arbitrio,* at his own discretion. His will is his sufficient and ultimate reason. He need assign no other reason for his conduct than his own free choice. Within this limit he is still responsible to God; but within this limit he is not responsible *to man,* nor *is man responsible for him.*[15]

1. Thus a man has an entire right to use his own *body* as he will, provided he do not so use it as to interfere with the rights of his neighbor. He may go where he will and stay where he please; he may work or be idle; he may pursue one occupation or another or no occupation at all; and it is the concern of no one else, if he leave inviolate the rights of everyone else; that is, if he leave everyone else in the undisturbed enjoyment of those means of happiness bestowed upon him by the Creator.

It seems almost trifling to argue a point which is, in its nature, so evident upon inspection. If, however, any additional proof be required, the following considerations will readily suggest themselves. It is asserted that every individual has an equal and ultimate right with every other individual, to the use of his body, his mind, and all the other means of happiness with which God has endowed him. But suppose it otherwise. Suppose that one individual has a right to the body or mind or means of happiness of another. That is, suppose that A has a right to use the body of B according to his, that is, A's, *will.* Now if this be true it is true universally; hence, A

---

[15] The 1865 edition has the following inserted sentence: "In other words, every man has a right to himself."

has the control over the body of B, and B has control over the body of C, C of that of D, &c., and Z again over the body of A; that is, every separate will has the right of control over some other body or intellect besides its own, and has no right of control over its own body or intellect. Whether such is the constitution of human nature, or, if it be not, whether it would be an improvement upon the present constitution, may be easily decided.

And if it be said that to control one man's body by another man's will is impossible for that every man acts as he will, since he cannot do anything unless he *will* do it, it may be answered that the term *will* is used here in a different sense from that intended in the preceding paragraph. Everyone must see that a man who, out of the various ways of employing his body set *before him by his Creator,* chooses that which he prefers is in a very different condition from him who is debarred from all choice excepting that he may do what his fellow man appoints, or else must suffer what his fellow man chooses to inflict. Now the true condition of a human being is that in which his will is influenced by no other circumstances than those which arise from the constitution under which his Creator has placed him. And he who for his own pleasure places his fellow man under any other conditions of existence, is guilty of the most odious tyranny, and seems to me to arrogate to himself the authority of the Most High God.

But it may be said that in this case the individual may become chargeable to the community. To this I answer, not unless the community *assume* the charge. If every man be left to himself but is obliged to respect the rights of others; if he do not labor, a remedy is provided in the laws of the system—he will very soon starve; and if he prefer starvation to labor he has no one to blame but himself. While the law of reciprocity frees him from the control of society, it discharges society from any responsibility for the result of his actions upon himself. I know that society undertakes to support the indigent and helpless and to relieve men in extreme necessity. This, however, is a conventional arrangement into which men who choose have a right to enter; and having entered into it, they are bound by its provisions. If they become responsible for the support of the individual's life they have a right over his power of labor to an extent sufficient to cover that responsibility. And he who has become a member of such a society has surrendered voluntarily his control over his body *to this amount*. But as he has done it *voluntarily*, such a convention proceeds upon the concession that the *original right* vests in the individual.

2. The same remarks apply to the use of the *intellect*.

If the preceding observations are just it will follow that every man, within the limit before suggested, has a right to use his intellect as he will. He may investigate whatever subjects he will and in what manner soever he will and may come to such conclusions as his investigations may teach and may publish those conclusions to those who are willing to hear them, provided he interfere with the happiness of no other human being. The denial of this right would lead to the same absurdities as in the former case.

If it be said that the individual may by so doing involve himself in error and thus diminish his own happiness, the answer is at hand, namely, for this the constitution of things provides its appropriate and adequate punishment. He who imbibes error suffers in his own person the consequences of error, which are misfortune and loss of respect. And besides, as for his happiness society is not in this case responsible: there can be no reason derived from the consideration of *his happiness* why society should interfere with the free use of this instrument of happiness, which the Creator has intrusted solely to the individual himself.

But it may be asked, has not society a right to oblige men to acquire a certain amount of intellectual cultivation? I answer, men have a right to form a society upon such conditions as they please; [16] and, of course, so to form it that it shall be necessary in order to enjoy its privileges for the individual to possess a certain amount of knowledge. Having formed such a society, everyone is bound by its provisions so long as he remains a member of it; and the enforcing of its provisions upon the individual is no more than obliging him to do what he, for a sufficient consideration, voluntarily contracted to

---

[16] The 1865 edition: "please, subject always to the social laws under which God has placed us; and so to"

do. And society may rightfully enforce this provision in either of two ways: it may either withhold from every man who neglects to acquire this knowledge the benefits of citizenship; or else it may grant these benefits to everyone and oblige everyone to possess the assigned amount of knowledge. In this case there is no violation of reciprocity; for the same requirements are made of all and everyone receives his full equivalent in the results of the same law upon others. More than this the individual could not justly require. He could not justly demand to be admitted to rights which presuppose certain intellectual attainments, and which can only be, with safety to others, enjoyed by those who have made these attainments, unless he be willing to conform to the condition necessary to that enjoyment.[17]

3. I have thus far considered man only in his relations to the present life. So far as I have gone I have endeavored to show that provided the individual interfere not with the rights of others, he has a right to use his own body and mind as he thinks will best promote his own happiness; that is, as he will. But if he have this right, within these limits, to pursue his *present happiness,* how much more incontrovertible must be his right to use his body and mind in such manner, as he supposes will best promote his eternal happiness! And besides, if for the sake of his own happiness he have a right to the unmolested enjoyment of whatever God has given him, how much more is he entitled to the same unmolested enjoyment for the sake of obeying God, and fulfilling the highest obligation of which he is susceptible!

We say, then, that every man, provided he does not interfere with the rights of his neighbor, has a right, so far as his neighbor is concerned, to worship God or not to worship him; and to worship him in any manner that he will, and that for the abuse of this liberty he is accountable only to God.

If it be said that by so doing a man may ruin his own soul, the answer is obvious; for this ruin the individual himself, and not *society,* is responsible. And moreover, as religion consists in the temper of heart, which force cannot affect—and not in external

[17] See Appendix (G) for additional passage in the 1865 edition.

observance, which is all that force can affect—no application of force can change our relations to God or prevent the ruin in question. All application of force must then be gratuitous mischief.

To sum up what has been said—all men are created with an equal right to employ their faculties of body or of mind in such a manner as will promote their own happiness, either here or hereafter; or, which is the same thing, every man has a right to use his own powers of body or of mind in such a manner as he will; provided he do not use them in such manner as to interfere with the rights of his neighbor.

The exceptions to this law are easily defined.

1. The first exception is in the case of infancy.

By the law of nature a parent is under obligation to support his child and is responsible for his actions. He has, therefore, a right to control the actions of the child so long as this responsibility exists. He is under obligation to render that child a suitable member of the community; and this obligation he could not discharge unless the physical and intellectual liberty of the child were placed within his power.

2. As the parent has supported the child during infancy, he has, probably, by the law of nature, a right to his services during youth or for so long a period as may be sufficient to insure an adequate remuneration. When, however, this remuneration is received, the right of the parent over the child ceases forever.

3. This right he may, if he sees fit, transfer to another, as in the case of apprenticeship. But he can transfer the right for no longer time than he holds it. He can, therefore, negotiate it away for no period beyond that of the child's minority.

4. A man may transfer his right over his own labor for a limited time and for a satisfactory equivalent. But this transfer proceeds upon the principle that the original right vests in himself and it is, therefore, no violation of that right. He has, however, no right to transfer the services of any other person except his child; nor of his child except under the limitations above specified.

In strict accordance with these remarks is the memorable sentence in the commencement of the Declaration of Independence, "We hold these truths to be self-evident: that all men are created equal; that they are endowed by their Creator with certain inalienable rights; that among these are life, liberty, and the pursuit of happiness." That the equality here spoken of is not of the means of happiness, but in the right to use them as we will, is too evident to need illustration.

Section II · Modes in Which Personal Liberty May Be Violated[18]

Personal liberty may be violated in two ways: 1. By the individual; 2. By society.

PART FIRST. *Of the violation of personal liberty by the* INDIVIDUAL. The most common violation of personal liberty under this head is that which exists in the case of *Domestic Slavery.*

Domestic slavery proceeds upon the principle that the master has a right to control the actions, physical and intellectual, of the slave for his own, that is, the master's, individual benefit; and of course, that the happiness of the master, when it comes in competition with the happiness of the slave, extinguishes in the latter the right to pursue it. It supposes, at best, that the relation between master and slave is not that which exists between man and man, but is a modification, at least, of that which exists between man and the brutes.

Now this manifestly supposes that the two classes of beings are created with dissimilar rights: that the master possesses rights which have never been conceded by the slave; and that the slave has no rights at all over the means of happiness which God has given him whenever these means of happiness can be rendered available to the service of the master. It supposes that the Creator intended one human being to govern the physical, intellectual, and moral actions of as many other human beings as by purchase he can bring within his physical power; and that one human being may thus acquire a right to sacrifice the happiness of any number of other human beings for the purpose of promoting his own.

Slavery thus violates the personal liberty of man as a *physical, intellectual,* and *moral being.*

[18] See Appendix (H) for version of Section II in the 1865 edition, entitled "Of the Violation of Personal Liberty By the Individual."

1. It purports to give to the master a right to control the *physical* labor of the slave not for the sake of the happiness of the slave, nor upon terms mutually satisfactory to the parties, but for the sake of the happiness of the master. It subjects the amount of labor, and the kind of labor and the remuneration for labor entirely to the will of the one party to the entire exclusion of the will of the other party.

2. But if this right in the master over the slave be conceded, there are of course conceded with it all other rights necessary to insure its possession. Hence inasmuch as the slave can be held in this condition only while he remains in a state of comparative mental imbecility, it supposes the master to have the right to control his intellectual development just as far as may be necessary to secure entire subjection. Thus it supposes the slave to have no right to use his intellect for the production of his own happiness; but only to use it in such manner as may be consistent with his master's profit.

3. And moreover, inasmuch as the acquisition of the knowledge of his duty to God could not be freely made without the acquisition of other knowledge, which might, if universally diffused, endanger the control of the master, slavery supposes the master to have the right to determine how much knowledge of his duty a slave shall obtain, the manner in which he shall obtain it, and the manner in which he shall discharge that duty after he shall have obtained a knowledge of it. It thus subjects the duty of man to God entirely to the will of man; and this for the sake of pecuniary profit. It renders the eternal happiness of the one party subservient to the temporal happiness of the other. And this principle is commonly recognized by the laws of all slaveholding countries.

If argument were necessary to show that such a system as this must be at variance with the ordinance of God, it might be easily drawn from the effects which it produces both upon *morals* and upon *national wealth.*

1. Its effects must be disastrous upon the *morals* of both parties. By presenting objects on whom passion may be satiated without resistance and without redress it tends to cultivate in the master, pride, anger, cruelty, selfishness and licentiousness. By accustoming the slave to subject his moral principles to the will of another it tends

to abolish in him all moral distinctions; and thus fosters in him lying, deceit, hypocrisy, dishonesty, and a willingness to yield himself up to minister to the appetites of his master. That in all slaveholding countries there are exceptions to this remark, and that there are principles in human nature which, in many cases, limit the effects of these tendencies may be gladly admitted. Yet that such is the *tendency of slavery, as slavery,* we think no reflecting person can for a moment hesitate to allow.

2. The effects of slavery on *national wealth* may be easily seen from the following considerations:

1. Instead of imposing upon *all* the necessity of labor, it restricts the number of laborers, that is, of producers, within the smallest possible limit by rendering labor disgraceful.

2. It takes from the laborers the *natural stimulus* to labor, namely the desire in the individual of improving his condition; and substitutes in the place of it that motive which is the least operative and the least constant, namely the fear of punishment without the consciousness of moral delinquency.

3. It removes as far as possible, from both parties, the disposition and the motives to *frugality*. Neither the master learns frugality from the necessity of labor, nor the slave from the benefits which it confers. And hence while the one party wastes from ignorance of the laws of acquisition, and the other because he can have no motive to economy, capital must accumulate but slowly if indeed it accumulate at all.

And that such are the tendencies of slavery is manifest from observation. No country not of great fertility can long sustain a large slave population. Soils of more than ordinary fertility cannot sustain it long after the first richness of the soil has been exhausted. Hence slavery in this country is acknowledged to have impoverished many of our most valuable districts; and hence it is continually migrating from the older settlements to those new and untilled regions where the accumulated manure of centuries of vegetation has formed a soil whose productiveness may, for awhile, sustain a system at variance with the laws of nature. Many of our free and of our slaveholding

States were peopled at about the same time. The slaveholding States had every advantage, both in soil and climate, over their neighbors. And yet the accumulation of capital has been greatly in favor of the latter. If anyone doubt whether this difference be owing to the use of slave labor, let him ask himself what would have been the condition of the slaveholding States at this moment, if they had been inhabited from the beginning by an industrious yeomanry; each one holding his own land and each one tilling it with the labor of his own hands.

But let us inquire what is the doctrine of revelation on this subject.

The moral precepts of the Bible are diametrically opposed to slavery. They are, Thou shalt love thy *neighbor* as *thyself,* and *all things whatsoever* ye would that men should do unto you, do ye even so unto them.

1. The application of these precepts is universal. Our neighbor is *everyone whom we may benefit*. The obligation respects *all things whatsoever*. The precept, then, manifestly extends to *men as men,* or *men* in *every condition;* and if to all things whatsoever, certainly to a thing so important as the right to personal liberty.

2. Again. By this precept it is made our duty to cherish as tender and delicate a respect for the right which the meanest individual possesses over the means of happiness bestowed upon him by God, as we cherish for our own right over our own means of happiness or as we desire any other individual to cherish for it. Now were this precept obeyed it is manifest that slavery could not in fact exist for a single instant. The principle of the precept is absolutely subversive of the principle of slavery. That of the one is the entire equality of right; that of the other, the entire absorption of the rights of one in the rights of the other.

If anyone doubt respecting the bearing of the Scripture precept upon this case, a few plain questions may throw additional light upon the subject. For instance—

1. Do the precepts and the spirit of the Gospel allow me to derive my support from a system which extorts labor from my fellow men without allowing them any voice in the equivalent which they shall

receive; and which can only be sustained by keeping them in a state of mental degradation and by shutting them out, in a great degree, from the means of salvation?

2. Would the master be willing that another person should subject him to slavery for the same reasons and on the same grounds that he holds his slave in bondage?

3. Would the gospel allow us, if it were in our power, to reduce our fellow citizens of our own color to slavery? But the gospel makes no distinction between men on the ground of color or of race. God has made of *one blood all the nations that dwell on the earth*. I think that these questions will easily ascertain the gospel principles on this subject.

But to this it is *objected* that the gospel never *forbids* slavery; and still more, that by prescribing the duties of masters and servants it tacitly *allows* it. This objection is of sufficient importance to deserve attentive consideration.

The following will, I think, be considered by both parties a fair statement of the teaching of the New Testament on this subject. The moral *principles* of the gospel are directly subversive of the principles of slavery; but on the other hand, the gospel *neither commands* masters to manumit their slaves *nor authorizes* slaves to free themselves from their masters; and also, it goes further, and *prescribes* the duties suited to both parties in their present condition.

First. Now if this be admitted it will, so far as I see, be sufficient for the argument. For if the gospel be diametrically opposed to the *principle* of slavery, it must be opposed to the *practice* of slavery; and therefore, were the principles of the gospel fully adopted, slavery could not exist.

Secondly.[19] 1. I suppose that it will not be denied that God has a right to inform us of his will in any manner that he pleases; and that the intimation of his will, in what manner soever signified, is binding upon the conscience.

2. Hence God may make known to us his will either directly or indirectly; and if that *will* be only distinctly signified it is as binding in the one case as in the other. Thus he may, in express terms, forbid

[19] The section indicated between nn. 19 and 20 did not appear in the 1835 edition.

a certain course of conduct; this is forbidding it *directly;* or else he may command certain duties or impose certain obligations with which that course of conduct is manifestly inconsistent; this is forbidding it *indirectly.* It is sufficient in either case, in order to constitute the obligation, that the will of God be known.

3. The question, then, resolves itself into this: Has God imposed obligations upon men which are inconsistent with the existence of domestic slavery? That he has may, I think, be easily shown.

a. He has made it our duty to proclaim the gospel to all men, without respect to circumstance or condition. If it be our duty to *proclaim the gospel* to every creature, it must be our duty to *give* to every creature every means for attaining a knowledge of it; and yet more imperatively, not to place any obstacles in the way of their attaining that knowledge.

b. He has taught us that the *conjugal* relation is established by himself; that husband and wife are joined together by God; and that man may not put them asunder. The marriage contract is a contract for life and is dissoluble only for one cause, that of conjugal infidelity. Any system that interferes with this contract and claims to make it anything else than what God has made it is in violation of his law.

c. God has established the *parental and filial* relations and has imposed upon parents and children appropriate and peculiar duties. The child is bound to honor and obey the parent; the parent to support and educate the child and to bring him up in the nurture and admonition of the Lord. With these relations and obligations no created being has a right to interfere. A system which claims authority to sever these relations and to annihilate these obligations must be at variance with the will of God.

4. That the Christian religion does establish these relations and impose these obligations will not, I think, be disputed. Now they either are or are not inconsistent with the existence of domestic slavery. If they are inconsistent with the existence of slavery, then slavery is *indirectly forbidden* by the Christian religion. If they are not inconsistent with it, then that interference with them which slavery exercises is as uncalled for as it would be in any other case;

and is the infliction of just so much gratuitous, inexcusable, and demoralizing misery. And as we have before said, what is indirectly forbidden in the Scripture is as *truly forbidden* as though it were directly forbidden.

But it may be asked, Why was this manner of forbidding it chosen in preference to any other? I reply that this question we are not obliged to answer. It is enough for us to show that it is *forbidden*. It is this which establishes the obligation, and this obligation cannot be in the least affected by the reason which may be given for the manner in which God has seen fit to reveal it.

The reason *may be* that slavery is a social evil; and that in order to eradicate it a change must be effected in the society in which it exists, and that this change would be better effected by the inculcation of the principles themselves which are opposed to slavery than by the inculcation of a direct precept. Probably all social evils are thus most successfully remedied.[20]

We answer, again, this very course which the gospel takes on this subject seems to have been the only one that could have been taken in order to effect the universal abolition of slavery. The gospel was designed, not for one race, or for one time, but for all races and for all times. It looked not at the abolition of this form of evil for that age alone, but for its universal abolition. Hence the important object of its Author was to gain it a lodgment in every part of the known world; so that by its universal diffusion among all classes of society it might quietly and peacefully modify and subdue the evil passions of men; and thus, without violence, work a revolution in the whole mass of mankind. In this manner alone could its object, a universal moral revolution, have been accomplished. For if it had forbidden the *evil* instead of subverting the *principle;* if it had proclaimed the unlawfulness of slavery and taught slaves to *resist* the oppression of their masters; it would instantly have arrayed the two parties in deadly hostility throughout the civilized world; its announcement would have been the signal of servile war; and the very name of the Christian religion would have been forgotten amidst the agitations of universal bloodshed. The fact, under these

[20] Concludes material not found in the 1835 edition.

circumstances, that the gospel does not forbid slavery affords no reason to suppose that it does not mean to prohibit it; much less does it afford ground for belief, that Jesus Christ intended to *authorize it*.

3. It is important to remember that two grounds of moral obligation are distinctly recognized in the gospel. The first is our duty to man as man; that is, on the ground of the relation which men sustain to each other: the second is our duty to man as a creature of God; that is, on the ground of the relation which we all sustain to God. On this latter ground many things become our duty which would not be so on the former. It is on this ground that we are commanded to return good for evil, to pray for them that despitefully use us, and when we are smitten on one cheek to turn also the other. To act thus is our duty, not because our fellow man has a right to claim this course of conduct of us, nor because he has a right to inflict injury upon us, but because such conduct in us will be well pleasing to God. And when God prescribes the course of conduct which will be well pleasing to him, he by no means acknowledges the right of abuse in the injurious person, but expressly declares, Vengeance is mine, and *I will repay it, saith the Lord*. Now it is to be observed that it is precisely upon this latter ground that the slave is commanded to obey his master. It is never urged, like the duty of obedience to parents, *because it is right;* but because the cultivation of meekness and forbearance under injury will be well pleasing unto God. Thus servants are commanded to be obedient to their own masters, "in singleness of heart, *as unto Christ;*" "doing the *will of God* from the heart, with good will doing service *as to the Lord, and not to men.*" *Eph.* vi, 5–7. "Servants are commanded to count their masters worthy of all honor, that the name of *God and his doctrine be not blasphemed.*" 1 *Tim.* vi, 1. "Exhort servants to be obedient to their own masters," &c., *"that they may adorn the doctrine of God our Saviour in all things."* *Titus* iii, 9. The manner in which the duty of servants or slaves is inculcated, therefore, affords no ground for the assertion that the gospel authorizes one man to hold another in bondage, any more than the command to honor the king, when that king was Nero, authorized the tyranny of the emperor; or than the command to turn the other cheek when one is

smitten justifies the infliction of violence by an injurious man.*

In a word, if the gospel rule of conduct be directly at variance with the existence of slavery; if the relations which it establishes and the obligations which it enforces are inconsistent with its existence; if the manner in which it treats it is the only manner in which it could attempt its utter and universal extermination; and if it inculcates the duty of slaves on principles which have no connection with the question of the right of masters over them; I think it must be conceded that the precepts of the gospel in no manner countenance, but are entirely opposed to, the institution of domestic slavery.

Before closing this part of the subject, it may be proper to consider the question, What is the duty of masters and slaves under a condition of society in which slavery now exists?

I. As to masters.

If the system be wrong, as we have endeavored to show, if it be at variance with our duty both to God and to man, it must be abandoned. If it be asked, When? I ask again, When shall a man begin to cease doing wrong? Is not the answer always, *Immediately?* If a man is injuring *us* do we ever doubt as to the time when *he* ought to cease? There is then no doubt in respect to the time when we ought to cease inflicting injury upon others.

But it may be said, immediate abolition would be the greatest possible injury to the slaves themselves. They are not competent to self-government.

This is a question of fact, which it is not within the province of moral philosophy to decide. It very likely may be so. So far as I know, the facts are not sufficiently known to warrant a full opinion on the subject. We will, therefore, suppose it to be the case and ask, What is the duty of masters *under these circumstances?*

1. The situation of the slaves in which this obstacle to their emancipation consists is not by their *own act,* but by the *act of their masters;* and therefore the *masters are bound to remove it.* The slaves

---

* I have retained the above paragraph, though I confess that the remarks of Professor Taylor, of the Union Theological Seminary of Virginia, have led me seriously to doubt whether the distinction to which it alludes is sustained by the New Testament.

were brought here without their own consent, they have been continued in their present state of degradation without their own consent, and *they* are not responsible for the consequences. If a man
have done injustice to his neighbor and have also placed impediments
in the way of remedying that injustice, he is as much under obligation to remove the impediments in the way of justice as he is to
do justice. Were it otherwise, a man might, by the accumulation
of injury, at last render the most atrocious injury innocent and right.

2. But it may be said, this cannot be done unless the slave is held
in bondage until the object be accomplished. This is also a question
of fact, on which I will not pretend to decide. But suppose it to be
so, the question returns, What then is the duty of the master? I
answer, supposing such to be the fact, it may be the duty of the
master to hold the slave; not, however, *on the ground of right over
him* but of *obligation to him,* and of obligation *to him* for the
purpose of accomplishing a particular and specified good. And of
course he who holds him for any other purpose, holds him wrongfully and is guilty of the sin of slavery. In the meanwhile, he is innocent *in just so far as* he, in the fear of God, holds the slave, not for
the good of the master, but for the good of the slave, and with the
entire and honest intention of accomplishing the object as soon as
he can and of liberating the slave as soon as the object is accomplished. He thus admits the slave to equality of right. He does unto
another as he would that another should do unto him; and thus
acting, though he may *in form* hold a fellow creature in bondage,
he is *in fact* innocent of the crime of violation of liberty. This opinion,
however, proceeds upon the supposition that the facts are as above
stated. As to the question of fact, I do not feel competent to a decision.

II. The *duty of slaves* is also explicitly made known in the Bible.
They are bound to obedience, fidelity, submission, and respect to
their masters not only to the good and kind but also to the unkind
and froward; not, however, on the ground of *duty to man,* but on
the ground of *duty to God.* This obligation extends to everything
but matters of conscience. When a master commands a slave to do
wrong the slave ought not to obey. The Bible does not, as I suppose,
authorize resistance to injury; but it commands us to refuse obedi-

ence in such a case and suffer the consequences, looking to God alone to whom vengeance belongeth. Acting upon these principles, the slave may attain to the highest grade of virtue and may exhibit a sublimity and purity of moral character which in the condition of the master is absolutely unattainable.

Thus we see that the Christian religion not only forbids slavery, but that it also provides the only method in which, after it has once been established, it may be abolished, and that with the entire safety and benefit to both parties. By instilling the right moral dispositions into the bosom of the master and of the slave, it teaches the one the duty of reciprocity and the other the duty of submission; and thus without tumult, without disorder, without revenge, but by the real moral improvement of both parties restores both to the relation towards each other intended by their Creator.

Hence if anyone will reflect on these facts and remember the moral law of the Creator and the terrible sanctions by which his laws are sustained, and also the provision which in the gospel of reconciliation He has made for removing this evil after it has once been established; he must, I think, be convinced of the imperative obligation which rests upon him to remove it without the delay of a moment. The Judge of the whole earth will do justice. He hears the cry of the oppressed and he will, in the end, terribly vindicate right. And on the other hand, let those who suffer wrongfully bear their sufferings with patience, committing their souls unto him as unto a *faithful Creator*.

PART II. *The right of personal liberty may be violated* by SOCIETY.

As the right to use the means of happiness which God has given him in such manner as he will, provided he do not violate the corresponding rights of others, is conferred upon the individual by his Creator, it is manifest that no being but the Creator can rightly restrict it. The individual is just as truly, in this sense, independent of society as he is of individuals. Society is composed of individuals and can have no other rights than the individuals of which it is composed, only in just so far as the individual voluntarily, and for an equivalent, has conceded to it, in given and limited respects, some of the rights of which he was originally possessed. Whenever society interferes with these original rights, unless in the cases in which they have been voluntarily ceded, then the right of personal liberty is violated. Thus the Declaration of Independence, above quoted, after having asserted the universality of the equality of men by virtue of their creation, and that they are endowed by their Creator with certain inalienable rights, among which are life, liberty, and the pursuit of happiness, proceeds to state, "that, to secure these rights, governments were instituted among men, deriving their just powers from the *consent of the governed*" (that is, by the concession of the individual to society), "that, when any form of government becomes destructive of these ends, it is the right of the people to alter or to abolish it, and to institute a new government, laying its foundation in such principles, and organizing its powers in such form, as to them shall seem most likely to effect their safety and happiness."

SOCIETY may violate the personal rights of the individual.

1. By depriving him unjustly of his *physical liberty* or any of his means of physical happiness. This is done, first, whenever any individual is imprisoned or punished, except for crime.

2. Whenever, although he may have been guilty of crime, he is imprisoned or punished without a fair and impartial trial; for as every man is presumed to be innocent until he shall have been proved to be guilty, to imprison or molest him without such proof is to imprison or molest him while he is innocent. This remark, however, does not apply to the detention of prisoners in order to trial. The detention in this case is not for the purposes of punishment, but simply to prevent escape, and is a necessary means for the execution of justice. It is also no injustice; for it is a power over their persons which the individuals have, for mutual good, conceded to society.

3. Inasmuch as every individual has the right to go where he pleases under the limitations above specified, this right is violated not merely by confining him to a particular place, but also by forbidding his going to any particular place within the limits of the society to which he belongs or by forbidding him to leave it when and how he pleases. As his connection with the society to which

he belongs is a voluntary act, his simple will is an ultimate reason why he should leave it; and the free exercise of this will cannot, without injustice, be restrained.

The great clause in the Magna Charta on this general subject is in these memorable words: "Let no freeman be imprisoned, or disseized, or outlawed, or in any manner injured or proceeded against by us, otherwise than by the legal judgment of his peers, or by the law of the land." And the full enjoyment of this right is guaranteed to every individual in this country and in Great Britain by the celebrated act of Habeas Corpus: by which, upon a proper presentation of the case before a judge, the judge is under obligation, if there be cause, to command the person who has the custody of another to bring him immediately before him; and is also obliged to set the prisoner at large unless it appear to him that he is deprived of his liberty for a satisfactory reason.

2. Society may violate the rights of the individual by restraining his *intellectual* liberty.

I have before stated that a man has the right to the use of his intellect in such manner as he pleases, provided he interfere not with the rights of others. This includes *first,* the right to pursue what studies he pleases; and *secondly*, to publish them when and where he pleases, subject to the above limitation.

1. This right is violated, first, when society, or government, which is its agent, prohibits any course of study or investigation to which the inclination of the individual may determine him.

2. When government prohibits him from publishing these results and from attempting, by the use of argument, to make as many converts to his opinions as he can, in both cases within the limits specified. If it be said that men may thus be led into error, the answer is, For this error the individuals themselves, and not their neighbor, are responsible; and therefore the latter has no authority to interfere.

These remarks apply to those cases only in which the use of the individual's intellect is without injury to the rights of others. They, however, by the terms of the case, exclude those modes of intellectual employment which *do thus interfere*. It is obvious that a man has no more right to restrict by the use of his intellect my just control over the means of happiness bestowed upon me than by the use of his body or the use of his property. What I have said, therefore, in no manner precludes the right of society to restrict the use of the individual's intellect in those cases where this violation exists.

But when this violation is supposed to exist, by what rule is society to be governed so as, in the exercise of the right of restraint, to avoid infringement of the law of intellectual liberty? I am aware that the decision of this question is attended with great difficulties. I shall, however, endeavor to suggest such hints as seem to me to throw light upon it in the hope that the attention of someone better able to elucidate it may be thus more particularly attracted to the discussion.

1. Society is bound to protect those rights of the individual which he has committed to its charge. Among these, for instance, is reputation. As the individual relinquishes the right of protecting his own reputation, as well as his property, society undertakes to protect it for him.

2. Society has the right to prevent its own destruction. As without society individual man would almost universally perish; so men, by the law of self-preservation, have a right to prohibit those modes of using a man's mind, as well as those of using his body, by which society would be annihilated.

3. As society has the right to employ its power to prevent its own dissolution, it also has the same right to protect itself from causeless injury. A man has no more right to carry on a trade by which his neighbor is annoyed than one by which he is poisoned. So if the employment of a man's intellect be not of such a character as to be positively fatal, yet if it be positively mischievous and if such be its manifest tendency, society has a right to interfere and prohibit it.

4. It is, however, a general principle, that society is not to interfere while the individual has in himself the means of repelling, or of rendering nugatory, the injury. Whenever, therefore, although the publication of opinions be confessedly injurious,[21] the injury is of such a nature that every individual can protect himself from it, so-

---

[21] The 1835 edition: "injurious, as erroneous opinions always must be, yet if they be of such a nature that every . . . from them, in this case, society leaves"

ciety leaves the individual to the use of that power which he still retains, and which is sufficient to remedy the evil.

If I mistake not, these principles will enable us to distinguish between those cases in which it is, and those in which it is not, the duty of society to interfere with the freedom of the human intellect.

1. Whenever the individual possesses within himself the means of repelling the injury, society should not interfere. As, for instance, so far as an assertion is false, and false simply, as in philosophical or mathematical error, men have, in their own understandings and their instinctive perception of truth, a safeguard against injury. And besides this, when discussion is free, error may be refuted by argument; and in this contest truth has always, from the constitution of things, the advantage. It needs not, therefore, physical force to assist it. The *confutation* of error is also decisive. It reduces it absolutely to nothing. Whereas the *forcible prohibition of discussion* leaves things precisely as they were and gives to error the additional advantage of the presumption that it could not be answered by argument; that is, that it is the truth.

2. But suppose the matter made public is also injurious, and is either false or, if true, is of such a nature as directly to tend to the destruction of individual or social happiness, and the individual has not in himself the power of repelling the injury. Here, the facts being proved, society is bound to interfere and impose such penalty and render such redress as shall, if possible, remunerate the injured party, or at least prevent the repetition of the offence.

Under this head, several cases occur:

1. If a man use his intellect for the purpose of destroying his neighbor's reputation, it is the duty of society to interfere. There is here a manifest injury inasmuch as reputation is a means of happiness, and as much the property of an individual, as his house or lands, or any other result of his industry. He has, besides, no method of redress within himself; for he may be ruined by a general assertion which is in its nature incapable of being disproved. As if A asserted that B had stolen; this, if believed, would ruin B; but he could not disprove it unless he could summon all the men with whom, in his whole life, he had ever had any pecuniary transactions. Besides, if he

could do this, he could never convey the facts to all persons to whom A had conveyed the scandal. Were such actions allowed, everyone might be deprived of his reputation, one of his most valuable means of happiness. It is the duty of society, therefore, in this case to guard the rights of the individual by granting him redress and preventing the repetition of the injury.

2. Inasmuch as men are actuated by various passions, which are only useful when indulged within certain restraints, but which, when indulged without these restraints, are destructive of individual right as well as of society itself; society has a right to prohibit the use of intellect for the purpose of exciting the passions of men beyond those limits. As he is guilty who robs another, so is he also guilty who incites another to robbery; and still more, he who incites not one man but a multitude of men to robbery. Hence society has a right to prohibit obscene books, obscene pictures, and everything of which the object and tendency is to promote lasciviousness. On the same ground it has a right to prohibit incendiary and seditious publications and everything which would provoke the enmity or malice of men against each other.

The reason of this is, first, injury of this kind cannot be repelled by argument for it is not addressed to the reason; and the very mention of the subject excites those imaginations from which the injury to society arises. As the evil is susceptible of no other remedy than prohibition, and as the welfare of society requires that a remedy be found, prohibition is the right and duty of society.

Another reason, applicable to most publications of this sort, is found in the nature of the parental relation. The parent, being the guardian of his child's morals, has the right of directing what he shall and what he shall not read. Hence all the parents of a community, that is, society at large, have a right to forbid such books as shall, in their opinion, injure the moral character of their children.

3. Again. Society may be dissolved not merely by the excitation of unlawful passion, but by the removal of moral restraint. Everyone must see that if moral distinctions were abolished society could not exist for a moment. Men might be gregarious, but they would cease to be social. If anyone, therefore, is disposed to use his intellect for

the purpose of destroying in the minds of men the distinction between virtue and vice, or any of those fundamental principles on
which the existence of society depends, society has a right to interfere and prohibit him.

This right of society is founded, first, upon the right of self-
preservation; and secondly, upon the ground of common sense.
Society is not bound to make, over and over again, an experiment
which the whole history of man has proved always to end in licentiousness, anarchy, misery, and universal bloodshed. Nor can any
man claim a right to use his mind in a way which must, if allowed,
produce unmixed misery and violation of right wherever its influence is exerted.

Besides, in this, as in the other cases specified, society has no means
of counteracting the injury by argument, because such appeals are
made, not to the reason and the conscience, but to the rapacious
passions of men; and also, because those persons who would listen
to such suggestions would rarely if ever be disposed to read, much
less to examine and reflect upon, any argument that could be offered.

But it may be objected that a society constituted on these principles might check the progress of free inquiry and under the pretext
of injurious tendency limit the liberty of fair discussion.

To this it may be answered—

It is no objection to a rule, that it is capable of abuse; for this
objection will apply to all laws and to all arrangements that man
has ever devised. In the present imperfect condition of human nature
it is frequently sufficient that a rule prevents greater evil than it
inflicts.

It is granted that men may suppose a discussion injurious when
it is not so and may thus limit, unnecessarily, the freedom of inquiry.
But let us see in what manner this abuse is guarded against.

The security in this case is the trial by jury. When twelve men
taken by lot from the whole community sit in judgment, and specially when the accused has the right of excepting, for cause, to as
many as he will, he is sure of having, at least, an impartial tribunal.
These judges are themselves under the same law which they administer to others. As it is not to be supposed that they would wish to

abridge their own personal liberty, it is not to be supposed that they would be willing to abridge it for the sake of interfering with that of their neighbor. The question is, therefore, placed in the hands of as impartial judges as the nature of the case allows. To such a tribunal no reasonable man can, on principle, object. To their decision every candid man would, when his duty to God did not forbid, readily submit.

Now as it must be granted that no man has a right to use his intellect to the injury of a community, the only question in any particular case is whether the use complained of is injurious in such a sense as to require the interference of society. It surely does not need argument to show that the unanimous decision of twelve men is more likely to be correct than the decision of one man; and specially that the decision of twelve men who have no personal interest in the affair is more likely to be correct than that of one man who is liable to all the influences of personal vanity, love of distinction, and pecuniary emolument. There surely can be no question whether, in a matter on which the dearest interests of others are concerned, a man is to be a judge in his own case, or whether as impartial a tribunal as the ingenuity of man has ever devised shall judge for him. If it be said that twelve impartial men are liable to error, and by consequence to do injustice, it may be answered, How much more liable is *one,* and he a *partial* man, to err and to do injustice! If, then, a system of trial of this sort not only must prevent more injury than it inflicts, but is free from all liability to injury, except such as results from the acknowledged imperfections of our nature, the fault, if it exist, is not in the rule but in the nature of man, and must be endured until the nature of man be altered.

And I cannot close this discussion without remarking that a most solemn and imperative duty seems to me to rest upon judges, legislators, jurors, and prosecuting officers in regard to this subject. We hear, at the present day, very much about the liberty of the press, the freedom of inquiry, and the freedom of the human intellect. All these are precious blessings—by far too precious to be lost. But it is to be remembered that no liberty can exist without restraint; and the remark is as true of intellectual as of physical liberty. As there could be no physical liberty if everyone, both bad and good, did what he would, so there would soon be no liberty, either physical or intellectual, if every man were allowed to publish what he would. The man who publishes what will inflame the licentious passions or subvert the moral principles of others is undermining the foundations of the social fabric; and it is kindness neither to him nor to society quietly to look on until both he and we are crushed beneath the ruins. The danger to liberty is pre-eminently greater, at the present day, from the licentiousness than from the restriction of the press. It therefore becomes all civil and judicial officers to act as the guardians of society; and, unawed by popular clamor and unseduced by popular favor, resolutely to defend the people against their worst enemies. Whatever may be the form of a government, it cannot long continue free after it has refused to acknowledge the distinction between the liberty and the licentiousness of the press. And much as we may execrate a profligate writer, let us remember that the civil officer who, from pusillanimity, refuses to exercise the power placed in his hands to restrain abuse deserves at least an equal share of our execration.

THIRDLY.[22] The right of *religious liberty* may be violated by society.

We have before said, that every individual has the right to pursue his own happiness by worshipping his Creator in any way that he pleases, provided he do not interfere with the rights of his neighbor.

This includes the following things: He is at liberty to worship God in any form that he deems most acceptable to Him, to worship individually or socially, and to promote that form of worship which he considers acceptable to God by the promulgation of such sentiments as he believes to be true, provided he leave the rights of his neighbors unmolested; and of this liberty he is not to be restricted, unless such molestation be made manifest to a jury of his peers.

As a man is at liberty to worship God individually or in societies collected for that purpose, if his object can be secured, in his own opinion, by the enjoyment of any of the facilities for association granted to other men for innocent purposes, he is entitled to them

[22] At this point the textual revision in the 1865 edition ends.

just as other men are. The general principle applicable to the case I suppose to be this: A man, in consequence of being religious, that is, of worshipping God, acquires no human right whatever; for it is, so far as his fellow men's rights are concerned, the same thing whether he worship God or not. And on the other hand, in consequence of being religious, he loses no right, and for the same reason. And therefore, as men are entitled to all innocent facilities which they need for prosecuting an innocent object, a religious man has the same right to these facilities for promoting his object; and it is the business of no one to inquire whether this be religious, scientific, mechanical, or any other, so long as it is *merely innocent*.

Now this right is violated by society—

1. By forbidding the exercise of all religion; as in the case of the French Revolution.

2. By forbidding or enforcing the exercise of *any* form of religion. Insofar as an act is religious society has no right of control over it. If it interfere with the rights of others, this puts it within the control of society, and this alone, and solely for this reason. The power of society is, therefore, in this case, exercised simply on the ground of *injury perpetrated* and proved, and not on account of the truth or falseness, the goodness or badness, of the religion in the sight of the Creator.

3. By inflicting disabilities upon men or depriving them of any of their rights as men because they are or are not religious. This violation occurs in all cases in which society interferes to deny to religious men the same privileges for promoting their happiness by way of religion as they enjoy for promoting their happiness in any other innocent way. Such is the case when religious societies are denied the right of incorporation, with all its attendant privileges, for the purposes of religious worship and the promotion of their religious opinions. Unless it can be shown that the enjoyment of such privileges interferes with the rights of others the denial of them is a violation of religious liberty. Depriving clergymen of the elective franchise is a violation of a similar character.

4. By placing the professors of any peculiar form of religion under any disabilities; as, for instance, rendering them ineligible to office,

or in any manner making a distinction between them and any other professors of religion or any other men. As society has no right to inflict disabilities upon men on the ground of their worshipping God in *general,* by consequence it has no right to inflict disabilities on the ground of worshipping God in any manner in *particular.* If the whole subject is without the control of society, a part of it is also without its control. Different modes of worship may be more or less acceptable to God; but this gives to no man a right to interfere with those means of happiness which God has conferred upon any other man.

The question may arise here whether society has a right to provide by law for the support of religious instruction. I answer, If the existence of *religious instruction* be necessary to the existence of society and if there *be no other mode of providing for its support* but by legislative enactment, then I do not see any more violation of principle in such enactment than in that for the support of common schools; provided that no one were obliged to attend unless he chose and that everyone were allowed to pay for that form of worship which he preferred. There are other objections, however, to such a course, aside from that arising from the supposed violation of civil liberty.

1. It cannot be shown that religious teachers cannot be supported without legislative aid. The facts teach a different result.

2. The religion of Christ has always exerted its greatest power when, entirely unsupported, it has been left to exert its own peculiar effect upon the consciences of men.

3. The support of religion by law is at variance with the genius of the gospel. The gospel supposes every man to be purely voluntary in his service of God, in his choice of the mode of worship of his religious teachers and of the compensation which he will make to them for their services. Now all this is reversed in the supposition of a ministry supported by civil power. We therefore conclude that although such support might be provided without interference with civil liberty, it could not be done without violation of the spirit of the gospel. That is, though the state might be desirous of affording aid to the church, the church is bound, on principle, resolutely and steadfastly to protest against in any manner receiving it.

4. And I think that the facts will show that this view of the subject is correct. The clergy, as a profession, are better remunerated by voluntary support than by legal enactment. When the people arrange the matter of compensation with their clergymen themselves, there are no rich and overgrown benefices, but there are also but few miserably poor curacies. The minister, if he deserve it, generally lives as well as his people. If it be said that high talent should be rewarded by elevated rank in this profession as in any other, I answer that such seems to me not to be the genius of the gospel. The gospel presents no inducements of worldly rank or of official dignity and it scorns to hold out such motives to the religious teacher. I answer again, official rank and luxurious splendor, instead of adding to, take from the real influence of a teacher of religion. They tend to destroy that moral hardihood which is necessary to the success of him whose object it is to render men better; and while they surround him with all the insignia of power, enervate that very spirit on which moral power essentially depends. And besides, a religion supported by the government must soon become the tool of the government; or at least must be involved and implicated in every change which the government may undergo. How utterly at variance this must be with the principles of Him who declared, "My kingdom is not of this world," surely need not be illustrated.

Section I · The Right of Property

I. DEFINITION of the right of property.

The abstract right of property is the right to use something in such manner as I choose.

But inasmuch as this right of use is common to all men, and as one may choose to use his property in such a way as to deprive his neighbor of this or of some other right, the right to use as I choose is limited by the restriction that I do not interfere with the rights of my neighbor. The right of property, therefore, when thus restricted, is the right to use something as I choose, provided I do not so use it as to interfere with the rights of my neighbor.

Thus we see that, from the very nature of the case, the right of property is exclusive; that is to say, if I have a right to anything this right excludes everyone else from any right over that thing; and it imposes upon everyone else the obligation to leave me unmolested in the use of it within those limits to which my right extends.

II. On what the right of property is founded.

The right of property is founded on the will of God as made known to us by *natural conscience,* by *general consequences,* and by *revelation.*

Everything which we behold is essentially the property of the Creator; and he has a right to confer the use of it upon whomsoever, and under what restrictions soever, he pleases. We may know in what relations he wills us to stand towards the things around us by the principles which he has implanted within us and by the result produced in individuals and communities by the different courses of conduct of which men are capable.

Now God signifies to us his will on this subject—

First. By the decisions of natural conscience. This is known from several circumstances.

1. All men, as soon as they begin to think, even in early youth and infancy, perceive this relation. They immediately appropriate certain things to themselves; they feel injured if their control over

those things is violated and they are conscious of guilt if they violate this right in respect to others.

2. The relation of property is expressed by the possessive pronouns. These are found in all languages. So universally is this idea diffused over the whole mass of human action and human feeling that it would be scarcely possible for two human beings to converse for even a few minutes on any subject or in any language without the frequent use of the words which designate the relation of possession.

3. Not only do men feel the importance of sustaining each other in the exercise of the right of property, but they manifestly feel that he who violates it has done wrong, that is, has violated obligation and hence deserves punishment on the ground, not simply of the *consequences* of *the act,* but of the *guiltiness of the actor.* Thus if a man steal other men are not satisfied when he has merely made restitution, although this may perfectly make up the loss to the injured party. It is always considered that something more is due either from God or from man as a *punishment for the crime.* Hence the Jewish law enjoined *tenfold* restitution in cases of theft and modern law inflicts fines, imprisonment, and corporal punishment for the same offence.

Secondly. That God wills the possession of property is evident from the general consequences which result from the existence of this relation.

The existence and progress of society, nay, the very existence of our race, depends upon the acknowledgment of this right.

Were not every individual entitled to the results of his labor and to the exclusive enjoyment of the benefits of these results—

1. No one would labor any more than was sufficient for his own individual subsistence because he would have no more right than any other person to the value which he had created.

2. Hence there would be no accumulation; of course no capital, no tools, no provision for the future, no houses, and no agriculture. Each man, alone, would be obliged to contend, at the same time with the elements, with wild beasts, and also with his rapacious fellow men. The human race under such circumstances could not long exist.

3. Under such circumstances the race of man must speedily perish or its existence be prolonged, even in favorable climates, under every accumulation of wretchedness. Progress would be out of the question; and the only change which could take place would be that arising from the pressure of heavier and heavier penury, as the spontaneous productions of the earth became rarer from improvident consumption without any correspondent labor for reproduction.

4. It needs only to be remarked, in addition, that just in proportion as the right of property is held inviolate, just in that proportion civilization advances and the comforts and conveniences of life multiply. Hence it is that in free and well ordered governments, and specially during peace, property accumulates, all the orders of society enjoy the blessings of competence, the arts flourish, science advances, and men begin to form some conception of the happiness of which the present system is capable. And, on the contrary, under despotism, when law spreads its protection over neither house, land, estate, nor life, and specially during civil wars, industry ceases, capital stagnates, the arts decline, the people starve, population diminishes, and men rapidly tend to a state of barbarism.

Thirdly. The Holy Scriptures treat of the right of property as a thing acknowledged and direct their precepts against every act by which it is violated and also against the tempers of mind from which such violation proceeds. The doctrine of revelation is so clearly set forth on this subject that I need not delay for the sake of dwelling upon it. It will be sufficient to refer to the prohibitions in the decalogue against stealing and coveting and to the various precepts in the New Testament respecting our duty in regard to our neighbor's possessions.

I proceed, in the next place, to consider—

III. The modes in which the right of property may be acquired. These may be divided into two classes: first, direct; second, indirect.

First. Direct.

1. *By the immediate gift of God.*

When God has given me a desire for any object and has spread this object before me, and there is no rational creature to contest my claim, I may take that object and use it as I will, subject only to the limitation of those obligations to Him and to my fellow creatures which have been before specified. On this principle is founded my right to enter upon wild and unappropriated lands, to hunt wild game, to pluck wild fruit, to take fish, or anything of this sort. This right is sufficient to exclude the right of any subsequent claimant; for if it has been given to me, that act of gift is valid until it can be shown by another that it has been annulled. A grant of this sort, however, applies only to an individual so long as he continues the *locum tenens,* and no longer. He has no right to enter upon unappropriated land, and leave, it and then claim it afterward by virtue of his first possession. Were it otherwise, any individual might acquire a title to a whole continent and exclude from it all the rest of his species.

2. *By the labor of our hands.*

Whatever value I have created by my own labor or by the innocent use of the other means of happiness which God has given me is mine. This is evident from the principle already so frequently referred to; namely, that I have a right to use for my own happiness whatever God has given me, provided I use it not to the injury of another. Thus if I catch a deer or raise an ear of corn upon land otherwise unappropriated, that deer or that corn is mine. No reason can possibly be conceived why any other being should raise a claim to them which could extinguish or even interfere with mine.

This, however, is not meant to assert that a man has a right to anything more than to the *results of his labor.* He has no right, of course, to the results of the *labor of another.* If by my labor I build a mill and employ a man to take the charge of it, it does not follow that he has a right to all the profits of the mill. If I, by my labor and frugality, earn money to purchase a farm and hire a laborer to work upon it, it does not follow that he has a right to all the produce of the farm. The profit is in this case to be divided between us. He has a right to the share which fairly belongs to *his labor* and I have a right to the share that belongs to me as the proprietor and possessor of that which is the result of my antecedent labor. It would be as unjust for *him to have the whole profit* as for *me to have the whole of it.* It is fairly a case of partnership, in which each party receives his share of the result upon conditions previously and voluntarily agreed upon. *This is the general principle of wages.*

Secondly. The right of property may be acquired indirectly.

1. *By exchange.*

Inasmuch as I have an exclusive right to appropriate, innocently, the possessions which I have acquired by the means stated above, and inasmuch as every other man has the same right, we may, if we choose, voluntarily exchange our right to particular things with each other. If I cultivate wheat and my neighbor cultivates corn and we, both of us, have more of our respective production than we wish to use for ourselves, we may, on such terms as we can agree upon, exchange the one for the other. Property held in this manner is held rightfully. This exchange is of two kinds: first, barter, where the exchange on both sides consists of commodities; and second, bargain and sale, where one of the parties gives, and the other receives, *money* for his property.

2. *By gift.*

As I may thus rightfully part with, and another party rightfully receive, my property, for an equivalent rendered, so I may, if I choose, part with it without an equivalent; that is, merely to gratify my feelings of benevolence or affection or gratitude. Here I voluntarily confer upon another the right of ownership and he may rightfully receive and occupy it.

3. *By will.*

As I have the right to dispose of my property as I please during my lifetime and may exchange it or give it as I will at any time previous to my decease, so I may give it to another, on the condition that he shall not enter into possession until after my death. Property acquired in this manner is held rightfully.

4. *By inheritance.*

Inasmuch as persons frequently die without making a will, society, upon general principles, presumes upon the manner in which the deceased would have distributed his property had he made a will. Thus it is supposed that he would distribute his wealth among his widow and children; or in failure of these, among his blood relations; and in proportions corresponding to their degree of consanguinity. Property may be rightfully acquired in this manner.

5. *By possession.*

In many cases, although a man have no moral right to property, yet he may have a right to exclude others from it; and others are under obligation to leave him unmolested in the use of it. Thus a man has by fraud obtained possession of a farm and the rightful owners have all died: now although the present holder has no just title to the property, yet if it were to be taken from him and held by another, the second would have no better title than the first; and a third person would have the same right to dispossess the second and in turn be himself dispossessed, and so on forever; that is, there would be endless controversy without any nearer approximation to justice; and hence it is better that the case be left as it was in the first instance; that is, in general possession gives a right, so far as man is concerned, to unmolested enjoyment unless someone else can establish a better title.

6. And hence in general I believe it will hold that while merely the laws of society do not give a man any *moral right* to property, yet when these laws have once assigned it to him; this simple fact imposes a *moral obligation* upon all other men to leave him in the undisturbed possession of it. I have no more right to set fire to the house of a man who has defrauded an orphan to obtain it than I have to set fire to the house of any other man.

To sum up what has been said—property may be *originally* acquired either by the gift of God or by our own labor: it may be *subsequently* acquired either by exchange or by gift during life or by will; but in these cases of transfer of ownership *the free consent of the original owner* is necessary to render the transfer morally right; and lastly, where the individual has not acquired property justly, yet mere possession, though it alters not his moral right to possession, yet it is a sufficient bar to molestation unless some other claimant can prefer a better title. These, I think, comprehend the most important modes by which the right of property can be acquired.

That principles somewhat analogous to these are in accordance with the laws of God is, I think, evident from observation of the

history of man. The more rigidly these principles have been carried
into active operation, the greater amount of happiness has been
secured to the individual, and the more rapidly do nations advance
in civilization and the more successfully do they carry into effect
every means of mental and moral cultivation. The first steps that
were taken in the recovery of Europe from the misery of the Dark
Ages consisted in defining and establishing the right of property
upon the basis of equitable and universal law. Until something of
this sort is done, no nation can emerge from a state of barbarism.*

And hence we see the importance of an able, learned, upright,
and independent judiciary and the necessity to national prosperity
of carrying the decisions of law into universal and impartial effect.
It not unfrequently happens that, for the purposes of party, the
minds of the people are inflamed against the tribunals whose duty
it is to administer justice; or else, on the other hand, for the same
purpose, a flagrant violation of justice by a popular favorite is looked
upon as harmless. Let it be remembered that society must be dissolved unless the supremacy of the law be maintained. "The voice
of the law" will cease to be "the harmony of the world," unless "all
things," both high and low, "do her reverence." How often has even-
handed justice commended the chalice to the lips of the demagogue;
and he has been the first to drink of that cup which he supposed himself to be mingling for others!

Section II · Modes in Which the Right of Property May Be Violated By the Individual

I have already remarked that the right of property, so far as it extends, is exclusive both of the individual and of society. This is true in
respect to both parties. Thus whatever I own, I own exclusively both
of society and of individuals; and whatever either individuals or
society own, they own exclusively of me. Hence the right of property
is equally violated by taking viciously either public or private property; and it is equally violated by taking viciously whether the aggressor be the public or an individual. And moreover, it is exclusive

* Robertson's Preliminary Dissertation to the History of Charles V.

to *the full amount of what is owned*. It is, therefore, as truly a violation of the right of property to take a little as to take much; to purloin a book or a penknife as to steal money; to steal fruit as to steal a horse; to defraud the revenue as to rob my neighbor; to overcharge the public as to overcharge my brother; to cheat the post office as to cheat my friend.

It has already been observed that a right to the property of another can be acquired only by his own voluntary choice. This follows immediately from the definition of the right of property. But in order to render this choice of right available, it must be influenced by no motives presented wrongfully by the receiver. Thus if I demand a man's purse on the alternative that I will shoot him if he deny me, he may surrender it rather than be shot; but I have no right to present such an alternative, and the consent of the owner renders it no less a violation of the right of property. If I inflame a man's vanity in order to induce him to buy of me a coach which he does not want, the transaction is dishonest; because I have gained his will by a motive which I had no right to use. So if I represent an article in exchange to be different from what it is, I present a false motive and gain his consent by a lie. And thus, in general, as I have said, a transfer of property is morally wrong where the consent of the owner is obtained by means of a vicious act on the part of the receiver.

The right of property may be violated—

1. By taking property *without the knowledge* of the owner, or *theft*. It is here to be remembered that the consent of the owner is necessary to any transfer of property. We do not vary the nature of the act by persuading ourselves that the owner will not care about it, or that he would have no objection, or that he will not know it, or that it will never injure him to lose it. All this may or may not be; but none of it varies the moral character of the transaction. The simple question is, Has the *owner consented to the transfer?* If he have not, so long as this circumstance, essential to a righteous transfer, is wanting, whatever other circumstances exist it matters not— the taking of another's property is theft.

2. By taking the property of another by consent *violently obtained*.

Such is the case in highway robbery. Here we wickedly obtain control over a man's life, and then offer him the alternative of death or delivery of his property. Inasmuch as the consent is no more voluntary than if we tied his hands and took the money out of his pocket, the violation of property is as great. And besides this, we assume the power of life and death over an individual over whom we have no just right whatever. In this case, in fact, we assume the unlimited control over the life and possessions of another and, on pain of death, oblige him to surrender his property to our will. As, in this case, there is a double and aggravated violation of right, it is in all countries considered deserving of condign punishment and is generally rendered a capital offence.

3. By consent *fraudulently* obtained, or cheating.

This may be of two kinds:

1. Where no *equivalent is offered,* as when a beggar obtains money on false pretenses.

2. Where the *equivalent is different from what it purports to be;* or where the consent is obtained by an immoral act on the part of him who obtains it. As this includes by far the greatest number of violations of the law of property, it will occupy the remainder of this section and will require to be treated of somewhat at length.

We shall divide it into two parts:—1. *Where the equivalent is material; 2. Where the equivalent is immaterial.*

I. WHERE THE EQUIVALENT IS MATERIAL. This is of two kinds:—1. *Where the transfer is perpetual; 2. Where the transfer is temporary.*

FIRST. *Where the transfer of property on both sides is perpetual.* This includes *the law of buyer and seller.*

The principal laws of buyer and seller will be seen from a consideration of the relation in which they stand to each other. The seller, or merchant, is supposed to devote his time and capital to the business of supplying his neighbors with articles of use. For his time, risk, interest of money, and skill he is entitled to an advance on his goods; and the buyer is under a correspondent obligation to allow that advance except in the case of a change in the market price, to be noticed subsequently.

Hence, 1. The seller is under obligation to furnish goods of the same quality as that ordinarily furnished at the same prices. He is paid for his skill in purchasing and of course he ought to possess that skill, or to suffer the consequences. If he furnish goods of this quality and they are, so far as his knowledge extends, free from any defect, he is under obligation to do nothing more than to offer them. He is under no obligations to explain their adaptation and direct the judgment of the buyer, unless by the law of benevolence. Having furnished goods to the best of his skill, and of the ordinary quality, his responsibility ceases, and it is the business of the buyer to decide whether the article is adapted to his wants. If, however, the seller have purchased a bad article and have been deceived, he has no right to sell it at the regular price on the ground that he gave as much for it as for what should have been good. The error of judgment was *his* and in his own profession; and *he* must bear the loss by selling the article for what it is worth. That this is the rule is evident from the contrary case. If he had, by superior skill, purchased an article at much less than its value, he would consider himself entitled to the advantage, and justly. Where he is entitled, however, to the benefit of his skill, he must under correspondent circumstances suffer from the want of it. Hence we say that a seller is under obligation to furnish goods at the market price and of the market quality, but is under no obligation to assist the judgment of the buyer unless the article for sale is defective, and then he is under obligation to reveal it.

The only exception to this rule is when, from the conditions of the sale, it is known that no guaranty is offered; as when a horse is sold at auction, without any recommendation. Here every man knows that he buys at his own risk and bids accordingly.

2. Everyone who makes it his business to sell is not only *bound* to sell, but is also *at liberty* to sell, at the market price. That he is *bound* to sell thus is evident from the fact that he takes every means to persuade the public that he sells thus; he would consider it a slander were anyone to assert the contrary; and were the contrary to be believed his custom would soon be ruined. Where a belief is so widely circulated and so earnestly inculcated by the seller, he is

manifestly under obligation to fulfill an expectation which he has been so anxious to create.

He is also *at liberty* to sell at the market price; that is, as he is obliged to sell without remuneration, or even with loss, if the article fall in price while in his possession, so he is at liberty to sell it at above a fair remuneration if the price of the article advances. As he must suffer in case of the fall of merchandise, he is entitled to the correspondent gain if merchandise rises; and thus his chance on both sides is equalized. Besides, by allowing the price of an article to rise with its scarcity, the rise itself is in the end checked; since by attracting an unusual amount of products to the place of scarcity the price is speedily reduced again to the ordinary and natural equilibrium of supply and demand.

It should, however, be remarked that this rule applies mainly to those whose occupation it is to traffic in the article bought and sold. A dealer in chinaware is bound to sell chinaware at the market price; but if a man insist upon buying his coat, he is under no such obligation for this is not his business. Should he put himself to inconvenience by selling his apparel to gratify the whim of his neighbor, he may, if he will, charge an extra price for this inconvenience. The rule applies in any other similar case. It would, however, become an honest man fairly to state that he did not sell at the market price, but that he charged what he chose as a remuneration for his trouble.[23]

3. While the seller is under no obligation to set forth the quality of his merchandise, yet he is at liberty to do so, confining himself to truth. He has, however, no right to influence the will of the buyer by any motives aside from those derived from the real value of the article in question.

Thus he has no right to appeal to the fears or hopes or avarice of the buyer. This rule is violated when, in dealings on the exchange, false information is circulated for the purpose of raising or depressing the price of stocks. It is violated by speculators, who monopolize an article to create an artificial scarcity and thus raise the price while the supply is abundant. The case is the same when a salesman looks upon a stranger who enters his store and deliberately calculates how

[23] This paragraph appears four paragraphs later in the 1835 edition.

he shall best influence and excite and mislead his mind so as to sell the greatest amount of goods at the most exorbitant profit. And in general, any attempt to influence the mind of the purchaser by motives aside from those derived from the true character of the article for sale are always doubtful, and generally vicious.

It is in vain to reply to this that if this were not done men could not support their families. We are not inquiring about the support of families, but about a question of right. And it is obvious that were this plea allowed, it would put an end to all questions of morals; for there never was an iniquity so infamous as not to find multitudes who were ready to justify it on this plea. But we altogether deny the validity of the plea. Were men to qualify themselves properly for their business and to acquire and exert a suitable skill in the management of it, that skill being beneficially exerted for the community at large, men would find it for their interest to employ it. He who understood his own profession well and industriously and honestly put his talents into requisition never stood in need of chicanery in order to support either himself or his family.

These remarks have been made with respect to the *seller*. But it is manifest that they are just as applicable to the *buyer*. Both parties are under equally imperative and correspondent obligations. If the seller be bound to furnish an article of ordinary quality and to sell it at the market price, that is, if he be obliged to exert his skill for the benefit of the buyer and to charge for that skill and capital no more than a fair remuneration, then the buyer is under the same obligation freely and willingly to pay that remuneration. It is disgraceful to him to wish the seller to labor for him for nothing or for less than a fair compensation. If the seller has no right by extraneous considerations to influence the motives of the buyer, the buyer has no right by any such considerations to influence the motives of the seller. The buyer is guilty of fraud if he underrate the seller's goods or by any of the artifices of traffic induces him to sell at less than a fair rate of profit. " 'Tis naught, 'tis naught, saith the buyer; but when he goeth his way, then he boasteth." Such conduct is as dishonest and dishonorable now as it was in the days of Solomon.

It has also been observed above that when the seller knows of any defect in his product, he is bound to declare it. The same rule, of course, applies to the buyer. If he know that the value of the article has risen, without the possibility of the owner's knowledge, he is bound to inform him of this change in its value. The sale is otherwise fraudulent. Hence all purchases and sales affected in consequence of secret information procured in advance of our neighbor are dishonest. If property rise in value, by the providence of God, while in my neighbor's possession, that rise of value is as much his as the property itself; and I may as honestly deprive him of the one, without an equivalent, as of the other.[24]

The ordinary pleas by which men excuse themselves for violation of the moral law of property are weak and wicked. Thus when men sell articles of a different quality from that which their name imports—as when wines or liquors are diluted or compounded; when the ordinary weight or measure is curtailed; or where employers defraud ignorant persons of their wages, as I am told is sometimes the case with those who employ certain classes of laborers —it is common to hear it remarked, "The competition is so great, that we could sell nothing, unless we adopted these methods;" or else, "The practice is universal, and if we did not do thus, other persons would, and so the evil would not be diminished." To all this, it is sufficient to reply: The law of God is explicit on this subject. "Thou shalt love thy neighbor as thyself;" and God allows of no excuses for the violation of his commands; "He hath shewed it unto them; therefore they are without excuse." These pleas are either true or false. If false, they ought to be abandoned. If true, then the traffic itself must be given up; for no man has any right to be engaged in any pursuit in violation of the laws of God.

A bargain is concluded when both parties have signified to each other their will to make the transfer; that is, that each chooses to part with his own property and to receive the property of the other in exchange. Henceforth, all the risk of loss and all the chances of gain are, of course, mutually transferred; although the articles themselves remain precisely as they were before. If a merchant buy a cargo of tea; after the sale, no matter where the tea is, the chances

[24] This paragraph and the next appear three paragraphs earlier in the 1835 edition.

of loss or gain are his and they are as much his in one place as in another.

So if the article, after the sale, have become injured before I take actual possession of it, I bear the loss; because, the right of ownership being vested in me, I could have removed it if I chose, and no one had a right, without my direction, to remove it.

The only exception to this exists in the case where, by custom or contract, the obligation to deliver is one of the conditions of the sale. Here the seller, of course, charges more for assuming the responsibility to deliver and he is to bear the risk for which he is fairly paid. It is frequently a question, When is the act of delivery completed? This must be settled by precedent; and can rarely be known in any country until a decision is had in the courts of law. As soon as such a case is adjudicated the respective parties govern themselves accordingly.

SECONDLY,[25] *when the transfer of property is temporary*. In this case, the borrower pays a stipulated equivalent for the use of it.

That he should do so is manifestly just, because the property in the hands of the owner is capable of producing an increase and the owner, if he held it, would derive the benefit of that increase. If he part with this benefit for the advantage of another, it is just that the other should allow him a fair remuneration. If the borrower could not, after paying this remuneration, grow richer than he would be without the use of his neighbor's capital, he would not borrow. But inasmuch as he, by the use of it, can be benefited, after paying for the use, no reason can be conceived why he should not pay for it.

The remuneration paid for the use of capital in the form of money is called *interest;* when in the form of land or houses, it is called *rent*.

The principles on which the rate of this remuneration is justly fixed are these: The borrower pays, first, for the use; and secondly, for the risk.

1. *For the use.*

Capital is more useful, that is, it is capable of producing a greater remuneration, at some times than at others. Thus a flour mill in some

[25] Heading numbered "Part II" in the 1865 edition.

seasons is more productive than in others. Land in some places is capable of yielding a greater harvest than in others. And thus at different times the same property may be capable of bringing in a very different income. And in general, where the amount of capital to be loaned is great and the number of those who want to borrow small, the interest will be low; and where the number of borrowers is great and the amount of capital small, the rate of interest will be high. The reasons of all this are too obvious to need illustration.

2. *For the risk.*

When an owner parts with his property it is put under the control of the borrower and passes, of course, beyond the control of the owner. Here there arises a risk over which he has no control. It varies with the character of the borrower for prudence and skill and with the kind of business in which he is engaged. Property in ships is exposed to greater risk than property in land. A man would consider the chance of having his property returned much better, if employed in the building of dwelling houses, than in the manufacture of gunpowder. Now as all these circumstances of risk may enter more or less into every loan, it is evident that they must, in justice, vary the rate at which a loan may be procured.[26]

Hence I think that the *rate* of interest, of every sort, being liable to so many circumstances of variation, should not in any case be fixed by law; but should be left in all cases to the discretion of the parties concerned.

This remark applies as well to loans of money as to loans of other property, because the reasons apply just as much to these as to any other. If it be said, men may charge exorbitant interest, I reply, so they may charge exorbitant rent for houses and exorbitant hire for horses. And, I ask, how is this evil of exorbitant charges in other cases remedied? The answer is plain. We allow a perfectly free competition and then the man who will not loan his property unless at an exorbitant price is underbidden, and his own rapacity defeats and punishes itself.

And, on the contrary, by fixing a legal rate of interest, we throw the whole community into the power of those who are willing to

---

[26] See Appendix (1) for four additional sentences appearing in the 1865 edition.

violate the law. For as soon as the actual value of money is more than the legal value, those who consider themselves under obligation to obey the laws of the land will not loan; for they can employ their property to better advantage. Hence if all were obedient to the law, as soon as property arrived at this point of value, loans would instantly and universally cease. But as some persons are willing to evade the law, they will loan at illegal interest; and as the capital of those who are conscientious is withdrawn from the market and an artificial scarcity is thus produced, those who are not conscientious have it in their power to charge whatever they choose.

Again, when we pay for money loaned, we pay, first, for the use, and, second, for the risk; that is, we pay literally a premium of insurance. As both of these vary with difference of time and with different individuals, there is a *double* reason for variation in the rate of interest. When we have a house insured we pay only for the risk; and hence there is here only a *single* cause of variation. But while all governments have fixed the rate of *interest* by law, they have never fixed the rate of *insurance;* which, being less variable, is more properly subject to a fixed rule. This is surely inconsistent; is it not also unjust?

Nevertheless, for the sake of avoiding disputes and errors of ignorance it might be wise for society to enact, by law, what shall be the rate of interest in cases where no rate is otherwise specified. This is the extent of its proper jurisdiction; and doing anything further is, I think, not only injurious to the interests of the community, but also a violation of the right of property. While, however, I hold this to be true, I by no means hold that, the laws remaining as they are, any individual is justified in taking or giving more than the legal rate of interest. When conscience does not forbid, it is the business of a good citizen to obey the laws; and the faithful obedience to an unwise law is generally the surest way of working its overthrow.

We shall now proceed to consider the laws which govern this mode of transfer of property.

The loan of *money.*

1. The *lender* is bound to demand no more than a fair remuneration for the use of his capital and for the risk to which it is exposed.

2. He is bound to make use of no unlawful means to influence the decision of the borrower. The principles here are the same as those which should govern the permanent exchange of property. All rumors and false alarms and all combinations of capitalists to raise by a monopoly the price of money are manifestly dishonest; nor are they the less so because *many persons may enter* into them or because they have the skill or the power to evade the laws of the land.

3. The *borrower* is bound to pay a just equivalent, as I have stated above; and he is equally forbidden to use any dishonest motives to influence the decision of the lender.

4. Inasmuch as the risk of the property is one part of the consideration for which the owner receives remuneration and as this is in every case supposed to be a specified quantity, the borrower has no right to expose the property of another to any risk not contemplated in the contract. Hence he has no right to invest it in a more hazardous trade or to employ it in a more hazardous speculation than that for which he borrowed it; and if he do, he is using it in a manner for which he has paid no equivalent. He is also under obligation to take all the care to avoid losses which he would take if the property were his own and to use the same skill to conduct his affairs successfully.

5. He is also bound to repay the loan exactly according to the terms specified in the contract. This requires that he pay the full sum promised and that he pay it precisely at the time promised. A failure in either case is a breach of the contract.

The question is often asked, whether a debtor is morally liberated by an act of insolvency. I think not, if he ever afterward have the means of repayment. It may be said, this is oppressive to debtors; but, we ask, is not the contrary principle oppressive to creditors; and are not the *rights* of one party just as valuable and just as much *rights* as those of the other? It may also be remarked that, were this principle acted upon, there would be fewer debtors and vastly fewer insolvents. The amount of money actually lost by insolvency is absolutely enormous; and it is generally lost by causeless, reckless speculation, by childish and inexcusable extravagance, or by gambling and profligacy, which are all stimulated into activity by the facility of credit and the facility with which debts may be cancelled by acts of insolvency. The more rigidly contracts are observed, the more rapidly will the capital of a country increase, the greater will be the inducements to industry, and the stronger will be the barriers against extravagance and vice.

Of the loan of *other property*.

The principles which apply in this case are very similar to those which have been already stated.

1. The *lender* is bound to furnish an article which, so far as he knows, is adapted to the purposes of the borrower. That is, if the thing borrowed has any internal defect he is bound to reveal it. If I loan a horse to a man who wishes to ride forty miles today which I know is able to go but thirty, it is a fraud. If I let to a man a house which I know to be in the neighborhood of a nuisance or to be in part uninhabitable from smoky chimneys, and do not inform him, it is fraud. The loss in the value of the property is mine and I have no right to transfer it to another.

2. So the lender has a right to charge the market price arising from the considerations of use, risk, and variation in supply and demand. This depends upon the same principles as those already explained.

3. The *borrower* is bound to take the same care of the property of another as he would of his own; to put it to no risk different from that specified or understood in the contract; and to pay the price, upon the principle stated above. Neither party has any right to influence the other by any motives extraneous to the simple business of the transfer.

4. The borrower is bound to return the property loaned precisely according to the contract. This includes both time and condition. He must return it at the time specified, and in the condition in which he received it, ordinary wear and tear only excepted. If I hire a house for a year and so damage its paper and paint that before it can be let again it will cost half the price of the rent to put it in repair, it is a gross fraud. I have, by negligence or other cause, de-

frauded the owner of half his rent. It is just as immoral as to pay him the whole and then pick his pocket of the half of what he had received.

The important question arises here, If a loss happen while the property is in the hands of the borrower, on whom shall it fall? The principle I suppose to be this:

1. If it happen while the property is subject to the use specified in the contract, the owner bears it; because it is to be supposed that he foresaw the risk, and received remuneration for it. As he was paid for the risk, he, of course, has assumed it, and justly suffers it.

2. If the loss happen in consequence of any use not contemplated in the contract, then the borrower suffers it. He having paid nothing for insurance against this risk, there is nobody but himself to sustain it and he sustains it accordingly. Besides, were any other principle adopted it must put an end to the whole business of loaning; for no one would part with his property temporarily, to be used in any manner the borrower pleased, and be himself responsible for all the loss. If a horse die while I am using it well, and for the purpose specified, the owner suffers. If it die by careless driving, I suffer the loss. He is bound to furnish a good horse, and I a competent driver.

3. So, on the contrary, if a *gain* arise unexpectedly. If this gain was one which was contemplated in the contract, it belongs to the borrower. If not, he has no equitable claim to it. If I hire a farm I am entitled, without any additional charge for rent, to all the advantages arising from the rise in the price of wheat or from my own skill in agriculture. But if a mine of coal be discovered on the farm I have no right to the benefit of working it; for I did not hire the farm for this purpose.

The case of insurance.

Here no transfer of property is made and, of course, nothing is paid for use. But the owner chooses to transfer the risk of use from himself to others and to pay, for their assuming this risk, a stipulated equivalent. The loss to society of property insured is just the same as when it is uninsured. A town is just as much poorer when property is destroyed that is insured, provided it be insured in the town as though no insurance were effected. The only difference is that the loss is equalized. Ten men can more easily replace one hundred dollars apiece who have nine hundred remaining than the eleventh can replace his whole property of one thousand.

The rule in this case is simple. The insured is bound fully to reveal to the insurer every circumstance within his knowledge which could in any measure affect the value of the risk; that is to say, the property must be, so far as he knows, what it purports to be, and the risks none other than such as he reveals them. If he expose the property to other risks the insurance is void; and the underwriter, if the property be lost, refuses to remunerate him; and if it be safe, he returns the premium. If the loss occur within the terms of the policy the insurer is bound fully and faithfully to make remuneration precisely according to the terms of the contract.

As to the rate of insurance very little need be said. It varies with every risk and is made up of so many conflicting circumstances that it must be agreed upon by the parties themselves. When the market in this species of traffic is unrestrained by monopolies the price of insurance, like that of any other commodity, will regulate itself.

II. *Next, where the equivalent is* IMMATERIAL, as where one party pays remuneration for some service rendered by the other.

The principal cases here are these: That of master and servant and that of principal and agent.

1. Of *master and servant.*

1. The *master* is bound to allow to the servant a fair remuneration. This is justly estimated by uniting the considerations of labor, skill, and fidelity, varied by the rise and fall of the price of such labor in the market. As this, however, would be liable to inconvenient fluctuation, it is generally adjusted by a rate agreed upon by the parties.

2. He is bound to allow him all the privileges to which moral law or established usage entitles him unless something different from the latter has been stipulated in the contract; and he is at liberty to require of him service upon the same principles.

3. The *servant* is bound to perform the labor assigned him by usage or by contract (matters of conscience only excepted), with all the skill which he possesses, making the interests of the employer his own. If either party fail—that is, if the master demand service

for which he does not render compensation or if the servant receive wages for which he does not render the stipulated equivalent—there is a violation of the right of property. Thus also, there is a violation of right if the master do not fulfill the terms of the contract just as it was made; as, for instance, if he do not pay a servant punctually. When the service is performed the wages belong to the servant and the master has no more right to them than to the property of anyone else. Thus saith St. James: "The hire of your laborers that have reaped your fields, that is *kept back* by fraud, crieth, and the cry is come into the ears of the Lord of Sabaoth." And, on the contrary, the servant is bound to use his whole skill and economy in managing the property of his master, and if he destroy it by negligence or fault, he ought to make restitution.

2. Of *principal and agent.*

It frequently happens that in the transaction of business duties devolve upon an individual which are to be discharged in different places at the same time. In other cases, in consequence of the subdivision of labor, he requires something to be done for him which another person can do better than himself. In both cases, either from necessity or for his own convenience and interest, he employs other men as agents.

Agencies are of two kinds; *first,* where the principal simply employs another to fulfill his own (that is, the principal's) will. Here the principal's will is the rule both as to the object to be accomplished and the manner in which, and the means whereby, it is to be accomplished. *Secondly.* Where the principal only designates the objects to be accomplished, reposing special trust in the skill and fidelity of the agent as to the means by which it is to be accomplished. Such I suppose to be the case in regard to professional assistance.

The laws on this subject respect, *first,* the relation existing between the principal and the community; and *secondly,* the relation existing between the principal and agent.

I. The principal is bound by the acts of the agent while the agent is employed in the business for which the principal has engaged him; but he is responsible no farther.

Thus it is known that a merchant employs a clerk to receive money on his account. For his clerk's transactions in this part of his affairs he is responsible; but he would not be responsible if money were paid to his porter or coachman, because he does not employ them for this purpose. Hence if the clerk be unfaithful and secrete the money, the merchant suffers; if the coachman receive the money and be unfaithful, the payer suffers. It is the merchant's business to employ suitable agents; but it is the business of his customers to apply to those agents only whom he has employed.

An important question arises here, namely, When is it to be understood that a principal has employed an agent? It is generally held that if the principal acknowledge himself responsible for the acts of the agent, he is hereafter held to be responsible for similar acts until he gives notice to the contrary.

II. Laws arising from the relation subsisting between the principal and the agent.

1. The laws respecting compensation are the same as those already specified and therefore need not be repeated.

2. The agent is bound to give the same care to the affairs of the principal as to his own. He is another self and should act in that capacity. The necessity of this rule is apparent from the fact that no other rule could be devised either by which the one party would know what justly to demand or the other when the demands of justice were fulfilled.

Hence if an agent do not give all the care to the affairs of his principal that he would do to his own and loss occur, he ought to sustain it. If a lawyer lose a cause through negligence or palpable ignorance he ought, in justice, to suffer the consequences. He receives fees for conducting the cause to the best of his ability and, by undertaking to conduct it, puts it out of the power of the client to employ anyone else. Thus, if he neglect it and, by neglecting it, his client is worse off than if he had not undertaken it, he accepts fees for really injuring his neighbor. He ought to bear the loss which has occurred by his own fault.

A question frequently arises here of considerable importance. It is, When is he obliged to obey the instructions of his principal; and when is he obliged to act without regard to them? Although this question does not come under the right of property, it may be as well to notice it here as anywhere else.

The question, I suppose, is to be answered by deciding to which of the above specified kinds of agencies the case to be considered belongs.

1. If it be *simple* agency, that is, where the agent undertakes merely to execute the will of the principal, and in the manner and by the means specified by the principal, he must obey *implicitly* (conscience only excepted), unless some fact material to the formation of a judgment has come to light after giving the order which, if known, would have necessarily modified the intention of the principal. This is the law of the military service. Here, even when the reason for disobedience of orders is ever so clear and an agent disobeys, he does it at his own risk; and hence the modifying facts should be obvious and explicit, in order to justify a variation from the instructions.

2. When the agency is of the other kind, and the will of the principal is only supposed to direct the end, while the means and manner are to be decided upon by the professional skill of the agent, I suppose that the agent is not bound to obey the directions of his principal. He is supposed to know more on the subject and to be better able to decide what will benefit his principal than the principal himself; and he has no right to injure another man, even if the other man desire it; nor has he a right to lend himself as an instrument by which another man, by consequence of his ignorance, shall injure himself. Besides, every man has a professional reputation to sustain, on which his means of living depend. He has no right to injure this for the sake of gratifying another, especially when by so gratifying the other, he shall ruin himself also. A physician has no right to give his patient drugs which will poison him because a patient wishes it. A lawyer has no right to bring a cause into court in such a manner as will ensure the loss of it because his client insists upon it. The professional agent is bound to conduct the business of his profession to the best of his ability. This is the end of his responsibility. If it please his client, well; if not, the relation must cease and the principal must find another agent.

A representative in Congress is manifestly an agent of the latter of these two classes. He is chosen on account of his supposed legislative ability. Hence he is strictly a professional agent; and on these principles he is under no sort of obligation to regard the instructions of his constituents. He is merely bound to promote their best interests, but the *manner* of doing it is to be decided by his superior skill and ability.[27]

But secondly, is he bound to resign his seat if he differ from them in opinion? This is a question to be decided by the constitution of the country under which he acts. Society, that is, the whole nation, have a right to form a government as they will; and to choose representatives *during good behavior,* that is, for as long a time as they and their representatives entertain the same views; or, setting aside this mode for reasons which may seem good to themselves, to elect them for a *certain period of service.* Now if they have chosen the latter mode they have bound themselves to abide by it and have abandoned the former. If they elect him during pleasure, he is *so elected.* If they, on the contrary, elect him for two years or for six years, *he is so elected.* And so far as I can discover, here the question rests. It is in the power of society to alter the tenure of office if they please; but until it be altered neither party can claim anything *more* or *different from* what that tenure actually and virtually expresses.

Section III · *The Right of Property as Violated By Society*

I have already stated that whatever a man possesses he possesses exclusively of every man and of all men. He has a right to use his property in such a manner as will promote his own happiness, provided he do not interfere with the rights of others. But with this right society may interfere as well as individuals; and the injury is here the greater, inasmuch as it is remediless. In this world the individual knows of no power superior to society, and from its decisions, even when unjust, he has no appeal. A few suggestions on this part of the subject will close the present chapter.

I have mentioned that the individual has a right to use his

[27] See Appendix (J) for sentences added in the 1865 edition.

property innocently, as he will, exclusively of any man or of all men. It is proper to state here that this right is apparently modified by his becoming a member of society. When men form a civil society they mutually agree to confer upon the individual certain benefits upon certain conditions. But as these benefits cannot be attained without incurring some expenses, as, for instance, those of courts of justice, legislation, &c., it is just that every individual who enters the society and thus enjoys these benefits should pay his portion of the expense. By the very act of becoming a member of society he renders himself answerable for his portion of that burden without the incurring of which, society could not exist. He has his option to leave society or to join it. But if he join it, he must join it on the same conditions as others. He demands the benefit of laws and of protection; but he has no right to demand what other men have purchased unless he will pay for it an equitable price.

From these principles it will follow that society has a natural right to require every individual to contribute his portion of those expenses necessary to the existence of society.

Besides these, however, the members of a society have the power to agree together to contribute for objects which, if not essential to the existence, are yet important to the well being of society. If they so agree, they are bound to fulfill this agreement; for a contract between the individual and society is as binding as one between individual and individual. Hence if such an agreement be made society has a right to enforce it. This, however, by no means decides the question of the original wisdom of any particular compact; much less is it meant to be asserted that the individual is bound by the acts of a majority when that majority has exceeded its power. These subjects belong to a subsequent chapter. What is meant to be asserted here is that there may arise cases in which society *may* rightfully oblige the individual to contribute for purposes which are not *absolutely necessary to the existence* of society.

The difference which we wish to establish is this: In the case of whatever is necessary to the existence of society, society has a natural right to oblige the individual to bear his part of the burden; that is, it has a right over his property to this amount without obtaining any concession on his part. Society has, manifestly, a right to whatever is necessary to its own existence.

Whatever, on the other hand, is not necessary to the existence of society, is not in the power of society unless it has been conferred upon it by the will of the individual. That this is the rule is evident from the necessity of the case. No other rule could be devised which would not put the property of the individual *wholly* in the power of society; or, in other words, absolutely destroy the liberty of the individual.

If such be the facts it will follow that society has a right over the property of the individual for all purposes necessary to the existence of society; and secondly, in all respects in which the individual has conferred that power, but only for the purposes for which it was conferred.

And hence, 1. It is the duty of the individual to hold his property always subject to these conditions; and for such purposes freely to contribute his portion of that expense for which he, in common with others, is receiving an equivalent. No one has any more right than another to receive a consideration without making a remuneration.

2. The individual has a right to demand that no impositions be laid upon him unless they come under the one or the other of these classes.

3. He has a right to demand that the burdens of society be laid upon individuals according to some equitable law. This law should be founded, as nearly as possible upon the principle that each one should pay in proportion to the benefits which he receives from the protection of society. As these benefits are either personal or pecuniary, and as those which are personal are equal, it would seem just that the variation should be in proportion to property.

If these principles be just it is evident that society may violate the right of individual property in the following ways:

1. By taking, through the means of government, which is its agent, the property of the individual arbitrarily, or merely by the will of the executive. Such is the nature of the exactions in despotic governments.

2. When, by arbitrary will or by law, it takes the property of the individual for purposes which, whether good or bad, are not necessary to the existence of society when the individuals of society have not consented that it be so appropriated. This consent is never to be *presumed* except in the case of *necessary* expenditures, as has been shown. Whenever this plea cannot be made good society has no right to touch the property of the individual unless it can show the constitutional provision. Were our government to levy a tax to build churches, it would avail nothing to say that churches were wanted or that the good of society demanded it; it would be an invasion of the right of property until the article in the constitution could be shown, granting to the government power over property for this very purpose.

3. Society, even when the claim is just, may violate the rights of the individual by adopting an inequitable rule in the distribution of the public burdens. Every individual has an equal right to employ his property unmolested in just such manner as will innocently promote his own happiness. That is, it is to society a matter of indifference in what way he employs it. Provided it be innocent, it does not come within the view of society. Hence in this respect all modes of employing it are equal. And the only question to be considered in adjusting the appropriation is, How much does he ask society to protect? and by this rule it should, as we have said before, be adjusted. If, then, besides this rule, another be adopted; and an individual be obliged, besides his *pro rata* proportion, to bear a burden levied *on his particular calling* to the exemption of *another,* he has a right to complain. He is obliged to bear a double burden, and one portion of the burden is laid for a cause over which society professes itself to have no jurisdiction.

4. Inasmuch as the value of property depends upon the unrestrained use which I am allowed to make of it for the promotion of my individual happiness, society interferes with the right of property if it in any manner abridge any of these. One man is rendered happy by accumulation, another by benevolence; one by promoting science, another by promoting religion. Each one has a right to use what is his own exactly as he pleases. And if society interfere by di-

recting the manner in which he shall appropriate it, it is an act of injustice. It is as great a violation of property, for instance, to interfere with the purpose of the individual in the appropriation of his property for religious purposes, as it is to enact that a farmer shall keep but three cows or a manufacturer employ but ten workmen.

CHARACTER is the present intellectual, social, and moral condition of an individual. It comprehends his actual acquisitions, his capacities, his habits, his tendencies, his moral feelings, and everything which enters into a man's state for the present, or his powers for attaining to a better state in the future.

That character in this sense is by far the most important of all the possessions which a man can call his own is too evident to need discussion. It is the source of all that he either suffers or enjoys here, and of all that he either fears or hopes for hereafter.

If such be the fact, benevolence would teach us the obligation to do all in our power to improve the character of our neighbor. This is its chief office. This is the great practical aim of Christianity. Reciprocity merely prohibits the infliction of any injury upon the character of another.

The reasons of this prohibition are obvious. No man can injure his own character without violating the laws of God and also creating those tendencies which result in violation of the laws of man. He who in any manner becomes voluntarily the cause of this violation is a partaker—and, not unfrequently, the largest partaker—in the guilt. As he who tempts another to suicide is in the sight of God guilty of murder, so he who instigates another to wickedness by producing those states of mind which necessarily lead to it is in the sight of God held responsible in no slight degree for the result.

Again, consider the motives which lead men to injure the character of each other. These are either pure malice or reckless self-gratification.

First, malice. Some men so far transcend the ordinary limits of human depravity as to derive a truly fiendlike pleasure from alluring and seducing from the paths of virtue the comparatively innocent, and to exult over the moral desolations which they have thus accomplished. "They will compass sea and land to make one proselyte, and when he is made, they make him tenfold more the child of hell than themselves." It is scarcely necessary to add that language has no terms of moral indignation that are capable of branding with adequate infamy conduct so intensely vicious. It is wickedness without excuse and without palliation. Or, secondly, take the more favorable case. One man wishes to accomplish some purpose of self-gratification, to indulge his passions, to increase his power, or to feed his vanity; and he proceeds to accomplish that purpose by means of rendering another immortal and accountable moral creature degraded forever—a moral pest henceforth on earth, and both condemned and the cause of condemnation to others throughout eternity. Who has given this wretch a right to work so awful a ruin among God's creatures for the gratification of a momentary and an unholy desire? And will not the Judge of all, when he maketh inquisition for blood, press to the lips of such a sinner the bitterest dregs of the cup of trembling?

With this, all the teaching of the sacred Scriptures is consonant. The most solemn maledictions in the Holy Scriptures are uttered against those who have been the instruments of corrupting others. In the Old Testament, Jeroboam is signalized as a sinner of unparalleled atrocity, because he *made Israel to sin*. In the New Testament the judgment of the Pharisees has been already alluded to. And, again, "Whosoever shall break the least of these commandments, and shall *teach men so,* shall be called least in the kingdom of heaven." By comparison with the preceding verse, the meaning of this passage is seen to be that, as the doing and teaching the commandments of God is the great proof of virtue, so the breaking them and the teaching others to break them is the great proof of vice. And in the Revelation, where God is represented as taking signal vengeance upon Babylon, it is because "she did *corrupt the earth* with her wickedness."

The moral precept on this subject, then, is briefly this: We are forbidden, for any cause or under any pretense or in any manner, willingly to vitiate the character of another.

This prohibition may be violated in two ways:

1. By weakening the moral restraints of men.
2. By exciting their evil passions.

I. BY WEAKENING THE MORAL RESTRAINTS OF MEN.

It has been already shown that the passions of men were intended to be restrained by conscience; and that the restraining power of conscience is increased by the doctrines and motives derived from natural and revealed religion. Whoever, therefore, in any manner renders obtuse the moral sensibilities of others, or diminishes the power of that moral truth by which these sensibilities are rendered operative, inflicts permanent injury upon the character of his fellow men. This also is done by all wicked example; for, as we have seen before, the sight of wickedness weakens the power of conscience over us. It is done when, either by conversation or by writing, the distinctions between right and wrong are treated with open scorn or covert contempt; by all conduct calculated to render inoperative the sanctions of religion, as profanity or Sabbath breaking; by ridicule of the obligations of morality and religion under the names of superstition, priestcraft, prejudices of education; or by presenting to men such views of the character of God as would lead them to believe that He cares very little about the moral actions of his creatures but is willing that everyone shall live as he chooses; and that therefore the self-denials of virtue are only a form of gratuitous, self-inflicted torture.

It is against this form of moral injury that the young need to be specially upon their guard. The moral seducer, if he be a practiced villain, corrupts the principles of his victim before he attempts to influence his or her practice. It is not until the moral restraints are silently removed and the heart left defenseless that he presents the allurements of vice, and goads the passions to madness. His task is then easy. If he have succeeded in the first effort, he will rarely fail in the second. Let every young man, especially every young woman, beware of listening for a moment to any conversation of which the object is to show that the restraints of virtue are unnecessary, or to diminish in aught the reverence and obedience which are due from the creature to the law of the Creator.

II. We injure the characters of men BY EXCITING TO ACTION THEIR EVIL DISPOSITIONS.

1. *By viciously stimulating their imaginations*. No one is corrupt in action until he has become corrupt in imagination. And, on the

other hand, he who has filled his imagination with conceptions of vice, and who loves to feast his depraved moral appetite with imaginary scenes of impurity, needs but the opportunity to become openly abandoned. Hence, one of the most nefarious means of corrupting men is to spread before them those images of pollution by which they will in secret become familiar with sin. Such is the guilt of those who write, or publish, or sell, or lend vicious books, under whatever name or character, and of those who engrave, or publish, or sell, or lend, or exhibit obscene or lascivious pictures. Few instances of human depravity are marked by deeper atrocity than that of an author or a publisher who, from literary vanity or sordid love of gain, pours forth over society a stream of moral pollution, either in prose or in poetry.

And yet there are not only men who will do this, but what is worse, there are men, yes, and women, too, who if the culprit have possessed talent will commend it, and even weep tears of sympathy over the infatuated genius who was so sorely persecuted by that unfeeling portion of the world, who would not consider talent synonymous with virtue, and who could not applaud the effort of that ability which was exerted only to multiply the victims of vice.

2. *By ministering to the appetites of others.* Such is the relation of the power of appetite to that of conscience that where no positive allurements to vice are set before men, conscience will frequently retain its ascendancy. While, on the other hand, if allurement be added to the power of appetite, reason and conscience prove a barrier too feeble to resist their combined and vicious tendency. Hence, he who presents the allurements of vice before others, who procures and sets before them the means of vicious gratification, is in a great degree responsible for the mischief which he produces. Violations of this law occur in most cases of immoral traffic, as in the sale and manufacture of intoxicating liquors, the sale of opium to the Chinese, &c. Under the same class is also comprehended the case of female prostitution.

3. *By using others to minister to our vicious appetites.* We cannot use others as ministers to our vices without rendering them corrupt, and frequently inflicting an incurable wound upon their moral

nature. For the sake of a base and wicked momentary gratification, the vicious man willingly ruins forever an immortal being who was but for him innocent; and, yet more, not unfrequently considers this ruin a matter of triumph. Such is the case in seduction and adultery, and in a modified degree in all manner of lewdness and profligacy.

4. *By cherishing the evil passions of men.* By passion, in distinction from appetite, I mean the spiritual in opposition to the corporeal desires. It frequently happens that we wish to influence men who cannot be moved by an appeal to their reason or conscience, but who can be easily moved by an appeal to their ambition, their avarice, their party zeal, their pride, or their vanity. An acquaintance with these peculiarities of individuals is frequently called *understanding human nature, knowing the weak sides of men,* and is by many persons considered the grand means for great and masterly effect. But he can have but little practical acquaintance with a conscience void of offense who does not instinctively feel that such conduct is unjust, mean, and despicable. It is accomplishing our purposes by means of the moral degradation of him of whom we profess to be the friends. It is manifestly doing a man a greater injury than simply to rob him. If we stole his money, he would be injured only by being made poorer. If we procure his services or his money in this manner, we also make him poorer; and we besides cultivate those evil dispositions which already expose him to sharpers; and also render him more odious to the God before whom he must shortly stand.

Nor do the ordinary excuses on this subject avail. It may be said, men would not give to benevolent objects but from these motives. Suppose it true. What if they did not? They would be as well off *morally* as they are now. A man is no better, after having refused from avarice, who at length gives from vanity. His avarice is no better, and his vanity is even worse. It may be said, the cause of benevolence could not be sustained without it. Then, I say, let the cause of benevolence perish. God never meant one party of his creatures to be relieved by our inflicting moral injury upon another. If there be no other way of sustaining benevolence, God did not mean that benevolence should be sustained. But it is not so. The appeal to men's better feelings is the proper appeal to be made to men. It will, when properly made, generally succeed; and if it do not, our responsibility is at an end.

I cannot leave this subject without urging it upon those who are engaged in promoting the objects of benevolent associations. It seems to me that no man has a right to present any other than an innocent motive to urge his fellow men to action. Motives derived from party zeal, from personal vanity, from love of applause, however covertly insinuated, are not of this character. If a man by exciting such feelings sold me a horse at twice its value, he would be a sharper. If he excite me to *give* from the same motives, the action *partakes* of the same character. The cause of benevolence is holy: it is the cause of God. It needs not human chicanery to approve it to the human heart. Let him who advocates it, therefore, go forth strong in the strength of Him whose cause he advocates. Let him rest his cause upon its own merits, and leave every man's conscience to decide whether or not he will enlist himself in its support. And, besides, were men conscientiously to confine themselves to the merits of their cause, they would much more carefully weigh their undertakings before they attempted to enlist others in support of them. Much of that fanaticism which withers the moral sympathies of man would thus be checked at the outset.

CHAPTER FOURTH

OF JUSTICE AS IT RESPECTS REPUTATION

It has been already remarked that every man is by the laws of his Creator entitled to the physical results of his labor; that is, to those results which arise from the operation of those laws of cause and effect, which govern the material on which he operates. Thus if a man form several trees into a house, the result of this labor, supposing the materials and time to be his own, are his own also. Thus, again, if a man study diligently, the amount of knowledge which he gains is at his own disposal; and he is at liberty innocently to use it as he will. And in general if a man be industrious, the immediate results of industry are his, and no one has any right to interfere with them.

But these are not the only results. There are others springing from those laws of cause and effect which govern the opinions and actions of men toward each other, which are frequently of as great importance to the individual as the physical results. Thus if a man have built a house, the house is his. But if he have done it well, there arises in the minds of men a certain opinion of his skill, and a regard toward him on account of it, which may be of more value to him than even the house itself; for it may be the foundation of great subsequent good fortune. The industrious student is entitled not merely to the use of that knowledge which he has acquired but also to the esteem which the possession of that knowledge gives him among men. Now these secondary and indirect results, though they may follow other laws of cause and effect, are yet as truly effects of the original cause, that is, of the character and actions of the man himself, and they as truly belong to him, as the primary and direct results of which we have before spoken. And, hence, to diminish the esteem in which a man is held by his fellows, to detract from the reputation which he has thus acquired, is as great a violation of justice, nay, it may be a far greater violation of justice, than robbing him of money. It has, moreover, the additional aggravation of conferring no benefit upon the aggressor beyond that of the gratification of a base and malignant passion.

But, it may be said, the man has a reputation greater than he deserves, or a reputation for that which he does not deserve. Have I not a right to diminish it to its true level?

We answer, The objection proceeds upon the concession that the man *has a reputation*. That is, men have such or such an opinion concerning him. Now the rule of property, formerly mentioned, applies here. If a man be in possession of property, though unjustly in possession, this gives to no one a right to seize upon that property for himself, or to seize it and destroy it, unless he can himself show a better title. The very fact of possession bars every other claimant except that claimant whom the present possessor has defrauded. So in this case, if this reputation injures the reputation of another, the other has a right to set forth his own claims; and anyone else has a right when prompted by a *desire of doing justice to the injured* to state the facts as they are; but where this element of desire to do justice does not enter, no man has a right to diminish the esteem in which another is held simply because *he may believe* the other to have more than he deserves.

The moral rule on this subject I suppose to be this: We are forbidden to utter anything which will be injurious to the reputation of another, except for adequate cause. I say *for adequate cause* because occasions may occur in which it is as much our duty to speak, as it is at other times our duty to be silent. The consideration of these cases will be a subsequent concern. The precept thus understood applies to the cases in which we speak either *from no sufficient motive,* or *from a bad motive*. It is merely an extension of the great principle of the law of reciprocity, which commands us to have the same simple desire that every other man should enjoy unmolested the esteem in which he is held by men, that we have to enjoy unmolested the same possession ourselves.

I do not here consider the cases in which we utter, either willfully or thoughtlessly, injurious *falsehood* respecting another. In these cases the guilt of lying is superadded to that of slander. I merely here consider slander by itself; it being understood that when what is asserted is false, it involves the sin of lying besides the violation of the law of reciprocity which we are here endeavoring to enforce.

The precept includes several specifications. Some of them it may be important to enumerate.

I. It prohibits us from giving publicity to the bad actions of men without cause. The guilt here consists in *causelessly giving publicity*. Of course it does not include those cases in which the man himself gives publicity to his own bad actions. He has himself diminished his reputation, and his act becomes a part of public indiscriminate information. We are at liberty to mention this, like any other fact, when the mention of it is demanded; but not to do it for the sake of injuring him. So whenever his bad actions are made known by the providence of God, it comes under the same rule. Thus I may know that a man has acted dishonestly. This alone does not give me liberty to speak of it. But if his dishonesty have been proved before a court of justice, it then becomes really a part of his reputation, and I am at liberty to speak of it in the same manner as of any other fact. Yet even here, if I speak of it with pleasure or with a desire of injury I commit sin.

Some of the reasons for this rule are the following:

1. The very act itself is injurious to the slanderer's own moral character, and to that of him who lends himself to be his auditor. Familiarity with wrong diminishes our abhorrence of it. The contemplation of it in others fosters the spirit of envy and uncharitableness, and leads us in the end to exult in, rather than sorrow over, the faults of others.

2. In the present imperfect state, where every individual, being fallible, must fail somewhere, if everyone were at liberty to speak of all the wrong and all the imperfection of everyone whom he knew, society would soon become intolerable from the festering of universal ill will. What would become of families, of friendships, of communities, if parents and children, husbands and wives, acquaintances, neighbors, and citizens, should proclaim every failing which they knew or heard of respecting each other? Now there can no medium be established between telling everything, and forbidding everything to be told which is told without adequate cause.

3. We may judge of the justice of the rule by applying it to ourselves. We despise the man who, either thoughtlessly or maliciously,

proclaims what he considers, either justly or unjustly, our failings. Now, what can be more unjust or more despicable than to do that which our own conscience testifies to be unjust and despicable in others?

II. The same law forbids us to utter general conclusions respecting the characters of men, drawn from particular bad actions which they may have committed. This is manifest injustice, and it includes, frequently, lying as well as slander. A single action is rarely decisive of character, even in repect to that department of character to which it belongs. A single illiberal action does not prove a man to be covetous, any more than a single act of charity proves him to be benevolent. How unjust, then, must it be to proclaim a man destitute of a whole class of virtues because of one failure in virtue! How much more unjust on account of one fault to deny him all claim to any virtue whatsoever! Yet such is frequently the very object of calumny. And in general this form of vice is added to that just noticed. Men first, in violation of the law of reciprocity, make public the evil actions of others; and then, with a malignant power of generalization, proceed to deny their claims, not only to a whole class of virtues, but not unfrequently to all virtue whatsoever. The reasons in this case are similar to those just mentioned.

III. We are forbidden to *judge,* that is, to assign unnecessarily bad motives to the actions of men. I say unnecessarily, for some actions are in their nature such that to presume a good motive is impossible.

This rule would teach us, first, to presume no unworthy motive when the action is susceptible of an innocent one.

And secondly, never to ascribe to an action which we confess to be good any other motive than that from which it proposes to proceed.

This is the rule by which we are bound to be governed in our own *private opinions* of men. And if from any circumstances we are led to entertain any doubts of the motives of men, we are bound to retain these doubts within our own bosoms unless we are obliged for some sufficient reason to disclose them. But if we are obliged to adopt this rule respecting *our own opinions of others,* by how much more are we obliged to adopt it in the *publication* of our opinions! If we are not allowed unnecessarily to suppose an unworthy motive, by how much less are we allowed to circulate it, and thus render it universally supposed! "Charity thinketh no evil, rejoiceth not in iniquity."

The reasons for this rule are obvious:

1. The motives of men, unless rendered evident by their actions, can be known to God alone. They are, evidently, out of the reach of man. In assigning motives unnecessarily, we therefore undertake to assert as fact what we at the outset confess that we have not the means of knowing to be such; which is in itself falsehood: and we do all this for the sake of gratifying a contemptible vanity or a wicked envy; or, what is scarcely less reprehensible, from a thoughtless love of talking.

2. There is no offense by which we are excited to a livelier or more just indignation than by the misinterpretation of our own motives. This quick sensitiveness in ourselves should admonish us of the guilt which we incur, when we traduce the motives of others.

IV. By the same rule we are forbidden to lessen the estimation in which others are held, by ridicule, mimicry, or by any means by which they are brought into contempt. No man can be greatly respected by those to whom he is the frequent subject of laughter. It is but a very imperfect excuse for conduct of this sort to plead that we do not mean any harm. What *do* we mean? Surely reasonable beings should be prepared to answer this question. Were the witty calumniator to stand concealed and hear himself made the subject of remarks precisely similar to those in which he indulges respecting others, he would have a very definite conception of what *others mean*. Let him, then, carry the lesson home to his own bosom.

Nor is this evil the less for the veil under which it is frequently and hypocritically hidden. Men and women propagate slander under the cover of secrecy, supposing that by uttering it under this injunction the guilt is of course removed. But it is not so. The simple question is this: Does my duty either to God or to man require me to publish this which will injure another? If it do, publish it wherever that duty requires, and do it fearlessly. If it do not, it is just as great guilt to publish it to one as to another. We are bound in all such cases to ask ourselves the question, Am I under obligation to tell this fact to this person? If not, I am under the contrary obligation to be silent. And still more. This injunction of secrecy is generally nothing better than the mere dictate of cowardice. We wish to gratify our love of detraction, but are afraid of the consequences to ourselves. We therefore converse under this injunction, that the injury to another may be with impunity to ourselves. And hence it is that in this manner the vilest and most injurious calumnies are generally circulated.

And lastly, if all this be so, it will be readily seen that a very large portion of the ordinary conversation of persons, even in many respects estimable, is far from being innocent. How very common is personal character, in all its length and breadth, the matter of common conversation! And in this discussion men seem to forget that they are under any other law than that which is administered by a judge and jury. How commonly are characters dissected with apparently the only object of displaying the power of malignant acumen possessed by the operator, as though another's reputation were made for no other purpose than the gratification of the meanest and most unlovely attributes of the human heart! Well may we say with the apostle James, "If any man offend not *in word,* the same is a perfect man, able to bridle the whole body." Well may we tremble before the declaration of the blessed Saviour: "For every idle word that men speak, they shall give an account in the day of judgment."

The following extract from Bishop Wilson on this subject breathes the spirit of true Christian philanthropy: "It is too true, that some evil passion or other, and to gratify our corruption, is the aim of most conversations. We love to speak of past troubles; hatred and ill will make us take pleasure in relating the evil actions of our enemies. We compare, with some degree of pride, the advantages which we have over others. We recount, with too sensible a pleasure, the worldly happiness which we enjoy. This strengthens our passions, and increases our corruption. God grant that I may watch against a weakness that has such evil consequences! May I never hear, and never repeat with pleasure, such things as may dishonor

God, hurt my own character, or injure my neighbor!"—*Bishop Wilson's Sacra Privata.*

The precepts of the Scriptures on this subject are numerous and explicit. It will be necessary here to refer only to a few, for the sake of illustrating their general tendency: "Judge not, that ye be not judged: for with what judgment ye judge, ye shall be judged; and with what measure ye mete, it shall be measured to you again. And why beholdest thou the mote that is in thy brother's eye, but considerest not the beam that is in thine own eye?" *Matthew* vii, 1–5. "Let all bitterness, and wrath, and clamor, and evil-speaking, be put away from you." *Ephesians* iv, 31. "Speak evil of no man." *Titus* iii, 2. "He that will love life, and see good days, let him refrain his tongue from evil." 1 *Peter* iii, 10.

See also *James,* third chapter, for a graphic delineation of the miseries produced by the unlicensed use of the tongue.

Secondly. I have thus far considered the cases in which *silence* respecting the evil actions of others is our duty. It is our duty when we have no just cause, either for speaking at all, or for speaking to the particular person whom we address. But where there is a sufficient cause, we are under an equally imperative obligation to speak, wherever and whenever that cause shall demand it. The common fault of men is that they speak when they should be silent and are silent only when they should speak.

The plain distinction in this case is the following: We are forbidden causelessly to injure another, even if he have done wrong. Yet whenever justice can be done or innocence protected in no other manner than by a course which must injure him, we are under no such prohibition. No man has a right to expect to do wrong with impunity; much less has he a right to expect that in order to shield him from the past consequences of his actions injustice should be done to others, or that other men shall by silence deliver up the innocent and unwary into his power.

The principle by which we are to test our own motives in speaking of that which may harm others, is this: When we utter anything which will harm another, and we do it either without cause, or with pleasure, or thoughtlessly, we are guilty of calumny. When we do it with *pain and sorrow for the offender,* and from the sincere motive of *protecting the innocent,* of *promoting the ends of public justice,* or *for the good of the offender himself,* and speak of it only *to such persons* and *in such manner* as is consistent with these ends, we may speak of the evil actions of others and yet be wholly innocent of calumny.

We are therefore bound to speak of the faults of others,

1. *To promote the ends of public justice.* He who conceals a crime against society renders himself a party to the offense. We are bound here not merely to speak of it, but also to speak of it to the proper civil officer in order that it may be brought to trial and punishment. The ordinary prejudice against informing is unwise and immoral. He who *from proper motives* informs against crime, performs an act as honorable as that of the judge who tries the cause, or of the juror who returns the verdict. That this *may be done* from improper motives alters not the case. A judge *may* hold his office for the love of money, but this does not make the office despicable.

2. *To protect the innocent.* When we are possessed of a knowledge of certain facts in a man's history, which if known to a third person would protect him from important injury, it may frequently be our duty to put that person on his guard. If A knows that B, under the pretense of religion, is insinuating himself into the good opinion of C for the purpose of gaining control over his property, A is bound to put C upon his guard. If I know that a man who is already married is paying his addresses to a lady in another country, I am bound to give her the information. So, if I know of a plan laid for the purpose of seduction, I am bound to make use of that knowledge to defeat it. All that is required here is that I know what I assert to be fact; and that I use it simply for the purposes specified.

3. *For the good of the offender himself.* When we know of the crimes of another, and there is some person—for instance, a parent, a guardian, or instructor—who might by control or advice be the means of the offender's reformation, it is our duty to give the necessary information. It is frequently the greatest kindness that we can manifest to both parties. Were it more commonly practiced, the allurements to sin would be much less attractive, and the hope

of success in correcting the evil habits of the young, much more encouraging. No wicked person has a right to expect that the community will keep his conduct a secret from those who have a right specially to be informed of it. He who does so is partaker in the guilt.

4. Though we may not be at liberty to make public the evil actions of another, yet no obligation exists to conceal his fault by maintaining toward him our former habits of intimacy. If we know him to be unworthy of our confidence or acquaintance, we have no right to act a lie by conducting toward him in public or in private as though he were worthy of it. By associating with a man we give to the public an assurance that we know of nothing to render him unworthy of our association. If we falsify this assurance we are guilty of deception, and of a deception by which we benefit the wicked at the expense of the innocent, and, so far as our example can do it, place the latter in the power of the former. And still more, if we associate on terms of voluntary intimacy with persons of known bad character, we virtually declare that such offenses constitute no reason why the persons in question are not good enough associates for us. We thus virtually become the patrons of their crime.

5. From what has been remarked we see what is the nature of a historian's duty. He has to do with facts which the individuals themselves have made public, or which have been made public by the providence of God. He records what has already been made known. What has not been made known, therefore, comes not within his province; but whatever has been made known comes properly within it. This latter he is bound to use, without either fear, favor, or affection. If, from party zeal or sectarian bigotry, or individual partiality, he exaggerate, or conceal, or misrepresent, if he "aught extenuate, or set down aught in malice," he is guilty of calumny of the most inexcusable character. It is calumny perpetrated deliberately, under the guise of impartiality, and perpetrated in a form intended to give it the widest publicity and the most permanent duration.

These remarks have had respect principally to the publication of injurious truth or falsehood by conversation. But it will be immediately seen that they apply with additional force to the publication of whatever is injurious *by the press*. If it be wrong to injure my neighbor's reputation within the limited circle of my acquaintance, how much more wrong must it be to injure it throughout a nation! If it be, by universal acknowledgment, mean to underrate the talents or vilify the character of a personal rival, how much more so that of a political opponent! If it would be degrading in me to do it myself, by how much is it less degrading to cause it to be done by others, and to honor or dishonor with my confidence and reward with political distinction those who do it? Because a man is a political opponent, does *he* cease to be a creature of God; and do *we* cease to be under obligations to obey the law of God in respect to him? or rather, I might ask, do men think that political collisions banish the Deity from the throne of the universe? Nor do these remarks apply to political dissensions alone. The conductor of a public press possesses no greater privileges than any other man, nor has he any more right than any other man to use, or suffer to be used, his press for the sake of gratifying personal pique, or avenging individual wrong, or holding up individuals without trial to public scorn. Crime against society is to be punished by society, and by society alone; and he who conducts a public press has no more *right,* because he has the physical power, to inflict pain than any other individual. If one man may do it because he has a press, another may do it because he has muscular strength; and thus the government of society is brought to an end. Nor has he even a right to publish cases of individual vice, unless the providence of God has made them public before. While they are out of sight of the public they are out of his sight, unless he can show that he has been specially appointed to perform this service.[28]

---

[28] See Appendix (к) for additional sentence in the 1865 edition.

Every individual by necessity stands in most important relations both to the past and to the future. Without a knowledge of what has been and of what, so far as his fellow men are concerned, will be, he can form no decision in regard to the present. But this knowledge could never be attained unless his constitution were made to correspond with his circumstances. It has therefore been made to correspond. There is on the one hand in men a strong *a priori* disposition to tell the truth; and it controls them, unless some other motive interpose; and there is on the other hand a disposition to believe what is told, unless some counteracting motive is supposed to operate.

Veracity has respect to the PAST AND PRESENT, or to the FUTURE. We shall consider them separately.

CHAPTER FIRST

VERACITY AS IT RESPECTS THE PAST AND PRESENT

VERACITY, in this sense, always has respect to a *fact,* that is, to something done, or to something which we believe to be doing.

Moral truth consists in our intention to convey to another, to the best of our ability, the conception of a fact exactly as it exists in our own minds.

Physical truth consists in conveying to another the conception of a fact precisely as it actually exists, or existed.

These two, it is evident, do not always coincide.

I may innocently have obtained an incorrect conception of a fact myself, and yet may intend to convey it to another precisely as it exists in my own mind. Here, then, is a *moral* truth, but a *physical* untruth.

Or, again, I may have a correct conception of a fact, supposing it to be an incorrect one, but may convey it to another with the intention to deceive. Here, then, is a moral falsehood, and a physical truth. Pure truth is communicated only when I have a correct conception of a fact, and communicate it intentionally to another precisely as it exists in my own mind.

The law on this subject demands that when we profess to convey a fact to another, we to the best of our ability convey to him the impression which exists in our own minds. This implies, first, that we convey the impression which exists, and not another; and, secondly, that we convey that impression without diminution or exaggeration. In other words we are obliged, in the language of jurisprudence, to tell the truth, the whole truth, and nothing but the truth.

This law, therefore, forbids—

1. *The utterance as truth of what we know to be false.* I say the utterance *as truth,* for we sometimes imagine cases for the sake of illustration, as in parables of fictitious writing, where it is known beforehand that we merely address the imagination. Since we utter it as fiction and do not wish it to be believed, there is no falsehood if it be not true.

2. *Uttering as truth what we do not know to be true.* Many things which men assert they cannot know to be true; such, for instance, are, in many cases, our views of the motives of others. There are many other things which may be probable, and we may be convinced that they are so, but of which we cannot arrive at the certainty. There are other things which are merely matters of opinion, concerning which every several man may hold a different opinion. Now in any such case, to utter as truth what we cannot know, or have not known to be truth, is falsehood. If a man utter anything as truth, he assumes the responsibility of ascertaining it to be so. If he who makes the assertion be not responsible, where shall the responsibility rest? And if any man may utter what he chooses under no responsibility, there is the end of all credibility.

But, it will be said, are we never to utter anything which we do not know to be true? I answer: we are never to utter *as truth* what we do *not know to be true.* Whatever is a matter of probability we may utter as a matter of probability; whatever is a matter of opinion we may state as a matter of opinion. If we convey to another a conception as true, of which we have only the impression of probability, we convey a different conception from that which exists in our own minds, and of course we do, in fact, speak falsely.

3. *Uttering what may be true in fact, but uttering it in such a manner as to convey a false impression to the hearers.*

As, *a*. By *exaggerating* some or all of the circumstances attendant upon the facts.

b. By *extenuating* some or all of the circumstances attendant upon the facts.

c. By exaggerating some and extenuating others.

d. By stating the facts just as they existed, but so arranging them as to leave a false impression upon the hearer. As, for instance, I might say, A entered B's room, and left it at ten o'clock; within five minutes after he left it, B discovered that his watch had been stolen. Now, although I do not say that A stole B's watch, yet, if I intentionally so arrange and connect these facts as to leave a false impression upon the mind of the hearer, I am guilty of falsehood. This is a crime to which pleaders and partial historians, and all prejudiced narrators, are specially liable.

4. As the crime here considered consists in making a false impression with intention to deceive, the same effect may be produced by the tones of the voice, a look of the eye, a motion of the head, or anything by which the mind of another may be influenced. The same rule, therefore, applies to impressions made in this manner, as to those made by words.

5. As this rule applies to our intercourse with men as intelligent agents, it applies to our intercourse with men under all the possible relations of life. Thus it forbids parents to lie to children, and children to lie to parents; instructors to pupils, and pupils to instructors; the old to the young, and the young to the old; attorneys to jurors, and jurors to attorneys; buyers to sellers, and sellers to buyers. That is, the obligation is universal and cannot be annulled by any of the complicated relations in which men stand to each other.

Nor can it be varied by the considerations often introduced, that the person with whom we are conversing has no right to know the truth. This is a sufficient reason why we should not tell the truth, but it is no reason why we should tell a falsehood. Under such circumstances we are at liberty to refuse to reveal anything, but we are not at liberty to utter what is false.

The reason for this is the following: The obligation to veracity does not depend upon the right of the inquirer to know the truth. Did our obligation depend upon this, it would vary with every person with whom we conversed; and in every case before speaking we should be at liberty to measure the extent of our neighbor's right, and to tell him truth or falsehood accordingly. And, inasmuch as the person whom we address would never know at what rate we estimated his right, no one would know how much to believe, any more than we should know how much truth we were under obligation to tell. This would at once destroy every obligation to veracity. On the contrary, inasmuch as we are under obligation to utter nothing but the truth in consequence of our relations to God, this obligation is never affected by any of the circumstances under which we are called upon to testify. Let no one, therefore, excuse himself on the ground that he tells only innocent lies. It cannot be innocent to do that which God has forbidden. "Lie not one to another, brethren, seeing ye have put off the old man with his deeds."

That obedience to this law is demanded by the will of God is manifest from several considerations:

1. We are created with a disposition to speak what is true, and also to believe what is spoken. The fact that we are thus constituted conveys to us an intimation that the Creator wills us to obey this constitution. The intention is as evident as that which is manifested in creating the eye for light and light for the eye.

2. We are created with a moral constitution by which (unless our moral susceptibility shall have been destroyed) we suffer pain whenever we violate this law, and by which also we receive pleasure whenever, under circumstances which urge to the contrary, we steadfastly obey it.

3. We are so constituted that obedience to the law of veracity is absolutely necessary to our happiness. Were we to lose either our feeling of obligation to tell the truth, or our disposition to receive as truth whatever is told to us, there would at once be an end to

all science and all knowledge, beyond that which every man had obtained by his own personal observation and experience. No man could profit by the discoveries of his contemporaries, much less by the discoveries of those men who have gone before him. Language would be useless, and we should be but little removed from the brutes. Everyone must be aware, upon the slightest reflection, that a community of entire liars could not exist in a state of society. The effects of such a course of conduct upon the whole show us what is the will of God in the individual case.

4. The will of God is abundantly made known to us in the holy Scriptures. I subjoin a few examples:

"Thou shalt not bear false witness against thy neighbor." *Ex.* xx, 16. "Lying lips are an abomination to the Lord." *Prov.* vi, 16. "Keep thy tongue from evil, and thy lips that they speak no guile." *Psalm* xxxiv, 13. Those that speak lies are called children of the devil, that is, followers, imitators of the actions of the devil. *John* viii, 44. See also the cases of Ananias and Sapphira, and of Gehazi. *Acts* v, and 2 *Kings* v, 20–27. "All liars shall have their portion in the lake that burneth with fire and brimstone." *Rev.* xxi, 8. "There shall in no wise enter therein (into heaven) anything that maketh a lie." *Ibid.,* verse 27.

From what has been said, the importance of strict adherence to veracity is too evident to need further remark. I will, however, add that the evil of falsehood in small matters, in lies told to amuse, in petty exaggerations, and in complimentary discourse, is not by any means duly estimated. Let it be always borne in mind that he who knowingly utters what is false tells a lie; and a lie, whether white, or of any other color, is a violation of the command of that God by whom we must be judged. And let us also remember that there is no vice which more easily than this stupefies a man's conscience. He who tells lies frequently will soon become a habitual liar; and a habitual liar will soon lose the power of readily distinguishing between the conceptions of his imagination and the recollections of his memory. I have known a few persons who seemed to have arrived at this most deplorable moral condition. Let everyone, therefore, beware of even the most distant approaches to this detestable vice. A volume might easily be written on the misery and loss of character which have grown out of a single lie; and another volume of illustrations of the moral power which men have gained by means of no other prominent attribute than that of bold, unshrinking veracity.

If lying be thus pernicious to ourselves, how wicked must it be to teach it, or specially to require it of others! What shall we say, then, of parents who, to accomplish a momentary purpose, will not hesitate to utter to a child the most flagitious falsehoods? Or what shall we say of those heads of families who direct their children or servants deliberately to declare that they are not at home, while they are quietly sitting in their parlor or their study? What right has anyone, for the purpose of securing a momentary convenience, or avoiding a petty annoyance, to injure forever the moral sentiments of another? How can such a man or woman expect to hear the truth from those whom they have deliberately taught to lie? The expectation is absurd; and the result will show that such persons in the end drink abundantly of the cup which they themselves have mingled. Before any man is tempted to lie, let him remember that God governs this universe on the principles of veracity, and that the whole constitution of things is so arranged as to vindicate truth and to expose falsehood. Hence the *first* lie always requires a multitude of lies to conceal it, each one of which plunges the criminal into more inextricable embarrassment, and at last all of them will combine to cover him with shame. The *inconveniences* of truth, aside from the question of guilt and innocence, are infinitely less than the *inconveniences* of falsehood.

CHAPTER SECOND

VERACITY IN RESPECT TO THE FUTURE

THE future is, within some conditions, subject to our power. We may, therefore, place ourselves under moral obligations to act within those conditions in a particular manner. When we make a promise we voluntarily place ourselves under such a moral obligation. The law of veracity obliges us to fulfill it.

This part of the subject includes *promises* and *contracts*.

I. OF PROMISES.

In every promise, two things are to be considered: the *intention* and the *obligation*.

1. *The intention*. The law of veracity in this respect demands that we convey to the promisee the intention as it exists in our own minds. When we inform another that we *intend* to do a service for him tomorrow, we have no more right to lie about this intention than about any other matter.

2. *The obligation*. The law of veracity obliges us to fulfill the intention just as we made it known. In other words, we are under obligation to satisfy precisely the expectation which we voluntarily excited. The rule of Dr. Paley is as follows: "A promise is binding in the sense in which the promiser supposed the promisee to receive it."

The modes in which promises may be violated, and the reasons for believing the obligation to fulfill promises to be enforced by the law of God, are so similar to those mentioned in the preceding chapter that I will not repeat them.

I therefore proceed to consider in what cases promises are not binding. The following are, I think, among the most important:

Promises are not binding—

1. *When the performance is impossible*. We cannot be under obligation to do what is plainly out of our power. The moral character of such a promise will, however, vary with the circumstances under which the promise was made. If I knew nothing of the impossibility and honestly expressed an intention which I designed to fulfill, I am, at the bar of conscience, acquitted. The providence of

God has interfered with my intention and I am not to blame. If, on the other hand, I knew of the impossibility, I have violated the law of veracity. I expressed an intention which I did not mean to fulfill. I am bound to make good to the other party all the loss which he may have sustained by my crime.

2. *When the promise is unlawful.* No man can be under *obligation* to violate *obligation;* for this would be to suppose a man to be *guilty for not being guilty.* Much less can he be under obligation to violate his obligations to God. Hence promises to lie, to steal, or in any manner to violate the laws of society, are not binding. And the duty of every man who has placed himself under any such obligation is at once to confess his fault, to declare himself free from his engagement, and to endeavor to persuade others to do the same. Here, as in the former instance, there are two cases. Where the unlawfulness was *not known,* the promiser is under no other obligation than that of informing the promisee of the facts as soon as possible. Where the unlawfulness *was known* to the promiser and not to the promisee, I think that the former is bound to make good the loss to the latter, if any occur. When it is known to both parties, either is at liberty to disengage himself, and neither is under any obligation to make any restitution; for the fault is common to both and each should bear his own share of the inconvenience.

3. *Promises are not binding where no expectation is voluntarily excited by the promiser.* He is bound only to fulfill the expectation which he *voluntarily excites;* and if he have excited none, he has made no promise. If A tell B that he shall give a horse to C, and B without A's knowledge or consent inform C of it, A is not bound. But if he directed B to give the information, he is as much bound as though he informed C himself.

4. *Promises are not binding when they are known by both parties to proceed upon a condition, which condition is subsequently by the promiser found not to exist.* As, if A promise to give a beggar money on the faith of his story, and the story be subsequently found to be a fabrication, A in such a case is manifestly not bound.

5. As the very conception of a promise implies an obligation entered into between two intelligent moral agents, I think there

can be no such obligation entered into where one of the parties is not a moral agent. I do not think we can properly be said to make a promise to a brute, nor to violate it. I think the same is true of a madman. Nevertheless, expediency has, even in such cases, always taught the importance of fulfilling expectation which we voluntarily excite. I think, however, that it stands on the ground of expediency and not of obligation. I do not suppose that anyone would feel guilty for deceiving a madman in order to lead him to a madhouse.

These seem to me to be the most common cases in which promises are not binding. The mere inconvenience to which we may be exposed by fulfilling a promise is not a release. We are at liberty beforehand to enter into the obligation, or not. No man need promise unless he please, but having once promised, he is holden until he be morally liberated. Hence, as after the obligation is formed it cannot be recalled, prudence would teach us to be extremely cautious in making promises. Except in cases where we are, from long experience, fully acquainted with all the ordinary contingencies of an event, we ought never to make a promise without sufficient opportunity for reflection. It is a good rule to enter into no important engagement on the same day in which it is first presented to our notice. And I believe that it will be generally found that those who are most careful in promising are the most conscientious in performing; and that, on the contrary, those who are willing on all occasions to pledge themselves on the instant have very little difficulty in violating their engagements with correspondent thoughtlessness.

OF CONTRACTS.

The peculiarity of a *contract* is that it is a *mutual* promise: that is, we promise to do one thing on the condition that another person does another.

The rule of interpretation, the reasons for its obligatoriness, and the cases of exception to the obligatoriness, are the same as in the preceding cases, except that it has a specific condition annexed by which the obligation is limited.

Hence, after a contract is made, while the other party performs his part, we are under obligation to perform our part; but if either party fail, the other is, by the failure of the condition essential to the contract, liberated.

But this is not all. Not only is the one party liberated by the failure of the other party to perform his part of the contract; the first has, moreover, upon the second, a claim for damages to the amount of what he may have suffered by such failure.

Here, however, it is to be observed that a distinction is to be made between a simple contract, that is, a contract to do a particular act, and a contract by which we enter upon a relation established by our Creator. Of the *first* kind, are ordinary mercantile contracts to sell or deliver merchandise at a particular place, for a specified sum, to be paid at a particular time. Here, if the price be not paid we are under no obligation to deliver the goods; and if the goods be not delivered we are under no obligation to pay the price. Of the *second* kind are the contract of civil society and the marriage contract. These, being appointed by the constitution under which God has placed us, may be dissolved only for such reasons as he has appointed. Thus society and the individual enter mutually into certain obligations with respect to each other; but it does not follow that either party is liberated by *every* failure of the other. The case is the same with the marriage contract. In these instances, each party is bound to fulfill its part of the contract, notwithstanding the failure of the other.

It is here proper to remark that the obligation to veracity is precisely the same under what relations soever it may be formed. It is as binding between individuals and society, on both parts, and upon societies and societies, as it is between individuals. There is no more excuse for a society when it violates its obligation to an individual, or for an individual when he violates his obligations to a society, than in any other case of deliberate falsehood. By how much more are societies or communities bound to fidelity in their engagements with each other, since the faith of treaties is the only barrier which interposes to shield nations from the appeal to bloodshed in every case of collision of interests! And the obligation is the same under what circumstances soever nations may treat with each other. A civilized people has no right to violate its solemn obligations because the other party is uncivilized. A strong nation has no right to lie to a weak nation. The simple fact that two communities of moral agents have entered into engagements binds both of them equally in the sight of their common Creator. And He who is the Judge of all in His holy habitation will assuredly avenge, with most solemn retributions, that violation of faith in which the peculiar blessings bestowed upon one party are made a reason for inflicting misery upon the other party with whom he has dealt less bountifully. Shortly before the death of the Duke of Burgundy, the pupil of Fenelon, a cabinet council was held at which he was present, to take into consideration the expediency of violating a treaty; which it was supposed could be done with manifest advantage to France. The treaty was read; and the ministers explained in what respects it operated unfavorably, and how great an accession of territory might be made to France by acting in defiance of its solemn obligations. *Reasons of state* were, of course, offered in abundance to justify the deed of perfidy. The Duke of Burgundy heard them all in silence. When they had finished, he closed the conference by laying his hand upon the instrument and saying with emphasis, *"Gentlemen, there is a treaty."* This single sentiment is a more glorious monument to his fame than a column inscribed with the record of a hundred victories.

It is frequently said, partly by way of explanation and partly by way of excuse for the violation of contracts by communities, that corporate bodies have no conscience. In what sense this is true it is not necessary here to inquire. It is sufficient to know that every one of the *corporators* has a conscience, and is responsible to God for obedience to its dictates. Men may mystify before each other, and they may stupefy the monitor in their own bosoms, by throwing the blame of perfidy upon each other; but it is yet worthy to be remembered that they act in the presence of a Being with whom the night shineth as the day, and that they must appear before a tribunal where there will be "no shuffling." For beings acting under these conditions, there surely can be no wiser or better course than that of simple, unsophisticated verity, under what relations soever they may be called upon to act.

I. *The theory of oaths.*

It is frequently of the highest importance to society that the facts relating to a particular transaction should be distinctly and accurately ascertained. Unless this could be done, neither the innocent could be protected nor the guilty punished; that is, justice could not be administered and society could not exist.

To almost every fact, or to the circumstances which determine it to be fact, there must, from the laws of cause and effect, and from the social nature of man, be many witnesses. The fact can, therefore, be generally known if the witnesses can be induced to testify, and to testify the truth.

To place men under such circumstances that upon the ordinary principles of the human mind they shall be most likely to testify truly, is the design of administering an oath.

In taking an oath, besides incurring the ordinary civil penalties incident to perjury, he who swears calls upon God to witness the truth of his assertions; and also, either expressly or by implication, invokes upon himself the judgments of God if he speak falsely. The ordinary form of swearing in this country and in Great Britain is to close the promise of veracity with the words, "So help me God;" that is, may God only help me so as I tell the truth. Inasmuch as without the help of God we must be miserable for time and for eternity; to relinquish his help if we violate the truth is, on this condition, to imprecate upon ourselves the absence of the favor of God, and, of course, all possible misery forever.

The theory of oaths, then, I suppose to be as follows:

1. Men naturally speak the truth when there is no counteracting motive to prevent it; and, unless some such motive be supposed to supervene, they expect the truth to be spoken.

2. When, however, by speaking falsely some immediate advantage can be gained or some immediate evil avoided, they will frequently speak falsely.

3. But when a greater good can be gained or a greater evil

avoided by speaking the truth than could possibly be either gained or avoided by speaking falsely, they will, on the ordinary principles of the human mind, speak the truth. To place them under such circumstances is the design of an oath.

4. Now as the favor of God is the source of every blessing which man can possibly enjoy, and as his displeasure must involve misery utterly beyond the grasp of our limited conceptions, if we can place men under such circumstances that by speaking falsely they relinquish all claim to the one, and incur all that is awful in the other, we manifestly place a stronger motive before them for speaking the truth than can possibly be conceived for speaking falsehood. Hence it is supposed, on the ordinary principles of the human mind, that men under such circumstances will speak the truth.

Such I suppose to be the theory of oaths. There can be no doubt that if men acted upon this conviction, the truth would be, by means of oaths, universally elicited.

But inasmuch as men may be required to testify whose practical conviction of these great moral truths is at best but weak and who are liable to be more strongly influenced by immediate than by ulterior motives, human punishments have always been affixed to the crime of perjury. These, of course, vary in different ages and in different periods of society. The most equitable provision seems to be that of the Jewish law, by which the perjurer was made to suffer precisely the same injury which he had designed to inflict upon the innocent party. The Mosaic enactment seems intended to have been in regard to this crime unusually rigorous. The judges are specially commanded not to spare, but to exact an eye for an eye, a tooth for a tooth. It certainly deserves serious consideration whether modern legislators might not derive important instruction from this feature of Jewish jurisprudence.

II. *The lawfulness of oaths.* On this subject, a diversity of opinion has been entertained. It has been urged by those who deny the lawfulness of oaths—

1. That oaths are frequently forbidden in the New Testament; and that we are commanded to use *yes* for our affirmative, and *no*

for our negative; for the reason that "whatsoever is more than these cometh of evil, or of the evil one."

2. That no man has a right to peril his eternal salvation upon a condition which from intellectual or moral imbecility he would be so liable to violate.

3. That no one has a right to oblige another to place himself under such conditions.

4. That the frequent use of oaths tends, by abating our reverence for the Deity, to lessen the practical feeling of the obligation to veracity.

5. That no reason can be assigned why this crime should be treated so differently from every other. Other crimes, so far as man is concerned, are left to *human* punishments; and there can be no reason why this crime should involve the additional punishment intended by the imprecation of the loss of the soul.

6. It is said that those sects who never take an oath are as fully believed upon their simple affirmation as any others; nay, that false witness among them is more rare than among other men taken at random. This is, I believe, acknowledged to be the fact.

Those who defend the lawfulness of oaths urge, on the contrary—

1. That those passages in the New Testament which have been referred to forbid, not judicial oaths, but merely profanity.

2. That our Saviour responded when examined upon oath. This, however, is denied by the other party to be a fair interpretation.

3. That the Apostles on several occasions call God to witness when they are attesting to particular facts. The instances adduced are such phrases as these: "God is my witness;" "Behold, before God I lie not." The example in this case is considered sufficient to assure us of the lawfulness of this sort of appeal.

4. That the importance of truth to the purposes of justice warrants us in taking other measures for the prevention of perjury than are taken for the prevention of other crimes, and specially as this is a crime to the commission of which there may always exist peculiarly strong temptations.

These are, I believe, the principal considerations which have been urged on both sides of the question. It seems to me to need a more thorough discussion than can be allowed to it in this place. One thing, however, seems evident, that the multiplication of oaths demanded by the present practice of most Christian nations is not only very wicked, but that its direct tendency is to diminish our reverence for the Deity; and thus in the end to lead to the very evil which it is intended to prevent.

III. *Interpretation of oaths.*

As oaths are imposed for the safety of the party administering them, they are to be interpreted as he understands them. The person under oath has no right to make any mental reservation, but to declare the truth, precisely in the manner that the truth, the whole truth, and nothing but the truth, is expected of him. On no other principle would we ever know what to believe or to expect from a witness. If, for the sake of personal friendship, or personal advantage, or from fear of personal inconvenience, or from the excitement of party partiality, he shrink from declaring the whole truth, he is as truly guilty of perjury as though he swore falsely for money.

IV. *Different kinds of oaths.*

Oaths respect either the past or the future, that is, are either assertory or promissory.

1. The oath respecting the past is definite. A transaction either took place or it did not take place, and we either have or have not some knowledge respecting it. It is therefore in our power either to tell what we know, or to tell what and in how much we do not know. This is the proper occasion for an oath.

2. The oath respecting the future is of necessity *indefinite,* as when we promise upon oath to discharge *to the best of our ability* a particular office. Thus the parties may have very different views of what is meant by discharging an office *according to the best of our ability;* or this obligation may conflict with others, such as domestic or personal obligations; and the incumbent may not know, even with the best intentions, which obligation ought to take the precedence, that is, what is the best of his ability. Such being the case, who that is aware of the frailty of human nature will dare to peril his eternal salvation upon the performance to the best of

his ability of any official duty? And if these allowances be understood by both parties, how are they to be limited; and if they be not limited, what is the value of an oath? Such being the case, it is at best doubtful whether promissory oaths of office ought ever to be required. Much less ought they to be required, as is frequently the case, in the most petty details of official life. They must be a snare to the conscience of a thoughtful man; and must tend to obliterate moral distinctions from the mind of him who is, as is too frequently the case, unfortunately thoughtless. Why should one man, who is called upon to discharge the duties of a constable, or of an overseer of common schools, or even of a counselor or a judge, be placed under the pains and perils of perjury or under peril of his eternal salvation, any more than his neighbor, who discharges the duty of a merchant, of an instructor of youth, a physician, or a clergyman? It seems to me that no man can take such an oath of office, upon reflection, without such mental reservation as must immediately convince him that the requirement is nugatory; and, if so, that it must be injurious.

It has already been remarked that the very fact that our Creator has constituted us with a capacity for a particular form of happiness, and has provided means for the gratification of that desire, is in itself an intimation that he intended that this desire should be gratified. But, as our happiness is the design of this constitution, it is equally evident that he intended this desire to be gratified only in such manner as would conduce to this result; and that in estimating that result we must take into view the whole nature of man as a rational and accountable being, and not only man as an individual but man also as a society.

1. The subject upon which we now enter presents a striking illustration of the truth of these remarks. On the one hand, it is evident that the principle of sexual desire is a part of the constitution of man. That it was intended to be gratified is evident from the fact that without such gratification the race of man would immediately cease to exist. Again, if it were not placed under restrictions, that is, were promiscuous intercourse permitted, the race would perish from neglect of offspring and universal sterility. Thus universal celibacy and unlimited indulgence would both equally defeat the end of the Creator. It is, therefore, as evident that our Creator has imposed a limit to this desire as a part of our constitution, as that he has implanted within us the desire itself. It is the object of the *law of chastity to explain and enforce this limit.*

2. As it is manifestly the object of the Creator that the sexes should live together and form a society with each other in many respects dissimilar to every other society, producing new relations and imposing new obligations, the laws of this society need to be particularly explained. *This is the law of marriage.*

3. As the result of marriage is children, a new relation arises out of this connection, namely, the relation of parent and child. This imposes special obligations upon both parties, namely, *the duties and rights of parents, and the duties and rights of children.*

This class of duties will therefore be treated of in the following order:

Chapter 1. The general duty of chastity.
     "   2. The law of marriage.
     "   3. The rights and duties of parents.
     "   4. The rights and duties of children.

CHAPTER FIRST
THE GENERAL DUTY OF CHASTITY [29]

THE sexual appetite being a part of our constitution, and a limit to the indulgence of it being fixed by the Creator, the business of moral philosophy is to ascertain this limit.

The moral law on this subject is as follows:

The duty of chastity limits the indulgence of this desire *to individuals who are exclusively united to each other for life.*

Hence it forbids—

1. Adultery, or intercourse between a married person and every other person except that person to whom he or she is united for life.

2. Polygamy, or a plurality of wives or of husbands.

3. Concubinage, or the temporary cohabitation of individuals with each other.

4. Fornication, or intercourse with prostitutes, or with any individual under any other condition than that of the marriage covenant.

5. Inasmuch as unchaste desire is strongly excited by the imagination, the law of chastity forbids all impure thoughts and actions; all unchaste conversation, looks, or gestures; the reading of obscene or lascivious books, and everything which would naturally produce in us a disposition of mind to violate this precept.

That the above is the law of God on this subject is manifest, both from natural and from revealed religion.

The law as above recited contains two restrictions:

1. That the individuals be exclusively united to each other; and—
2. That this exclusive union be for life.

---

[29] See Appendix (L) for chapter as condensed for the 1865 edition.

Let us examine the indications of natural religion upon both of these points.

I. The indulgence of the desire referred to is by the law of God restricted to individuals exclusively united to each other. This may be shown from several considerations.

1. The number of births of both sexes under all circumstances and in all ages has been substantially equal. Now if single individuals be not exclusively united to each other, there must arise an inequality of distribution, unless we adopt the law of promiscuous concubinage. But as the desire is universal, it cannot be intended that the distribution should be unequal; for thus, many would from necessity be left single. And the other alternative, promiscuous concubinage, would very soon lead, as we have already remarked, to the extinction of society.

2. The manifest design of nature is to increase the human species in the most rapid ratio consistent with the conditions of our being. That is always the most happy condition of a nation, and that nation is most accurately obeying the laws of our constitution in which the number of the human race is most rapidly increasing. Now it is certain that under the law of chastity as it has been explained, that is, where individuals are exclusively united to each other, the increase of population will be more rapid than under any other circumstances.

3. That must be the true law of the domestic relations which will have the most beneficial effect upon the maintenance and education of children. Under the influence of such a law as I have described, it is manifest that children will be incomparably better provided for than under that of any other. The number of children produced by a single pair thus united will ordinarily be as great as can be supported and instructed by two individuals. And, besides, the care of children under these circumstances becomes a matter not merely of duty but of pleasure. On the contrary, just insofar as this law is violated, the love of offspring diminishes. The care of a family, instead of a pleasure, becomes an insupportable burden; and in the worst states of society children either perish by multitudes from neglect or are murdered by their parents in infancy. The number of human beings who perish by infanticide in heathen countries is

almost incredible. And in countries not heathen it is a matter of notoriety that neglect of offspring is the universal result of licentiousness in parents. The support of foundlings in some of the most licentious districts in Europe has become so great a public burden as to give rise to serious apprehension.

4. There can be no doubt that man is intended to derive by far the greatest part of his happiness from society. And of social happiness, by far the greatest, the most exquisite, and the most elevating portion, is that derived from the domestic relations; not only those of husband and wife, but those of parent and child, of brother and sister, and those arising from the more distant gradations of collateral kindred. Now human happiness in this respect can exist only in proportion to our obedience to the law of chastity. What domestic happiness can be expected in a house continually agitated by the ceaseless jealousy of several wives and the interminable quarrels of their several broods of children? How can filial love dwell in the bosoms of children the progeny of one father by several concubines? This state of society existed under the most favorable circumstances in the patriarchal age; and its results even here are sufficiently deplorable. No one can read the histories of the families of Abraham, Isaac, and Jacob, and David, without becoming convinced that no deviation can be made from the gospel law of marriage without creating a tendency to wrangling without end, to bitterness and strife, nay, to incest and murder. And if this be the result of polygamy and concubinage, in what language is it possible to describe the effects of universal licentiousness? By this, the very idea of home would be abolished. The name of parent would signify no more in man than in the brutes. Man, instead of being social, would become nothing more than a gregarious animal, distinguished from his fellow animals by nothing else than greater intellectual capacity and the more disgusting abuse of it.

5. No reason can be assigned why the intellectual, moral, and social happiness of the one sex is not as valuable in the sight of the Creator as that of the other. Much less can any reason be assigned why the one sex should be to the other merely a source of sensual gratification. But just as we depart from the law of chastity as it has

been here explained, woman ceases to be the equal and the companion of man and becomes either his timid and much abused slave, or else the mere instrument for the gratification of his lust. No one can pretend to believe that the Creator ever intended that one human being should stand in such a relation as this to any other human being.

II. The second part of the law of chastity requires that this union should be for life.

Some of the reasons for this are as follows:

1. In order to domestic happiness it is necessary that both parties should cultivate a spirit of conciliation and forbearance, and mutually endeavor to conform their individual peculiarities to each other. Unless this be done, instead of a community of interests there will arise incessant collision. Now nothing can tend more directly to the cultivation of a proper temper than the consideration that this union is indissoluble. A mere temporary union, liable to be dissolved by every ebullition of passion, would foster every impetuous and selfish feeling of the human heart.

2. If the union be not for life, there is no other limit to be fixed to its continuance than the will of either party. This would speedily lead to promiscuous concubinage, and all the evils resulting from it of which I have already spoken.

3. Children require the care of both parents until they have attained to maturity; that is, generally during the greater part of the lifetime of their parents, at least during all that period of their life in which they would be most likely to desire a separation. Besides, the children are the joint property of both parents; and if the domestic society be dissolved, they belong to one no more than to the other; that is, they have no protector, but are cast out defenseless upon the world.

4. Or, if this be not the case, and they are protected by one parent, they must suffer an irreparable loss by the withdrawment of the other parent from his or her share of the parental responsibility. In general the care would fall upon the mother, whose parental instincts are the stronger, but who is, from her peculiar situation, the less able to protect them. The whole tendency of every licentious

system is to take advantage of the parental tenderness of the mother; and because she would rather die than leave her children to perish, basely to devolve upon her a burden which she is wholly unable to sustain.

5. Parents themselves in advanced years need the care of their children, and become dependent in great measure for their happiness upon them. But all this source of happiness is dried up by any system which allows of the disruption of the domestic society and the desertion of offspring simply at the will of the parent.

The above considerations may perhaps be deemed sufficient to establish the *general* law, and to show what is the will of the Creator on this subject. But it may be suggested that all these consequences need not follow *occasional* aberrations, and that individual cases of licentious indulgence should be exempted from the general rule. To this I answer—

1. The severity of the punishment which God has affixed to the crime in general, shows how severe is his displeasure against it. God is no respecter of persons, but he will visit upon everyone the strict reward of his iniquity. And he does thus act. In woman, this vice is immediately fatal to character; and in man, it leads directly to those crimes which are the sure precursors of temporal and eternal perdition.

2. The God who made us all, and who is the Father and the Judge of his creatures, is omniscient; and he will bring every secret thing into judgment. Let the seducer and the profligate remember that each must stand, with his victim and his partner in guilt, before the Judge of quick and dead, where a recompense will be rendered to every man according to his deeds.

3. Let it be remembered that a female is a moral and accountable being, hastening with us to the bar of God; that she is made to be the center of all that is delightful in the domestic relations; that by her very nature she looks up to man as her protector, and loves to confide in his hands her happiness for life; and that she can be ruined only by abusing that confidence, proving false to that reliance, and using the very loveliest trait in her character as the instrument of her undoing. And then let us consider the misery into which a loss

of virtue must plunge the victim and her friends forever; the worth of that soul which, unless a miracle interpose, must by the loss of virtue be consigned to eternal despair; and I ask whether in the whole catalogue of human crime there be one whose atrocity more justly merits the deepest damnation than that which, for the momentary gratification of a lawless appetite, will violate all these obligations, outrage all these sympathies, and work out so widespreading, so interminable a ruin?

Such is the lesson of natural religion on this subject.

III. The precepts of revealed religion may be very briefly stated:

1. The seventh commandment is, "Thou shalt not commit adultery." *Ex.* xx, 14. By the term adultery is meant every unlawful act and thought. The Mosaic law enacted that he who seduced a woman should marry her. *Ex.* xxii, 16, 17. This is, doubtless, the equitable rule; and there is no reason why it should not be strictly enforced now, both by the civil law and by the opinions of the community.

2. The punishment of adultery was, under the same law, death to both parties. *Lev.* x, 22. *Deut.* xxii, 22. That this should now be enforced, no one will contend. But it is sufficient to show in what abhorrence the crime is held by the Creator.

3. The consequences of whoredom and adultery are frequently set forth in the prophets, and the most awful judgments of God are denounced against them. This subject is also treated with graphic power by Solomon, in the book of Proverbs. See *Proverbs* v, 3–29; vii, 5–26.

4. Our Saviour explains the law of chastity and marriage in his sermon on the mount, and declares it equally to respect unclean thoughts and actions: "Ye have heard that it hath been said by them of old time, thou shalt not commit adultery. But I say unto you, that whosoever looketh on a woman to lust after her, hath committed adultery with her already in his heart. And if thy right eye offend thee (or cause thee to offend), pluck it out and cast it from thee; for it is profitable for thee that one of thy members should perish, and not that thy whole body should be cast into hell." *Matt.* v, 27–32. That is, as I suppose, eradicate from your bosom every impure thought, no matter at what sacrifice; for no one who

cherishes impurity, even in thought, can be an inheritor of the kingdom of heaven.

Uncleanness is also frequently enumerated among the crimes which exclude men from the kingdom of heaven:

Ephesians v, 5, 6: "No whoremonger or unclean person hath any inheritance in the kingdom of Christ and God."

Galatians v, 19–21: "Now, the works of the flesh are manifest, which are these: adultery, fornication, uncleanness, lasciviousness; of the which I tell you before, as I have told you in times past, that they which do such things shall not inherit the kingdom of God."

Colossians iii, 5, 6: "Mortify, therefore, your members, which are upon the earth: fornication, uncleanness, inordinate affections; for which things' sake, the wrath of God cometh upon the children of disobedience."

Let every one remember, therefore, that whoever violates this command violates it in defiance of the most clearly revealed command of God, and at the peril of his own soul. He must meet his act, and the consequences of it, at that day when the secrets of all hearts are made manifest, when every hidden thing will be brought to light, and when God will judge every man according to his deeds.

I remarked above that the law of chastity forbade the indulgence of impure or lascivious imaginations, the harboring of such thoughts in our minds, or the doing of anything by which such thoughts should be excited. Of no vice is it so true as of this, that "lust, when it is cherished, bringeth forth sin; and sin, when it is finished, bringeth forth death." Licentiousness in outward conduct never appears, until the mind has become defiled by impure imaginations. When, however, the mind has become thus defiled, nothing is wanted but suitable opportunity to complete the moral catastrophe. Hence the necessity of the most intense vigilance in the government of our thoughts and in the avoiding of all books, and all pictures, and all society, and all conduct and actions of which the tendency is to imbue our imaginations with anything at variance with the purest chastity. Whatever in other respects may be the fascinations of a book, if it be impure or lascivious let it be eschewed. Whatever be the accomplishments of an acquaintance, if he or she be licentious in conversation or action let him or her be shunned. No man can take fire in his bosom, and his clothes not be burned. We cannot mingle with the vile, let that vileness be dressed in ever so tasteful a garb, without becoming defiled. The only rule of safety is to avoid *the appearance of evil;* for thus alone shall we be able to avoid the reality. Hence it is that a licentious theatre (and the tendency of all theatres is to licentiousness), immodest dancing, and all amusements and actions which tend to inflame the passions, are horribly pernicious to morals. It would be interesting to learn on what principle of morals a virtuous woman would justify her attendance upon an amusement, in which she beholds before her a once lovely female uttering covert obscenity in the presence of thousands, and where she is surrounded by hundreds of women, also once lovely but now abandoned, whose ruin has been consummated by this very means, and who assemble in this place with the more certain assurance of thus being able most successfully to effect the ruin of others.

It has been already remarked in the preceding section that the law of chastity forbids all sexual intercourse between persons who have not been exclusively united for life. In the act of marriage two persons under the most solemn circumstances are thus united; and they enter into a mutual contract thus to live in respect to each other. This relation having been established by God, the contract thus entered into has all the solemnity of an oath. Hence he who violates it is guilty of a twofold crime: first, the violation of the law of chastity; and secondly, of the law of veracity—a veracity pledged under the most solemn circumstances.

But this is by no means all that is intended by the institution of marriage. By the contract thus entered into, a society is formed of a most interesting and important character, which is the origin of all civil society; and in which children are prepared to become members of that great community. As our principal knowledge of the nature and obligations of this institution is derived from the sacred Scriptures, I shall endeavor briefly to explain the manner in which they treat of it, without adding anything to what I have already said, in regard to the teaching of natural religion.

I shall consider, first, the nature of this contract, and, secondly, the duties which it enjoins, and the crimes which it forbids.

First. The nature of the contract.

1. The contract is for life, and is dissoluble for one cause only,— the cause of whoredom:

Matthew xix, 3–6, 9. "Then came some of the Pharisees to him, and, tempting him, asked, Can a man, upon every pretense, divorce his wife? He answered, Have ye not read, that at the beginning, when the Creator made man, he formed a male and female; and said, for this cause shall a man leave father and mother, and adhere to his wife; and they two shall be one flesh. Wherefore, they are no longer two, but one flesh. What then God hath conjoined, let not man separate. Wherefore, I say unto you, whosoever divorceth his wife, except for whoredom, and marrieth another, committeth adultery." I use here the translation of Dr. Campbell, which, I think, conveys more exactly than the common version the meaning of the original.

2. We are here taught that marriage, being an institution of God, is subject to *his laws* alone, and not to the laws of man. Hence the civil law is binding upon the conscience only insofar as it corresponds to the law of God.

3. This contract is essentially mutual. By entering into it the members form a society, that is, they have something in common. Whatever is thus in common belongs equally to both. And on the contrary, what is not thus surrendered remains as before in the power of the individual.

4. The basis of this union is *affection*. Individuals thus contract themselves to each other on the ground not merely of mutual regard, but also of a regard stronger than that which they entertain for any other persons else. If such be not the condition of the parties, they cannot be united with any fair prospect of happiness. Now such is the nature of the human affections that we derive a higher and a purer pleasure from rendering happy those whom we love than from self-gratification. Thus a parent prefers self-denial for the sake of a child to self-indulgence. The same principle is illustrated in every case of pure and disinterested benevolence. This is the essential element on which depends the happiness of the married state. To be in the highest degree happy, we must each prefer the happiness of another to our own.

5. I have mentioned above that, this being a voluntary compact and forming a peculiar society, there are some things which by this compact each surrenders to the other, and also other things which are not surrendered. It is important that these be distinguished from each other.

I remark, then—

a. Neither party surrenders to the other any control over anything appertaining to the conscience. From the nature of our moral constitution, nothing of this sort can be surrendered to any created being. For either party to interfere with the discharge of those duties which the other party really supposes itself to owe to God is therefore wicked and oppressive.

b. Neither party surrenders to the other anything which would violate prior and lawful obligations. Thus a husband does not promise to subject his professional pursuits to the will of his wife. He has chosen his profession, and if he pursue it lawfully it does not interfere with the contract. So also his duties as a citizen are of prior obligation; and if they really interfere with any others, those subsequently formed must be construed in subjection to them. Thus also the filial duties of both parties remain in some respects unchanged after marriage, and the marriage contract should not be so interpreted as to violate them.

c. On the other hand, I suppose that the marriage contract binds each party, whenever individual gratification is concerned, to prefer the happiness of the other party to its own. If pleasure can be enjoyed by both, the happiness of both is increased by enjoying it in common. If it can be enjoyed but by one, each should prefer that it be enjoyed by the other. And if there be sorrow to be endured or inconvenience to be suffered, each should desire, if possible, to bear the infliction for the sake of shielding the other from pain.

d. And, as I have remarked before, the disposition to do this arises from the very nature of the principles on which the compact is formed, from unreserved affection. This is the very manner in which affection always displays itself. This is the very means by which affection is created "She loved me for the dangers I had seen, and I loved her that she did pity them."—SHAKESPEARE. And this is the only course of conduct by which affection can be retained. And the manifestation of this temper is under all circumstances obligatory upon both parties.

6. As, however, in all societies there may be differences of opinion even where the harmony of feeling remains unimpaired, so there may be differences here. Where such differences of opinion exist, there must be some ultimate appeal. In ordinary societies such questions are settled by a numerical majority. But as in this case such a decision is impossible, some other principle must be adopted. The

right of deciding must rest with either the one or the other. As the husband is the individual who is responsible to civil society, as his intercourse with the world is of necessity greater, the voice of nature and of revelation unite in conferring the right of ultimate authority upon him. By this arrangement the happiness of the wife is increased no less than that of the husband. Her power is always greatest in concession. She is graceful and attractive while meek and gentle; but when angered and turbulent she loses the fascination of her own sex, without attaining to the dignity of the other.

> "A woman moved is like a fountain troubled,
> Muddy, ill-seeming, and bereft of beauty."   SHAKES.

Secondly. I come now to speak of the *duties* imposed by the marriage relation.

I. The marriage relation imposes upon both parties equally the duty of chastity.

1. Hence it forbids adultery, or intercourse with any other person than that one to whom the individual is united in marriage.

2. And, hence, it forbids all conduct in married persons, or with married persons, of which the tendency would be to diminish their affection for those to whom they are united in marriage, or of which the tendency would be to give pain to the other party. This is evident from what we have before said. For if the contract itself proceed upon the principle of entire and exclusive affection, anything must be a violation of it which destroys or lessens that affection; and that which causes this affection to be doubted produces to the party in which the doubt exists the same misery that would ensue from actual injury.

The crime of adultery is of an exceedingly aggravated nature. As has been before remarked, aside from being a violation of the law of chastity it is also a violation of a most solemn contract. The misery which it inflicts upon parents and children, relatives and friends, the total annihilation of domestic happiness and the total disruption of parental and filial ties which it necessarily produces, mark it for one of the basest forms of human atrocity. Hence, as might be expected, it is spoken of in Scriptures as one of those crimes on which God has set the seal of his peculiar displeasure. In addition to the passages already quoted on this subject, I barely mention the following:

Matthew v, 28. "Whosoever looketh on a woman to cherish impure desire, hath committed adultery with her already in his heart." *Hebrews* xiii, 4. "Marriage is honorable in all, and the bed undefiled; but whoremongers and adulterers God will judge." *Revelations* xxi, 8. "Murderers and the lascivious shall have their part in the lake that burneth with fire and brimstone, which is the second death." Throughout the writings of the prophets, in numberless instances, this crime is singled out as one for which God visits with the most awful judgments both nations and individuals. And if any one will reflect that the happiness and prosperity of a country must depend on the virtue of the domestic society more than on anything else, he cannot fail to perceive that a crime which by a single act sunders the conjugal tie and leaves children worse than parentless must be attended with more abundant and remediless evils than almost any other that can be named. The taking of human life can be attended with no consequences more dreadful. In the one case the parental tie is broken but the victim is innocent; in the other the tie is broken with the additional aggravation of an irretrievable moral stain, and a widespreading dishonor that cannot be washed away.

II. The law of marriage enforces the duty of mutual affection.

Affection toward another is the result of his or her actions and temper toward us. Admiration and respect may be the result of other manifestations of character, but nothing is so likely as evidence of affection toward ourselves to produce in us affection toward others.

Hence the duty of cultivating affection imposes upon each party the obligation to act in such manner as to excite affection in the bosom of the other. The rule is, "As ye would that others should do unto (or be affected towards) you, do ye even so unto (or be ye so affected towards) them." And the other gospel rule is here also verified: "Give, and it shall be given unto you, good measure, pressed down, and heaped together, and running over, shall men give into your bosom." To cultivate affection, then, is not to strive to excite it by any direct effort of abstract thinking, but to show by the whole tenor of a life of disinterested goodness that our happiness is really promoted by seeking the happiness of another. It consists in restraining our passions, in subduing our selfishness, in quieting our irritability, in eradicating from our minds everything which could give pain to an ingenuous spirit, and in cherishing a spirit of meekness, forbearance, forgiveness, and of active, cheerful, and incessant desire for the happiness of those whom we love. At no less price than this can affection be purchased; and those who are willing to purchase it at this price will rarely have reason to complain of the want of it.

III. The law of marriage imposes the duty of mutual assistance.

In the domestic society as in every other there are special duties devolving upon each member; this is no more than to say that it is not the duty of every member of a society to do everything. So here, there are duties devolving of right upon the husband, and other duties devolving of right upon the wife. Thus it is the duty, in the first instance, of the husband to provide for the wants of the family; and of the wife to assume the charge of the affairs of the household. His sphere of duty is *without,* her sphere of duty is *within*. Both are under obligation to discharge these duties, specially because they are parties to this particular compact. The Apostle Paul affirms that he who does not provide for his own, specially for those of his own house, hath denied the faith and is worse than an infidel. That man is worthily despised who does not qualify himself to support that family of which he has voluntarily assumed the office of protector.[30] Nor surely is that woman less deserving of contempt who, having consumed the period of youth in frivolous reading, dissipating amusement, and in the acquisition of accomplishments which are to be consigned immediately after marriage to entire forgetfulness, enters upon the duties of a wife with no other expectation, than that of being a useless and prodigal appendage to a household, ignorant of her duties and of the manner of discharging them; and with no other conceptions of the responsibilities which she has assumed than such as have been acquired from a life of childish

[30] See Appendix (M) for condensation of remainder of paragraph in the 1865 edition.

caprice, luxurious self-indulgence, and sensitive, feminine, yet thoroughly finished selfishness. And yet I fear that the system of female education at present in vogue is, in many respects, liable to the accusation of producing precisely this tendency.

I have remarked that the duties of the husband and wife are thus, in the first instance, apportioned. Yet if one be disabled, all that portion of the duty of the disabled party which the other can discharge falls upon that other. If the husband cannot alone support the family, it is the duty of the wife to assist him. If the wife is through sickness unable to direct her household, the husband is bound insofar as it is possible to assume her care. In case of the death of either, the whole care of the children devolves upon the survivor; nor has the survivor a right to devolve it upon another person if he or she can discharge it alone.

IV. The law of marriage, both from Scripture and from reason, makes the husband the head of the domestic society. Hence when difference of opinion exists (except as stated above, where a paramount obligation binds) the decision of the husband is ultimate. Hence the duty of the wife is submission and obedience. The husband, however, has no more right than the wife to act unjustly, oppressively, or unkindly; nor is the fact of his possessing authority in the least an excuse for so acting. But as differences of opinion are always liable to exist, and as in such case one or the other party must yield to avoid the greatest of all evils in such a society—continual dissension—the duty of yielding devolves upon the wife. And it is to be remembered that the act of submission is in every respect as dignified and as lovely as the act of authority; nay, more, it involves an element of virtue which does not belong to the other. It supposes neither superior excellence nor superior mind in the party which governs; but merely an official relation, held for the mutual good of both parties and of their children. The teaching of Scripture on this subject is explicit; see 1 *Peter* iii, 1-7: "Likewise, ye wives, be in subjection to your own husbands, that if any obey not the word, they also may, without the word, be won by the conversation of the wives; while they behold your chaste conversation united with respect. Whose adorning, let it not be that *outward* adorning of plaiting the hair, and of wearing of gold, and of putting on of apparel; but let it be *the inward disposition of the mind,* which is not corruptible, even the ornament of a *meek and quiet spirit,* which is, in the sight of God, of great price. Likewise, ye husbands, dwell with your wives according to knowledge, as with the weaker party; rendering respect to them, as heirs with you of the grace of life." That is, if I understand the passage, conduct toward them as knowing that they are weak, that is, needing support and protection; and, at the same time, rendering them all that respect which is due to those who are as much as yourselves heirs to a blessed immortality. A more beautiful exhibition of the duties of the marriage relation cannot be imagined.

I shall close this chapter with the following well known extract from a poet, whose purity of character and exquisite sensibility have done more than any other in our language, to clothe virtue in her own native attractiveness:

> Domestic happiness, thou only bliss
> Of Paradise, that has survived the fall!
> Though few now taste thee unimpaired and pure,
> Or, tasting, long enjoy thee! too infirm,
> Or too incautious, to preserve thy sweets
> Unmixed with drops of bitter, which neglect
> Or temper sheds into thy crystal cup:
> Thou art the nurse of virtue; in thine arms
> She smiles, appearing, as in truth she is,
> Heaven-born, and destined to the skies again.
> Thou art not known where pleasure is adored,
> That reeling goddess, with her zoneless waist
> And wandering eyes, still leaning on the arm
> Of novelty, her fickle, frail support;
> For thou art meek and constant, hating change:
> And finding in the calm of truth-tried love,
> Joys which her stormy rapture never yields.
> Forsaking thee, what shipwreck have we seen,
> Of honor, dignity, and fair renown!
> 'Till prostitution elbows us aside
> In all our crowded streets.   [Cowper,] *Task*.

CHAPTER THIRD

THE LAW OF PARENTS

THE adaptation of the physical and moral laws under which man is placed to the promotion of human happiness is beautifully illustrated in the relation which exists between the law of marriage and the law of parent and child. Were the physical or moral conditions of marriage different in any respect from those which exist, the evils which would ensue would be innumerable. And on the contrary, by accurately observing these conditions, we shall see that they not only contain a provision for the well-being of successive generations, but also establish a tendency to indefinite social progress.

For instance, we see that mankind are incapable of sustaining the relation of parent until they have arrived at the age of maturity, attained to considerable knowledge and experience, and become capable of such labor as will enable them to support and protect their offspring. Were this otherwise, were children liable to become parents—parent and child growing up together in physical and intellectual imbecility—the progress of man in virtue and knowledge would be impossible, even if the whole race did not perish from want and disease.

Again, the parent is endowed with a love of his offspring which renders it a pleasure to him to contribute to its welfare, and to give it by every means in his power the benefit of his own experience. And on the contrary, there is in the child, if not a correspondent love of the parent, a disposition to submit to the parent's wishes and to yield (unless its instincts have been mismanaged) to his authority. Were either of these dispositions wanting, it is evident that the whole social system would be disarranged, and incalculable misery entailed upon our race.

Again, it is evident that civil society is constituted by the surrender of the individual's personal desires and propensities to the good of the whole. It of course involves the necessity of self-restraint—that is, of habitual self-government. Now in this point of view the domestic society is designed to be, as has been frequently remarked, the nursery for the state.

Thus, the parent being of an age and having experience sufficient to control and direct the child, and being instinctively impelled to exert this control for the child's benefit, and the child being instinctively disposed to yield to his authority when judiciously exerted, the child grows up under a system in which he yields to the will of another, and thus he learns at home to submit to the laws of the society of which he is soon to become a member. And hence it is that the relaxation of parental authority has always been found one of the surest indications of the decline of social order, and the unfailing precursor of public turbulence and anarchy.

But still more, it is a common remark that children are influenced by example more readily than by any other means. Now by the marriage constitution this principle of human nature is employed as an instrument of the greatest possible good. We stated that the basis of the marriage covenant is affection, and that it supposes each party to prefer the happiness of the other to its own. While the domestic society is governed by this principle, it presents to the children a continual example of disinterestedness and self-denial, and of the happiness which results from the exercise of these virtues. And yet more, the affection of the parents prompts them to the exercise of the same virtues in behalf of their children; and, hence, the latter have before their eyes a constantly operating motive to the cultivation of these very dispositions. And, lastly, as the duty of the wife is submission, children are thus taught by the example of one whom they respect and love that submission is both graceful and dignified; and that it in no manner involves the idea of baseness or servility.

1. From these considerations we learn the relation which exists by nature between parents and children. It is the relation of a superior to an inferior. The *right* of the parent is to *command;* the *duty* of the child is to *obey.* Authority belongs to the one, submission to the other. This relation is a part of our constitution, and the obligation which arises from it is, accordingly, a part of our duty. It is not a mere matter of convenience or of expediency, but it belongs to the relations under which we are created and to the violation of it our Creator has affixed peculiar and afflicting penalties.

2. While this is the relation, yet the motive which should govern the obligation on both sides is affection. While the authority to command rests with the parent and the duty of submission is imposed upon the child, yet the parent is not at liberty to exercise this authority from caprice, or from love of power, or for his own advantage, but from simple love to the child and for the child's advantage. The constitution under which we are placed renders it necessary that the parent should exercise this power; but that parent abuses it, that is, he uses it for purposes for which it was not conferred, if he exercise it from any other motive than duty to God and love to his offspring.

3. This relation being established by our Creator, and the obligations consequent upon it being binding upon both parties, the failure in one party does not annihilate the obligations of the other. If a child be disobedient, the parent is still under obligation to act towards it for its own good and not to exert his authority for any other purpose. If a parent be unreasonable, this does not release the child; he is still bound to honor, and obey, and reverence his parent.

The duty of parents is, then, generally, to educate or to bring up their children in such a manner as they believe will be most for their future happiness, both temporal and eternal.

This comprehends several particulars:

I. Support, or maintenance.

That it is the duty of the parents to keep alive the helpless being whom they have brought into existence need not be proved. As to the expensiveness of this maintenance, I do not know that anything very definite can be asserted. The general rule would seem to be that the mode of life adopted by the parent would be that which he is required to provide for the child. This, however, would be modified by some circumstances. If a parent of large wealth brought up his family in meanness and ignorance so that they would be specially unfitted for the opulence which they were hereafter to enjoy, he would act unjustly. He is voluntarily placing them in circumstances of great temptation. So, on the other hand, if a parent destitute of means to render his children independent of labor brings them up, whether male or female, in idleness and expensiveness, he violates his duty as a parent; he is preparing them for a life not of happiness but of discontent, imbecility, and misery. The latter, owing to the natural weakness of parental affection, is by far the most common error, and is liable to become peculiarly prevalent in the social condition of this country.

II. EDUCATION.

1. *Physical education.* A parent is under obligation to use all the means in his power to secure to his children a good physical constitution. It is his duty to prescribe such food, and in such quantity, as will best conduce to their health; to regulate their labor and exercise so as fully to develop all the powers and call into exercise all the functions of their physical system; to accustom them to hardship and render them patient of labor. Everyone knows how greatly the happiness of a human being depends upon early physical discipline; and it is manifest that this discipline can be enforced by no one but a parent, or by one who stands in the place of a parent.

By the same rule we see the wickedness of those parents who employ their children in such service, or oblige them to labor in such manner, as will expose them to sickness, infirmity, disease, and premature death. In many manufacturing countries children are forced to labor before they are able to endure confinement and fatigue, or to labor vastly beyond their strength; so that the vigor of their constitution is destroyed even in infancy. The power of the parent over the child was given for the child's good, and neither to gratify the parent's selfishness nor to minister to his love of gain. It is not improper to add that the guilt and the shame of this abuse of the rights of children are equally shared between the parent who thus sells his child's health and life for gold and the heartless agent who thus profits by his wickedness. Nor is this form of violation of parental obligation confined to any one class of society. The ambitious mother who, for the sake of her own elevation or the aggrandizement of her family and without any respect to the happiness of her child, educates her daughter in all the trickery of fashionable fascination, dwarfing her mind and sensualizing her aspirations, for the chance of negotiating for her a profitable match, regardless of the character or habits of him to whom she is to be united for life, falls under precisely the same condemnations.

2. *Intellectual education.* A child enters into the world utterly ignorant, and possessed of nothing else than a collection of impulses and capabilities. It can be happy and useful only as this ignorance is dispelled by education, and these impulses and capabilities are directed and enlarged by discipline and cultivation. To some knowledge and discipline the parent has, from the necessity of the case, attained; and, at least, so much as this he is bound to communicate to his children. In some respects, however, this duty can be discharged more effectively by others than by the parent; and it may, therefore, very properly be thus devolved upon a teacher. The parental obligation requires that it be done either by a parent himself, or that he procure it to be done by another.

I have said that it can *in part* be discharged by the teacher. But, let it be remembered, it can be done *only in part.* The teacher is only the *agent;* the parent is the *principal.* The teacher does not remove from the parent any of the responsibility of his relation. Several duties devolve upon the one which cannot be rightfully devolved upon the other.

For instance—

1. He is bound to inform himself of the peculiar habits and reflect upon the probable future situation of his child, and deliberately to consider what sort of education will most conduce to his future happiness and usefulness.

2. He is bound to select such instructors as will best accomplish the results which he believes will be most beneficial.

3. He is bound to devote such time and attention to the subject as will enable him to ascertain whether the instructor of his child discharges his duty with faithfulness.

4. To encourage his child by manifesting such interest in his studies as shall give to diligence and assiduity all the assistance and benefit of parental authority and friendship.

5. And if a parent be under obligation to do this, he is, of course, under obligation *to take time to do it,* and so to construct the arrangements of his family and business that *it may be done.* He has

no right to say that *he has no time for these duties.* If God have required them of him, as is the fact, *he has time exactly for them;* and the truth is he has not time for those other occupations which interfere with them. If he neglect them, he does it to the injury of his children, and, as he will ascertain when it shall be too late, to his own disappointment and misery.

Nor let it be supposed that this will ever be done without bringing with it its own reward. God has always connected together indissolubly our own personal benefit and the discharge of every duty. Thus, in the present case, a parent who assiduously follows his children throughout the various steps of their education will find his own knowledge increased and his own education carried forward vastly beyond what he would at first have conceived. There are very few things which a child ought to learn from the study of which an adult will not derive great advantage, especially if he go through the process of simplification and analysis, which are so necessary in order to communicate knowledge to the mind of the young. And yet more. It is only thus that the parent will be able to retain that intellectual superiority which it is so much for the interest of both parties that he should, for a long time, at least, possess. It is an unfortunate circumstance for a child to *suppose* that he knows more than his parent; and if his supposition be true he will not be slow to entertain it. The longer the parent maintains his superiority in knowledge and wisdom, the better will it be for both parties. But this superiority cannot be retained if as soon as the parent enters upon active business he desist from all effort after intellectual cultivation, and surrenders himself a slave to physical labor while he devotes his child to mere intellectual cultivation, and thus renders intellectual intercourse between himself and his children almost impossible.

3. *Moral education.*

The eternal destiny of the child is placed in a most important sense in the hands of its parents. The parent is under obligation to instruct, and cause his child to be instructed, in those religious sentiments which he believes to be according to the will of God.

With his duty in this respect, until the child becomes able to decide for himself, no one has a right to interfere. If the parent be in error, the fault is not in teaching the child what he believes, but in believing what is false, without having used the means which God has given him to arrive at the truth. But, if such be the responsibility, and so exclusive the authority of the parent, it is manifest that he is under a double obligation to ascertain what is the will of God and in what manner the future happiness of an immortal soul may be secured. As soon as he becomes a parent his decisions on this subject involve the future happiness or misery not only of his own soul but also of that of another. Both considerations, therefore, impose upon him the obligation of coming to a serious and solemn decision upon his moral condition and prospects.

But besides that of making himself acquainted with the doctrines of religion, the relation in which he stands imposes upon the parent several other duties.

It is his duty—

1. To teach his child its duties to God and to man, and produce in its mind a permanent conviction of its moral responsibility. This is to be done not merely by direct but also by indirect precept, and by directing it to such trains of observation and reflection as shall create a correct moral estimate of actions and of their consequences. And specially should it be the constant effort of the parent to cultivate in his child a spirit of piety, or a right feeling toward God, the true source of every other virtue.

2. Inasmuch as the present state of man is morally imperfect, and every individual is a sharer in that imperfection, it is the duty of the parent to eradicate so far as is in his power the wrong propensities of his children. He should watch with ceaseless vigilance for the first appearances of pride, obstinacy, malice, envy, vanity, cruelty, revenge, anger, lying, and their kindred vices; and, by steadfast and unwearied assiduity, strive to extirpate them before they have gained firmness by age or vigor by indulgence. There cannot be a greater unkindness to a child than to allow it to grow up with any of its evil habits uncorrected. Everyone would consider a parent cruel

who allowed a child to grow up without having taken means to cure a limb which had been broken; but how much worse is an evil temper than a broken limb!

3. Inasmuch as precept will be of no avail without a correspondent example, a parent is under obligation, not only to set no example by which the evil dispositions of his child will be cherished, but to set such an example as will be most likely to remove them. A passionate, selfish, envious man must expect that, in spite of all his precepts, his children will be passionate, envious, and selfish.

4. Inasmuch as all our efforts will be fruitless without the blessing of God, that parent must be convicted of great neglect of duty who does not habitually pray for that direction which he needs in the performance of these solemn obligations; as well as for that blessing upon his efforts without which, though ever so well directed, they will be utterly in vain.

5. Inasmuch as the moral character of the child is greatly influenced by its associations and companions, it is the duty of the parent to watch over these with vigilance and to control them with entire independence. He is false to his trust if, for the sake of gratifying the desires of his child, or of conciliating the favor of others or avoiding the reputation of singularity or preciseness, he allow his child to form associations which he believes, or even fears, will be injurious to him. And on the other hand, if such be the duty of the parent, he ought to be considered as fully at liberty to perform it, without remark and without offense. In such matters he is the ultimate and the only responsible authority. He who reproaches another for the exercise of this authority is guilty of slander. He who from the fear of slander shrinks from exercising it is justly chargeable with a pusillanimity wholly unworthy of the relation which he sustains.

6. As the parent sustains the same relation to all his children, it is manifest that his obligations to them all are the same. Hence he is bound to exercise his authority with entire impartiality. The want of this must always end in jealousy, envy, and malice, and cannot fail to render the domestic society a scene of perpetual bickering and

contention. A striking exemplification of all this is recorded in the history of Joseph and his brethren.

If this be so, it is evident that the violation of parental obligation is more common, among even indulgent parents, than would generally be supposed.

1. Parents who render themselves slaves to fashionable society and amusement violate this obligation. The mother who is engaged in a perpetual round of visiting and company, and who, from the pressure of engagements to which she subjects herself, has no leisure to devote to the mental and moral culture of her children, violates her most solemn duties. She has no right to squander away in frivolous self-gratification the time which belongs to her offspring. She will reap the fruits of her folly when in a few years her children, having grown up estranged from her affection, shall thwart her wishes, disappoint her hopes, and neglect, if they do not despise, the mother who bare them.

2. The father who plunges into business so deeply that he has no leisure for domestic duties and pleasures, and whose only intercourse with his children consists in a brief and occasional word of authority, or a surly lamentation over their intolerable expensiveness, is equally to be pitied and to be blamed. What right has he to devote to other pursuits the time which God has allotted to his children? Nor is it any excuse to say that he cannot support his family in their present style of living without this effort. I ask, By what right can his family demand to live in a manner which requires him to neglect his most solemn and important duties? Nor is it an excuse to say that he wishes to leave them a competence. Is he under obligation to leave them that competence which he desires? Is it an advantage to them to be relieved from the necessity of labor? Besides, is money the only desirable bequest which a father can leave to his children? Surely, well cultivated intellects, hearts sensible to domestic affection, the love of parents and brethren and sisters, a taste for home pleasures, habits of order, regularity and industry, a hatred of vice and of vicious men, and a lively sensibility to the excellence of virtue are as valuable a legacy as an inheritance of property, simple

property purchased by the loss of every habit which could render that property a blessing.

3. Nor can thoughtful men be always exculpated from the charge of this violation. The duties of a parent are established by God, and God requires us not to violate them. While the social worship of God is a duty, it ought not to interfere with parental duty. Parents who spend that time *which belongs to their children* in offices of public social worship have mistaken the nature of their special obligation. I do not pretend to say what time or how much time any individual shall spend in any religious service. This question does not belong to the present discussion. But I say that this time must be taken out of that which belongs to ourselves; and it might easily be abstracted from that devoted to visiting, company, or idleness; it should not be taken from that which belongs by the ordinance of God to our children.

It will be easily seen that the fulfillment of these obligations in the manner I have suggested would work a very perceptible change in the whole fabric of society. It would check the eager desire of accumulation, repress the ardor of ambition, and allay the feverish thirst for selfish gratification. But it would render a family, in truth, *a society*. It would bring back parents and children to the relations to each other which God has established. It would restore to home a meaning, and to the pleasures of home a reality, which they are in danger of losing altogether. Forsaking the shadow of happiness, we should find the substance. Instead of a continual round of physical excitation, and the ceaseless pursuit of pleasures which, as everyone confesses, end in ennui and disappointment, we should secure

> "A sacred and home-felt delight,
> A sober certainty of waking bliss,"

of which, previously, we could have had no conception.

THE RIGHTS OF PARENTS.

The right of the parent over his child is, of course, commensurate with his duties. If he be under obligation to educate his child in such manner as he supposes will most conduce to the child's happiness and the welfare of society, he has from necessity the right to control the child in everything necessary to the fulfillment of this obligation. The only limits imposed are that he exert this control no further than is necessary to the fulfillment of his obligation, and that he exert it with the intention for which it was conferred. While he discharges his parental duties within these limits, he is by the law of God exempt from interference both from the individual and from society.

Of the duration of this obligation and this right.

1. In infancy, the control of the parent over the child is absolute; that is, it is exercised without any respect whatever to the wishes of the child.

2. When the child has arrived at majority, and has assumed the responsibility of its own conduct, both the responsibility and the right of the parent cease altogether.

The time of majority is fixed in most civilized nations by statute. In Great Britain and in the United States an individual becomes of age at his twenty-first year. The law, therefore, settles the rights and obligations of the parties so far as civil society is concerned, but does not pretend to decide upon the moral relations of the parties.

3. As the rights and duties of the parent at one period are absolute and at another cease altogether, it is reasonable to infer that the control of the parent should be exercised on more and more liberal principles, that a wider and wider discretion should be allowed to the child, and that his feelings and predilections should be more and more consulted, as he grows older; so that when he comes to act for himself he may have become prepared for the responsibility which he assumes by as extensive an experience as the nature of the case admits.

4. Hence I think that a parent is bound to consult the wishes of his child, in proportion to his age, whenever this can be done innocently; and also to vary his modes of enforcing authority so as to adapt them to the motives of which the increasing intellect of the child is susceptible. While it is true that the treatment proper for a young man would ruin a child, it is equally true that the treatment proper for a child might very possibly ruin a young man. The right of control, however, still rests with the parent, and the duty of obedi-

ence still is imposed upon the child. The parent is merely bound to exercise it in a manner suited to the nature of the being over whom it is to be exerted.

The authority of *instructors* is a delegated authority, derived immediately from the parent. He, for the time being, stands to the pupil *in loco parentis*. Hence the relation between him and the pupil is analogous to that between parent and child; that is, it is the relation of superiority and inferiority. The right of the instructor is to command; the obligation of the pupil is to obey. The right of the instructor is, however, to be exercised, as I before stated when speaking of the parent, for the pupil's benefit. For the exercise of it he is responsible to the *parent,* whose professional agent he is. He must use his own best skill and judgment in governing and teaching his pupil. If he and the parent cannot agree, the connection must be dissolved. But, as he is a professional agent, he must use his *own* intellect and skill in the exercise of his own profession, and in the use of it he is to be interfered with by no one.

I SHALL consider in this chapter the *duties* and the *rights* of children, and their *duration*.

THE DUTIES OF CHILDREN.

I. *Obedience.* By this I mean that the relation between parent and child obliges the latter to conform to the will of the former *because it is his will,* aside from the consideration that what is required seems to the child best or wisest. The only limitation to this rule is the limitation of conscience. A parent has no right to require a child to do what it believes to be wrong; and a child is under no obligation in such a case to obey the commands of a parent. The child must obey God, and meekly suffer the consequences. It has even in this case no right to *resist.*

The reasons of this rule are manifest.

1. The design of the whole domestic constitution would be frustrated without it. This design, from what has been already remarked, is to enable the child to avail itself both of the wisdom, and knowledge, and experience, of the parent; and also of that affection which prompts the parent to employ all these for the well-being of the child. But of these advantages the child can never avail himself unless he yield obedience to the parent's authority, until he have acquired that age and experience which are necessary to enable him to direct and to govern himself.

2. That this is the duty of children is made apparent by the precepts of the Holy Scriptures:

Exodus xx, 12. "Honor thy father and thy mother, that thy days may be long in the land which the Lord thy God giveth thee." This, as St. Paul remarks, *Eph.* vi, 2, 3, is the only commandment in the decalogue, to which a special promise is annexed.

In the book of Proverbs no duty is more frequently inculcated than this; and of no one are the consequences of obedience and disobedience more fully set forth.

A few examples may serve as a specimen:

Proverbs i, 8, 9. "My son, keep the instruction of thy father, and forsake not the law of thy mother. They shall be an ornament of grace (that is, a graceful ornament) unto thy head, and chains about thy neck."

Proverbs vi, 20. "Keep thy father's commandment, and forsake not the law of thy mother."

Proverbs xiii, 1. "A wise son heareth his father's instructions, but a scorner heareth not rebuke."

The same duty is frequently inculcated in the New Testament:

Ephesians vi, 1. "Children, obey your parents in the Lord, for *this is right.*" The meaning of the phrase "in the Lord" I suppose to be, in accordance with the will of the Lord.

Colossians iii, 20. "Children, obey your parents in all things, for this is well pleasing unto the Lord." The phrase "well pleasing unto the Lord" is here of the same meaning as "in the Lord," above.

The displeasure of God against those who violate this command is also frequently denounced in the Scriptures:

Deuteronomy xxvii, 16. "Cursed be he that setteth light by his father or his mother; and all the people shall say Amen."

Proverbs xv, 5. "A fool despiseth his father's instructions."

Proverbs xxx, 17. "The eye that mocketh at his father, and despiseth to obey his mother, the ravens of the valley shall pluck it out, and the young eagles shall eat it." That is, he shall perish by a violent death; he shall come to a miserable end.

From such passages as these, and I have selected only a very few from a great number that might have been quoted, we learn, 1. That the Holy Scriptures plainly inculcate obedience to parents as a command of God. He who is guilty of disobedience, therefore, violates not merely the command of man, but that also of God. And it is, therefore, our duty always to urge it and to exact it mainly on this ground.

2. That they consider obedience to parents as no indication of meanness and servility, but on the contrary as the most honorable and delightful exhibition of character that can be manifested by the young. It is a *graceful* ornament, which confers additional beauty upon that which was otherwise lovely.

3. That the violation of this commandment exposes the trans-

gressor to special and peculiar judgments. And, even without the light of revelation, I think that the observation of everyone must convince him that the curse of God rests heavily upon filial disobedience, and that his peculiar blessing follows filial obedience. And, indeed, what can be a surer indication of future profligacy and ruin than that turbulent impatience of restraint which leads a youth to follow the headlong impulses of passion in preference to the counsels of age and experience, even when conveyed in the language of tender and disinterested affection?

II. Another duty of children to parents is *reverence*. This is implied in the commandment, *"honor* thy father and thy mother." By reverence I mean that conduct and those sentiments which are due from an inferior to a superior. The parent is the superior, and the child the inferior, by virtue of the relation which God himself has established. Whatever may be the rank or the attainments of the child, and how much soever they may be superior to those of the parent, these can never abrogate the previous relation which God has established. The child is bound to show deference to the parent, whenever it is possible, to evince that he considers him his superior; and to perform for him services which he would perform for no other person. And let it always be remembered that in this there is nothing degrading, but everything honorable. No more ennobling and dignified trait of character can be exhibited than that of universal and profound filial respect. The same principle, carried out, would teach us universal and tender respect for *old age,* at all times and under all circumstances.

III. Another duty of children is *filial affection,* or the peculiar affection due from a child to a parent *because he is a parent.* A parent may be entitled to our love because he is a man, or because he is *such a man,* that is, possessing such excellences of character; but, besides all this, and aside from it all, he is entitled to our affection on account of the *relation in which he stands to us.* This imposes upon us the duty not only of hiding his foibles, of covering his defects, of shielding him from misfortune, and of seeking his happiness by what means soever Providence has placed in our power, but also of performing all this and all the other duties of which we have spoken *from love to him* because *he is our parent*—a love which shall render such services not a burden but a pleasure, under what circumstances soever it may be our duty to render them.

IV. It is the duty of the child, whenever it is by the providence of God rendered necessary, to support his parent in old age. That man would deserve the reputation of a monster who would not cheerfully deny himself in order to be able to minister to the comforts of the declining years of his parent.

THE RIGHTS OF CHILDREN

1. Children have a right to maintenance, and, as has been remarked before, a maintenance corresponding to the circumstances and condition of the parent.

2. They have a right to expect that the parent will exert his authority not for his own advantage, nor from caprice, but for the good of the child, according to his best judgment. If the parent act otherwise he violates his duty to his children and to God. This, however, in no manner liberates the child from his obligations to his parent. These remain in full force, the same as before. The wrong of one party is no excuse for wrong in the other. It is the child's misfortune, but it can never be alleviated by domestic strife, and still less by filial disobedience and ingratitude.

Of the duration of these rights and obligations.

1. *Of obedience.* The child is bound to obey the parent so long as he remains in a state of pupilage, that is, so long as the parent is responsible for his conduct and he is dependent upon his parent. This period, so far as society is concerned, as has been remarked, is fixed in most countries by statute. Sometimes, by the consent of both parties, it ceases before that period; at other times it continues beyond it. With the termination of minority, let it occur when it will, the duty of *obedience* ceases. After this, however, the advice of the parent is entitled to more deference and respect than that of any other person; but, as the individual now acts upon his own responsibility, it is only advice, since it has ceased to be authoritative.

2. The *conscience* of a child becomes capable of deliberate decision long before its period of pupilage ceases. Whenever this decision is fairly and honestly expressed, the parent ought not to in-

terfere with it. It is his duty to strive to convince his child if he think it to be in error; but if he cannot succeed in producing conviction he must leave the child, like any other human being, to obey God in the manner it thinks will be most acceptable to Him.

3. The obligation of *respect and affection* for parents never ceases, but rather increases with advancing age. As the child grows older, he becomes capable of more disinterested affection, and of the manifestation of more delicate respect; and as the parent grows older, he feels more sensibly the need of attention; and his happiness is more decidedly dependent upon it. As we increase in years it should, therefore, be our more assiduous endeavor to make a suitable return to our parents for their kindness bestowed upon us in infancy and youth, and to manifest by unremitting attention and delicate and heartfelt affection our repentance for those acts of thoughtlessness and waywardness which formerly may have grieved them.

That a peculiar insensibility exists to the obligations of the parental and filial relation is, I fear, too evident to need any extended illustration. The notion that a family is a society, and that a society must be governed, and that the right and the duty of governing this society rest with the parent, seems to be rapidly vanishing from the minds of men. In the place of it, it seems to be the prevalent opinion that children may grow up as they please; and that the exertion of parental restraint is an infringement upon the personal liberty of the child. But all this will not abrogate the law of God, nor will it avert the punishments which he has connected indissolubly with disobedience. The parent who neglects his duty to his children is sowing thickly, for himself and for them, the seeds of his future misery. He who is suffering the evil dispositions of his children to grow up uncorrected will find that he is cherishing a viper by which he himself will first be stung. That parent who is accustoming his children to habits of thoughtless caprice and reckless expenditure, and who stupidly smiles at the ebullitions of youthful passion and the indulgence in fashionable vice as indications of a manly spirit, needs no prophet to foretell that, unless the dissoluteness of his family leave him early childless, his gray hairs will be brought down with sorrow to the grave.

I remarked at the close of the last chapter that the duty of instructors was analogous to that of parents, and that they stood to pupils in a relation essentially *parental*. It is proper here to add that a pupil stands to his instructor in a relation essentially *filial*. His duty is obedience: first to his parent; and secondly to the professional agent to whom he has been committed by his parent. The equals in this relation are the parent and the instructor: to both of them is the pupil the inferior; and to both is he under the obligation of obedience, respect, and reverence.

Now such being the nature of the relation, it is the duty of the instructor to enforce obedience and of the pupil to render it. It would be very easy to show that on the fulfillment of this duty on the part of the instructor, the interests of education and the welfare of the young vitally depend. Without discipline there can be formed no valuable habit. Without it, when young persons are congregated together far away from the restraints of domestic society, exposed to the allurements of ever-present temptation and excited by the stimulus of youthful passion, every vicious habit must be cultivated. The young man may applaud the negligent and pusillanimous instructor; but, when that man, no longer young, suffers the result of that neglect and pusillanimity, it is well if a better spirit have taught him to mention the name of that instructor without bitter execration.

> In colleges and halls, in ancient days,
> There dwelt a sage called Discipline.
> His eye was meek and gentle, and a smile
> Played on his lips; and in his speech was heard
> Paternal sweetness, dignity, and love.
> The occupation dearest to his heart
> Was to encourage goodness. Learning grew,
> Beneath his care, a thriving, a vigorous plant.
> The mind was well informed, the passions held
> Subordinate, and diligence was choice.
> If e'er it chanced, as sometimes chance it must,
> That one, among so many, overleaped
> The limits of control, his gentle eye
> Grew stern, and darted a severe rebuke.
> His frown was full of terror, and his voice
> Shook the delinquent with such fits of awe,
> As left him not, till penitence had won

Lost favor back again, and closed the breach.
                    But Discipline at length,
O'erlooked and unemployed, grew sick, and died.
Then study languished, emulation slept,
And virtue fled. The schools became a scene
Of solemn farce, where ignorance in stilts,
His cap well lined with logic not his own,
With parrot tongue, performed the scholar's part,
Proceeding soon a graduated dunce.
                    What was learned,
If aught was learned in childhood, is forgot;
And such expense as pinches parents blue,
And mortifies the liberal hand of love,
Is squandered in pursuit of idle sports
And vicious pleasures.   [Cowper,] *Task*.

To this class belong the duties of magistrates and citizens. As these, however, would be but imperfectly understood without a knowledge of the nature of civil society and of the relations subsisting between society and the individual, it will be necessary to consider these latter before entering upon the former. I shall, therefore, attempt to explain, first, *The Nature and Limitations of Civil Society;* secondly, *Government, or the Manner in which the Obligations of Society are Discharged;* thirdly, *The Duties of Magistrates;* fourthly, *The Duties of Citizens.*

CHAPTER FIRST
OF CIVIL SOCIETY

As civil society is a somewhat complicated conception, it may be useful, in the first place, to consider the nature of a society in its simplest form. This chapter will therefore be divided into two sections. The first treats of the *constitution of a simple society;* the second, of the *constitution of civil society.*

Section I · Of a Simple Society

I. *Of the nature of a Simple Society.*

1. A society of any sort originates in a peculiar form of contract entered into between each several individual forming the society on the one part, and all the other members of the society on the other part. Each party promises to do certain things to or for the other, and puts itself under moral obligation to do so. Hence we see that conscience, or the power of recognizing moral obligation, is, in the very nature of things, essential to the existence of a society. Without it a society could not be formed.

2. This contract, like any other, respects those things, and those things only, in which the parties have thus bound themselves to each other. As the individual is under no obligation to belong to the society, but the obligation is purely voluntary, he is bound in no other

manner and for no other purpose than those in and for which he has bound himself. In all other respects he is as free as he was before.

3. Inasmuch as the formation of a society involves the idea of a moral obligation, each party is under moral obligation to fulfill its part of the contract. The society is bound to do what it has promised to every individual, and every individual is bound to do what he has promised to the society. If either party cease to do this, the compact, like any other mutual contract, is dissolved.

4. Inasmuch as every individual is, in all respects excepting those in which he has bound himself, as free as he was before, the society has no right to impose upon the individual any other obligation than those under which he has placed himself. For, as he has come under no such obligation to them, they have no more control over him than any other men. And, as *their whole power* is limited to that which has been conferred upon them by individuals, beyond this limit they are no society; they have no power; their act is really *out of the society,* and is, of course, binding upon no member of the society any more than upon any other man.

5. As every member of the society enters it upon the same terms, that is, as everyone comes under the same obligations to the society and the society comes under the same obligations to him, they are by consequence, so far as the society is concerned, all equals or fellows. All have equal rights, and all are subject to the same obligations.

6. That which defines the obligations under which the individual and the society have come, in respect to each other, is called the *constitution* of the society. It is intended to express the object of the association and the manner in which that object is to be accomplished: that is to say it declares what the individual promises to do for the society, what the society promises to do for the individual, and the object for which this association between the parties is formed.

7. As the union of individuals in this manner is voluntary, every member naturally has a right to dissolve the connection when he pleases; and the society have also a corresponding right. As, however, this would frequently expose both parties to inconvenience, it is common in the articles of the constitution or the form of compact to specify on what terms this may be done. When this part of the

agreement has thus been entered into, it of course becomes as binding as any other part of it.

II. *Of the manner in which such a society shall be governed.*

The object of any such association is to do something. But it is obvious that they can act only on one of three suppositions: by unanimity, by a minority, or by a majority. To expect *unanimity* in the opinions of a being so diversified in character as man is frivolous. To suspend the operation of many upon the decisions of one is manifestly unjust, would be subversive of the whole object of the association, and would render the whole society more inefficient than the separate individuals of which it is composed. To suppose a society to be governed by a *minority* would be to suppose a *less* number of equals superior in wisdom and goodness to a *greater* number, which is absurd. It remains, therefore, that every society must of necessity be governed by a *majority*.

III. *Of the limits within which the power of the majority is restricted.*

The majority, as we have just seen, is vested from necessity with the whole power of the society. But it derives its power wholly and exclusively from the society, and of course it can have no power beyond, or diverse from, that of the society itself. Now as the power of the society is limited by the concessions made by each individual respectively, and is bound by its obligations to each individual, the power of the majority is manifestly restricted within precisely the same limits.

Thus, to be more particular, a majority has no right to do anything which the individuals forming the society have not authorized the society to do:

1. They have no right to *change the object* of the society. If this be changed, another society is formed, and the individual members are, as at first, at liberty to unite with it or not.

2. They have no right to do anything *beyond,* or *different from,* the object of the society. The reasons are the same as in the former instance.

3. Nor have they a right to do anything in a *manner* different from that to which the members upon entering the society agreed.

The manner set forth in the constitution was that by which the individuals bound themselves, and they are bound by nothing else.

4. Nor have they a right to do anything which violates the principle of the entire social equality of the members. As all subjected themselves equally to the same rules, any act which supposes a difference of right is at variance with the fundamental principle of the compact.

And, hence, from the nature of the compact, it is obvious that while a majority act within the limits of the authority thus delegated to them, the individual is under a moral obligation to obey their decisions; for he has voluntarily placed himself under such obligation, and he is bound to fulfill it.

And, on the other hand, the society is bound to fulfill to the individual the contract which they have formed with him, and to carry forward the object of the association in the manner and in the spirit of the contract entered into. Nor is this a mere matter of form or of expediency: it is a matter of moral obligation voluntarily entered into; and it is as binding as any other contract formed under any other circumstances.

And, again, if the society or the majority act in violation of these engagements, or if they do anything not committed to them by the individual, such act is not binding upon any member; and he is under no more obligation to be governed by it than he would be if it were done by any other persons or if not done at all.

If these principles be correct, they will, I think, throw some light upon the question of the durability of corporations. A corporation is a society established for certain purposes which are to be executed in a certain manner. He who joins it, joins it under these conditions; and the whole power of the society consists in power to do these things in this manner. If they do anything else they, when doing it, are not this society but some other. And of course those, whether the minority or the majority, who act according to the original compact, are the society; and the others, whether more or less, are something else. The act of incorporation is governed by the same principles. It renders the persons so associated a body politic, and recognised in law, but it does not interfere with the original principles of such an association. The corporation, therefore, are the persons, whether more or less, who adhere to the original agreement; and any act declaring anything else to be the society is unjust and void.

But suppose them all to have altered their sentiments. The society is then of course dissolved. They may, if they choose, form another society; but they are not another, *of course,* nor can they be such until they form another organization.

Again, suppose that they have property given under the original association, and for the promotion of its objects, and the whole society, or a majority of them, have changed its objects. I answer, If a part still remain and prosecute the original object, they are the society; and the others, by changing the object, have ceased to be the society. The right of property vests with those who adhere to the original constitution. If all have changed the object, the society is dissolved; and all ownership so far as the property is concerned ceases. It therefore either belongs to the public or reverts to the heirs at law. A company of men united for another object, though retaining the same name, have no more right to inherit it than any other citizens. The right of a legislature to give it to them by special act is even very questionable. Legislatures are not empowered to bestow property upon men at will; and such grant, being beyond the power conceded to the legislator, seems to me to be null and void.

The principles of this section seem to me to demand the special attention of those who are at present engaged in conducting the business of voluntary associations. It should always be remembered that he who joins a voluntary association joins it for a specified object, and for no other. The association itself has one object, and no other. This object, and the manner in which it is to be accomplished, ought to be plainly set forth in the constitution. Now, when a majority attempt to do anything not comprehended within this object thus set forth, or in a manner at variance with that prescribed, they violate the fundamental article of the compact and the society is virtually dissolved. And against such infraction of right it is the duty of the individual to protest; and if it be persisted in, it is his duty to withdraw. And it seems to me that otherwise the whole benefit of voluntary associations will be lost; and if the whole society do it the society is changed, and it is changed in no manner the less because its original name is retained. If the objects of such associations be not restricted, their increasing complication will render them unmanageable by any form of agency. If an individual, when he unites with others for one object, knows not for how many objects nor for what modes of accomplishing them he shall be held responsible, who will ever unite in a benevolent enterprise? And if masses of men may be thus associated in every part of a country for one professed object and this object may be modified, changed, or exceeded, according to the will of an accidental majority, voluntary associations will very soon be transformed into the tools of intriguing and ambitious men and will thus become a curse instead of a blessing.

Section II · Of Civil Society

In order to consider this subject correctly it will be necessary to consider *society* as distinct from *government*. It may exist without a government. At some time it must have so existed. And in all cases government is merely the instrument by which it accomplishes its purposes. Government is the *agent*. Society is the *principal*.[31]

The first consideration which meets us in the discussion of this subject is that CIVIL SOCIETY IS AN INSTITUTION OF GOD; or in other words, it is the will of God that man should live in a state of society. This may be shown both from the *original impulses common to all men* and from the *necessities of man* arising out of the conditions of his present existence.

I. *From the original impulses of man.*

1. One of the strongest and most universal impulses of our nature is a general love for society. It commences, as everyone must have observed, with early infancy and continues, unabated, to the close of life. The poets can conceive of no situation more afflictive or more intolerable than that of a human being in a state of perfect loneliness. Hence solitary confinement is considered by all mankind as one of the severest forms of punishment. And hence a disposition to sepa-

---

[31] See Appendix (N) for remainder of section as it appears in the 1865 edition.

rate oneself from society is one of the surest indications of mental derangement. Now the natural result of this intense and universal impulse is a disposition to control such other desires as shall be inconsistent with it. Wherever these dispositions exist, a number of human beings will as readily and naturally form a society as they will do any other thing on which their happiness depends. A constitution of this sort manifestly shows what is the will of our Creator concerning us.

2. The various forms of human attachment illustrate the same truth.

Thus the attachment between the sexes at once forms a society, which is the origin of every other. Of this union the fundamental principle is a limited surrender of the happiness of each to that of the other and the consequent attainment of an increased return of happiness. From this arises the love of parents to children and that of children to parents and all the various modifications of affection resulting from collateral and more distant relationships.

Besides these, there must continually arise the feeling of friendship between individuals of similar habits and of correspondent pursuits; the love of benevolence toward those who need our succor or who awaken our sympathy; and the love of approbation, which will stimulate us to deny ourselves for the sake of acquiring the good opinion of those by whom we are surrounded. Now the tendency of all these instincts is manifestly twofold: *first,* as in the former instance, as these propensities can be gratified only by society, we shall be disposed to surrender whatever will be inconsistent with the enjoyment of society; and *secondly,* since it is, as we have seen before, in the very nature *of affection* to surrender our own personal gratification for the happiness of those whom we love, affection renders such a surrender one of the very sources of our individual happiness. Thus patriotism, which is only one form of the love of society, not only supposes a man to be willing to surrender something personal for the sake of something general, which he likes better, but also to derive happiness from that very surrender and to be actually happier when acting from these principles than from any other. It is almost needless to add that the Creator's intention in forming beings with such impulsions is too evident to be mistaken.

II. The same truth is taught from *the necessities imposed upon us by the conditions of our being.*

1. Suppose the human race, entirely destitute of these social principles, to have been scattered abroad over the face of the earth as mere isolated individuals. It is evident that under such circumstances the race must quickly have perished. Man thus isolated could never contend either with the cold of the northern or with the wild beasts of the temperate and warmer regions. He has neither muscular power nor agility nor instinct to protect him from the one, nor any natural form of clothing to shield him from the other.

2. But suppose that, by any means, the race of man could be continued. Without society, the progressive melioration of his condition would be impossible.

Without society there could be no *division of labor.* Everyone must do everything for himself, and at the greatest possible disadvantage. Without society there could be neither any *knowledge of* the *agents of nature* nor any *application* of them to the production of value. A man's instruments would be almost exclusively limited to his teeth and nails. Without society there could be no acknowledged *right of property.* Hence from these causes, there could be no accumulated *capital;* and each successive generation of men must, like the brutes, remain precisely in the condition of their predecessors. It is equally evident that under these circumstances there could exist no possibility of either intellectual or moral *improvement.* In fact, take the most civilized, intellectual, and moral condition in which man has ever existed, and compare it with the condition of man naked, wandering, destitute, exposed to the peltings of every tempest, and liable to become the prey of every ferocious beast, and the difference between these two conditions is wholly the result of society. If it be granted that God is benevolent and wills the *happiness* of man, nay, if it be even granted that God wills the *existence* of man, it must be conceded that He also wills that condition on which, not merely his happiness, but even his very existence depends.

Now if this be the fact, that is, if civil society be an institution of God, several important conclusions will be seen to follow from it:

1. A very important distinction may be observed between civil society and a simple or voluntary society such as is described in the last section. In a simple society the contract is voluntary and is, like any other society, dissolved at the pleasure of the parties; or it ceases to be binding upon either party if its conditions be violated by the other party. But civil society being an institution of God, specific duties are imposed upon both parties which remain unchanged even after the other party may, in various respects, have violated his part of the contract. In civil society we are under obligation to God as well as to man, and the former obligation remains even after the other has been annulled. In this respect it follows the analogy of the other relations established by God, as that of husband and wife, parent and child, in which the one party is bound to act in obedience to the will of God and according to the obligations of the relation whether the other party does so or not.

2. Civil society being an ordinance of God, it cannot be justly established upon any principles whatsoever, simply according to the will of the parties, but it must be established upon the principles which God has established. If it be established upon any other principles the evidence of his displeasure will be seen in the mutual evil which both parties suffer in consequence of violating a law of their being. Such is the case with marriage. This is a form of society established by God. Men have no right to enter into it as they please, but only according to the laws which God has established; and if they act otherwise, mutual misery will be the result.

3. If society be an ordinance of God it follows that every man who conforms to the social laws of God has a right to it. For if in the formation of civil society men are under obligation to act in obedience to the will of God, they have no right to construct it upon such principles as will exclude any man who is willing to obey the social laws of his Maker. No man can, therefore, justly be excluded from society unless he have committed some overt act by which he has forfeited this right. His original right is to be taken for granted; the proof of forfeiture rests with those who would exclude him. Hence it is not enough to say, if a man does not like this society he may go to another. So long as he violates none of his Maker's

social laws he has a right to *this* society, and he cannot be excluded from it without injustice. Any course of legislation, therefore, which obliges men to leave a society, unless their forfeiture of social right be proved, is oppressive and unjust.

4. As society is an ordinance of God, it is evidently the will of God that its existence be preserved. Hence society has a right to take all the means which may be necessary to prevent those crimes which, if permitted, must destroy society itself. Hence is derived its power to punish criminals, to enforce contracts, and to establish such forms of government as may best conduce to the well being of the social institution.

I suppose it to have been from a misconception of these principles that our forefathers erred. They conceived that in forming a civil society here in the wilderness they had a right to frame its provisions in such manner as they chose. Hence they made the form of religious belief a subject of civil legislation and assumed the right of banishing from their society those who differed from them in the mode of worshipping God. Their first assumption I conceive to be an error. If society be an ordinance of God, whenever and wherever men form it they must form it in obedience to his laws. But he has never intended that religious belief or religious practice, if they interfere not with the rights of others, should be subject to human legislation.

Secondly. OF THE NATURE AND LIMITATIONS OF THE CONTRACT entered into between the individual and civil society.

It has been already remarked that every society is essentially a mutual compact entered into between every individual and all the rest of those who form the society. As all these individuals enter the society upon the same terms, that is, put themselves under the power of society in the same respects, the power of the society over the individual is derived from the concession of every individual and is no other, and in no wise different from what these individuals have made it. And on the other hand, as every member of the society is a party to the contract which the society has made with the individual, every member of the society is bound faithfully to execute the contract thus entered into.

But as it was also remarked, this society differs from a simple or voluntary society inasmuch as it is an ordinance of God and it is subject to the laws which he has imposed upon it. That every man is *bound to become a member* of civil society need not be asserted; all that I affirm is that if men form a civil society they are bound to form it according to the laws which God has appointed. They cannot form it according to any other principles without violating the rights of their fellow men and disobeying the laws of God.

The question, then, which meets us as of the first importance is this: What are the laws under which God has subjected civil society? On this question I now proceed to offer a few suggestions, considering, first, what is *essential to the existence of society;* and secondly, what is merely *accidental*.

I. *Of what is essential to the existence of civil society.*

1. As God wills the existence of civil society, it is manifest that he must forbid whatever would be inconsistent with its existence. And on the other hand, he who chooses to enter society virtually contracts to abstain from whatever is, from the constitution of things, inconsistent with its existence. This, I think, is as evident as that a man cannot honestly enter into a contract to do any two things in their nature essentially at variance.

2. Suppose, now, a number of men to meet together to form a society, all being perfectly acquainted with the law of reciprocity and all perfectly inclined to obey it. I think it is manifest that such persons would have to *surrender nothing whatever* in order to form a civil society. Everyone would do just as he pleased, and yet everyone would enjoy fully all the benefit of the social nature of man; that is, everyone would enjoy all the blessings arising both from his individual and from his social constitution. This, I suppose, would be the most perfect state of human society of which we are able to conceive.

As, therefore, society in *its most perfect state may exist* without the individual's surrendering up the right to do anything which is consistent with the law of reciprocity, *the existence of society* presents no reason why he should surrender any right which he may enjoy consistently with this law. Whatever other reasons there may be, as those of benevolence, mercy, or religion, they belong not to this question. As every man has, originally, the right to do as he pleases, provided he interferes not with the rights of his neighbors, and as the existence of civil society presents no reason why this right should be restricted, it remains, notwithstanding the existence of such society, just as it was before; that is, the right vests, without change, in the individual himself.

3. Suppose, now, any individual to *violate the law* of reciprocity; as, for instance, that A steals the property of B or violates a contract into which they have mutually entered. If this be allowed, that is, if every man were to steal at will the property of his neighbor, it is manifest that the right of property would be at an end and every man would be obliged to retire as far as possible from every other man; that is, society would be dissolved.

4. Again, suppose that B takes the work of redress into his own hands, being at once his own legislator, judge, and executioner. From the native principles of the human heart it is evident that from being the aggrieved party, he would, in turn, become the aggressor. This would lead to revenge on the part of A—a revenge to be repeated by the other party, until it ended either in the destruction of one or of both. Hence every difference would lead to interminable war and unbridled ferocity; and society would cease, because every man would prefer quiet solitude to ceaseless hostility.

To allow oneself, therefore, in any violation of the law of reciprocity or to assume the right of redressing one's own wrongs is to pursue a course inconsistent with the existence of society; for were such a course to be pursued universally society could not exist.

Again, on the other hand, since in a company of morally imperfect beings injury is liable to occur, and since if injury were not prevented the virtuous would become the prey of the vicious and society would, as before, be destroyed by universal violence, it is manifestly necessary that injury be prevented, that is, that the virtuous be protected and that wrongs be redressed. But as we have shown that the rights of individual self-protection and redress are inconsistent with the existence of society and as the *individual* must not redress them, the duty devolves upon the other party, that is, upon society. Society is therefore bound to do for the individual what he has relinquished the right to do for himself; that is, to protect him from violation of the law of reciprocity or to redress his wrong, if this right be violated.

Hence we see the nature of the compact entered into between the individual and society. It essentially involves the following particulars:

1. Every individual, by entering society, promises that he will abstain from every violation of the law of reciprocity, which, if universally permitted, would destroy society. For if *he* be allowed to violate it the allowance to violate it must be extended *to all,* since all are equals; and thus society would be destroyed. But as by the destruction of society he would gain nothing but solitude, which he could enjoy without depriving others of what is to them a source of happiness, there can be no reason assigned why he should diminish their happiness to procure what he could equally well enjoy by leaving them alone. If he join the society he must conform to whatever is necessary to its existence; if he be unwilling to do so he must remain alone.

2. Every individual promises to surrender to society the right of self-protection.

3. And lastly, every individual promises to surrender to society the right to redress his own wrongs.

And on the other hand, society promises—

1. To protect the individual in the enjoyment of all his rights; that is, to enforce upon every individual, within certain limits, obedience to the law of reciprocity.

2. To redress wrongs whenever they may occur, either by obliging the offender to do justly or else by inflicting such punishment as may be most likely to prevent a repetition of the injury either by the offender or by others.

It is important here to remark that this surrender on the one part and this obligation on the other part are mutual and universal: that is to say, the individual on his part surrenders wholly and entirely the right either to defend or to redress himself; and on the other hand, society guarantees to defend him and to do him justice to the utmost; that is, no matter in how small a right and no matter at how great an expense.

Hence we see the antisocial tendency of all those secret societies of which the object, either avowed or in fact, is to protect the individual members in opposition to the laws, that is, in opposition to society. In this case, while the individual receives from civil society the same benefits as other men and expects from it the fulfillment of its part of the contract, he does not make, on his part, the correspondent surrender. He expects to be protected and redressed, but he reserves also the right of protecting and redressing himself, and it may be in opposition to the just operation of those laws which he enforces upon others.

And hence also, we see the obligation of everyone to exert himself to the uttermost in order to enforce the execution of the laws, no matter in how small a matter or in the case of how obscure an individual. The execution of the laws is what we all promise and we are all bound to fulfill it. And if laws are not executed, that is, if individuals be not protected and wrongs be not redressed by society, the individuals will redress them themselves, and thus society will be dissolved. The frequent occurrence of mobs, that is, of extralegal modes of redress for supposed grievances, are among the most decisive indications of a state of society verging towards dissolution.

But while this contract is thus universal and obligatory, it is to be remarked that it is so only in respect to those things in which the parties have respectively bound themselves. The individual, by entering into society, promises to abstain from whatever is inconsistent with the existence of society; but by entering into society he promises nothing more. Society promises to restrain and to redress whatever would be destructive to society, but it promises no more. In all other respects the parties are exactly in the situation in which they were before the establishment of society. Thus freedom, therefore, both of person, of intellect, and of conscience, remain, by the fact of the existence of society, untouched. Thus also freedom of property remains as before except simply insofar as a portion of every man's property is pledged to meet the necessary expenses of government. So long as he obey the law of reciprocity, society has no further demands upon him unless his assistance be demanded in enforcing this obedience upon others.

By this compact every individual is very greatly the gainer.

1. He promises to obey the law of reciprocity, which is the law of his nature, and by the obedience to which alone he can be happy.

2. He surrenders the right of self-protection, which without society he can exert in but a very imperfect manner and with nothing but the force of his individual arm; and he receives in return the right to wield in his defence the whole power of society.

3. He surrenders the right of redressing his own grievances and receives in return the right to have his grievances redressed, at whatever expense, by the whole power of the society.

And hence as God wills the happiness of man, we see another reason why society is in obedience to his will; and why the laws necessary to the existence of society may be considered, as they are in fact considered in the Scriptures, as enacted by His authority.

And again, we see that from the very nature of society the individual is perfectly within its physical power. This power of the whole, which they are bound to use only for his protection and defense, they may use for his injury and oppression. And as the whole power of the society is in the hands of the majority, the whole happiness of the individual or of the minority is always in the power of the majority. Hence we see there is no safeguard against oppression except that which exists in the conditions of the compact on which the society is formed and the feeling of moral obligation to observe that compact inviolably. That is to say, the real question of civil liberty is not concerning *forms* of government, but concerning the respective *limits* and *obligations of the individual and of society*. When these are correctly adjusted and inviolably observed there can be no oppression under any form of government. When these are not understood or not observed there will be tyranny, under any form whatsoever. And to a man of sense it is a matter of very small consequence whether oppression proceed from one or from many; from a hereditary tyrant or from an unprincipled majority. The latter is rather the more galling and surely at least as difficult of remedy.

And supposing the limits to have been correctly adjusted, it is obvious that they will be of no avail unless there be in the community sufficient virtue to resist the temptations which continually occur to violate them. In the absence of this the best constitution is valueless or worse than valueless. Hence we see the necessity of individual virtue to the existence of civil freedom. And hence whatever tends to depress the standard of individual virtue, saps the very foundations of liberty. And hence religion, in its purest form, and under its most authoritative sanctions, is the surest hope of national as well as of individual happiness.

II. *Of the accidental modifications of civil society.*

I have thus far treated of what is *essential* to the social compact. Without such a contract as I have suggested society could not exist. I by no means, however, intend to assert that these limits are exclusive; and that men, in forming society, may not enter into contract in other respects besides those which I have stated.

Some of the incidental additions to the original forms of contract are the following:

1. After having adjusted the limits of the respective obligations both of the society and of the individual, men may choose whatever form of government they please for the purpose of carrying forward the objects of society. But having adopted a particular form of government, they bind themselves to whatever is necessary to the existence of that government. Thus if men choose a republican form of government, in which the people are acknowledged to be the immediate fountain of all power, they come under obligation to educate their children intellectually and morally; for without intellectual and moral education such a form of government cannot long exist. And as the intellectual education of the young can be made properly a subject of social enactment, this duty may be enforced by society. And the only reason why religious education does not come under the same rule is that it is not, for reasons which have been before given, a subject for social enactment.

2. I have said that by the essential principles of the social compact every man is bound to contribute his part to the expenses of civil society; but that beyond this he is not in any respect bound. Still, this does not exclude other forms of contract. Men may, *if they choose,* agree to hold their whole property subject to the will of the

whole, so that they shall be obliged to employ it, not each one for his own good, but each one for the benefit of the whole society. I say that such a state of things *might* exist, but it is manifest that it is not *essential* to society; and that, being not essential, it is by no means *to be presumed;* and that it cannot exist justly unless this right have been expressly conceded by the individual to society. If society exert such a power when it has not been expressly conceded to it, it is tyranny. The common fact has been that society has presumed upon such powers and has exercised them without reflection and very greatly to social and individual injury.

3. Men have very generally been disposed to take for granted these accidental powers and to question or limit the essential powers of society. An instance in point occurs in the question of war. The very idea of war supposes the society to have the right of determining the moral relations in which the individuals of one nation shall stand to the individuals of another nation. Now this power of society over the individual has never, that I know of, been questioned. And yet I think it would be very difficult to establish it. The moral precept is, "If thine enemy hunger, feed him; if he thirst, give him drink." And I do not see that society has a right to abrogate this command or to render void this obligation; or that any moral agent has the right to commit to other individuals the power of changing his moral relations to any creature of God. Forgiveness and charity to men are dispositions which we owe to God. And I do not see that society has any more right to interfere with the manifestation of these dispositions than with the liberty to inculcate them and to teach them.

To conclude. Whatever concessions on the part of the individual and whatever powers on the part of society are *necessary* to the existence of society must, by the very fact of the existence of society, be taken for granted. Whatever is not thus necessary is a matter of concession and mutual adjustment; and has no right to be presumed unless it can be shown to have actually been surrendered. That is, in general, a man is bound by what he has agreed to; but he is not bound by anything else.

I think no one can reflect upon the above considerations without

being led to the conclusion that the cultivation of the moral nature
of man is the grand means for the improvement of society. This
alone teaches man, whether as an individual or as a society, to respect
the rights of man as an individual or as a society. This teaches
everyone to observe inviolate the contract into which, as a member
of society, he has entered. Now since, as we have before shown, the
light of conscience and the dictates of natural religion are insufficient
to exert the requisite moral power over man, our only hope is in
that revelation of his will which God has made in the Holy Scriptures. In these books we are taught that all our duties to man are
taken under the immediate protection of Almighty God. On pain
of his eternal displeasure he commands us to love every man as
ourselves. Here he holds forth the strongest inducements to obedience and here he presents the strongest motives, not merely to reciprocity, but also to benevolence. It is lamentable to hear the levity
with which some politicians and, as they would persuade us to
believe them to be, *statesmen,* speak of the religion of Jesus Christ;
to observe how complacently they talk of using it as an instrument,
convenient enough for directing the weak, but which a man of sense
can well enough do without; and which is a mere appendage to the
forces that, by his constitution, are destined to act upon man. A
more profound acquaintance with the moral and social nature of
man would, as it seems to me, work a very important change in
their views of this subject.

WE have thus far treated merely of the constitution of a society, of the contract entered into between the individual and society, and of the obligations hence devolving upon each. The obligations of society are to protect the individual from infractions of the law of reciprocity and to redress his wrongs if he have been injured.

But it is manifest that this obligation cannot be discharged by the whole of society as a body. If a man steal from his neighbor, the whole community cannot leave their occupations to detect, to try, and to punish the thief. Or if a law is to be enacted respecting the punishment of theft, it cannot be done by the whole community, but must of necessity be entrusted to delegates. On the principle of division of labor it is manifest that this service be both more cheaply and more perfectly done by those who devote themselves to it than by those who are, for the greater part of the time, engaged in other occupations.

Now I suppose a government to be that system of delegated agencies by which these obligations of society to the individual are fulfilled.

And moreover, as every society may have various engagements to form with other independent societies, it is convenient, in general, that this business should be transacted by this same system of agencies. These two offices of government, though generally united, are in their nature distinct. Thus we see in our own country, the State Governments are to a considerable degree entrusted with the first, while a *part* of the former and *all* the latter power, rest in the general government.

A government thus understood is naturally divided into three parts.

1. An individual may from ignorance violate the rights of his neighbor and thus innocently expose himself to punishment. Or if he violate his neighbor's rights maliciously, and justly merit punishment, a punishment may be inflicted more severe than the nature

of the case demands. To avoid this it is necessary that the various forms of violation be as clearly as possible defined and also that the penalty be plainly and explicitly attached to each. This is a *law*. This, as we have shown, must be done by delegates. These delegates are called a *legislature* and the individual members of it are *legislators*.

From what we have said, their power is manifestly limited. They have no power except to execute the obligations which society has undertaken to fulfill towards the individual. This is all that society has conferred, for it is all that society had to confer.

If legislators originate any power in themselves or exercise any power conferred for any purpose different from that for which it was conferred, they violate right and are guilty of tyranny.

2. But suppose a law to be enacted, that is, a crime to be defined and the penalty to be affixed. It has reference to no particular case for, when enacted, no case existed to be affected by it. Suppose now an individual to be accused of violating this law. Here it is necessary to apply the law to this particular case. In order to do this we must ascertain, first, whether the accused did commit the act laid to his charge; secondly, whether the act, if it be proved to have been done, is a violation of the law; that is, whether it come within the description of actions which the law forbids; and thirdly, if this be proved it is necessary to declare the punishment which the law assigns to this particular violation. This is the *judicial* branch of the government.

3. After the law has been thus applied to this particular case it is necessary that it be carried into effect. This devolves upon the third, or the *executive* branch of a government.

Respecting all of these three branches of government it may be remarked in general that they are essentially *independent* of each other; that each one has its specific duties marked out by society, within the sphere of which duties it is responsible to *society* and to society *alone*. Nor is this independence at all affected by the mode of its appointment. Society may chose a way of appointing an agent, but that is by no means a surrender of the claim which it has upon the agent. Thus society may impose upon a legislature or an executive the duty of appointing a judiciary; but the judiciary is just as much *independent* of the *executive* or of the *legislature* as though it were appointed in some other way. Society, by conferring upon one branch the *right of appointment,* has conferred upon it *no other right.* The judge, although appointed by the legislator, is as independent of him as the legislator would be if appointed by the judge. Each, within his own sphere, is under obligation to perform precisely those duties assigned by society and no other. And hence arises the propriety of establishing the tenure of office in each several branch independently of the other.

The two first of these departments are frequently subdivided.

Thus the legislative department is commonly divided into two branches, chosen under dissimilar conditions, for the purpose of exerting a check upon each other by representing society under different aspects and thus preventing partial and hasty legislation.

The judiciary is also generally divided. The *judges* explain and interpret *the law;* while it is the province of the *jury* to ascertain *the facts.*

The executive is generally sole, and executes the law by means of subordinate agents. Sometimes, however, a council is added for the sake of advice, without whose concurrence the executive cannot act.

Sometimes the fundamental principles of the social compact are expressed and the respective powers of the different branches of the government are defined and the mode of their appointment described, in a written document. Such is the case in the United States. At other times these principles and customs have grown up in the progress of society and are the deductions drawn from, or principles established by, uncontested usage. The latter is the case in Great Britain. In either case, such principles and practices, whether expressed or understood, are called the *constitution* of a country.

Nations differ widely in the mode of selection to office and in the tenure by which office is held. Thus under some constitutions the government is wholly hereditary. In others it is partly hereditary and partly elective. In others it is wholly elective.

Thus in Great Britain the executive and one branch of the legislature are hereditary; the other branch of the legislature is elective.

The judiciary is appointed by the executive, though they hold office, except in the case of the lord high chancellor, during good behavior.

In the United States the executive and both branches of the legislature are elective. The judiciary is appointed by the executive, by and with the advice and consent of the senate. In the State Government, the mode of appointment is various.

If it be asked, Which of these is the preferable form of government? the answer, I think, must be conditional. The best form of government for any people *is the best that its present moral and social condition renders practicable.* A people may be *so entirely surrendered to the influence of passion* and so feebly *influenced by moral restraint* that a government which relied upon moral restraint could not exist for a day. In this case, a subordinate and inferior principle yet remains—*the principle of fear;* and the only resort is to a government of force, or a military despotism. And such do we see to be the fact. An anarchy always ends in this form of government. After this has been established and habits of subordination have been formed, while the moral restraints are yet too feeble for self-government, a hereditary government, which addresses itself to the imagination and strengthens itself by the influence of domestic connections and established usage, may be as good a form as a people can sustain. As they advance in intellectual and moral cultivation, it may advantageously become more and more elective; and, in a suitable moral condition, it may be wholly so. For beings who are willing to govern themselves by moral principle, there can be no doubt that a government relying upon moral principle is the true form of government. There is no reason why a man should be oppressed by taxation and subjected to fear who is willing to govern himself by the law of reciprocity. It is surely better for an intelligent and moral being to do right from his own will than *to pay another to force him* to do right. And yet, as it is better that he should do right than wrong even though he be forced to it, it is well that he should pay others to force him if there be no other way of insuring his good conduct. God has rendered the blessing of freedom inseparable from moral restraint in the individual; and hence it is vain for a people to expect to be free unless they are first willing to be virtuous.

It is on this point that the question of the permanency of the present form of government of the United States turns. That such a form of government requires, of necessity, a given amount of virtue in the people cannot, I think, be doubted. If we possess that required amount of virtue, or if we can attain to it, the government will stand; if not, it will fall. Or if we now possess that amount of virtue, and do not maintain it, the government will fall. There is no self-sustaining power in *any form of social organization*. The only self-sustaining power is in individual virtue. And the form of a government will always adjust itself to the moral condition of a people. A virtuous people will, by their own moral power, frown away oppression and, under any form of constitution, become essentially free. A people surrendered up to their own licentious passions must be held in subjection by force; for everyone will find that force alone can protect him from his neighbors; and he will submit to be oppressed if he may only be protected. Thus in the feudal ages the small independent landholders frequently made themselves slaves of *one* powerful chief to shield themselves from the incessant oppression of *twenty*.

CHAPTER THIRD

THE DUTY OF THE OFFICERS OF A GOVERNMENT

FROM what has been said, the duties of the officers of a government may be stated in a few words.

It will be remembered that a government derives its authority from society, of which it is the agent; that society derives its authority from the compact formed by individuals; that society and the relations between society and individuals are the ordinance of God: of course the officer of a government, as the organ of society, is bound as such by the law of God and is under obligation to perform the duties of his office in obedience to this law. And hence it makes no difference how the other party to the contract may execute their engagements; he, as the servant of God, set apart for this very thing, is bound, nevertheless, to act precisely according to the principles by which God has declared that this relation should be governed.

The officers of a government are *Legislative, Judicial,* and *Executive.*

I. *Of legislative officers.*

1. It is the duty of a legislator to understand the social principles of man, the nature of the relation which subsists between the individual and society, and the mutual obligations of each. By these are his power and his obligations limited; and unless he thus inform himself, he can never know respecting any act whether it be just or whether it be oppressive. Without such knowledge he can never act with a clear conscience.

2. It is the duty of a legislator to understand the precise nature of the compact which binds together the *particular society* for which he legislates. This involves the general conditions of the social compact, and something more. It generally specifies conditions which the former does not contain and, besides, establishes the limit of the powers of the several branches of the government. He who enters upon the duties of a legislator without such knowledge is not only wicked, but contemptible. He is the worst of all empirics; he offers to prescribe for a malady, and knows not whether the medicine he uses be a remedy or a poison. The injury which he inflicts is not on an in-

dividual, but on an entire community. There is probably no method in which mischief is done so recklessly and on so large a scale, as by ignorant and thoughtless and wicked legislation. Were these plain considerations duly weighed there would be somewhat fewer candidates for legislative office and a somewhat greater deliberation on the part of the people in selecting them.

3. Having made himself acquainted with his powers and his obligations, he is bound to exert his power precisely within the limits by which it is restricted and for the purposes for which it was conferred, to the best of his knowledge and ability and for the best good of the whole society. He is bound impartially to carry into effect the principles of the general and the particular compact just *in those respects* in which the carrying them into effect is *committed to him*. For the action of others he is not responsible, unless he has been made so responsible. He is not the organ of a *section* or of a *district,* much less of a *party,* but of the *society at large.* And he who uses his power for the benefit of a section or of a party is false to his duty, to his country, and to his God. He is engraving his name on the adamantine pillar of his country's history to be gazed upon forever as an object of universal detestation.

4. It is his duty to leave everything else undone. From no plea of present necessity or of peculiar circumstances may he overstep the limits of his constitutional power, either in the *act itself,* or the *purpose* for which the act is done. The moment he does this, he is a tyrant. Precisely the power *committed to him* exists, and *no other.* If he may exercise one power not delegated, he may exercise another, and he may exercise all; thus, on principle, he assumes himself to be the fountain of power; restraint upon encroachment ceases and all liberty is henceforth at an end. If the powers of a legislator are insufficient to accomplish the purposes of society, inconveniences will arise. It is better that these should be endured until the necessity of some modification be made apparent, than to remedy them on principles which destroy all liberty and thus remove one inconvenience by taking away the possibility of ever removing another.[32]

[32] See Appendix (o) for paragraph added in the 1865 edition.

II *Of judicial officers.*

1. The judicial officer forms an independent branch of the government, or a separate and distinct agent, for executing a particular part of the contract which society has made with the individual. As I have said before, it matters not how he is appointed: as soon as he is appointed he is the agent of society and of society alone.

The judge, precisely in the same manner as the legislator, is bound by the principles of the social contract; and by those of the particular civil compact of the society in whose behalf he acts. This is the limit of his authority; and it is on his own responsibility if he transcend it.

2. The provisions of this compact, as they are embodied in laws, he is bound to enforce.

And hence we see the relation in which the judge stands to the legislator. Both are equally limited by the principles of the original compact. The acts of both are valid insofar as they are authorized by that compact. Hence if the legislator violate his trust and enact laws at variance with the constitution, the judge is bound not to enforce them. The fact that the one has violated the constitution imposes upon the other no obligation to do the same. Thus the judge, inasmuch as he is obliged to decide upon the constitutionality of a law before he enforces it, becomes accidentally, but in fact, a co-ordinate power without whose concurrence the law cannot go into effect.

Hence we see that the duty of a judge is to understand,

1. The principles of that contract from which he derives his power;

2. The laws of the community whose agent he is;

3. To explain these laws without fear, favor, or affection; and to show their bearing upon each individual case without bias either toward the individual or toward society; and,

4. To pronounce the decision of the law according to its true intent.

5. As the jury are a part of the judicial agents of the government, they are bound in the same manner to decide upon the facts according to their best knowledge and ability with scrupulous and impartial integrity.

III. *Of executive officers.*

The executive office is either *simple* or *complex.*

1. *Simple;* as where his only duty is to perform what either the legislative or judicial branches of the government have ordered to be done.

Such is the case with sheriffs, military officers, &c.

Here the officer has no right to question the *goodness* or *wisdom* of the law; since for these he is not responsible. His only duty is to execute it so long as he retains his office. If he believe the action required of him to be morally wrong or at variance with the constitution, he should resign. He has no right to hold the office and refuse to perform the duties which others have been empowered to require of him.

2. *Complex;* where legislative and executive duties are imposed upon the same person; as where the chief magistrate is allowed a vote on all acts of the other branches of the legislature.

As far as his duties are legislative he is bound by the same principles as any other legislator.

Sometimes his power is limited to a vote on mere constitutional questions; and at others it extends to all questions whatsoever. Some times his assent is absolutely necessary to the passage of all bills; at others it is only conditionally necessary, that is, the other branches may, under certain circumstances, enact laws without it.

When this legislative power of the executive has been exerted within its constitutional limits, he becomes merely an executive officer. He has no other deliberative power than that conferred upon him by the constitution. He is under the same obligations as any other executive officer to execute the law, unless it seem to him a violation of moral or constitutional obligation. In that case it is his duty to resign. He has no more right than any other man to hold the office while he is, from any reason whatever, unable to discharge the duties which the office imposes upon him. That executive officer is guilty of gross perversion of official and moral obligation who, after the decision of the legislative or judicial branch of a government has been obtained, suffers his own personal views to influence him in the discharge of his duty. The exhibition of such a disposition is a manifest indication of an entire disqualification for office. It shows that a man is either destitute of the ability to comprehend the nature of his station or fatally wanting in that self-government so indispensably necessary to him who is called to preside over important business.

And not only is an executive officer bound to exert no other power than that committed to him; he is also bound to exert that power for no other purposes than those for which it was committed. A power may be conferred for the public good; but this by no means authorizes a man to use it for the gratification of individual love or hatred; much less for the sake of building up one political party or of crushing another. Political corruption is in no respect the less wicked because it is so common. Dishonesty is no better policy in the affairs of state than in any other affairs; though men may persuade themselves and others to the contrary.

FROM what has already been stated, it will be seen that the duties of a citizen are of two kinds: first, as an individual; and, second, as a member of society. A few remarks on each of these will close this part of the subject.

FIRST. *As an individual.*

Every citizen,[33] *as an individual, is bound to observe in good faith the contract which he has made with society.* This obliges him—

1. To observe the law of reciprocity in all his intercourse with others.

The nature of this law has been already explained. It is only necessary to remark that society furnishes an additional reason for observing it—a reason founded both in voluntary compact and also in the necessity of obedience to our own happiness. It may also be added that the nature of the law of reciprocity binds us not merely to avoid those acts which are destructive to *the existence* of society, but also those which would *interfere with its happiness.* The principle is in all cases the same. If we assume the right to interfere with the smallest means of happiness possessed by our neighbor, the admission of that assumption would excuse every form of interference.

2. To surrender the right of redressing his wrongs wholly to society. This has been considered already in treating of the social compact. Aggression and injury in no case justify retaliation. If a man's house be attacked he may, so far as society is concerned, repel the robber, because here society is unable, at the instant, to assist him; but he is at liberty to put forth no other effort than that necessary to protect himself or to secure the aggressor for the purpose of delivering him over to the judgment of society. If after having secured him we put him to death, this is murder.

3. To obey all laws made in accordance with the constituted powers of society. Hence we are in no manner released from this obligation by the conviction that the law is unwise or inexpedient. We have

---

[33] See Appendix (P) for sentence as it appears in 1865 edition, and for following two sentences as replaced in the 1865 edition.

confided the decision of this question to society and we must abide by that decision. To do otherwise would be to constitute every man the judge in his own case; that is, to allow every man to obey or disobey as he pleased while he expected from *every other man* implicit obedience. Thus though a man were convinced that laws regulating the rate of interest were inexpedient, this would give him no right to violate these laws. He must obey them until he be able to persuade society to think as he does.

SECONDLY. *The citizen is under obligations as a constituent member of society.* By these obligations, on the other hand, he is bound to fulfill the contract which he has made with every individual.

Hence he is bound—

1. To use all the necessary exertion to secure to every individual, from the highest and most powerful to the lowest and most defenseless, the full benefit of perfect protection in the enjoyment of his rights.

2. To use all the necessary exertion to procure for every individual just and adequate redress for wrong.

3. To use all the necessary exertion to carry into effect the laws of civil society and to detect and punish crime, whether committed against the individual or against society. Wherever he knows these laws to be violated he is bound to take all proper steps to bring the offenders to justice.

And here it is to be remarked that he is to consider not merely his property, but his personal service, pledged to the fulfillment of this obligation. He who stands by and sees a mob tear down a house is a partaker in the guilt. And if society knowingly neglect to protect the individual in the enjoyment of his rights, every member of that society is in equity bound, in his proportion, to make good that loss, how great soever it may be.

4. It is the duty of the citizen to bear, cheerfully, his proportionate burden of the public expense. As society cannot be carried on without expense, he, by entering into society, obliges himself to bear his proportion of it. And besides this, there are but few modes in which we receive back so much for what we expend as when we pay money for the support of civil government. The gospel, I think, teaches us

to go farther and be ready to do more than we are compelled to do by law. The precept, "If a man compel thee to go a mile, go with him twain," refers to labor in the public service and exhorts us to do *more* than can be in equity demanded of us.

5. Besides this, I think a citizen is under moral obligation to contribute his proportion to every effort which affords a reasonable prospect of rendering his fellow citizens wiser and better. From every such successful effort he receives material benefit both in his person and estate. He ought to be willing to assist others in doing that from which he himself derives important advantage.

6. Inasmuch as society enters into a moral obligation to fulfill certain duties, which duties are performed by agents whom the society appoints; for their faithful discharge of those duties society is morally responsible. As this is the case, it is manifestly the duty of every member of society to choose such agents as in his opinion will truly and faithfully discharge those duties to which they are appointed. He who, for the sake of party prejudice or personal feelings, acts otherwise and selects individuals for office without regard to these solemn obligations, is using his full amount of influence to sap the very foundations of society and to perpetrate the most revolting injustice.

Thus far we have gone upon the supposition that society has exerted its power *within its constituted* limits. This, however, unfortunately, is not always the case. The question then arises, What is the duty of an individual when such a contingency shall arise?

Now there are but three courses of conduct in such a case, for the individual to pursue: passive obedience, resistance, and suffering in the cause of right:

1. *Passive obedience* in many cases would be manifestly wrong. We have no right to obey an unrighteous law, since we must obey God at all hazards. And aside from this, the yielding to injustice forms a precedent for wrong, which may work the most extensive mischief to those who shall come after us. It is manifest, therefore, that passive obedience cannot be the rule of civil conduct.

2. *Resistance by force.*

Resistance to civil authority by a single individual would be absurd. It can succeed only by the combination of all the aggrieved against the aggressors, terminating in an appeal to physical force; that is, by civil war.

The objections to this course are the following:

1. It is at best uncertain. It depends mainly on the question, which party is, under the present circumstances, the stronger? Now the oppressor is as likely to be the stronger as the oppressed, as the history of the world has abundantly shown.

2. It dissolves the social fabric and thus destroys whatever has thus far been gained in the way of social organization. But it should be remembered that few forms of society have existed for any considerable period in which there does not exist much that is worthy of preservation.

3. The cause of all oppression is the wickedness of man. But civil war is in its very nature a most demoralizing process. It never fails to render men more wicked. Can it then be hoped that a form of government can be created, by men already worse than before, better than that which their previous but less intense wickedness rendered intolerable?

4. Civil war is of all evils which men inflict upon themselves the most horrible. It dissolves not only social but domestic ties, overturns all the security of property, throws back, for ages, all social improvement, and accustoms men to view without disgust and even with pleasure all that is atrocious and revolting. Napoleon, accustomed as he was to bloodshed, turned away with horror from the contemplation of civil war. This, then, cannot be considered the way designed by our Creator for rectifying social abuses.

3. The third course is that of *suffering in the cause of right*. Here we act as we believe to be right, in defiance of oppression, and bear patiently whatever an oppressor may inflict upon us.

The advantages of this course are—

1. It preserves entire whatever exists that is valuable in the present organization.

2. It presents the best prospect of ultimate correction of abuse by appealing to the reason and the conscience of men. This is surely a more fit tribunal to which to refer a moral question than the tribunal of physical force.

3. It causes no more suffering than is actually necessary to accom-

plish its object; for whenever men are convinced of the *wickedness* of oppression, the suffering, of itself, ceases.

4. Suffering in the cause of right has a manifest *tendency* to induce the injurious to review their conduct under all the most favorable circumstances for conviction. It disarms pride and malevolence and enlists sympathy in favor of the sufferer. Hence its tendency is to make men better.

5. And experience has shown that the cause of civil liberty has always gained more by martyrdom than by war; it has rarely happened that during civil war the spirit of true liberty has not declined. Such was the case in the time of Charles I in England. How far the love of liberty had declined in consequence of civil war is evident from the fact that Cromwell succeeded immediately to unlimited power and Charles II returned with acclamation, to inflict upon the nation the most odious and heartless tyranny by which it was ever disgraced. During *the suffering for conscience* under his reign the spirit of liberty revived, hurled his brother from the throne, and established British freedom upon a firm and, we trust, an immovable foundation.

6. Everyone must be convinced, upon reflection, that this is really the course indicated by the highest moral excellence. Passive obedience may arise from servile fear; resistance, from vainglory, ambition, or desire of revolution. Suffering for the sake of right can arise only from a love of justice and a hatred of oppression. The real spirit of liberty can never exist, in any remarkable degree, in any nation where there is not this willingness to suffer in the cause of justice and liberty. Ever so little of the spirit of martyrdom is always a more favorable indication for civilization than ever so much dexterity of party management or ever so turbulent protestation of immaculate patriotism.

CHAPTER FIRST

GENERAL OBLIGATION AND DIVISION OF THE SUBJECT

WE have thus far considered merely the law of reciprocity; that is, the law which prevents our interference with those means of happiness which belong to our neighbor from the fact that they are the gift of God to him. But it is manifest that this is not the only law of our present constitution. Besides being obliged to abstain from doing wrong to our neighbor, we are also obliged to do him good; and a large part of our moral probation actually comes under this law.

The law of benevolence, or the law which places us under obligation to be the instruments of happiness to those who have no claim upon us on the ground of reciprocity, is manifestly indicated by the circumstances of our constitution.

1. We are created under a constitution in which we are of necessity dependent upon the benevolence of others. Thus we are all exposed to sickness, in which case we become perfectly helpless, and when, were it not for the kindness of others, we must perish. We grow old and by age lose the power of supporting ourselves. Were benevolence to be withdrawn, many of the old would die of want. The various injuries arising from accident as well as from disease teach us the same lesson. And besides, a world in which every individual is subject to death must abound with widows and orphans, who, deprived by the hand of God of their only means of support, must frequently either look for sustenance and protection to those on whom they have no claim by the law of reciprocity, or they must die. Now as we live under a constitution in which these things are of daily occurrence, and many of them by necessity belonging to it, and as we are all equally liable to be in need of assistance, it must be the design of our Creator that we should, under such circumstances, help each other.

2. Nor do these remarks apply merely to the necessity of physical

support. Much of the happiness of man depends upon intellectual and moral cultivation. But it is generally the fact that those who are deprived of these means of happiness are ignorant of their value; and would, therefore, remain forever deprived of them were they not awakened to a conviction of their true interests by those who have been more fortunate. Now as we ourselves owe our intellectual happiness to the benevolence, either near or more remote, of others, it would seem that an obligation was imposed upon us to manifest our gratitude by extending the blessings which we enjoy to those who are destitute of them. We frequently cannot requite our actual benefactors, but we always may benefit others less happy than ourselves; and thus, in a more valuable manner, promote the welfare of the whole race to which we belong.

3. This being manifestly an obligation imposed upon us by God, it cannot be affected by any of the actions of men; that is, we are bound by the law of benevolence, irrespective of the character of the recipient. It matters not though he be ungrateful or wicked or injurious; this does not affect the obligation under which we are placed by God to treat our neighbor according to the law of benevolence. Hence in all cases we are bound to govern ourselves, not by the treatment which we have received at his hands, but according to the law by which God has directed our intercourse with him to be governed.

And yet more. It is evident that many of the virtues most appropriate to human nature are called into exercise only by the miseries or the vices of others. How could there be sympathy and mercy, were there no suffering? How could there be patience, meekness, and forgiveness, were there no injury? Thus we see that a constitution which involves, by necessity, suffering, and the obligation to relieve it, is that which alone is adapted to the perfection of our moral character in our present state.

This law of our moral constitution is abundantly set forth in the Holy Scriptures.

It is needless here to speak of the various passages in the Old Testament which enforce the necessity of mercy and charity. A single text from our Saviour's Sermon on the Mount will be sufficient for my purpose. It is found *Luke* vi, 32–36, and *Matthew* v, 43–48. I quote the passage from Luke:

"If ye love them that love you, what thank have ye? for sinners also love those that love them. And if ye do good to those that do good to you, what thank have ye? for sinners also do even the same. And if you lend to them of whom ye hope to receive, what thank have ye? for sinners also lend to sinners, to receive as much again. But love ye your enemies, and do good, and lend, hoping for nothing again; and your reward shall be great, and ye shall be the children of the Highest, for he is kind unto the unthankful and to the evil. Be ye, therefore, merciful, as your Father in heaven is merciful." In Matthew it is said, "Love your enemies, bless them that curse you, do good to them that hate you, and pray for them that despitefully use you and persecute you; that ye may be the children of (that is, that ye may imitate) your Father which is in heaven, for he maketh his sun to rise upon the evil and upon the good, and sendeth rain upon the just and upon the unjust."

The meaning of this precept is obvious from the context. To be merciful is to promote the happiness of those who have no claim upon us by the law of reciprocity, and from whom we can hope for nothing by way of remuneration. We are to be merciful *as our Father* who is in heaven *is merciful*.

1. God is the independent source of happiness to everything that exists. None can possibly repay him and yet his bounty is unceasing. All his perfections are continually employed in promoting the happiness of his creation. Now we are commanded to be imitators of him; that is, to employ all our powers, not for our own gratification, but for the happiness of others. We are to consider this not as an onerous duty but as a privilege; as an opportunity conferred upon us of attaining to some resemblance to the Fountain and Author of all excellence.

2. This precept teaches us that our obligation is *not altered by the character of the recipient*. God sends rain on the just and on the unjust and causeth his sun to shine on the evil and on the good. "God commandeth his love to us, in that, while we were yet sinners, Christ died for us." In imitation of this example, we are com-

manded to do good to, and promote the happiness of, the evil and the wicked. We are to comfort them when they are afflicted; to relieve them when they are sick; and specially, by all the means in our power, to strive to reclaim them to virtue. We are not, however, to give a man the means of breaking the laws of God; as to furnish a drunkard with the means of intemperance: this would be to render ourselves partakers of his sin. What is here commanded is merely the relieving his misery as a *suffering human creature*.

3. Nor is our obligation altered by the *relation in which the recipient may stand to us*. His being our enemy in no manner releases us from obligation. Every wicked man is the enemy of God; yet God bestows even upon such the most abundant favors.

"God so loveth the world, that he sent his only begotten Son, that whosoever believeth on him should not perish, but have everlasting life." Jesus Christ spent his life in acts of mercy to his bitterest enemies. He died praying for his murderers. So we are commanded to love our enemies, to overcome evil with good, and to follow the example of St. Paul, who declares to the Corinthians, "I desire to spend and be spent for you; though the more abundantly I love you, the less I be loved."

In a word, God teaches us in the Holy Scriptures that all our fellow men are his creatures as well as ourselves; and hence that we are not only under obligation under all circumstances to act just as he shall command us, but that we are specially under obligation to act thus to our fellow men, who are not only our brethren, but who are also under his special protection. He declares that they are all his children; that by showing mercy to them we manifest our love to him; and that this manifestation is the most valuable when it is the most evident that we are influenced by no other motive than love to him.

Shakespeare has treated this subject very beautifully in the following passages:

> 'Tis mightiest in the mightiest; it becomes
> The throned monarch better than his crown.
> His *sceptre* shows the force of *temporal power,*
> The attribute to awe and majesty,
> Wherein doth sit the *dread and fear of kings:*

But *mercy* is *above* the *sceptred sway*.
It is enthroned in the *heart* of kings.
It is an attribute of God himself;
And earthly power doth then show likest God's
When mercy seasons justice.

Mer. of Venice, Act 4, *Scene* 1.

Alas! alas!
Why all the souls that are, were forfeit once;
And He that might the advantage best have took,
Found out the remedy. *How would you be,*
If He, who is the top of judgment, should
But judge you as you are?

Measure for Measure, Act 2, *Scene* 2.

The Scriptures enforce this duty upon us for several reasons:

1. From the example of God. He manifests himself to us as bound-less in benevolence. He has placed us under a constitution in which we may, at humble distance, imitate him. This has to us all the force of law, for we are surely under obligation to be as good as we have the knowledge and the ability to be. And as the goodness of God is specially seen in mercy to the wicked and the injurious, by the same principles we are bound to follow the same example.

2. We live, essentially and absolutely, by the bounty and forbear-ance of God. It is meet that we should show the same bounty and forbearance to our fellow men.

3. Our only hope of salvation is in the forgiveness of God—of that God whom we have offended more than we can adequately conceive. How suitable is it, then, that we forgive the little offenses of our fellow men against us! Our Saviour illustrates this most beautifully in his parable of the two servants, *Matthew* xviii, 23–35.

4. By the example of Christ, God has shown us what is that type of virtue which in human beings is most acceptable in his sight. This was an example of perfect forbearance, meekness, benevolence, and forgiveness. Thus we are not only furnished with the rule but also with the exemplification of the manner in which the rule is to be kept.

5. These very virtues which are called forth by suffering from the wickedness and injury of our fellow men are those which God specially approves, and which he declares essential to that character

which shall fit us for heaven. Blessed are the *merciful*, for they shall obtain mercy. Blessed are the *meek*, blessed are the *peacemakers*, &c. A thousand such passages might easily be quoted.

6. God has declared that our forgiveness with him depends upon our forgiveness of others. "If ye forgive not men their trespasses, neither will your Father, who is in heaven, forgive you your trespasses." "He shall have judgment without mercy, that showeth no mercy; but mercy rejoiceth against judgment;" that is, a merciful man rejoices, or is confident, in the view of the judgment day.

If it be asked, What is the Christian limit to benevolence, I answer that no definite rule is laid down in the Scriptures, but that merely the principle is inculcated. All that we possess is God's, and we are under obligation to use it all as He wills. His will is that we consider every talent as a trust and that we seek our happiness from the use of it, not in self-gratification, but in ministering to the happiness of others. Our doing thus he considers as the evidence of our love to him; and therefore he fixes no definite amount which shall be abstracted from our own immediate sources of happiness for this purpose, but allows us to show our consecration of all to him just as fully as we please. If this be a privilege, and one of the greatest privileges, of our present state, it would seem that a truly grateful heart would not ask *how little* but rather *how much* may I do to testify my love for the God who preserves me and the Saviour who has redeemed me.

And inasmuch as our love to God is more evidently displayed in kindness and mercy to the wicked and the injurious than to any others, it is manifest that we are bound, by this additional consideration, to practice these virtues toward *them* in preference to any others.

And hence we see that benevolence is a *religious* act in just so far as it is done from love to God. It is lovely and respectable and virtuous when done from sympathy and natural goodness of disposition. It is *pious* only when done from love to God.

CHAPTER SECOND

OF BENEVOLENCE TO THE UNHAPPY

A MAN may be simply unhappy from either his *physical* or his *intellectual* condition. We shall consider these separately.

Section I · Unhappiness from Physical Condition

The occasions of unhappiness from this cause are simple poverty, or the mere want of the necessities and conveniences of life; and sickness and decrepitude, either alone, or when combined with poverty.

1. *Of poverty.* Simple poverty, or want, so long as a human being has the opportunity of labor sufficiently productive to maintain him, does not render him an object of charity. "If a man will not work, neither shall he eat," is the language no less of reason than of revelation. If a man be indolent the best discipline to which he can be subjected is to suffer the evils of penury. Hence all that we are required to do in such a case is to provide such a person with labor and to pay him accordingly. This is the greatest kindness both to him and to society.

2. Sometimes, however, from the dispensations of Providence, a human being is left so destitute that his labor is insufficient to maintain him. Such is frequently the case with widows and orphans. This forms a manifest occasion for charity. The individuals have become, by the dispensation of God, unable to help themselves, and it is both our duty and our privilege to help them.

3. *Sickness.* Here the ability to provide for ourselves is taken away and the necessity of additional provision is created. In such cases, the rich stand frequently in need of our aid, our sympathy, and our services. If this be the case with them, how much more must it be with the poor, from whom the affliction which produces suffering takes away the power of providing the means necessary for alleviating it! It is here that the benevolence of the gospel is peculiarly displayed. Our Saviour declares, "inasmuch as ye have done it unto one of the least of these, ye have done it unto me." Bishop Wilson, on this

passage, has the following beautiful remark: " '*Inasmuch*' (*as often*); who, then, would miss any *occasion?* '*The least;*' who, then, would despise *any object?* '*To me;*' so that, in serving the *poor,* we serve *Jesus Christ.*"

4. *Age* also frequently brings with it *decrepitude* of body, if not imbecility of mind. This state calls for our sympathy and assistance and all that care and attention which the aged so much need, and which it is so suitable for the young and vigorous to bestow.

The above are, I believe, the principal occasions for the exercise of benevolence towards man's *physical* sufferings. We proceed to consider the principles by which our benevolence should be regulated. These have respect both to the recipient and to the benefactor.

I. Principles which relate to the *recipient.*

It is a law of our constitution that every benefit which God confers upon us is the result of labor, and generally of labor in advance; that is, a man pays for what he receives, not *after* he has received it, but *before.* This rule is universal and applies to physical, intellectual, and moral benefits, as will be easily seen upon reflection.

Now so universal a rule could not have been established without both a good and a universal reason; and hence we find, by experience, that labor, even physical labor, is necessary to the healthful condition of man as a physical, an intellectual, and a moral being. And hence it is evident that the rule is just as applicable to the poor as to the rich. Or to state the subject in another form: Labor is either a benefit or a curse. If it be a curse, there can be no reason why every class of men should not bear that portion of the infliction which God assigns to it. If it be a benefit, there can be no reason why every man should not enjoy his portion of the blessing.

And hence it will follow that our benevolence should co-operate with this general law of our constitution.

1. Those who are poor but yet able to support themselves should be enabled to do so by means of labor, and on no other condition. If they are too indolent to do this, they should suffer the consequences.

2. Those who are unable to support themselves *wholly* should be assisted *only insofar as* they are thus unable. Because a man cannot

do *enough* to support himself, there is no reason why he should do *nothing*.

3. Those who are unable to do anything should have everything done for them which their condition requires. Such are infants, the sick, the disabled, and the aged.

Benevolence is intended to have a moral effect upon the recipient by cultivating kindness, gratitude, and universal benevolence among all the different classes of men. That mode of charity is therefore most beneficial to its object which tends in the highest degree to cultivate the kinder and better feelings of his nature. Hence it is far better for the needy for us to administer alms ourselves, than to employ others to do it for us. The gratitude of the recipient is but feebly exercised by the mere fact of the relief of his necessities unless he also have the opportunity of witnessing the temper and spirit from which the charity proceeds.

II. Principles which relate to the *benefactor*.

The Christian religion considers charity as a means of moral cultivation *specially* to the benefactor. It is always, in the New Testament, classed with prayer, and is governed essentially by the same rules. This may be seen from our Saviour's Sermon on the Mount.

Hence, 1. That method of charity is always the best which calls into most active exercise the virtues of self-denial and personal sacrifice as they naturally arise from kindness, sympathy and charity, or universal love to God and man. And, on the contrary, all those modes of benevolence must be essentially defective in which the distresses of others are relieved without the necessary exercise of these virtues.

2. As charity is a religious service and an important means of cultivating love to God, and as it does this in proportion as all external and inferior motives are withdrawn, it is desirable also that, insofar as possible, it be done secretly. The doing of it in this manner removes the motives derived from the love of applause and leaves us simply those motives which are derived from love to God. Those modes of benevolence which are, in their nature, the farthest removed from human observation are, *cæteris paribus,* the most favorable to the cultivation of virtue and are, therefore, always to be preferred.

Hence, in general, those modes of charity are to be preferred which most successfully teach the object to relieve himself, and which tend most directly to the moral benefit of both parties. And, on the contrary, those modes of charity are the worst which are the farthest removed from such tendencies.

These principles may easily be applied to some of the ordinary forms of benevolence.

I. *Public provision for the poor by poor laws* will be found defective in every respect.

1. It makes a provision for the poor because he is *poor*. This, as I have said, gives no claim upon charity.

2. It in no manner teaches the man to help himself; but, on the contrary, tends to take from him the natural stimulus for doing so.

3. Hence its tendency is to multiply paupers, vagrants, and idlers. Such have been its effects, to an appalling degree, in Great Britain; and such, from the nature of the case, must they be everywhere. It is taking from the industrious a portion of their earnings and conferring them, without equivalent, upon the idle.

4. It produces no feeling of gratitude toward the benefactor, but the contrary. In those countries where poor rates are the highest, the poor will be found the most discontented and lawless and the most inveterate against the rich.

5. It produces no moral intercourse between the parties concerned, but leaves the distribution of bounty to the hand of an official agent. Hence what is received is claimed *by the poor* as a matter of right; and the only feeling elicited is that of displeasure because it is so little.

6. It produces no feeling of sympathy or of compassion *in the rich;* but, being extorted by force of law, is viewed as a mere matter of compulsion.

Hence every principle would decide against poor laws as a means of *charity*. If, however, the society undertake to control the capital of the individual and manage it as they will, and by this management make paupers by thousands, I do think they are under *obligation* to support them. If, however, they insist upon pursuing this course, it would be better that every poorhouse should be a workhouse; and that the poor rates should always be given as the wages of some form of labor.

I would not, however, be understood to decide against all public provision for the necessitous. The aged and infirm, the sick, the disabled, and the orphan, in the failure of their relatives, should be relieved, and relieved cheerfully and bountifully, by the public. I only speak of provision for the *poor because they are poor,* and do not refer to provision made for *other reasons.* Where the circumstances of the recipient render him *an object of charity,* let him be relieved freely and tenderly. But if he be *not an object of charity,* to make public provision for him is injurious.

II. *Voluntary associations for purposes of charity.*

Some of the inconveniences arising from poor-laws are liable to ensue from the mode of conducting these institutions.

1. They do not make the *strongest* appeal to the moral feelings of the recipient. Gratitude is much diminished when we are benefited by a public charity instead of a private benefactor.

2. This is specially the case, when a charity is *funded* and the almoner is merely the official organ of a distribution in which he can have but a comparatively trifling personal interest.

3. The moral effect upon the giver is much less than it would be if he and the recipient were brought immediately into contact. Paying an annual subscription to a charity has a very different effect from visiting and relieving, with our own hands, the necessities and distresses of the sick and the afflicted.

I by no means, however, say that such associations are not exceedingly valuable. Many kinds of charity cannot well be carried on without them. The comparatively poor are thus enabled to unite in extensive and important works of benevolence. In many cases, the expenditure of capital necessary for conducting a benevolent enterprise requires a general effort. I however say that the rich, who are able to labor personally in the cause of charity, should never leave the most desirable part of the work to be done by others. They should be their own almoners. If they will not do this, why then let them furnish funds to be distributed by others; but let them remember that they are losing by far the most valuable, that is, they are losing the *moral* benefit which God intended them to enjoy. God meant every man to be charitable as much as to be prayerful; and he never intended that the one duty, any more than the other, should be done by a deputy. The same principles would lead us to conclude what, I believe, experience has always shown to be the fact, that a fund for the support of the poor of a town has always proved a nuisance instead of a benefit. And in general, as charity is intended to be the means of moral improvement to both parties, and specially to the benefactor, those modes of charity which do not have in view the cultivation of moral excellence are in this respect essentially defective.

Section II · Of Unhappiness from Intellectual Condition

To an intellectual being in a cultivated state of society, a certain amount of knowledge may be considered a necessary of life. If he do not possess it he is shut out from a vast source of enjoyment; is liable to become the dupe of the designing and to sink down into mere animal existence. By learning how to read, he is enabled to acquire the whole knowledge which is contained within a language. By writing, he can act where he cannot be personally present; and can also benefit others by the communication of his own thoughts. By a knowledge of accounts, he is enabled to be just in his dealings with others and to be assured that others are just in their dealings with him.

So much as this may be considered necessary; the rest is not so. The duty of thus educating a child belongs, in the first instance, to the parent. But since as so much knowledge as this is indispensable to the child's happiness, if the parent be unable to furnish it, the child becomes, insofar, *an object of charity*. And as it is for the benefit of the whole society that every individual should be thus far instructed, it is properly also a subject of social regulation. And hence provision should be made, at public expense, for the education of those who are unable to procure it.

Nevertheless, this education is a valuable consideration to the receiver; and hence our former principle ought not to be departed from. Although the provision for this degree of education be properly made a matter of public enactment, yet everyone should contribute to it *insofar as he is able*. Unless this be done he will cease to value it and it will be merely a premium on idleness. And hence I think it will be found that large permanent funds for the purpose of general education are commonly injurious to the cause of education itself. A small fund, annually appropriated, may be useful to stimulate an unlettered people to exertion, but it is probably useful for no other purpose. A better plan, perhaps, would be to oblige each district to support schools at its own expense. This would produce the greatest possible interest in the subject and the most thorough supervision of the schools. It is generally believed that the school funds of some of our older states have been injurious to the cause of common education.

Insofar, then, as education is necessary to enable us to accomplish the purposes of our existence and to perform our duties to society, the obligation to make a provision for the universal enjoyment of it comes within the law of benevolence. Beyond this it may very properly be left to the arrangements of Divine Providence; that is, everyone may be left to acquire as much more as his circumstances will allow. There is no more reason why all men should be educated alike than why they should all dress alike or live in equally expensive houses. As civilization advances and capital accumulates and labor becomes more productive, it will become possible for *every man* to acquire more and more intellectual cultivation. In this manner, the condition of all classes is to be improved; and not by the impracticable attempt to render the education of all classes at any one time alike.

While I say this, however, I by no means assert that it is not a laudable and excellent charity to assist, in the acquisition of knowledge, any person who gives promise of peculiar usefulness. Benevolence is frequently exerted under such circumstances with the greatest possible benefit and produces the most gratifying and the most abundant results. There can surely be no more delightful mode of charity than that which raises from the dust modest and despairing talent and enables it to bless and adorn society. Yet on such a subject as this it is manifest that *no general* rule can be given. The duty must be determined by the respective condition of the parties. It is, however, proper to add that aid of this kind should be given with discretion; and never in such a manner as to remove from genius the necessity of depending on itself. The early struggle for independence is a natural and a salutary discipline for talent. Genius was given, not for the benefit of its possessor, but for the benefit of others. And the sooner its possessor is taught the necessity of exerting it to practical purpose, the better is it for him and the better for society. The poets tell us much of the amount of genius which has been nipped in the bud by the frosts of adversity. This doubtless is true; but let it not be forgotten that, by the law of our nature, early promise is frequently delusive. The poets do not tell us how great an amount of genius is also withered by the sun of prosperity. It is probable that a greater proportion of talent is destroyed or rendered valueless by riches than by poverty; and the rapid mutations of society, I think, demonstrate this to be the fact.

The same principles will, in substance, apply to the case in which for a particular object, as for the promotion of religion, it is deemed expedient to increase the proportion of professionally educated men.

In this as in every other instance, if we would be truly useful, our charities must be governed by the principles which God has marked out in the constitution of man.

The general principle of God's government is that for all valuable possessions we must render a consideration, and experience has taught that it is impossible to vary from this rule without the liability of doing injury to the recipient. The reason is obvious; for we can scarcely, in any other manner, injure another so seriously, as by leading him to rely on anyone else than himself or to feel that the public are under obligations to take charge of him.

Hence charity of this sort should be governed by the following principles:

1. The recipient should receive no more than is necessary, with his own industrious exertions, to accomplish the object.

2. To loan money is better than to give it.

3. It should be distributed in such manner as most successfully to cultivate the good dispositions of both parties.

Hence private and personal assistance, when practicable, has some advantages over that derived from associations. And hence such supervision is always desirable as will restrict the charity to that class of persons for whom it was designed, and as will render it of such a nature that those of every other class would be under the least possible temptation to desire it.

And in arranging the plan of such an association, it should always be borne in mind that the sudden change in all the prospects of a young man's life which is made by setting before him the prospect of a professional education is one of the severest trials of human virtue.

Public provision for *scientific* education does not come under the head of *benevolence*. Inasmuch, however, as the cultivation of science is advantageous to all classes of a community, it is for the *interest of the whole* that it be cultivated. But the means of scientific education, as philosophical instruments, libraries, and buildings, could never be furnished by instructors without rendering this kind of education so expensive as to restrict it entirely to the rich. It is therefore wise for a community to make these provisions out of the common stock, so that a fair opportunity of improvement may be open to all. When, however, the public fails to discharge this duty it is frequently, with great patriotism and benevolence, assumed by individuals. I know of no more interesting instances of expansive benevolence that those in which wealth is appropriated to the noble purpose of diffusing over all coming time, "the light of science and the blessings of religion." Who can estimate the blessings which the founders of Oxford and Cambridge universities have conferred upon the human race!

CHAPTER THIRD

BENEVOLENCE TO THE WICKED

WE now come to treat of a form of benevolence in which other elements are combined. What is our duty to our fellow men who are *wicked?*

A wicked man is, from the nature of the case, unhappy. He is depriving himself of all the pleasures of virtue; he is giving strength to those passions which, by their ungovernable power, are already tormenting him with insatiable and ungratified desire; he is incurring the pains of a guilty conscience here, and he is, in the expressive language of the Scriptures, "treasuring up wrath, against the day of wrath and of righteous indignation." It is manifest, then, that no one has stronger claims upon our pity than such a fellow creature as this.

So far, then, as a wicked man is miserable or unhappy, he is entitled to our pity and, of course, to our love and benevolence. But this is not all. He is also wicked; and the proper feeling with which we should contemplate wickedness is that of disgust, or moral indignation. Hence a complex feeling in such a case naturally arises—that of benevolence, because he is unhappy; and that of moral indignation, because he is sinful. These two sentiments, however, in no manner conflict with, but on the contrary, if properly understood, strengthen each other.

The fact of a fellow creature's wickedness affects not our obligation to treat him with the same benevolence as would be demanded in any other case. If he is necessitous or sick or afflicted or ignorant, our duty to relieve and sympathize with and assist and teach him are the same as though he were virtuous. God sends his rain on the *evil* and on the *good*.

But especially, as the most alarming source of his misery is his moral character, the more we detest his wickedness, the more strongly would benevolence urge us to make every effort in our power to reclaim him. This surely is the highest exercise of charity; for virtue is the true solace against all the evils incident to the present life, and it is only by being virtuous that we can hope for eternal felicity.

We are bound, then, by the law of benevolence, to labor to reclaim the wicked—

1. By example, by personal kindness, by conversation, and by instructing them in the path of duty and persuading them to follow it.

2. As the most efficacious mode of promoting moral reformation yet discovered is found to be the inculcation of the truth of the Holy Scriptures; it is our imperative duty to bring these truths into contact with the consciences of men. This duty is, by our Saviour, imposed upon all his disciples: "Go ye into all the world, and preach *the gospel to every creature."*

3. As *all men* are our brethren, and as all men equally need moral light, and as experience has abundantly shown that all men will be both wicked and unhappy without it, this duty is binding upon every man towards the whole human race. The sentiments of Dr. Johnson on this subject in his letter on the translation of the Scriptures into the Gaelic language, are so apposite to my purpose that I beg leave to introduce them here, though they have been so frequently published. "If obedience to the will of God be necessary to happiness, and knowledge of his will necessary to obedience, I know not how he that withholds this knowledge, or delays it, can be said to love his neighbor as himself. He that voluntarily continues in ignorance is guilty of all the crimes which that ignorance produces; as, to him that should extinguish the tapers of a light-house, might be justly imputed the calamities of shipwrecks. Christianity is the highest perfection of humanity; and as no man is good but as he wishes the good of others, no man can be good in the highest degree who wishes not to others the largest measures of the greatest good."—*Life, Anno* 1766.

We see, then, that insofar as wicked men are by their wickedness miserable, benevolence renders it our duty to reclaim them. And to such benevolence the highest rewards are promised. "They that turn many to righteousness shall shine as the stars for ever and ever." But this is not all. If we love our Father in heaven it must pain us to see his children violating his just and holy laws, abusing his goodness, rendering not only themselves but also his other children miserable, and exposing themselves and others to his eternal displeasure. The love of God would prompt us to check these evils and to teach our brethren to serve and love and reverence our common Father, and to become his obedient children both now and forever.

Nor is either of these sentiments inconsistent with the greatest moral aversion to the crime. The more hateful to us is the conduct of those whom we love, the more zealous will be our endeavors to bring them back to virtue. And surely the more we are sensible of the evil of sin against God, the more desirous we must be to teach his creatures to love and obey him.

The perfect exemplification of both of these sentiments is found in the character of our Lord and Saviour Jesus Christ. While in all his conduct and teachings we observe the most intense abhorrence of every form of moral evil, yet we always find it combined with a love for the happiness, both temporal and spiritual, of man; which in all its bearings transcends the limits of finite comprehension. This is the example which God has held forth for our imitation. It would be easy to show that the improvement of the moral character of our fellow men is also the surest method of promoting their physical, intellectual, and social happiness.

CHAPTER FOURTH

BENEVOLENCE TOWARD THE INJURIOUS [34]

THE cases to be considered here are three:

I. Where injury is committed by an individual upon an individual.

II. Where injury is committed by an individual upon society.

III. Where injury is committed by a society upon a society.

I. Where an injury is committed by an individual upon an individual.

In this case the offender is guilty of wickedness and of violation of our personal rights.

1. Insofar as the action is *wicked*, it should excite our moral detestation, just as in the case in which wrong is done to anyone else.

2. Insofar as the wicked man is *unhappy*, he should excite our pity and our active effort to benefit him.

3. As the cause of this unhappiness is *moral* wrong, it is our duty to reclaim him.

4. Inasmuch as the injury is done *to us*, it is our duty *to forgive* him. On this condition alone can we hope to be forgiven.

5. Yet more; inasmuch as the injury is done *to us*, it gives us an opportunity of exercising special and peculiar virtue. It is therefore our special duty to overcome it *by good;* that is, the duty of reclaiming him from wrong rests specially *upon us;* and it is to be fulfilled by manifesting toward him particular kindness and the most cheerful willingness to serve him. "Be *not overcome* of evil, but *overcome evil* with *good.*" That is, it is *our* special duty, by an exhibition of peculiar benevolence, to reclaim the injurious person to virtue.

Such is plainly the teaching of the Holy Scriptures. It will require but a few words to show that this is the course of conduct indicated by the conditions of our being.

1. I think that everyone must acknowledge this to be the course pointed out by the *most exalted virtue*. Every man's conscience testifies that to reward evil with good is noble, while the opposite course is mean. There is nothing more strongly indicative of littleness of spirit than revenge.

[34] See Appendix (Q) for the 1865 edition revision of the portion of this chapter preceding the final section on brutes.

2. This mode of treating injuries has a manifest *tendency* to put an end to injury and every form of ill will:

For, 1. No man can long continue to injure him who requites injury with nothing but goodness.

2. It improves the heart of the offender and thus not only puts an end to the injury at that particular time, but also greatly diminishes the probability of its recurrence at any subsequent time. Were this course universally pursued there would be done on earth the least possible injury.

3. It improves, in the most signal manner, the offended person himself; and thus renders it less likely that he will ever commit an injury himself.

In a word, the *tendency* of this mode of treating an injurious person is to diminish indefinitely the liability to injury and to render all parties both happier and better.

On the contrary, the tendency of retaliation is exactly the reverse. We should consider,

1. That the offender is a creature of God and we are bound to treat him as God has commanded. Now no treatment which we have received from another gives us, by the law of God, any right to treat him in any other manner than with kindness. That he has violated his duty toward us and toward God affords no reason why we should be guilty of the same crimes.

2. The tendency of retaliation is to increase and foster and multiply wrongs, absolutely without end. Such, we see, is its effect among savage nations.

3. Retaliation renders neither party better, but always renders both parties worse. The offended party who retaliates does a mean action when he might have done a noble one.

Such, then, is the scriptural mode of adjusting *individual* differences.

II. When the *individual* has committed an injury against *society*.

Such is the case when an offender has violated a law of society and comes under its condemnation. In what way and on what principles is society bound to treat him?

1. The crime being one which, if permitted, would greatly injure

if not destroy society, it is necessary that it be prevented. Society has, therefore, a right to take such measures as will insure its prevention. This prevention may always be secured by solitary confinement.

But this being done, *society* is under the same obligations to the offender as the *several individuals* composing the society are under to him. Hence—

2. They are bound to seek his happiness by *reclaiming* him; that is, to direct all treatment of him, while under their care, with distinct reference to his moral improvement. This is the law of benevolence and it is obligatory no less on societies than on individuals. Everyone must see that the tendency of a system of prison discipline of this kind must be to diminish crime; while that of any other system must be, and always has been, to increase it.

Nor is this chimerical. The whole history of prisons has tended to establish precisely this result. Prisons which have been conducted on the principle of retaliation have everywhere multiplied felons; while those which have been conducted on the principle of rendering a prison a school of moral reformation have, thus far, succeeded beyond even the anticipations of their friends. Such a prison is also the greatest terror to a wicked man; and it ceases not to be so until he becomes at least comparatively virtuous. The whole experience of John Howard is summed up by himself in a single sentence: "It is in vain to punish the wicked, unless you seek to reclaim them."

By what I have said above I would not be understood to deny the right of society to punish *murder* by death. This right, I think, however, is to be established, not by the principles of natural law, but by the command of God to Noah. The precept in this case seems to me to have been given to the whole human race and to be still obligatory.

III. Where one *society* violates the rights of another *society*. The principles of the gospel, already explained, apply equally to this as to the preceding cases.

1. The *individual* has, by the law of God, no right to return evil for evil; but is bound to conduct towards every other *individual,* of what nation soever, upon the principle of charity.

2. The individual has no right to authorize society to do anything

contrary to the law of God; that is to say, men connected in societies are under the same moral law as individuals. What is forbidden to the one is forbidden also to the other.

3. Hence I think we must conclude that an injury is to be treated in the same manner; that is, that we are under obligation to forgive the offending party and to strive to render him both better and happier.

4. Hence it would seem that all wars are contrary to the revealed will of God and that the individual has no right to commit to society, nor society to commit to government, the power to declare war.

Such, I must confess, seems to me to be the will of our Creator; and hence that to all arguments brought in favor of war, it would be a sufficient answer that God has forbidden it and that no consequences can possibly be conceived to arise from keeping his law, so terrible as those which must arise from violating it. God commands us to love every man, alien or citizen, Samaritan or Jew, as ourselves; and the act neither of society nor of government can render it our duty to violate this command.

But let us look at the arguments offered in support of war.

The miseries of war are acknowledged. Its expense, at last, begins to be estimated. Its effects upon the physical, intellectual, and moral condition of a nation are deplored. It is granted to be a most calamitous remedy for evils and the most awful scourge that can be inflicted upon the human race. It will be granted, then, that the resort to it, if not necessary, must be intensely wicked; and that if it be not in the highest degree useful it ought to be universally abolished.

It is also granted that the universal abolition of war would be one of the greatest blessings that could be conferred upon the human race. As to the *general principle,* then, there is no dispute. The only question which arises is whether it be not necessary for one nation to act upon the principle of offense and defense so long as other nations continue to do the same?

I answer, *first.* It is granted that it would be better for man in general if wars were abolished and all means, both of offense and defense, abandoned. Now this seems to me to admit that this is the law under which God has created man. But this being admitted, the question seems to be at an end; for God never places men under circumstances in which it is either wise or necessary or innocent to violate his laws. Is it for the advantage of him who lives among a community of thieves to steal; or for one who lives among a community of liars to lie? On the contrary, do not honesty and veracity under these very circumstances give him additional and peculiar advantages over his companions?

Secondly. Let us suppose a nation to abandon all means, both of offense and of defense, to lay aside all power of inflicting injury and to rely for self-preservation solely upon the justice of its own conduct and the moral effect which such a course of conduct would produce upon the consciences of men. How would such a nation *procure redress of grievances?* and how would it *be protected from foreign aggression?*

I. *Of redress of grievances.* Under this head would be comprehended violation of treaties, spoliation of property, and ill treatment of its citizens.

I reply, 1. The very fact that a nation relied solely upon the justice of its measures and the benevolence of its conduct would do more than anything else *to prevent* the occurrence of injury. The moral sentiment of every community would rise in opposition to injury inflicted upon the just, the kind, and the merciful. Thus by this course the probabilities of aggression are rendered *as few* as the nature of man will permit.

2. But suppose injury to be done. I reply, the proper appeal for moral beings upon moral questions is not to physical force, but to the consciences of men. Let the wrong be set forth, but be set forth in the spirit of love; and in this manner, if in any, will the consciences of men be aroused to justice.

3. But suppose this method to fail. Why, then, let us suffer the injury. This is the preferable evil of the two. Because they have injured us a *little,* it does not follow that we should injure ourselves *much.* But it will be said, what is then to become of our national honor? I answer, first, if we have acted justly we surely are not dishonored. The dishonor rests upon those who have done wickedly. I answer again, national honor is displayed in forbearance, in for-

giveness, in requiting faithlessness with fidelity and grievances with kindness and good will. These virtues are surely as delightful and as honorable in nations as in individuals.

But it may be asked, what is to prevent repeated and continued aggression? I answer, first, not instruments of destruction, but the moral principle which God has placed in the bosom of every man. I think that obedience to the law of God on the part of the injured is the surest preventive against the repetition of injury. I answer, secondly, suppose that acting in obedience to the law of benevolence will not prevent the repetition of injury, will acting upon the principle of retaliation prevent it? This is really the true question. The evil tempers of the human heart are allowed to exist, and we are inquiring in what manner shall we suffer the least injury from them; whether by obeying the law of benevolence or that of retaliation? It is not necessary, therefore, to show that by adopting the law of benevolence we shall not *suffer at all;* but that by adopting it we shall suffer *less* than by the opposite course; and that a nation would actually thus suffer less upon the whole than by any other course cannot, I think, be doubted by anyone who will calmly reflect upon the subject.

II. How would such a nation be protected from external attack and entire subjugation? I answer, by adopting the law of benevolence a nation would render such an event in the highest degree improbable. The causes of national war are most commonly the love of plunder and the love of glory. The first of these is rarely, if ever, sufficient to stimulate men to the ferocity necessary to war, unless when assisted by the second. And by adopting as the rule of our conduct the law of benevolence, all motive arising from the second cause is taken away. There is not a nation in Europe that could be led on to war against a harmless, just, forgiving, and defenseless people.

But suppose such a case really should occur, what are we then to do? I answer, is it certain that we can do better than suffer injury with forgiveness and love, looking up to God, who, in his holy habitation, is the Judge of the whole earth? And if it be said, we shall then all be subjected and enslaved, I answer again, have wars prevented men from being subjected and enslaved? Is there a nation on the continent of Europe that has not been overrun by foreign troops several times, even within the present century? And still more, is it not most commonly the case that the very means by which we repel a despotism from abroad only establishes over us a military despotism at home? Since, then, the principle of retaliation will not with any certainty save a country from conquest, the real question, as before, is, by obedience to which law will a nation be most likely to escape it, by the law of retaliation, or that of benevolence? It seems to me that a man who will calmly reflect will see that the advantages of war, even in this respect, are much less than they have been generally estimated.

I however would by no means assert that forgiveness of injuries alone is a sufficient protection against wrong. I suppose the real protection to be active benevolence. The Scriptures teach us that God has created men, both as individuals and as societies, under the law of benevolence, and that he intends this law to be obeyed. Societies have never yet thought of obeying it in their dealings with each other; and men generally consider the allusion to it as puerile. But this alters not the law of God, nor the punishments which he inflicts upon nations for the violation of it. This punishment I suppose to be war. I believe aggression from a foreign nation to be the intimation from God that we are disobeying the law of benevolence, and that this is his mode of teaching nations their duty, in this respect, to each other. So that aggression seems to me in no manner to call for retaliation and injury, but rather to call for special kindness and good will. And still farther, the requiting evil with good tends just as strongly to the cessation of all injury in nations as in individuals. Let any man reflect upon the amount of pecuniary expenditure and the awful waste of human life which the wars of the last hundred years have occasioned, and then I will ask him whether it be not evident that the one hundredth part of this expense and suffering, if employed in the honest effort to render mankind wiser and better, would long before this time have banished wars from the earth and rendered the civilized world like the garden of Eden.

If this be true it will follow that the cultivation of a military spirit is injurious to a community, inasmuch as it aggravates the source of the evil, the corrupt passions of the human heart, by the very manner in which it attempts to correct the evil itself.

I am aware that all this may be *called* visionary, romantic, and chimerical. This, however, neither *makes* it so nor *shows* it to be so. The time *to apply* these epithets will be when the justness of their application has been proved.[35] And if it be said, these principles may all be very true, but you can never induce nations to act upon them; I answer, If they be true, then God requires us thus to act; and if this be the case, then that nation will be the happiest and the wisest which is the first to obey his commandments. And if it be said that though all this be so, yet such is the present state of man that until his social character be altered, the necessity of wars will exist; I answer; first, it is a solemn thing to meet the punishments which God inflicts for the transgression of his laws. And secondly, inasmuch as the reason for this necessity arises from the social wickedness of man, we are under imperative obligations to strive to render that wickedness less; and, by all the means in our power, to cultivate among nations a spirit of mutual kindness, forbearance, justice, and benevolence.

NOTE. I should be guilty of injustice to one class of my fellow creatures if I should close this treatise upon human duty without a single remark upon our obligations to *brutes*.

Brutes are sensitive beings, capable of, probably, as great degrees of physical pleasure and pain as ourselves. They are endowed with instinct which is probably a form of intellect inferior to our own, but which, being generically unlike to ours, we are unable to understand. They differ from us chiefly in being destitute of any moral faculty.

We do not stand to them in the relation of equality. "Our right is paramount, and must extinguish theirs." We have, therefore, a right to use them to promote our comfort, and may innocently take their life if our necessities demand it. This right over them is given to us by the revealed will of God. But inasmuch as they, like ourselves, are

---

[35] See Appendix (R) for remainder of paragraph as it appears in the 1835 edition.

the creatures of God, we have no right to use them in any other manner than that which God has permitted. They, as much as ourselves, are under his protection.

We may, therefore, use them, 1. For our necessities. We are designed to subsist upon animal food; and we may innocently slay them for this purpose.

2. We may use them for labor or for innocent physical recreation, as when we employ the horse for draught or for the saddle.

3. But while we so use them, we are bound to treat them kindly, to furnish them with sufficient food and with convenient shelter. He who cannot feed a brute well ought not to own one. And when we put them to death it should be with the least possible pain.

4. We are forbidden to treat them unkindly on any pretense, or for any reason. There can be no clearer indication of a degraded and ferocious temper than cruelty to animals. Hunting, in many cases, and horse racing seem to me liable to censure in this respect. Why should a man, for the sake of showing his skill as a marksman shoot down a poor animal which he does not need for food? Why should not the brute that is harming no living thing be permitted to enjoy the happiness of its physical nature unmolested? "There they are privileged; and he that hurts or harms them there is guilty of a wrong."

5. Hence all amusements which consist in inflicting pain upon animals, such as bullbaiting, cockfighting, &c., are purely wicked. God never gave us power over animals for such purposes. I can scarcely conceive of a more revolting exhibition of human nature than that which is seen when men assemble to witness the misery which brutes inflict upon each other. Surely nothing can tend more directly to harden men in worse than brutal ferocity.

APPENDIX

Whence Do We Derive Our Notion of the Moral Quality of Actions?

Before we attempt to answer this question, let us first inquire whether our notion of the moral quality of actions be original or derived.

By an *original* idea, I mean an idea which arises spontaneously in the human mind, by virtue of the constitution with which we were created, as soon as its appropriate object is presented. Thus the idea of color arises in us spontaneously as soon as a colored object is presented to our vision. No one can convey the idea of color to a blind man. Let him, however, be endowed with sight, and as soon as a colored object is presented to him the notion of color immediately arises. A *derived* idea, on the contrary, is the result of some preceding intellectual exercise. Thus the idea that the three angles of a triangle are equal to two right angles is a derived idea. Before I knew such to be the fact I had seen a hundred triangles, but this idea never arose in my mind. Afterwards, when I had studied Euclid's Elements, I passed through several mental acts which, together, resulted in the conviction that such a relation exists.

Now as all our ideas must be either original or derived, the question arises, To which of these classes does the moral idea—the idea of right and wrong—belong?

In attempting to answer this question, let us appeal in the first place to our own consciousness. We are all familiar with the ideas which we denominate right and wrong. In the first place, I think that these ideas are generally *distinct* from any others which we can contemplate. Compare them with the ideas of beauty and deformity, of utility and inutility, of joy and grief, of wisdom and folly, and the dissimilarity to which we refer must be at once obvious. The moral idea forms a class by itself entirely distinct from every other.

Secondly. The idea of right and wrong arises spontaneously whenever the appropriate objects are presented to us. Such objects are the actions of intelligent beings. A judge sentences to death a man whom he knows to be innocent; and as soon as we learn the facts, the idea of wrong arises unbidden within us. Another man employs his time and income in ministering to the perishing, whether his friends or enemies. As we contemplate such a life, there arises within us the notion of virtue, right, moral goodness. These ideas are not derived from reasoning. They are the necessary result of no previous mental state. There is nothing that intervenes between the cognition of the act and the spontaneous existence of the moral idea. The will cannot create it, nor can the will prevent its existence. If we are asked what is the cause of the rise of this idea under these circumstances, we can only answer we do not know; but such is the constitution by which we were endowed by our Creator.

We may also remark in passing that this idea arises only from the contemplation of the actions of intelligent beings. We never discover right or wrong, virtue or vice, in the actions of brutes. Nor is this idea occasioned by all the actions of men. For instance, a man in a shower shelters himself from rain by opening his umbrella. He uses the proper means for accomplishment of an end, and we say he acts *wisely*. We discover neither right nor wrong in the action. But if we see him steal an umbrella, there arises at once a different idea, the idea of wrong. Or, again, let him give up his umbrella to shelter a sick stranger from exposure, the idea of virtue, of right, arises at once—the opposite of that to which we last alluded.

Again. If it be said that the moral idea is derived, that is, that like the mathematical idea to which we have already referred, it is a necessary result from previous states of mind, the previous states of mind must be designated from which it emanates. I do not believe that this can be done. Indeed, if a man could not discover the quality of right and wrong in the actions of men, he could no more arrive at a knowledge of it by previous acts of mind than a blind man could attain the cognition of color by argument or illustration.

It seems, then, apparent that the idea of right and wrong, or the moral idea, arises spontaneously within us in virtue of the constitution with which we were endowed by our Creator, whenever its appropriate objects are present to our contemplation.

If this be so, it is plain that the moral idea is not derived from an exercise of the judgment, as some persons have supposed. Judgment can do no more than affirm a predicate of a subject, as that grass is green, or that an assertion is true. But the ideas of the predicate and subject must already have existed in the mind before a judgment could have been pronounced. Judgment could not account for the existence of an idea which must have been present to the mind before any act of judgment was possible. Nor, from a similar reason, can the idea of right and wrong be derived from association. Association can do no more than cause a desire or emotion or conception to be awakened by one object in preference to another. It can originate nothing, but can only act upon the ideas already present in the mind; and acts in different men in the most dissimilar manner, and differently, even in the same man, under dissimilar circumstances. There is nothing analogous to this in the rise of our ideas of right and wrong.

It has been said that an idea of right and wrong is derived from the idea of the greatest amount of happiness. Let us briefly consider this view of the subject.

First. When we appeal to our own consciousness, I think we must decide that the ideas are wholly dissimilar. They seem to me as different from each other as the ideas of form and color, of beauty and utility, or any other dissimilar ideas.

Secondly. If it be true that one gives origin to the other, then the idea of right and wrong can never exist unless it be preceded by the idea of the greatest amount of happiness. I appeal to the human consciousness and ask, Is this the fact? When the idea of wrong is called into existence by the commission of crime, or the returning evil for good, do we find that we previously determine that such an act would not be productive of the greatest amount of happiness? For myself, I must confess I can discover no such connections.

Thirdly. How can any finite being ever decide that any action will or will not produce the greatest amount of happiness? Of the future we are manifestly ignorant. Unless we know the consequences which would flow from two actions respectively throughout eternity, we could never determine which of the two would produce the greatest amount of happiness; that is, which was right and which was wrong.

Fourthly. Were we to determine the moral character of an action by the amount of happiness which it would produce, it would, I fear, tend to destroy all moral distinctions; for sometimes atrocious crimes have in the long run been the occasion of the happiest results. If an action is right because it produces the greatest amount of happiness, we must award to the treachery of Judas the praise of the greatest virtue.

The question then returns, Whence do we derive our idea of right and wrong, or our notion of the moral quality of actions? The view which we take of this subject is briefly as follows:

The moral idea, being original and simple, is incapable of definition. Like any other original idea, it arises by virtue of the constitution bestowed on us by the Creator, wherever its appropriate objects are presented to our contemplation. The question, then, to be answered is, What are the appropriate objects, on the contemplation of which the moral idea arises?

The answer which we venture to propose to this question is the following:

(B) *Book First, Chapter Second, Section II, 1865 edition:*

Of the States of Mind Which Immediately Emanate from the Idea of Right and Wrong

We have thus far considered that part of the action of conscience which discovers to us the quality of a human action as either right or wrong. We cannot, however, have failed to observe that as soon as this idea presents itself, other ideas accompany or follow it, without any will of our own, but purely in obedience to the laws of our moral constitution. To these let us attend.

1. In the first place, as soon as we perceive in an action a moral quality, there arises within us the feeling of *obligation*. If it be right, we feel an obligation to do it; if it be wrong, an obligation to refrain from doing it. This feeling of obligation we designate by the terms *ought* and *ought not*. We always consider the quality of the

action as the necessary cause of the obligation. Thus we say it is wrong to lie, therefore I *ought not* to lie; it is right to relieve the helpless, therefore I *ought* to do it. We see that *right* or *wrong* are qualities of the *action; ought* and *ought not* designate the mental state of the moral agent who takes cognizance of these qualities.

2. Intimately connected with this feeling of ought and ought not is the *impulse* to do or not to do the action in which we observe the moral quality. If the action is right, and we feel that we ought to do it, we are sensible of an impulse to do it. It is as though a voice within us was advising and sometimes even urging us to act; as if it said, Do it, do it: and if the action is wrong, and we feel that we ought not to do it, the voice within us is, Do it not, do it not. The action of conscience is in this respect analogous to that of passion. Thus when by a particular act we can gratify a passion, whether the act be right or wrong, passion urges us to do it. And thus it comes to pass that passion and conscience are frequently brought into direct collision. Conscience perceives in the act which passion urges us to do the element of wrong, and forbids us, saying, Do it not. The human being is thus placed between two impulses, free to determine to which he will yield, and it is upon this determination that his moral character depends.

3. This determination and its consequent action are attended by *results* either pleasant or painful. If we have successfully resisted the impulse of passion, and thus escaped temptation by obeying the impulse of conscience, this of itself is not only a source of pleasure, but pleasure of a peculiar kind. It is not like the pleasure derived from the sight of a beautiful object or from the successful pursuit of truth. It is the pleasure of innocence, of the consciousness of right, of victory over our inner propensities, and of just approbation and consciousness of good desert. If, on the contrary, we have obeyed the impulse of passion and disobeyed the impulse of conscience, the pain which we suffer is also distinct and peculiar. It is the pain of self-disapprobation, of shame, of consciousness of guilt, which we cannot wash away; of desert of punishment, which, much as we may desire it, we know not how to escape. Correspondent feelings are awakened by an act either of right or wrong, when done by another.

If he have done right, we feel for him a sentiment of respect and love, a desire to do him good, a hope and feeling that he will be somehow rewarded. If he have done wrong by obeying his passions instead of his conscience, we instinctively perceive that he has sunk by one step nearer to the level of brutes. We shrink from him with disrespect; we feel that he has deserved punishment; that he must yet meet it, and not unfrequently desire to punish him ourselves. And more than this: he who has done wrong feels that he deserves all this, and that if all the facts were known, all men would feel thus towards him.

4. Another state of mind which arises from the contemplation of the moral idea is *expectation*. We always expect some consequence to follow it. In this respect I think the moral idea differs from any other of which we are conscious. No other idea has respect to the future, or gives rise to any other distinct from itself. Thus we look upon a beautiful object; we are pleased: we afterwards, in an inferior degree, repeat the same pleasure by recollection. But here it ends. We look upon an ugly object; it displeases us; and the feeling of dislike may, as in the other case, be repeated by recollection: but it goes no farther. Another and different idea is not necessarily connected by our constitution with either.

5. This expectation, moreover, is of a *definite character*. I say definite; but by this I do not mean that we expect any particular event, but that events of a definite character will follow the doing of good, and that events of an opposite character will follow the doing of evil. We feel that such consequences are indissolubly linked to moral actions by a power which we can neither resist nor elude. We may strive to drown the memory of a crime, but we cannot forget it; and whenever it arises to our recollection, it is ever accompanied by the conviction that justice has a claim upon us, which somehow and somewhere must be satisfied.

6. This connection of the opposite results of dissimilar actions is *unchangeable*. We expect happiness as the reward of virtue, and misery as the wages of vice; and we cannot reverse them. To suppose an act of disinterested goodness to be punishable, and an act of deliberate wickedness to be deserving of reward, and that this

connection is a part of the constitution under which we are created, is unthinkable. A moral government established on such principles cannot be conceived. On the contrary, we are obliged to believe that happiness is unalterably connected with virtue, and misery as unalterably connected with vice.

7. I say we expect this with *certainty;* but this is not all. When I place water in the temperature of zero, I expect with *certainty* that it will freeze. When I plant seed in the ground, I expect with *certainty* that, under proper conditions, it will germinate. But in morals it is not merely *certainty*—it is *something more*. We feel not only that the appropriate consequent WILL, but that it MUST follow. Abolish this idea of the *necessary* connection between virtue and happiness, and wickedness and punishment, and all respect for the government of the universe would be prostrated.

The absolute certainty of the connection between virtue and vice, and their appropriate consequences, gives rise to one of the finest passages in the English language:

> Against the threats
> Of malice, or of sorcery, or the power
> Which erring men call chance, this I hold firm:
> Virtue may be assailed, but never hurt;
> Surprised by unjust force, but not enthralled;
> Yea, even that which mischief meant most harm,
> Shall in the happy trial prove most glory;
> But evil on itself shall back recoil,
> And mix no more with goodness; when, at last,
> Gathered like scum, and settled to itself,
> It shall be in eternal ceaseless change,
> Self-fed and self-consumed. If this fail,
> The pillared firmament is rottenness,
> And earth's base built on stubble.
>
> *Comus,* 585–598.

8. And it is worthy of remark that we derive a high degree of pleasure from the *contemplation of this connection*. We delight to see disinterested goodness rewarded, innocence protected, and wickedness overtaken by its appropriate punishment. When virtuous men under an arbitrary government have been exposed to the utmost peril, for no other cause than the pure love of liberty and

law, their deliverance is an occasion for national exultation. A case of this kind is related by Lord Macaulay, in his account of the trial of the nine Bishops, in the time of James II. During this memorable trial, the interest of the people was intense. When the jury appeared to render their verdict, the people of London were in breathless suspense. The verdict and the manner of its reception are thus described by the author in one of his most brilliant passages: "Sir Samuel Astry spoke: 'Do you find the defendants, or any of them, guilty of the misdemeanor whereof they are impeached, or not guilty?' Sir Roger Langley answered, 'Not guilty!' As the words passed his lips, Halifax sprang up and waved his hat. At that signal, benches and galleries raised a shout. In a moment, ten thousand persons who crowded the great hall replied with a still greater shout, which made the old oaken roof crack, and in another moment the innumerable throng without set up a third huzza, which was heard at Temple Bar. The boats which covered the Thames gave an answering cheer. A peal of gunpowder was heard on the water, and another and another, and so in a few moments the glad tidings went flying past the Savoy and the Friars to London Bridge and the forest of masts below. As the news spread, streets and squares, market-places and coffee-houses, broke forth into acclamations. Yet were the acclamations less strange than the weeping; for the feelings of men had been wound up to such a point, that at length the stern English nature, so little used to outward signs of emotions, gave way, and thousands sobbed aloud for very joy."—*History of England,* Vol. II., Chap. 8.

This expectation of certain results which must inevitably follow moral action, is frequently alluded to by the poets.

Thus Shakespeare puts into the mouth of Macbeth, when meditating the murder of Duncan, the following words:

> But in these cases,
> We still have judgment here; that we but teach
> Bloody instructions; which, being taught, return
> To plague the inventor. This even-handed justice
> Commends the ingredients of the poisoned chalice
> To our own lips.
>
> *Macbeth,* Act i., Scene 7.

9. The boldness of innocence and the timidity of guilt may both be traced to these facts in our moral constitution. The virtuous man is conscious of deserving from his fellow men nothing but reward. Whom, then, should he fear? The guilty man is conscious of desert of punishment, and is aware that as soon as his crime is known everyone will desire to punish him, and he is never sure but that everyone knows it. Whom, then, can he trust? And still more, this consciousness of desert of punishment is attended by a feeling of self-disapprobation and remorse, which depresses the spirit, and prostrates the courage of the offender, more than even the external circumstances by which he is surrounded. Thus, says Solomon, "The wicked flee when no man pursueth, but the righteous is bold as a lion."

> Thrice is he *armed* who hath his quarrel *just;*
> And he but *naked, though locked up in steel,*
> Whose conscience with injustice is corrupted.
> *Henry VI.,* Part 2, Act iii., Scene 2.

We learn, also, from the nature of our moral constitution, the reason why crime is with so great certainty detected.

A man, before the commission of a crime, can foresee no reason why he may not commit it without detection. He can perceive no reason why he should be suspected, and can imagine a thousand methods by which suspicion, if awakened, may be allayed. But he no sooner becomes guilty, than he finds his relations to his fellow men entirely reversed. He becomes suspicious of everyone, and sees every occurrence through a false medium. He cannot act like an innocent man. He either does too much or too little; and this difference in his conduct is frequently the means of his detection. When to this effect produced upon his own mind is added the fact, that every action must, by the condition of our being, be attended by antecedents and consequents wholly beyond our control, all of which lead directly to the discovery of the truth, it is not wonderful that the guilty so rarely escape. Hence it has grown into a proverb, "Murder will out;" and such do we generally find to be the fact.

The effect of guilt upon character has been frequently remarked. Thus Macbeth, after the murder of Duncan:

How is it with me when *every noise appalls me?*
Macbeth, Act ii., Scene 2.

Guiltiness will speak, though tongues were out of use.

Suspicion always haunts the guilty mind;
The thief doth fear each bush to be an officer.

The same fact is frequently referred to in the sacred Scriptures. The wicked is snared in the work of his own hands.

We hardly need remark that this expectation of consequences, necessarily connected with moral action, points us directly to a future life, and a day of certain retribution. We feel that goodness *must be* rewarded and wickedness punished, and that this retribution is inevitable. But this retribution takes place but imperfectly in the present world; there must, therefore, be another state of being, in which individuality shall be distinctly preserved, and an infallible tribunal, at which every action shall receive its due demerit at the hands of an omniscient and all-holy Judge. Thus saith the Scripture: "For we must all appear before the judgment-seat of Christ, that every one may receive the things done in his body according to that he hath done, whether it be good or bad" (2 *Cor.* v. 10.).

I close this section with the remarks of Mr. Webster in a trial for murder, as they powerfully enforce the view which we have taken on the subject.

"There is no evil that we cannot either face or fly from but the consciousness of duty disregarded. A sense of duty pursues us ever. It is omnipresent, like the Deity. If we take to ourselves the wings of the morning, and dwell in the uttermost parts of the sea, duty performed or duty violated is still with us for our happiness or our misery. If we say the darkness shall cover us, in the darkness as in the light our obligations are still with us. We cannot escape their power, nor fly from their presence. They are with us in this life, and they will be with us at its close; and in that scene of inconceivable solemnity, which lies yet further onward, we shall still find ourselves surrounded by the consciousness of duty, to pain us whenever it has been violated, and to console us so far as God may have given us grace to perform it." *

(c) *Book First, Chapter Fifth, 1865 edition. Quotation added:*

"Whatever," says Dr. Johnson, "withdraws us from the power of our senses; whatever makes the past, the distant, or the future predominate over the present, advances us in the dignity of thinking beings."—*Tour to the Hebrides, Iona.*

(D) *Book First, Chapter Seventh, Section I, 1865 edition. Text revised:*

To this it may be answered that this distinction, were it ever so true, does not invalidate the views which we have taken. It matters not whether the pains which we suffer from an action be monitory or prohibitory; either plainly indicates the will of the Creator, and this is all that he desires to make known to us. Having done this, he leaves us, as free and responsible agents, to take our own choice and act according to our own will. He makes known to us in this manner his will, but he does not prevent us from acting at variance with it if we so choose—being, however, always responsible to him for our actions.

(E) *Book First, Chapter Ninth, Section I, 1865 edition. Inserted paragraph:*

It is here worthy of special remark that the law of God was first made known to a rude and ignorant people. Its moral precepts were at first few and simple; and after these had become known, others were from time to time added, as the hearers were able to bear them. Thus in the beginning many practices were not forbidden which were afterwards disallowed. Various rites were at one time established which at a later time were annulled. Thus, by repeated

* Works, Vol. vi., p. 105. Boston: Little & Brown, 1857.

and increasing manifestations of moral truth, the nation was prepared for that fulness of time in which the whole will of God was
revealed, not only to the Hebrews, but to them, and through them,
to the whole human race. Thus "God who, at sundry times and in
divers manners, spake in times past to the fathers by the prophets,
hath in these last days spoken to us by his Son" from heaven. "And
the times of this ignorance God winked at, but *now* commandeth
all men everywhere to repent." Our Saviour particularly alludes to
the progressive development of the moral law, from the time in
which it was first made known by Moses. "Moses, for the hardness
of your hearts, suffered you to put away your wives, but from the
beginning it was not so. But *I* say unto you, whosoever shall put
away his wife, except it be for fornication, and marry another, committeth adultery. It hath been said by them of old time, Thou shalt
not forswear thyself, but shalt perform to the Lord thine oaths; but
I say to you, *swear not at all,"* etc.

(F) *Book First, Chapter Ninth, Section II, 1865 edition. Inserted
paragraph:*

And still more: in pity to our blindness and weakness, God has
invited us to ask him with childlike confidence for all the aid that
we need; and he has assured us that by his Spirit he will unfold to
us knowledge of our duty, and strengthen us to perform it. Thus,
weak, blind, and erring though we are, we may freely come to the
fountain of all wisdom and holiness, and derive all that will enable
us to serve him acceptably here and prepare us to dwell with him in
glory hereafter.

(G) *Book Second, Part Second, Class First, Chapter First, Section
I, 1865 edition. Inserted passage:*

And, moreover, the elements of a common education are necessary to everyone, and they must be acquired before the human being
arrives at manhood. If a parent is either unable or unwilling to
provide such instruction for his child, society may justly interpose,

and furnish for the child that education of which the selfishness of the parent would deprive it.

(H) *Book Second, Part Second, Class First, Chapter First, Section II, 1865 edition:*

Of the Violation of Personal Liberty by the Individual

The most common violation of personal liberty by the individual is that which exists in the case of domestic slavery.

Domestic slavery can only be justified upon one of the two following assumptions: either, 1st, that slavery is authorized by a general law under which human beings are constituted; or, 2d, that in some manner it has been signified to us by the Creator that one portion of the human race is made to be the slaves of the other portion.

Let us proceed and examine these assumptions in detail.

I. It is affirmed that one of the laws under which we have been created is that one human being has the right to reduce another human being to the condition called slavery. The person who is reduced from freedom to this condition has henceforth no right over either his body or mind. He can neither go nor stay where he chooses. He can neither labor nor rest for his own profit or pleasure, but must in both obey the will of another. He receives no wages, for he is disabled from holding any property. His oath can never be taken in evidence. He can form no contract. He cannot marry; and his only domestic relation is that of concubinage, subject to the will of another. He has no right over his own children; but they and their parents may at any moment be separated forever from each other at the will of him who has thus subjected them. The dominant party is at liberty to use the subjected party in such manner as may best gratify his own appetites and will. He may use the females as concubines; his children by them are his slaves and are, like their mother, chattels to be sold to the highest bidder. Resistance to such authority is punishable at the sole will of the owner, and, if he please, with instant death.

It may be supposed that a human being, reduced to this condition, if his mind were permitted by reading and reflection to estimate his condition, must be dissatisfied with it. Hence the power over the body once conceded gives to the dominant party the right over the mind of the other party. He may forbid the slave to learn to read or do anything whatever for his own improvement. He is best suited to his condition when he is merely a working animal; and anything which would render him less valuable in this respect may innocently be prohibited.

The knowledge of his relations to God and man as they are made known in the Scriptures would tend to the same result as intellectual cultivation. Nay, more; if there be a God, the authority of the dominant party cannot be absolute. He who has been enslaved would learn that he must obey *God* rather than *man;* and hence, in many cases, must refuse to obey the commands of him who is called his master. Hence the dominant party may forbid the other to attain to the knowledge of the Scriptures, or to receive religious instruction, only in such portions or in such manner as he may appoint; or, if he see fit, he may forbid it altogether. If, in obedience to what he considers to be the will of God, the subject party refuse to obey, he may be punished with stripes at the will of the other, or, it may be, with death. In a word, it has been decided by an eminent judge in the highest tribunal of a slaveholding state that a colored man possesses no right which a white man is under obligation to respect.

The manner in which the one party obtains this extraordinary power over the other party deserves to be remarked. Men go to Africa and excite wars between the native tribes. A village is sacked and burned. The aged and children, being useless, are slain. The able-bodied, both men and women, are seized, driven to the coast, and sold to the slave trader. They are then shipped, under circumstances of the most atrocious cruelty, and transported to a port in Christendom. As many as survive the horrors of the passage are sold by the slave dealer to the citizens of a Christian country, and all the right which he acquired over them by the burning of their village and murdering their dearest relatives is transferred to the purchaser. And this power is supposed to continue to the remotest generations. The offspring of a slave mother is in all respects a slave, though he or she be the child of a white man; nay, even of its master. And this continues indefinitely, even though, by licentiousness, it comes to pass that the slave is as white as his owner: and no matter how small a portion of Negro blood may be in his veins, he remains under the inexorable slave law. It is still a crime, punishable by the severest penalty, to teach him to read even the Word of God: he can own no property, earn for himself no wages, give no evidence, have no right in his own children, and is not and cannot be the husband of their mother.

It is in vain to say that these powers are not always exercised. Of course they are not, nor are the powers we possess over domestic animals always used to the utmost. But we prove from the laws on the statute book that they are all conceded, and, what is more, they are in very many cases exercised; and the legal right to exercise them stands unquestioned; and the attempt to effect any modification of the slave laws is universally resisted as an injurious and impertinent encroachment on the rights of the slaveowner.

Now this simple statement of the facts would seem sufficient to teach us that such an institution cannot be in obedience to the will of the Creator—most holy, most just, and most merciful. We all believe that God governs the universe by moral laws, and that moral laws in his estimation take precedence of all others. But on the principle on which domestic slavery is founded, physical force takes the precedence of moral law. It supposes that a man by physical force can reduce another to a condition in which he may act towards him in a manner which would be wrong had not physical force been exerted. And, again, as the parties may change places by force, it follows that then the moral law must be entirely reversed. The subjected party becomes dominant; and he, again, may do the reverse of what he had a right to do before the change; and the once dominant party, now having become subject, must submit to the same treatment which it before ministered to the other. How such an institution can consist with the moral government of a holy God, let any man judge.

But this is not all. Can it be supposed that a God of infinite love would establish, as the law for a race of intelligent creatures, a rule which can tend only to universal and endless war? Were such the law of humanity, our natural condition would be that of an internecine strife for superiority, both in nations and individuals—every man striving to enslave his brother and every nation to subdue to slavery its neighbor—and the parties subdued ever striving to regain what they had lost. How it is possible to reconcile such a law with the character of the all-loving God, I cannot conceive.

We arrive at the same conclusions by an observation of the moral and economical results of slavery.

Its effects must be disastrous on the morals of both parties. By presenting objects on whom passion may be satiated without resistance and without redress, it tends to cultivate in the one party pride, anger, cruelty, selfishness, and licentiousness. By accustoming the other party to submit entirely to the will of another, it tends to abolish in him all moral distinctions, and thus fosters in him lying, hypocrisy, dishonesty, and a willingness to yield himself up to gratify the appetites of another. That in all slaveholding countries there are exceptions to this remark, and that in some men moral principle may limit the effect of these tendencies, may be gladly admitted; yet that such is the tendency of the system as it is we think no reasonable person can hesitate to allow. Thomas Jefferson, himself a slaveholder, mentions them as the evident tendencies of slavery.

The effects of slavery upon national wealth are obvious.

Nations can increase in wealth only by industry and frugality. By labor we increase production, and by economy we are enabled to add the profits of the present year to those of the past. The greater and more universal the industry and economy of a nation, the more rapid will be its progress in the accumulation of wealth and all the means of physical happiness.

On the contrary, slavery, instead of imposing upon *all* the necessity of labor, restricts the *number* of laborers within the smallest possible limit, by treating labor as if it were disgraceful.

It takes from this diminished company of laborers the natural *stimulus* to labor—namely, the desire in man to improve his condition—and substitutes for it that motive which is the least operative and the least constant—the fear of punishment, without the consciousness of moral delinquency.

It removes from both parties the disposition and the motives to *frugality*. Neither the one party learns frugality from the necessity of labor, nor the other from the benefits it confers: and hence, when one party wastes from ignorance, and the other because he can have no motive to economy, capital must accumulate but slowly, if indeed it accumulate at all.

That such are the tendencies of slavery is manifest from observation. No country not of great fertility can long sustain a slave population. Soils even of more than ordinary fertility cannot sustain it long after their first fertility has been exhausted. Some of the most favored districts of this country, under the system of slavery, have become steadily *less* instead of *more* productive; and hence slavery is continually migrating from the older settlements to those new and untilled regions, where the accumulated fertility of centuries of vegetation has formed a soil whose productiveness may for a while sustain an institution at variance with the laws under which we have been created. Many of the free and the slaveholding states were peopled about the same time. The slaveholding states possessed every advantage of soil and climate over their neighbors; and yet the accumulation of capital, the progress of the people in general intelligence, as well as the improvement of the capabilities of the soil, have been greatly in favor of the latter. If any one doubt whether this difference has been owing to the use by one party of slave labor, let him ask himself what would have been the condition of the slaveholding states at this moment if they had been inhabited from the beginning by an industrious yeomanry; each individual owning his own land, and each one tilling it with the labor of his own hands.

These considerations seem sufficiently to indicate to us the will of the Creator. It could not have been his intention to give to man such power over his brother.

We may briefly look upon the subject from another point of view.

1. We presume every man holds himself amenable to moral law. I would, then, ask, What right can I acquire over another by burn-

ing his house and murdering his wife and children? Yet it is by this act, or acts like it, that the condition of a man is changed from that of a freeman to that of a slave. Such an act merits the severest punishment from God and man, instead of conferring upon the perpetrator the semblance of right over his victim. When the captor sells his captive to another, he has no right which he can transfer. The buyer can have no other right than the captor; and the captor having none, the buyer must be in the same condition. And if this be true of the captive himself, how much more must it be true of his wife and children. Every man has a right to himself; and neither the burning of a man's house, the murder of his family, nor the payment of money to the murderer, can in the least degree invalidate this right.

2. If this be the law of humanity, it is the law for every man; therefore every man may innocently exercise it. Every man, therefore, who by force can reduce his brother to this condition, may do it rightfully. Any nation may, in like manner, reduce another nation to bondage. I see not why this should not necessarily follow.

3. This being the law of humanity, it applies equally to the slave as to any other man. He not only has a right to freedom, if he can regain it by force, but he has the right, if he can gain it by force, to change places with his master, and make the master *his* slave. And he may do it by the same means. He was reduced to this condition by the burning of his house and the murder of his relatives; he has an equal right to reduce any other man to this condition by the same means. So far as I perceive, all these consequences flow from supposing this to be a law of humanity. We therefore must conclude that no such law exists, or could ever have been given to his creatures by a holy and all-loving Creator.

II. But, in the second place, it may be asserted that this is not a *universal* law, affecting equally every individual; but that it is special, and applies only to a portion of the race: that is, that to one portion has been given the right to reduce another portion to the condition of slavery. This assertion has been sustained by several considerations.

1. It has been said that Negroes—the persons generally enslaved

—are not men. It is granted that nations may be red, brown, olive, or tawny and be *men;* but that if *black,* they are *not men.* It is allowed that they may become skillful in any business; that they have immortal souls, and may become exemplary disciples of Christ; but that having complexions of this color they are not men. The simple statement of this reasoning renders any argument on the case unnecessary.

2. It is said that Negroes are as a class degraded men; stupid, incapable of education, and fit only for the simplest forms of labor; and therefore we may rightfully reduce them to the condition of slavery.

To this it may be answered—

1. We deny the assertion on which this reasoning is founded. The Africans are on the same level as other barbarous nations, and are equally capable of civilization. When under proper influences, they have attained to civilization as readily as other men.

2. If they are thus stupid and incapable of civilization, why, in all the slave states, is it made a crime to attempt to teach them the rudiments of education? This assertion can never be made with any effect until they have been allowed the same opportunities of cultivation as other men, and that then they, as a class, have shown themselves incapable of improvement.

3. But suppose the assertion to be true; it by no means justifies the inference that is drawn from it. Suppose it to be true, by what right could a man of ever so eminent intelligence reduce to slavery his neighbor who is ignorant, dull of apprehension, and apparently incapable of high cultivation? By what right can a civilized nation reduce a barbarous nation to slavery? Could we rightfully have reduced the Sandwich Islanders to slavery, instead of sending missionaries and teachers to raise them to the level of civilized and Christian communities, such as they really are now? Could we rightfully reduce to slavery the ignorant foreigners who are arriving daily by thousands on our shores, and who are commonly in nothing superior to the Africans now among us? Is it not our duty, as men and as Christians, to elevate the unfortunate, the ignorant, and the vicious to the same level as ourselves? Did the Samaritan make a slave of the wounded and helpless traveler? And shall we burn the house of a

simple peasant, murder his family, and claim a right by this crime to consign him and his posterity to interminable bondage? Our own ancestors were once as far below the civilization of Rome as the Africans are below our own. Nay, they were exposed for sale in the slave markets of the imperial city. Christianity redeemed them from captivity, and carried to their homes the benefits of knowledge and the blessings of religion, thus sowing the seeds of which the eminence of Great Britain is now the legitimate fruit. Had we not better imitate their example, instead of sending men to incite these ignorant people to murder and rapine, and consigning the survivors to slavery, from the horrors of which there is no hope of escape?

And again. Suppose Africans to be of a rank inferior in intelligence to ourselves, what *authority over them* does this difference confer upon us? The various races of men may differ in natural endowment. Are they all but one created to be the slaves of the most highly endowed nation? Or, if only some are created to be the slaves of the rest, where is the line to be drawn, on the one side of which are to be the masters, and on the other the slaves? It is said that, under all their present disadvantages, slaves are frequently as capable as their masters of managing an important plantation. And, besides, we suppose that there exist spiritual beings, possessed of powers vastly superior to ours. Does this superiority confer upon them any right to diminish the means of happiness which God has conferred upon us? Great and powerful as they are, are they not *ministering spirits* sent forth *to minister* to those who are heirs of salvation? If these glorious beings are *our ministers,* though in rank we be so far below them, least of all could we suppose them to have authority to diminish our happiness for the sake of increasing their own.

II. But, lastly, it has been said that slavery has been authorized by the holy Scriptures. This authority is supposed to be conferred by the Word of God, and from that we have a right to reduce our fellow men to this condition.

1. It is said that the African race was, immediately after the flood, condemned to slavery by Noah; that this malediction was a prophecy; and that we are authorized, nay, it is sometimes said, commanded, to accomplish its fulfillment.

Now with regard to this reason for slavery we remark, in the first place, that it proceeds upon a total misconception of the object of prophecy. A prophecy informs us of some event which shall occur in the future, for the purpose of teaching us the omniscience of God. By the prophet Isaiah, God appeals to prophecy in various cases for this very purpose. The foretelling of a future event confers upon no man the authority to take its fulfillment into his own hands; nor is the prophecy that a deed will be done any authority for the doing of it. No event was ever so distinctly foretold as the crucifixion of Christ, and yet the guilt of his murderers has always been considered as without parallel. The Apostle Peter declares, "Him, being delivered by the determinate counsel and foreknowledge of God, ye have taken and with *wicked hands* have crucified and slain." The part which Judas should take in this transaction is a matter of prophecy; and yet we are told, "Good had it been for that man if he had never been born."

"But let us inquire, Was the utterance of Noah a *prophecy?* Was it anything more than the wish of an angry man? I do not remember that Noah is ever in the Scriptures referred to as a prophet. Let us, however, turn to the passage. It is contained in *Genesis* ix. 20–25: "And Noah planted a vineyard; and he drank of the wine, and was drunken; and he was uncovered in his tent. And Ham, the father of Canaan, saw the nakedness of his father, and told his two brethren without. And Shem and Japheth took a garment, and laid it upon their shoulders, and went backwards, and covered the nakedness of their father. And Noah *awoke from his wine,* and knew what his younger son had done unto him: and he said, Cursed be *Canaan;* a servant of servants shall he be unto his brethren." This curse is afterwards twice repeated, saying that *Canaan* should be the servant of *both Shem and Japheth.*

Now, concerning this malediction, we remark, first:

1. The words in question were uttered by a man just awaking out of a drunken sleep. The Holy Spirit in no other case has made use of a mind in this condition for the purpose of revealing to us the will of God. We could never believe words so spoken to be a prophecy, unless it was expressly revealed.

2. The malediction refers not to Ham, but to Canaan. If it confers authority to enslave any one, it is only to Canaan that it refers; and no one, unless he can be proved to be a descendant of Canaan, could, in virtue of this malediction, even if it were a curse spoken by God, be reduced to slavery. It may also be observed that it was only concerning Shem and Japheth that these words were spoken: there is nothing said of their descendants, nor of the descendants of Canaan.

3. If it be said that though Canaan is spoken of *Ham* his father is intended, we reply, It is not so spoken; nor do we know of any reason why he should mention one and mean another, unless it be that he had not yet quite recovered his consciousness. And, if it really meant *Ham,* the malediction has never been fulfilled. The descendants of Ham, as they are given us in Genesis, were as free as those of Shem and Japheth. Among them were Assyria and Egypt, who, so far from being slaves to the Israelites, were their grievous oppressors, and to the latter of whom Israel was in bondage for four hundred years. Many of the descendants of Ham were among the most powerful nations of antiquity. It seems to me impossible to find any justification of the institution of slavery from anything that Noah ever said on the subject.

2. It has been said that slavery is authorized by the law of Moses, and by the teaching of the New Testament. We will first consider the bearing of the law of Moses.

The argument on this subject is substantially this: Moses recognized without rebuke the existence of slavery. He made various laws concerning it, and even allowed the Hebrews to hold slaves. Whatever God allows at one time, he allows for all times; therefore we at the present day may, without offense to him, hold slaves, and plead the Mosaic law for our permission. To us it seems that the facts are neither correctly stated, nor do they justify the inference that is drawn from them.

The facts in the case are these:

At the time when the law was given by Moses, slavery was universal, and had been so for ages. The people for whom he was appointed to legislate, were rude, ignorant, and sensual, strongly tending to idolatry, and much disposed, when anything unfortunate or displeasing occurred, to leave him and return again to Egypt. Many of the practices which they had brought with them from Egypt, though wrong, he did not directly prohibit; and our Saviour declares that he treated them in this manner on account of the hardness of their hearts. Had he at once directly forbidden their cherished practices, unless a miracle had interposed, they would have renounced his authority altogether. While he allowed the continuance of these practices, therefore, he placed them under such restrictions as should tend ultimately to abolish them. Such was the course which he pursued with regard to individual revenge. He did not forbid it, but established in its place the cities of refuge. He acted in the same manner with respect to divorce, to the power of the parent over the child, to polygamy, and other things. He did not directly abolish the wrong, but placed it under restrictions which would in the end lead to its disuse. And in general he acted upon the principle that his was a preparatory dispensation, on which light should shine at successive periods of the future, until the nation should be prepared for the perfect illumination that was to break forth in the preaching of Jesus of Nazareth. Our Saviour manifestly treats the Mosaic law as standing in this relation to himself.

Now it is precisely in this manner that Moses deals with slavery. While he allows its existence, and says that slaves may be held, he is very explicit as to the manner in which a slave is to be treated. He makes a distinction between a Hebrew and an alien slave; he establishes a septennial and jubilee year of release; he unites the slave with the master in all religious service; he confers upon him the right of circumcision; he enforces kind treatment by freeing the slaves in consequence of blemishes produced by punishment; he forbids the Israelite to return a fugitive slave to his master; he enacts that if a man bought a slave girl for the wife of his son, he must deal with her after the manner of daughters; and if he took another wife, her food, raiment, and duty of marriage he shall not diminish; and if he did not these, then he shall let her go free. His laws respecting usury, and various others, are of the same tendency.

1. Now if the laws of Moses furnish authority for slavery, they furnish authority for *just such slavery* as Moses permitted, and no

other. His laws respecting the treatment of slaves, their rights and privileges, are of just as much obligatoriness as the permission to hold slaves at all. If Moses authorizes slavery under special limitations and no other, then only slavery such as he permits can plead his authority. But everyone sees that to place slavery under such laws would be to abolish it in a single generation.

Let us not be deluded by the use of a word. We find slavery permitted in the Pentateuch; but the kind of slavery there permitted is clearly defined, and permission is given to no other. But men seem to suppose that they may establish an institution under such laws as they please, and if they only *call* it slavery, they may claim for it the authority of Moses. Thus, if Moses allowed a Hebrew to buy a slave girl for his wife, or the wife of his son, and was bound to concede to her the privileges of a wife, even if he married another; therefore a man may brutally violate or seduce a slave girl, and then sell his own offspring and its unfortunate mother at the auction-block, and plead in justification the authority of Moses.

2. If the laws of Moses are of unchangeable obligation, then we are not at liberty to select here and there a precept which we profess to obey, but we are under obligation to obey the whole of them; and we may indulge in every practice which they tolerate. The laws of circumcision, the passover, the going up to Jerusalem to worship, the cities of refuge, capital punishment for gathering of sticks on the Sabbath, are as much in force as ever; and we may innocently institute the laws of divorce, polygamy, as well as slavery, as among the first elements of our present civilization.

3. If the precepts and examples of Moses are of unalterable obligation, then whatever teaches any opposite doctrine is of course to be rejected. Now the New Testament is in many respects not only at variance with, but in opposition to, the precepts of the Old. Nay, our Saviour himself, in various cases, not only annuls the law of Moses, but inculcates moral precepts directly opposite to it.

Thus says our Lord: "It was said by them of old time—but *I* say unto you." Here there is direct and palpable opposition. One or the other must be abandoned. If the laws and precepts of Moses are of unchangeable obligation, the precepts of the New Testament must be surrendered, and the teachings of the Saviour of mankind become an absolute nullity. To such consequences do we necessarily arrive if we take the law of Moses as of unalterable obligation. It would seem, then, that the institution of slavery can find no support from the Hebrew legislator.

3. And, lastly, it has been said that the institution of slavery is sustained by the teachings of the New Testament. The argument presented on this subject is on this wise:

In the New Testament we find slavery nowhere directly prohibited; the duties of slaves are clearly specified; and we also find that the Apostle Paul returned a slave to his master. Slavery is therefore in harmony with the teachings of Christ and his apostles.

Now while we admit the above statements to be true, yet they are by no means the whole truth. While it is true that the New Testament does not prohibit slavery (except that it declares that man-stealers can never enter the kingdom of heaven), it inculcates doctrines entirely subversive of it. It teaches us the doctrine of universal humanity—that the whole race of men are equal in the sight of God, and are brethren of each other; that Christ died for the whole race without exception; that we are under obligation to love our neighbor as ourselves; nay, more, that we are to imitate the love of Christ to us, and love the evil and unthankful: "As I have loved you, that ye love one another." And in his account of the decisions of the last day, he has made the evidence of our love to him to depend upon our love to the most helpless of our brethren: "Inasmuch as ye have done it unto the *least* of these my brethren ye have done it unto me." But still more, our Saviour has inculcated such duties as are inconsistent with the existence of slavery. He has taught us that every one of our race is a distinct individual, responsible first of all to God. Every one of us must give an account of himself unto God. No man may require service or impose restrictions on another, and no man may render service to another which is at variance with the sovereign will of God. The domestic relations are under his own special charge. He has said of the marriage relation, "What God hath joined together, let not man put asunder;" and he who forcibly tears asunder those who are thus united for life, does it in defiance of the command of the eternal God. He has established the obligations of parents to bring up their children in the nurture and admonition of the Lord. And, finally, God requires every moral creature to consecrate to his service all his powers, whether of body or mind, and for so living he will be held responsible. But how can a man live thus who has no right to himself; but who, in the government of his body and mind, is subject to the will of another, having no right over himself or anything else which the other is bound to respect?

The whole of the facts, then, would seem to teach us that while the New Testament did not directly prohibit slavery, it inculcated moral principles which, just insofar as they are believed and obeyed, must lead to its entire overthrow. That such is the intention of our blessed Redeemer cannot, we think, admit of a doubt. We know what slavery was at the time of our Lord; and to suppose the holy Son of God to look with favor on such an institution seems almost like blasphemy.

The question then arises, Why did the Saviour adopt this method of abolishing slavery? Why did he not at once prohibit it, and declare that every slave throughout the world was at once free?

The answer is apparent. A social wrong, such as slavery, could be peacefully eradicated only by changing the mind of both master and slave, by teaching the one party the love of justice and the fear of God, and by elevating the other to the proper level of individual responsibility. Is not the method which our Saviour selected the only one by which the overthrow of slavery could be peacefully and permanently effected? The prohibition of slavery among the pagan population of the time could have led to nothing but servile war; and nothing essential would be gained, for the minds of men would remain as before; but by the inculcation of true moral principles, slavery would fall of itself, with harm to no one, while both parties would be rendered essentially better. Can anything more clearly illustrate the boundless love and the omniscient wisdom of the Saviour than his choice of this method for the accomplishment of his benevolent purpose?

We must bear in mind that the gospel was designed not for one race, or for one time, but for all races and for all times. It looked not at the abolition of this form of evil for that age alone, but for its universal abolition. Hence the important object of its author was to gain it a lodgment in every part of the known world, so that by its universal diffusion it might greatly and peacefully modify and subdue the evil passions of men, and thus without violence work a revolution in the whole mass of mankind. In this manner alone could its object, a universal moral revolution, have been accomplished. For if it had forbidden the *evil,* instead of subverting the principle—if it had proclaimed the unlawfulness of slavery, and taught slaves to resist the oppression of their masters—it would instantly have arrayed the two parties in deadly hostility. Throughout the civilized world its announcement would have been the signal of servile war, and the very name of the Christian religion would have been forgotten amidst the agitation of universal bloodshed. The fact, under these circumstances, that the gospel does not forbid slavery, affords no reason to suppose that it does not mean to prohibit it; least of all does it afford ground for the belief that Jesus Christ intended to authorize it.

Upon these principles the apostle acted in the case of Onesimus. By the civil law, Philemon had power over his service, and with this power St. Paul would not interfere. He wished Philemon to have an opportunity to act in the case according to the principles of the gospel. He therefore sends him back, not as a *slave,* but as a *brother beloved;* and enjoins him to treat Onesimus as he would treat *the apostle himself.* "Thou therefore receive him that is mine own bowels." "Receive him as myself." What kind of servitude was imposed on Onesimus after this, we can easily judge. It is in this manner that slavery was intended to cease everywhere, by the obedience to the principles of the gospel.

If it be said that we may infer the innocence of the institution from the fact that the New Testament prescribes distinctly the conduct proper for slaves, we answer, The inference is by no means justified by the premises. We are commanded to return good for evil, to pray for them that despitefully use us, and when we are smitten on one cheek to turn also the other. We are told that to act thus is well-pleasing to God. When God prescribes the course of conduct that will be well-pleasing to him, he by no means acknowledges the right of abuse in the injurious person, but expressly declares, "Vengeance is mine, and I will repay, saith the Lord." Thus servants are commanded to be obedient to their own masters in *singleness of heart as unto Christ,* with good will doing service as to the Lord and not unto man, that they may adorn the doctrine of God our Saviour in all things. The manner in which the duty of servants is inculcated affords no ground for the assertion that the gospel authorizes slavery, any more than the command to honor the king, when that king was Nero, authorized the tyranny of the emperor; or than the command to turn the other cheek, when one is smitten, justifies the infliction of violence by an injurious man.

In a word, if the principles of conduct which the gospel inculcates are directly at variance with the existence of slavery; if the relations which it establishes and the obligations which it enforces are inconsistent with its existence; if the manner in which it treats it is the only manner which could lead to its universal extermination; and if it inculcates the duty of slaves on principles which have no connection with the question of the right of masters over them—I think it must be conceded that the precepts of the gospel in no manner countenance, but are entirely opposed to, the institution of domestic slavery.

It may be proper in closing this discussion to consider the question, What is the duty of masters and slaves under a condition of society in which slavery now exists?

1. As to masters.

If the system be wrong, as we have endeavored to show; if it can be sustained by no principle, either of natural law or of revealed religion; if it be at variance with our duty both to God and man,— it must be abandoned. If it be asked, When? I ask, again, When shall a man cease to do wrong? Is not the answer, Always—*immediately?* If a man is injuring us, do we ever doubt in respect to the time when he ought to cease?

But it may be said that immediate abolition would be the greatest injury to the slaves themselves; they are incapable of self-support and of self-government.

Let us inquire into the facts. They, even under the most unfavorable circumstances, have supported themselves and their masters. They are able-bodied and willing to work for wages. If they are fairly paid for their labor, they are as able and willing to support themselves as the emigrants who are daily landing by thousands upon our shores. Labor is everywhere needed: they are willing and desirous to render it for a fair compensation, and this compensation will enable them to take care of themselves. Place them under the government and protection of good and wholesome laws, and they are disposed to be peaceable and law-abiding citizens. This has been abundantly proved by all the fair experiments that have been made for the last three or four years. It has also been proved that it is more profitable to employ men as freemen, and at fair wages, than to employ them under the lash as slaves.

But, it may be said, the laws of the state in which we live will not permit us to liberate our slaves, and if we liberated them they would be returned again to bondage. This may be so; but I ask, Who made these laws? Did not the slaveholders themselves? and cannot they unmake them? We cannot surely be innocent if we ourselves have placed it out of our power to do right.

But, it may be said, we are in favor of liberty; but we are the minority, and cannot control legislation on this subject. I ask, again, Have we yet done all in our power? Have we obeyed God in rendering to our slaves that which is just and equal? Have we treated them as human beings, soon, with ourselves, to stand before the judgment-seat of Christ? Have we taught them to read the Word of God, and given them every opportunity for obedience to its precepts? And yet more, have we publicly borne testimony against this wrong, and done all in our power to change the legislation under the protection of which the wrong has been perpetrated? Until we have done all this, we cannot, surely, be innocent of the guilt of slavery.

The duty of slaves is also explicitly made known in the Bible. The Scripture rule is this: it matters not how a man treats me, I am bound to treat him justly, kindly, and faithfully. They are thus bound to obedience, fidelity, and submission, not for the reason that the power of the master is founded in right, but on the ground of duty to God. This obligation extends to everything but matters of conscience. When a master commands a slave, or anyone else, to do wrong, he must refuse obedience and suffer the consequences, looking to God alone, to whom vengeance belongeth. Acting upon these principles the slave may attain to the highest grade of virtue, and exhibit a sublimity and purity of moral character which, in the condition of the master, is to him wholly unattainable.

Thus we see that the Christian religion not only forbids slavery, but that it provides the only method in which, after it has been once established, it may be abolished with entire safety and benefit to both parties. By instilling the right moral dispositions into the bosom of the master and of the slave, it teaches the one the duty of reciprocity and universal love, and the other the duty of faithfulness, patience, and submission; and thus, without disorder and revenge, but by the real moral improvement of both parties, restores both to the relation toward each other intended by the Creator.

If anyone will reflect on these facts and remember the moral laws of the Creator and the terrible sanctions by which these laws are vindicated, and also the benevolent provision which he has made for removing this evil after it has been once established, he must, I think, be convinced of the imperative obligation resting upon him to remove it without delay. The Judge of the whole earth will do justice. He hears the cry of the oppressed, and he will in the end terribly deliver them. The throne of iniquity can have no fellowship with him, though it frame mischief by a law. And, on the other hand, let those who suffer wrongfully bear their sufferings with patience, committing their souls to him as to a faithful Creator.

(1) *Book Second, Part Second, Class First, Chapter Second, Section II, 1865 edition. Four additional sentences:*

The risk is frequently removed by the custom of endorsing. Here another guarantees for the borrower the payment of his note. If the endorser be good, there is then no risk to be paid for. The endorser who assumes the risk is, however, entitled to a fair remuneration.

(J) *Book Second, Part Second, Class First, Chapter Second, Section II, 1865 edition. Additional sentences:*

Here, however, it is understood that the representative is *in good faith* using his best skill for the good of his constituents. If he act differently from selfishness or venality, he has violated the conditions on which he was elected, and is bound to resign immediately.

(K) *Book Second, Part Second, Class First, Chapter Fourth, 1865 edition. Additional sentence:*

Alexander Hamilton, in the trial of Henry Croswell, unfolds the true doctrine of liberty of the press in these remarkable words: "The liberty of the press consists in the right to publish, with impunity, the *truth,* with *good motives,* and for *justifiable ends,* whether it respects governments, magistrates, or individuals."

(L) *Book Second, Part Second, Class Second, Chapter First, 1865 edition:*

THE DUTY OF CHASTITY

THE moral law limits the indulgence of the sexual desire to individuals who are exclusively united to each other for life.

Hence it forbids adultery, polygamy, concubinage, or, in general, intercourse with one of the other sex, under any other condition than that of the marriage covenant.

Inasmuch as unchaste desire is strongly excited by the imagination, the law of chastity forbids all impure thoughts and actions, all unchaste conversation, looks and gestures, the reading of obscene or lascivious books, and everything which would naturally produce in us a tendency to violate this precept.

The law which we are to consider contains two restrictions. It requires that the individuals be exclusively united to each other, and that this union be during life.

Let us briefly examine the teachings of natural religion upon both of these points.

That it is the will of our Creator that the gratification of the sexual desire should be limited to those who are exclusively united to each other may be shown as follows:

1. The number of births of each sex is substantially equal. As at the beginning God created a male and a female, so has it ever been. This universal fact sufficiently indicates his will.

2. Under this restriction the race is most rapidly multiplied, and the health of the young most certainly secured.

3. The human infant is proverbially helpless, and on its entrance into this world needs all the comforts of an affectionate home, where everything will be done lovingly for its comfort and sustenance. And after its infancy is passed, it needs the watchful care of parents who will unite in rendering to it every needful office to guide it by their experience, restrain it by parental authority, and prepare it for its future situation in society. It is obvious that such a home can never be prepared for the offspring of disgraceful lust or promiscuous concubinage.

4. There can be no doubt that we were created to find a large part of our earthly happiness in domestic society, where all the relations of husband and wife, parents and children, brothers and sisters, combine to augment the happiness of every individual. But how can such happiness be enjoyed when the domestic society is constituted on any other principles than those which we have indicated?

5. No reason can be assigned why an individual of one sex is not as valuable in the sight of the Creator as an individual of the other, much less why the one sex should be the abused slave, or the object of sensual gratification for the other. But just as we depart from obedience to the law of chastity, is woman degraded to this condition. No one can suppose that the Creator intended one human being to stand in such a relation to another, while both are equally tending to the same solemn eternity.

II. The second requirement of the law of chastity is that the union be for life. Among the natural reasons for this requirement may be the following:

1. Nothing tends so strongly to cultivate that self-government and

mutual forbearance, which are essential to any connection of imperfect beings, as the conviction that the union is for life.

2. If the union be not for life, it must be liable to be dissolved at the will of either party. This would lead to all the evils of promiscuous concubinage of which we have spoken.

3. Children require the care of parents until they have arrived at an age at which they are competent to assume the care of themselves. But if the domestic society be dissolved, they belong to no one; they have no protector, and are cast helpless upon the world.

4. Or, if otherwise, they become the charge of one of the parents, and this will commonly be the mother, whose parental instincts are stronger, and who would frequently rather die than desert her offspring. The tendency of every licentious system is to take advantage of the maternal instincts of the mother for the purpose of devolving upon her a labor which she is least able to sustain.

5. Parents themselves in advanced age frequently need the care of their children, and are greatly dependent for their happiness upon them. But all this source of happiness is dried up by any system which allows of the disruption of the domestic society and the desertion of offspring at the will of both or either of the parents.

If it be suggested that though this may be the general rule, yet that occasional aberrations may be exempted from the general rule, it may be answered—

1. That the severity of the punishment which God has affixed to the crime displays his displeasure against it. In woman this crime is fatal to reputation, and a return to virtue seems almost hopeless; and in man it leads directly to those states of mind which are the sure precursors to destruction.

2. The Creator, who made us, and to whom we must give account, is no respecter of persons, and he will bring every secret thing into judgment. The seducer and his victim will shortly stand at the bar of that Judge who will render to every man according to his deeds.

3. Let it be remembered that a female is, like us, a moral and accountable being, hastening to the bar of God. Let us consider the worth of that soul which, unless a miracle interposes, must by the loss

of virtue be driven into that path which leads to endless despair; and we ask whether there be a crime whose atrocity more justly merits the deepest condemnation than that which, for the sake of a momentary gratification, will violate all these obligations, outrage all these sympathies, and work out so widespreading and interminable a ruin?

III. The precepts of revealed religion on this subject may be briefly stated.

1. The seventh commandment of the decalogue is, "Thou shalt not commit adultery." The term *adultery* here is intended to designate impurity of action of every kind.

2. Our Saviour, in reference to the law of chastity, in his Sermon on the Mount, teaches us fully the *extent* of this precept. "Ye have heard that it hath been said by them of old time, Thou shalt not commit adultery. But I say unto you, that whosoever shall look upon a woman to lust after her [to cherish impure desire] hath committed adultery with her already in his heart. And if thy right eye offend thee [cause thee to offend], pluck it out and cast it from thee; for it is profitable for thee that one of thy members should perish, and not that thy whole body should be cast into hell" (*Matt.* v. 27-33). That is, as I suppose, eradicate from your bosom every impure thought, no matter at what sacrifice; for no one who cherishes impurity even in thought can inherit the kingdom of heaven.

I need not multiply quotations from both the Old and New Testaments, which show that God has classed uncleanness among those crimes which especially bring down his judgments upon men. Let everyone, then, remember that whoever violates this command violates it in defiance of the most clearly revealed command of God, and at the price of his own soul.

I remarked above that the law of chastity forbade the indulgence of lascivious or impure imaginations, the harboring of such thoughts in the mind, or the doing of anything by which such thoughts could be excited. Licentiousness in outward conduct never appears until the mind has become defiled by impure imaginations. Hence the necessity of the utmost vigilance in the government of our thoughts, and in the avoiding of all books, all pictures, all society, and all conduct or actions, of which the tendency is to imbue our imaginations with anything at variance with the purest virtue. No man can take fire in his bosom and his clothes be not burned. Hence it is that immodest dancing, and all amusements and actions which tend to inflame the passions, are sadly pernicious to morals. It is not enough for a virtuous woman to say that she suffers no harm from such associations; if she knows that they are the occasions of ruin to others, she must charge herself with the crime of being accessory to the undoing of others. It was Cain who asked, "Am I my brother's keeper?"

(M) *Book Second, Part Second, Class Second, Chapter Second, 1865 edition. Condensation of remainder of paragraph:*

Nor surely is that woman less deserving of contempt who enters upon the duties of a wife with no other conceptions of the responsibilities which she has assumed than such as have been acquired from a life of childish caprice, luxurious self-indulgence, and sensitive, feminine, yet thoroughly finished selfishness.

(N) *Book Second, Part Second, Class Third, Chapter First, Section II, 1865 edition. Remainder of section:*

In presenting this subject we shall commence with the axiom which we have already frequently considered, namely, *Every man has a right to himself.* That is, every man has a right to his own body, and to his faculties both of body and mind; he is at liberty to use them as he will, subject only to his responsibility to God. Within this limitation, he may use them as he will, and for using them in any particular way he need give no other reason than that such is his choice. As this right is universal, and belongs just as much to my neighbor as to myself, my right over my own means of happiness, therefore, forbids me from interfering with the means of happiness bestowed upon another. Over my own faculties and the means of happiness which they present I am supreme; beyond these I have no right whatever.

The use of our faculties within the above limit produces results. To these results the individual also has a right. The man who on unoccupied land produces a crop of corn has a right to that corn. It is the joint product of his labor and the powers of the soil. His own labor enters into every particle of it. It is his as truly as his faculties themselves, and he has a right to dispose of it as he will.

2. But every man has the physical power in some way or other to violate the rights of his neighbor. He may deprive him of life; he may reduce him to subjection to his will; he may seize upon his property by force, or procure it by stealth, and in a thousand ways may violate the rights which have been conferred on him by the Creator. And, unfortunately, it is found to be the fact that men have the disposition in various degrees thus to injure each other; not that they love injury *for itself,* but choose injury of another only when it is necessary to the accomplishment of their unrestrained desires. When they have no personal desire to gratify, conscience teaches them to disapprove of injustice, and condemn the evildoer.

3. Under these circumstances the individual can protect himself from injury, or redress the injuries which he has suffered, by nothing but his own physical power. But this is manifestly insufficient. He who was able at first to violate right has commonly the power to violate it again, and to resist with effect the claims of the injured party. Should everyone attempt by his own arm to redress his wrongs or protect his rights, the world would present a scene of nothing but intolerable strife. And the strife would be commonly fruitless, for power is as likely to be united with wrong as with right. The contest would, therefore, have no tendency to the establishment of justice. But this is not all. It is impossible for us to redress our own grievances without awakening in ourselves the spirit of revenge. Vindictiveness only increases wrong, and renders the injurious person the injured. Thus is laid the foundation of contention, growing into interminable wrong and unappeasable malice. Such a condition of human beings would be nothing else than universal war.

4. How then can justice be administered? How can right be protected and injury redressed? I answer, Provision is made for this in the social nature of man. *Every man is so created as instinctively to*

commit to the community of his fellow men the protection of his rights and the redress of his wrongs; and his fellow men, on the other hand, instinctively assume this authority. They feel that they assume it innocently; nay more, they feel guilty if they do not exert it. Every man feels that he stands in this relation to society, and society feels that it stands in the corresponding relation to him. In this manner is the society of human beings established.

The human being thus surrenders the right to redress his wrongs and to protect his rights *by the prowess of his own arm,* and receives in return *the power of the whole community* to do this for him. Instead of measuring redress by his own exasperated feelings, redress is administered by those who have no personal interest in the matter and to whose decision the injurious person feels himself instinctively bound to submit. More than this, the Christian religion imposes upon us subjection to the civil power as a matter of moral duty, on the ground that society is an ordinance of God. "Let every soul be subject to the higher powers; for there is no power but of God; the powers that be are *ordained of God.* Whosoever, therefore, resisteth the power, *resisteth the ordinance of God.* Wherefore we must needs be subject, not only for wrath, but for conscience' sake" (*Rom.* xiii. 1, 2, 5).

5. The formation of a society on the principles stated above depends neither upon organization nor number; it exists wherever human beings exist. As soon as they associate together and form a community by themselves, they form a society on these principles, each individual surrendering himself to the whole, and the whole assuming the care of each individual. Thus we have heard of a case in which a company was crossing the wilderness of the West, and who, when far beyond the confines of civilization, found that one of their number had been murdered by a fellow traveler. They paused in their journey, all feeling that their first duty was to do justice. They arrested the suspected person, appointed a jury to examine the evidence and render a verdict accordingly. It was done immediately. The man was found guilty of murder, and was executed accordingly. They then proceeded on their journey.

Or, again. During one of the British expeditions to the polar regions, Dr. Richardson, the surgeon of the company, found himself in the depths of the wilderness, accompanied only by a midshipman, a sailor, and an Indian guide. The temper of the Indian had for some time been far from satisfactory; when, on one occasion, upon the return of Dr. Richardson and the sailor to the tent after an absence of some hours, they found the midshipman dead. He had been shot, and the Indian declared that he had shot himself.

Dr. Richardson and the sailor formed the only society within, perhaps, a circuit of a thousand miles. They proceeded to perform the functions of society in the case before them. They examined the body. It had been shot in the back, in a manner that showed that death by suicide was impossible. The Indian was evidently the murderer, and justly condemned to die. The sailor offered to be the executioner; but Dr. Richardson, as the superior officer, considered that the duty devolved on himself. He, therefore, as soon as the Indian entered the tent, shot him himself.

I think that while we all regret the necessity for these acts, we approve of the acts themselves. We believe that the executioners did not transcend their rightful authority. They acted innocently. They did no more than perform a deed of justice, and they acted from a stern conviction of duty. These were evidently the sentiments of Dr. Richardson, for he has related the transaction, with all its particulars, in his report of the expedition. I think that the common conscience of humanity acquits him of all blame in the occurrence.

6. It will be seen from what has been said that society *confers* no right upon any man; it only *secures to* him the enjoyment of rights already bestowed upon him by the Creator. The Creator who bestowed them has secured them to him by the constitution under which man was created. That society best fulfills its office which most perfectly protects the rights and redresses the wrongs of every individual, and where every individual confides these duties wholly to society.

Hence we see the error of the notion sometimes entertained, that property, nay, that even right and wrong, are merely the creatures of society. I know that men may declare that they will punish or reward particular actions, but this makes the actions neither right nor wrong. They may protect me in the enjoyment of my property, but they cannot make that *my* property which was not *mine* before they took action on the subject.

7. Inasmuch as every man has been created a constituent member of society, every man has a right to it. He may differ from the community in which he lives in various respects, and may hold opinions quite dissimilar from theirs; but so long as he violates no right he is entitled to all the privileges of the social state. His person and his property are under the protection of the community. He may be a foreigner, alone and friendless, yet society covers all his rights as a *man* under the shield of her protection. The infant of a day old is watched over and protected by the same benevolent power, and no man may lay upon it an unkind hand without exposing himself to the penalty of the laws which society has enacted for the protection of every individual.

Hence we see the error of those who suppose that any company of men who choose to organize a society for themselves, and who even may settle in the wilderness for this purpose, have a right to organize it upon such principles as they please. They have no right to form a society in violation of the social laws of man. God evidently intended that man should live in society, and of this right he cannot be deprived unless he violates some social law. His opinions and practices may differ from ours; but if he commits no injury, his right to the privileges of his social nature remains intact. It is not enough for us to say if he does not agree with us let him form some other society for himself. He has a right to *this* society, and so long as he interferes with the rights of no one, he is as free of this society as any other man.

It was in this respect, I suppose, that our Puritan forefathers erred. They came to this land, inhabited only by wandering savages, desiring freedom to worship God; and in establishing the foundations of their organization, assumed the authority to punish by banishment, or even by death, all those who differed from them in what they considered important religious opinions. They believed in *their own right* to worship God according to the dictates of their own consciences, but they did not allow this to be the *common right of all men.* Hence arose the banishment of Roger Williams, the severe treatment of Baptists, the execution of Quakers, and the harsh measures dealt out to dissentients from their own religious belief. A true conception of the nature of religious liberty would have taught them that the right which they so nobly claimed for *themselves* was equally the right of *every human being.*

8. We see from what has been stated that a vast difference exists between civil society and the voluntary societies and associations existing among men. Men belong to a voluntary society because they choose to unite with it: they select the object which they wish to accomplish; they adopt such means as they suppose will advance their purposes; they continue united as long as they see fit; and any member dissolves his connection with the society as he will, or they may all agree to abolish the society altogether.

On the contrary, it is not a matter of choice whether a man will or will not be a member of civil society. He becomes a member of it as soon as he begins to live, and society at once bestows upon him the full benefit of its protection. That protection he needs every moment of his life. This protection, which others afford to him, he is under obligations to unite in affording to others. He cannot free himself from his obligation, nor live without the protection of society. It is an influence which, like the atmosphere, surrounds him everywhere and always, and he can no more dissever himself from it than he can cease to breathe.

But it may be said that societies may err as well as individuals, and may impose unjust restrictions upon its members, or may even interfere with their obligations to God. This is true; and the question arises, What then is to be done? We see at once that the attempt is hopeless for the individual by force to overcome the power of society. He has the right to exhibit what he believes to be the truth before men, and gain as many converts to his opinions as he can. If he succeed in changing the opinions of his fellow citizens, they will agree with him, and the variance between the parties will cease. If he, however, is unable to do this, and cannot contend by force, what then shall he do? I see no other course open for him than to do whatever he believes to be right, dispassionately and boldly, and suffer the consequences. These may be suffering even to martyrdom; but if he suffer in the cause of right, he may in this manner do more to change the minds of men than by the most convincing argument. Persecution is apt to react powerfully upon the persecutor. Thus it was said in early days, "The blood of the martyrs was the seed of the church." It is from just such martyrdoms that the greatest and most important improvements in society have originated.

9. This relation of the individual to society is the foundation of some of the most interesting affections in our nature. As society is thus the source of innumerable blessings, we look up to it with gratitude, veneration, and love. It is to us a sort of parent, to whom we owe a vast debt of filial obedience. We all know the special regard in which we hold a neighbor, a townsman, a fellow citizen of our state or of the United States. Thus is formed the affection of patriotism, or love of country, one of the most ennobling virtues that can adorn our character. It is thus that we joyfully suffer the loss of all things, even life itself, for our native land; and the sentiment has for twenty centuries thrilled the hearts of thousands, *Dulce et decorum est pro patria mori.* This particular form of love of society gives us victory over the love of self, and raises us to the dignity not only of intelligent but of social and moral beings.

10. From this just and proper love of society, it not unnaturally follows that we are disposed to concede to it other forms of authority. Some of these tend to good, others to evil. Thus universal education is an undoubted blessing, and it can best be secured by confiding it to the public charge. The control of society over the labor of the individual, over his religious opinions, over his personal expenses, and over various other innocent acts, can work nothing but evil. Hence in respect to the claims of society an important distinction is to be taken. Society, without asking the consent of the individual, may properly tax him for his proportionate share of all the necessary expenses of the government. All that the citizen can rightfully claim is that no more than his proportionate part be demanded. A government can demand money for no other purpose, unless the authority to do so has been conferred on it by society. It is not sufficient for the majority to believe the object to be wise or benevolent: the ques-

tion, first of all, is, has power been conferred on them to act in the premises? Thus it may be supposed that the good order of society requires that churches be built and ministers of religion supported by law. All this would avail nothing until it first be shown that the power to support religion by law had been conferred by the people themselves on their legislators. Until the article of the constitution be shown by which this power is conferred, all such acts are usurpation and tyranny.

(o) *Book Second, Part Second, Class Third, Chapter Third, 1865 edition. Additional paragraph:*

The only exception to this is when an emergency arises for which the constitution has made no provision, and which must be met immediately. In such a case, the executive may be obliged to act on his own authority, submitting his conduct to the approval of his fellow citizens after the emergency shall have passed.

(p) *Book Second, Part Second, Class Third, Chapter Fourth, 1865 edition. Sentence revision and substitutions:*

Every individual is under obligation to observe in good faith the contract which he instinctively makes as soon as he becomes a member of society. Everyone expects that his neighbor shall refrain from every violation of his rights. This expectation imposes upon him the equal obligation to refrain from every violation of the rights of his neighbor.

(q) *Book Second, Part Second, Division Second, Chapter Fourth, 1865 edition:*

BENEVOLENCE TO THE INJURIOUS

THE teaching of the gospel in this case is explicit. Our Saviour has taught us that it is our duty to return good for evil. "If thine enemy hunger, feed him; and if he thirst, give him drink." We are to love our enemies, to bless those that curse us, and pray for those

that despitefully use us and persecute us. The gospel commands us
to love all men. If they violate this command, it furnishes us with
no reason for following their example. And still more, their ill conduct furnishes us with an opportunity for the exercise of special and
peculiar virtue. It is made our duty to overcome the wrong disposition of the evildoer by manifesting toward him particular kindness
and good will. It is our duty to *overcome* evil with good; that is, by
the exhibition of sincere good will to reclaim the injurious person
to virtue. There can be no doubt that such is the teaching of the
New Testament. It is, moreover, evident that such a course is indicated by the conditions of our being. This is evident from the slightest
consideration.

The conscience of every man bears witness that to overcome evil
with unchanged kindness is an act of the most exalted virtue; while
retaliation is ever an unfailing indication of meanness of spirit. We
cannot hope for the forgiveness of God, unless from the heart we
forgive all who have injured us.

Again: this method of treating an injurious person has a manifest
tendency to put an end to every form of ill will.

For, 1. No man can long continue in a course of injurious conduct
when he receives in return nothing but kindness.

2. By such conduct the heart of the offender is improved, and
there is less probability that he will repeat the injury.

3. It also improves the heart of the offended person, and thus
renders it less likely that he will ever commit an injury himself.

On the contrary, the tendency of retaliation is exactly the reverse.
It tends to increase and foster and multiply wrongs absolutely without end. It renders neither party better, but always renders both
parties worse. The offending party is aroused to revenge, and the
offended party who retaliates is so much the worse, as he has done a
mean action when he might have done a noble one.

We thus learn the temper which we should cultivate toward those
who injure us, and the conduct which should flow from such a
temper.

It, however, frequently happens that the injury may be of such
a nature that the peace of society demands its suppression. Society

was established for the very purpose of protecting rights and redressing wrongs. We may therefore, without any feeling of vindictiveness, deliver such an offender to the judgment of society. It is our duty to do this without the least feeling of vindictiveness or malice. Thus the Apostle Paul appealed to his rights as a Roman citizen for protection.

But when the case of injustice or violation of right is in the hands of society, the same principles should govern its action as in the case of the individual. The crime should be prevented, and the criminal should, if possible, be reclaimed. Those means should be adopted which will most directly tend to eradicate wrong habits, to cultivate and strengthen moral principles, to form habits of industry, and eventually restore the criminal to society a wiser, a better, and a useful man. The whole experience of John Howard is summed up by him in the simple sentence, "It is in vain to punish the wicked, unless you seek to reclaim them."

Secondly. If injury be done by one society to another, what is to be done?

Here there is no party to which we naturally appeal. Both parties are supreme. The common resort of nations in case of injury is war; that is, they declare their purpose to do each other the greatest injury by every means in their power. Hundreds of thousands of men are brought face to face for the express purpose of slaughtering each other, and of destroying the property of each other, which has been the accumulation of the labor of ages, and wherever this property is found, whether on land or at sea. This work of mutual destruction proceeds, giving unlimited indulgence to every evil passion, until one of the parties can endure it no longer; and then peace is restored by the weaker yielding to the stronger the matter in dispute. In such contests the loss of life in battle and by disease is frightful; the murder of innocent and unoffending men, women, and children is shocking to contemplate. And the demoralization of those engaged in actual warfare is such as we might expect from men associated for the very purpose of destruction, and from whom all ordinary restraints have been removed, and by whom all evil passions of the human heart may be exerted without control.

Strange as it may seem, yet even Christian nations seem to resort to this as the only method of dealing with a nation which they believe to have offered to them an injury. Yet I think no one can for a moment suppose that this work of universal destruction is in harmony with the precepts of the Prince of Peace. Can any other method be devised?

On this subject we beg leave to offer a few suggestions.

First. It is the duty of every society to present an example of strict justice in all its dealings with every other society; to refrain in all cases from injury; and when, from any cause, it has committed an injury, to make at once all needful reparation.

Secondly. It is the duty of every nation to manifest kindness and charity to every other nation; to relieve them when suffering from famine, or by any other afflictive dispensation of Divine Providence; to abstain from every form of aggression; and to desire the happiness of the whole human race as we desire our own.

Thirdly. A nation acting upon these principles would rarely suffer injury from its neighbors. But suppose injury to be offered. Suppose any nation to act at variance with the principles of national law and injure or rob any of our citizens. Are we not bound to use the whole power of the nation for the protection and redress of every member of the body politic?

I think we are. But this does not involve the necessity of war. It would be far better for us at once to assume the charge of remuneration for the injury inflicted, and present our claim to the offending nation. When the violence of passion has subsided, a calm appeal to the principles of right in the view of all the nations of the earth will commonly have a greater and better effect than can be obtained by war.

But suppose these means to fail: what then is to be done? Suppose a nation to hold itself amenable neither to the principles of national law or individual right. What course should we pursue when a case of the same kind occurs between individuals? When a man by his conduct renders it evident that he is governed by no principle of right, though we should cheerfully relieve him in distress, yet we should withdraw from all ordinary intercourse with him; we should, as far as possible, put it out of his power to do us an injury again. It seems to me that the same course might with advantage be pursued by a nation. If another nation in its treatment of our citizens held itself at liberty to act in defiance of all the rules of right, we might well refuse to have with it any intercourse. If this mode of treatment were universally adopted, the offending nation would suffer all the evils of entire isolation, and would soon see the importance of retracing its steps and yielding obedience to the principles of universal law.

But suppose an extreme case. If a nation in defiance of right, from love of conquest, or desire of territory, or any other wicked motive, should resolve on the subjugation of its unoffending neighbor with the intention of overthrowing a just government and establishing in its place the power of brute force: what then is to be done? The offending nation, abjuring all moral principles, lays aside its character as men, and, like inferior animals, appeals solely to physical force. As such, I think, they must be treated; and force must be repelled by force, just so far as it is necessary to resist their evil design. In this the whole people may unite, and strive to the utmost to transmit unharmed to their children the legacy of liberty which they have received from their fathers. Their object is simply to repel injury; and when this is accomplished the sword should be returned to its scabbard, and the offending nation be treated as brethren as soon as they have by their conduct shown themselves worthy of this relation.

(R) *Book Second, Part Second, Division Second, Chapter Fourth, 1835 edition. Remainder of paragraph:*

And if it be said, these principles may all be very true, but you can never induce nations to act upon them; I answer, this concession admits that such is the law of God. If this be the case, that nation will be the happiest and wisest which is the first to obey it. And if it be said, it would be wisest and best to obey the law of benevolence, but men will never obey it; I answer, here is manifestly the end of the argument. If we show men what is wisest and best, and according to the will of their Creator, we can do no more. If they disobey it, this is a matter to be settled between them and their God. It remains, however, to be seen whether God will or will not cause his laws to be obeyed; and whether omniscience and omnipotence have not the means of teaching his creatures submission to his will.

THE JOHN HARVARD LIBRARY

*The intent of
Waldron Phoenix Belknap, Jr.,
as expressed in an early will, was for
Harvard College to use the income from a
permanent trust fund he set up, for "editing and
publishing rare, inaccessible, or hitherto unpublished
source material of interest in connection with the
history, literature, art (including minor and useful
art), commerce, customs, and manners or way of
life of the Colonial and Federal Periods of the United
States . . . In all cases the emphasis shall be on the
presentation of the basic material." A later testament
broadened this statement, but Mr. Belknap's interests remained constant until his death.*

*In linking the name of the first benefactor of
Harvard College with the purpose of this later,
generous-minded believer in American culture the
John Harvard Library seeks to emphasize the importance of Mr. Belknap's purpose. The John Harvard
Library of the Belknap Press of Harvard University
Press exists to make books and documents
about the American past more readily
available to scholars and the
general reader.*